HUNTERS OF THE BURNING STONE

COLLECTED COMIC STRIPS
from the pages of

BBC DOCTOR WHO
MAGAZINE™

PANINI COMICS

CONTENTS

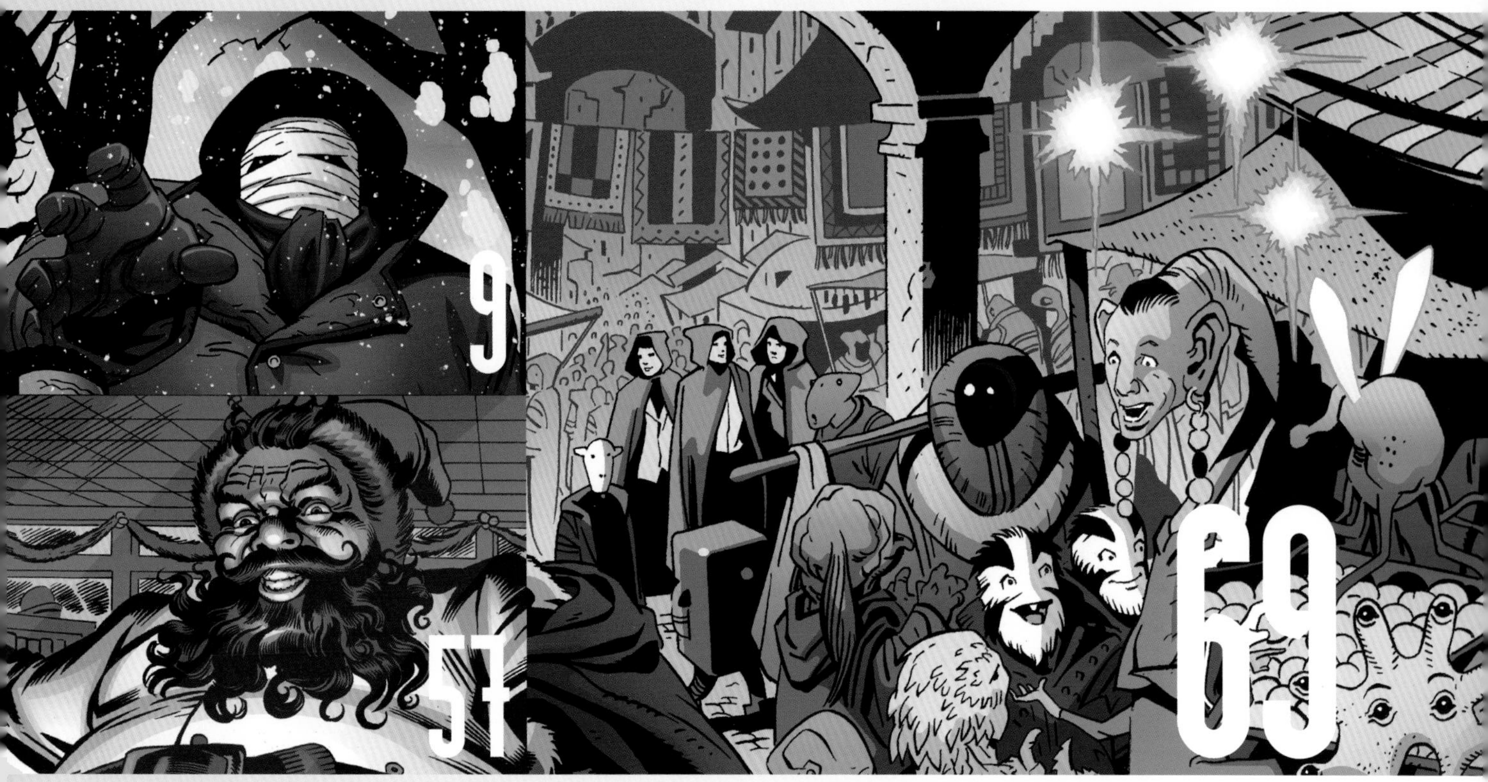

9
57
69

Project Editors **TOM SPILSBURY & SCOTT GRAY** Designer **PERI GODBOLD**
Cover pencils and inks by **DAVID A ROACH** Cover colours by **JAMES OFFREDI**

Head of Production **MARK IRVINE** Managing Editor **ALAN O'KEEFE** Managing Director **MIKE RIDDELL**

Special thanks to **STEVEN MOFFAT, MATT SMITH, KAREN GILLAN, ARTHUR DARVILL, GARY RUSSELL, CAROLINE SKINNER, RICHARD ATKINSON, PETER WARE, JOHN AINSWORTH, JASON LYTHGOE-HAY and all the writers and artists whose work is presented herein.**

FSC www.fsc.org MIX Paper from responsible sources FSC® C002386

PREVIOUSLY in THE CHAINS OF OLYMPUS...

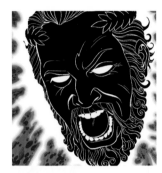

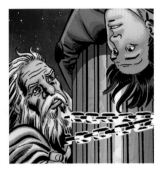

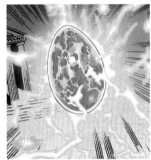

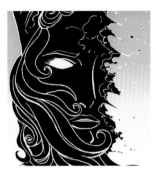

The Doctor, Amy and Rory travel to Athens in the year 410 BC. The city is attacked by a creature who appears to be Zeus. With the aid of Socrates, the Doctor discovers a "Belief Engine" – a device constructed from a golden metal with psychic properties. It has used the mind of an elderly woman to create the entire pantheon of Greek gods.

The Doctor and Socrates defeat Zeus, and Olympus is destroyed. The dying Athena, goddess of wisdom, tells the Doctor that there is a question he must answer: "What is buried in Man?"

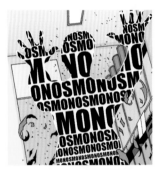

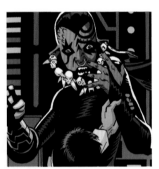

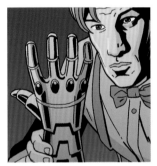

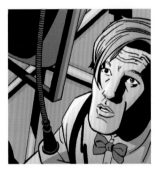

Modern-day London also comes under attack in a different way – people begin to be transformed into living names. The culprit is the alien artist Monos. He is using a gauntlet composed of psychic metal to transmit his identity into the bodies of London's population. The Doctor stops Monos and returns everyone to normal.

As he examines the gauntlet in the TARDIS, the Doctor is stunned by the appearance of someone on the monitor screen. He hears a warning: "I am so very, very sorry... but this next bit is going to hurt."

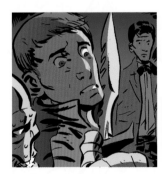

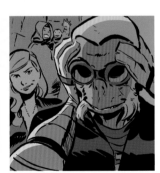

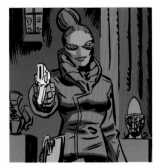

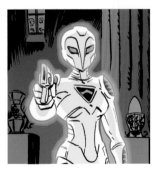

The time-travellers land in the alien spaceport Cornucopia; a society ruled by the ruthless Crime Lords. A giant Ziggurat has been hovering above the city for a century. It is another psychic metal construction. With the aid of master thief Horatio Lynk and a secretary called Miss Ghost, the Doctor, Amy and Rory defeat the Crime Lords and destroy the Ziggurat.

But the Doctor is aware that Miss Ghost is not what she seems. She reveals herself to be a woman in armour who has had a prior encounter with the Doctor. She vanishes after posing a familiar question to him: "What is buried in Man...?"

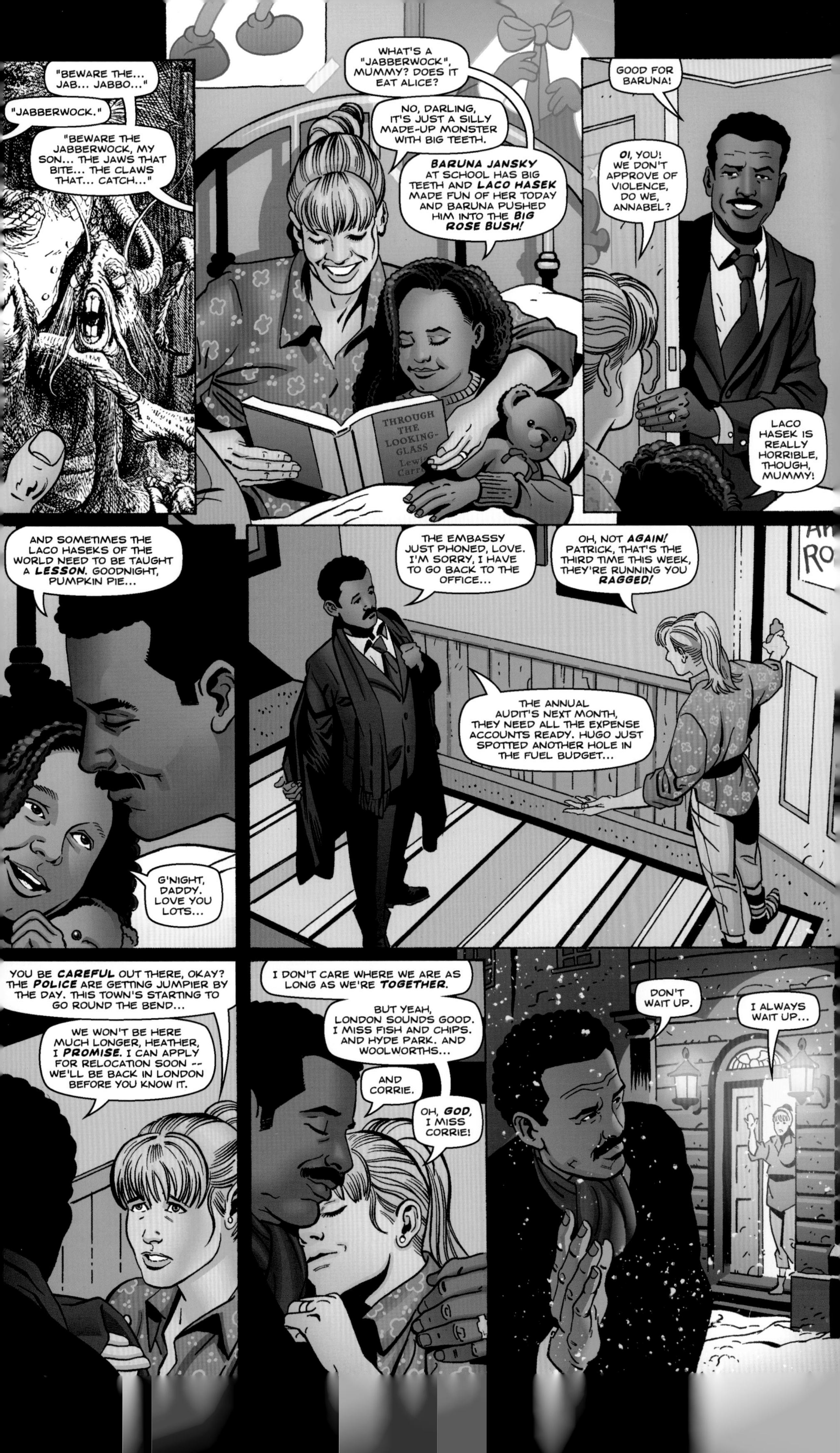
"BEWARE THE... JAB... JABBO..."
"JABBERWOCK."
"BEWARE THE JABBERWOCK, MY SON... THE JAWS THAT BITE... THE CLAWS THAT... CATCH..."
WHAT'S A "JABBERWOCK", MUMMY? DOES IT EAT ALICE?
NO, DARLING, IT'S JUST A SILLY MADE-UP MONSTER WITH BIG TEETH.
BARUNA JANSKY AT SCHOOL HAS BIG TEETH AND LACO HASEK MADE FUN OF HER TODAY AND BARUNA PUSHED HIM INTO THE BIG ROSE BUSH!
THROUGH THE LOOKING-GLASS
GOOD FOR BARUNA!
OI, YOU! WE DON'T APPROVE OF VIOLENCE, DO WE, ANNABEL?
LACO HASEK IS REALLY HORRIBLE, THOUGH, MUMMY!
AND SOMETIMES THE LACO HASEKS OF THE WORLD NEED TO BE TAUGHT A LESSON. GOODNIGHT, PUMPKIN PIE...
G'NIGHT, DADDY. LOVE YOU LOTS...
THE EMBASSY JUST PHONED, LOVE. I'M SORRY, I HAVE TO GO BACK TO THE OFFICE...
OH, NOT AGAIN! PATRICK, THAT'S THE THIRD TIME THIS WEEK, THEY'RE RUNNING YOU RAGGED!
THE ANNUAL AUDIT'S NEXT MONTH, THEY NEED ALL THE EXPENSE ACCOUNTS READY. HUGO JUST SPOTTED ANOTHER HOLE IN THE FUEL BUDGET...
YOU BE CAREFUL OUT THERE, OKAY? THE POLICE ARE GETTING JUMPIER BY THE DAY. THIS TOWN'S STARTING TO GO ROUND THE BEND...
WE WON'T BE HERE MUCH LONGER, HEATHER, I PROMISE. I CAN APPLY FOR RELOCATION SOON -- WE'LL BE BACK IN LONDON BEFORE YOU KNOW IT.
I DON'T CARE WHERE WE ARE AS LONG AS WE'RE TOGETHER.
BUT YEAH, LONDON SOUNDS GOOD. I MISS FISH AND CHIPS. AND HYDE PARK. AND WOOLWORTHS...
AND CORRIE.
OH, GOD, I MISS CORRIE!
DON'T WAIT UP.
I ALWAYS WAIT UP...

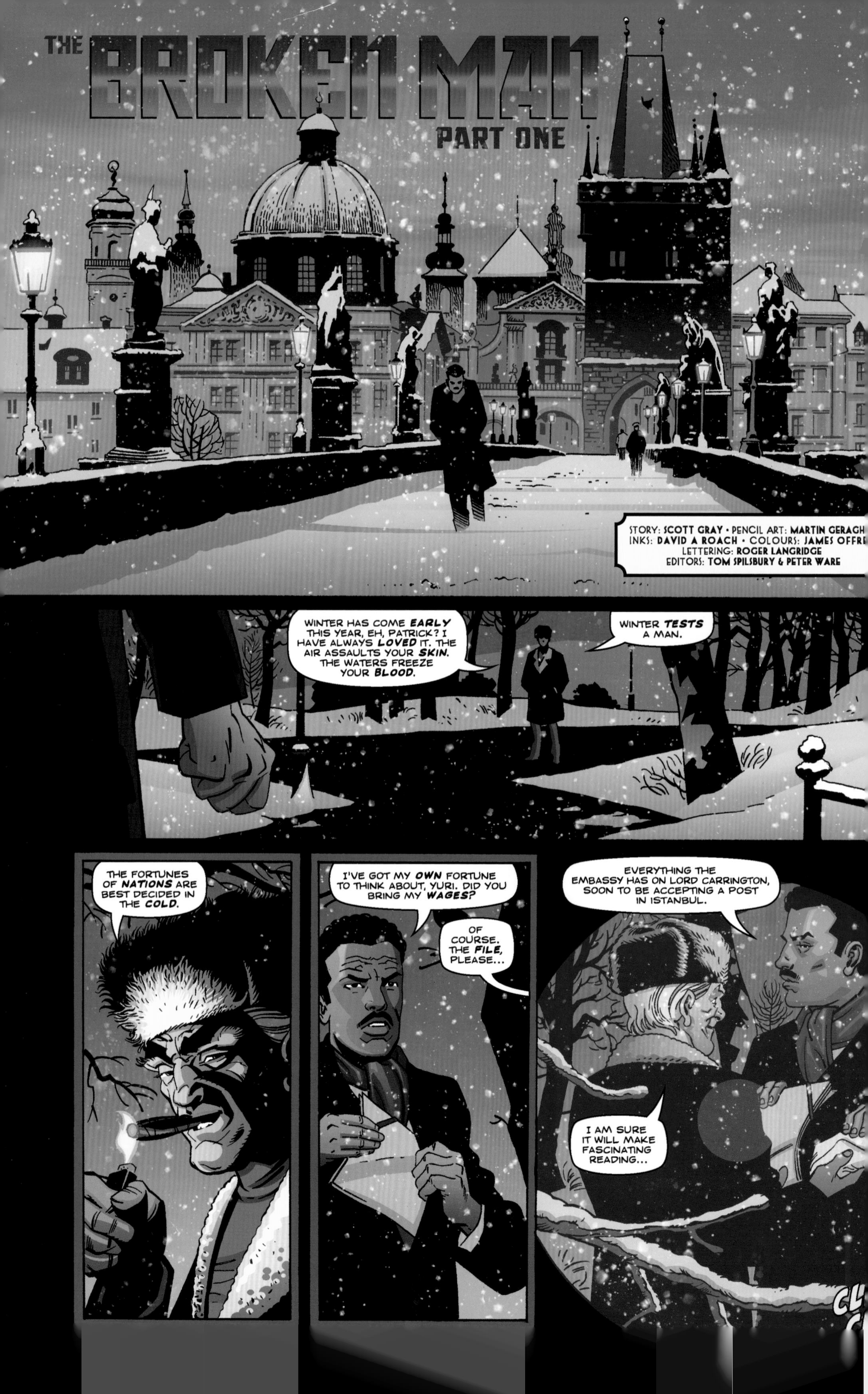
THE BROKEN MAN
PART ONE
STORY: SCOTT GRAY • PENCIL ART: MARTIN GERAGH
INKS: DAVID A ROACH • COLOURS: JAMES OFFRE
LETTERING: ROGER LANGRIDGE
EDITORS: TOM SPILSBURY & PETER WARE
WINTER HAS COME EARLY THIS YEAR, EH, PATRICK? I HAVE ALWAYS LOVED IT. THE AIR ASSAULTS YOUR SKIN. THE WATERS FREEZE YOUR BLOOD.
WINTER TESTS A MAN.
THE FORTUNES OF NATIONS ARE BEST DECIDED IN THE COLD.
I'VE GOT MY OWN FORTUNE TO THINK ABOUT, YURI. DID YOU BRING MY WAGES?
OF COURSE. THE FILE, PLEASE...
EVERYTHING THE EMBASSY HAS ON LORD CARRINGTON, SOON TO BE ACCEPTING A POST IN ISTANBUL.
I AM SURE IT WILL MAKE FASCINATING READING...

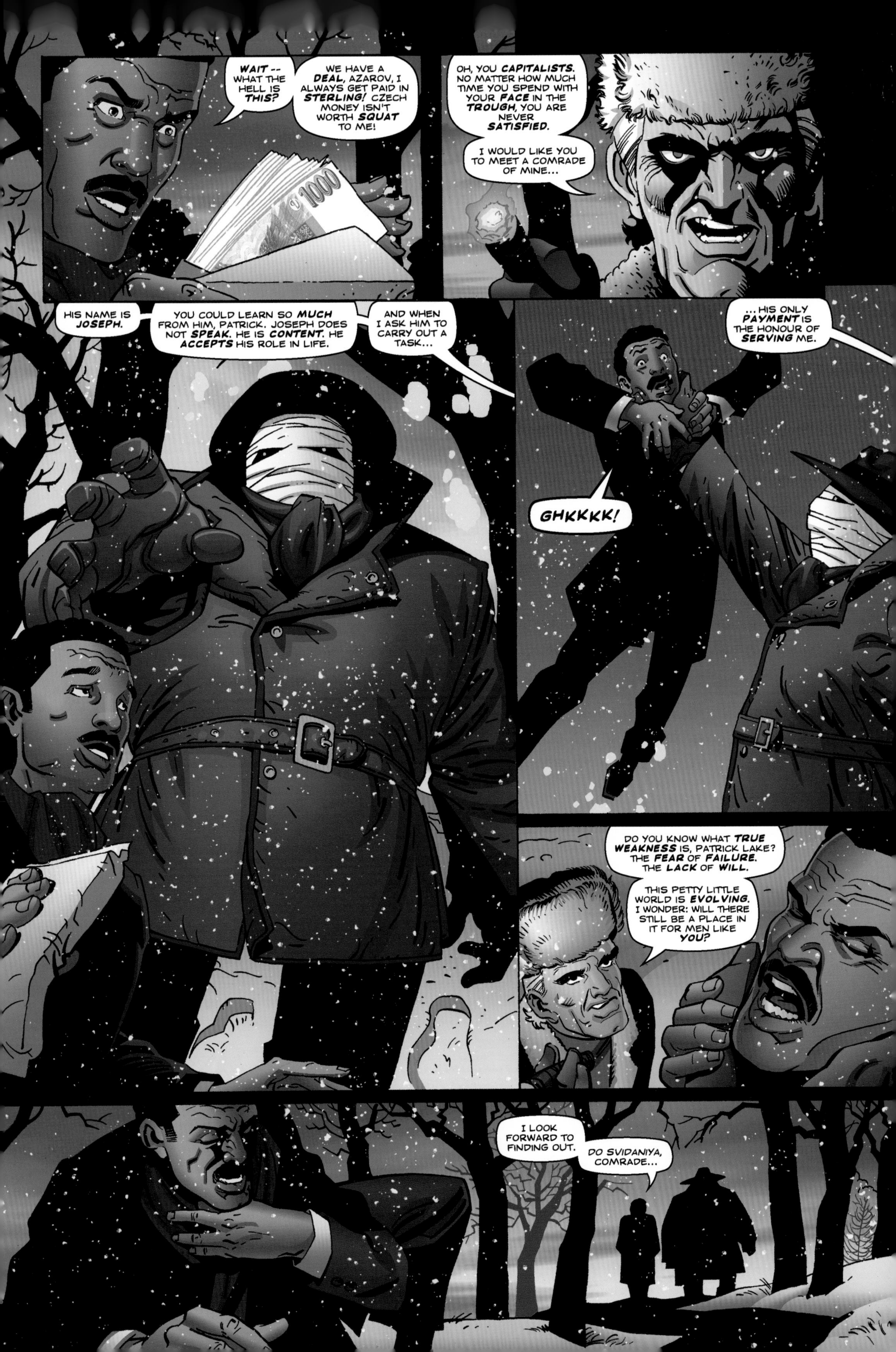
WAIT -- WHAT THE HELL IS THIS?
WE HAVE A DEAL, AZAROV, I ALWAYS GET PAID IN STERLING! CZECH MONEY ISN'T WORTH SQUAT TO ME!
OH, YOU CAPITALISTS. NO MATTER HOW MUCH TIME YOU SPEND WITH YOUR FACE IN THE TROUGH, YOU ARE NEVER SATISFIED.
I WOULD LIKE YOU TO MEET A COMRADE OF MINE...
HIS NAME IS JOSEPH.
YOU COULD LEARN SO MUCH FROM HIM, PATRICK. JOSEPH DOES NOT SPEAK. HE IS CONTENT. HE ACCEPTS HIS ROLE IN LIFE.
AND WHEN I ASK HIM TO CARRY OUT A TASK...
...HIS ONLY PAYMENT IS THE HONOUR OF SERVING ME.
GHKKKK!
DO YOU KNOW WHAT TRUE WEAKNESS IS, PATRICK LAKE? THE FEAR OF FAILURE. THE LACK OF WILL.
THIS PETTY LITTLE WORLD IS EVOLVING. I WONDER: WILL THERE STILL BE A PLACE IN IT FOR MEN LIKE YOU?
I LOOK FORWARD TO FINDING OUT.
DO SVIDANIYA, COMRADE...

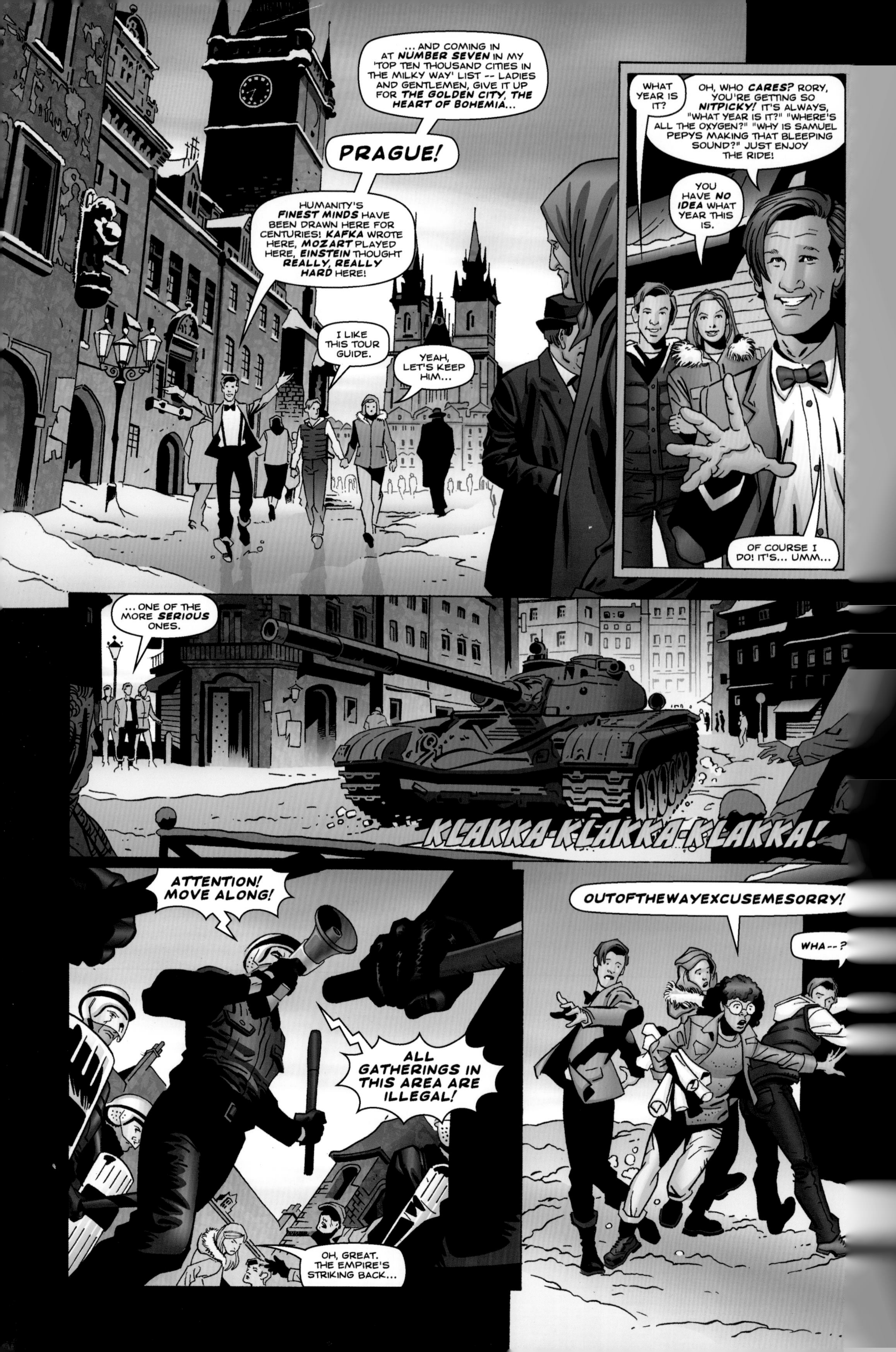

...AND COMING IN AT NUMBER SEVEN IN MY 'TOP TEN THOUSAND CITIES IN THE MILKY WAY' LIST -- LADIES AND GENTLEMEN, GIVE IT UP FOR THE GOLDEN CITY, THE HEART OF BOHEMIA...
PRAGUE!
HUMANITY'S FINEST MINDS HAVE BEEN DRAWN HERE FOR CENTURIES! KAFKA WROTE HERE, MOZART PLAYED HERE, EINSTEIN THOUGHT REALLY, REALLY HARD HERE!
I LIKE THIS TOUR GUIDE.
YEAH, LET'S KEEP HIM...
WHAT YEAR IS IT?
OH, WHO CARES? RORY, YOU'RE GETTING SO NITPICKY! IT'S ALWAYS, "WHAT YEAR IS IT?" "WHERE'S ALL THE OXYGEN?" "WHY IS SAMUEL PEPYS MAKING THAT BLEEPING SOUND?" JUST ENJOY THE RIDE!
YOU HAVE NO IDEA WHAT YEAR THIS IS.
OF COURSE I DO! IT'S... UMM...
...ONE OF THE MORE SERIOUS ONES.
KLAKKA-KLAKKA-KLAKKA!
ATTENTION! MOVE ALONG!
ALL GATHERINGS IN THIS AREA ARE ILLEGAL!
OH, GREAT. THE EMPIRE'S STRIKING BACK...
OUTOFTHEWAYEXCUSEMESORRY!
WHA--?

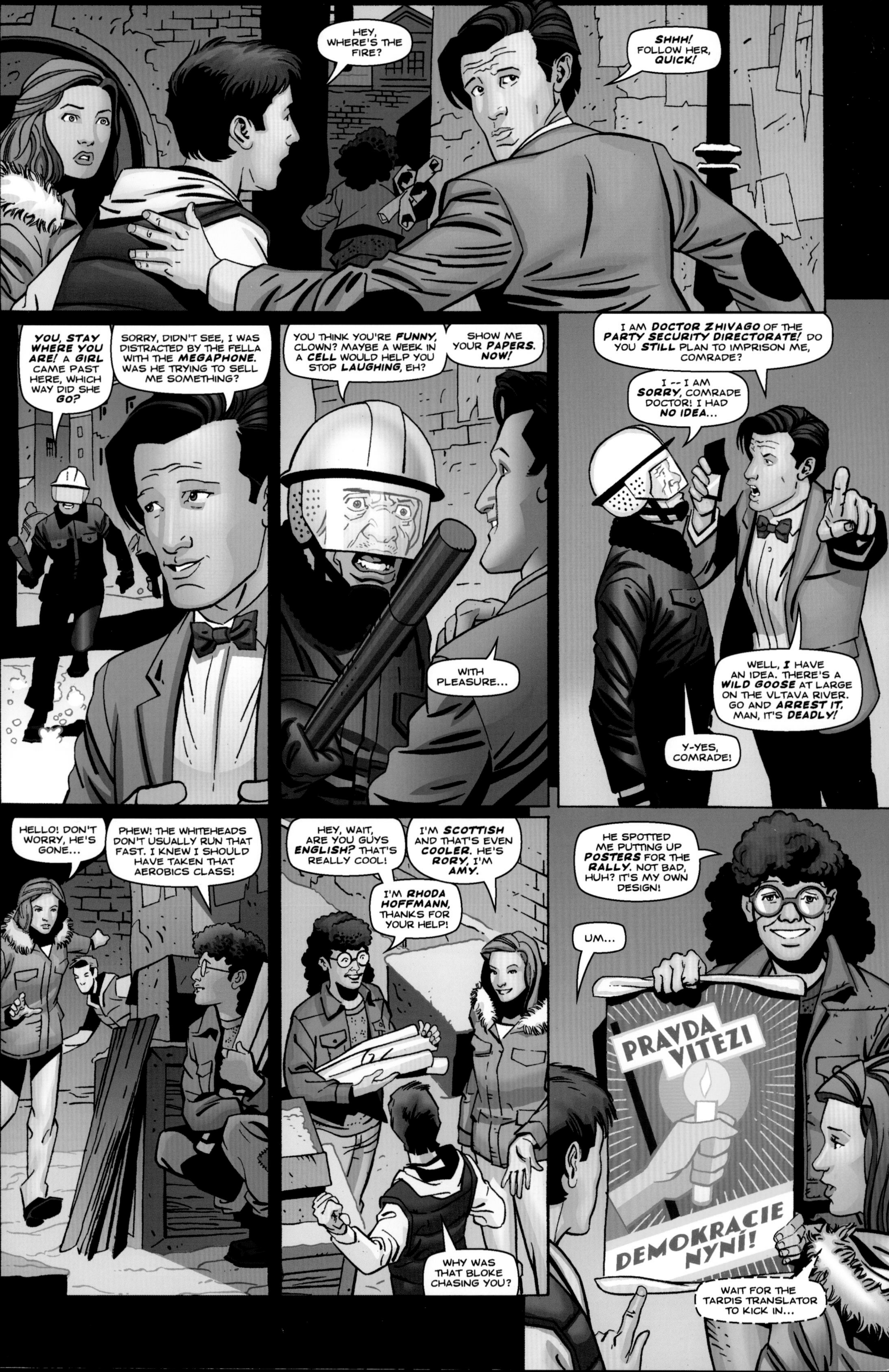
HEY, WHERE'S THE FIRE?
SHHH! FOLLOW HER, QUICK!
YOU, STAY WHERE YOU ARE! A GIRL CAME PAST HERE, WHICH WAY DID SHE GO?
SORRY, DIDN'T SEE, I WAS DISTRACTED BY THE FELLA WITH THE MEGAPHONE. WAS HE TRYING TO SELL ME SOMETHING?
YOU THINK YOU'RE FUNNY, CLOWN? MAYBE A WEEK IN A CELL WOULD HELP YOU STOP LAUGHING, EH?
SHOW ME YOUR PAPERS. NOW!
WITH PLEASURE...
I AM DOCTOR ZHIVAGO OF THE PARTY SECURITY DIRECTORATE! DO YOU STILL PLAN TO IMPRISON ME, COMRADE?
I -- I AM SORRY, COMRADE DOCTOR! I HAD NO IDEA...
WELL, I HAVE AN IDEA. THERE'S A WILD GOOSE AT LARGE ON THE VLTAVA RIVER. GO AND ARREST IT, MAN, IT'S DEADLY!
Y-YES, COMRADE!
HELLO! DON'T WORRY, HE'S GONE...
PHEW! THE WHITEHEADS DON'T USUALLY RUN THAT FAST. I KNEW I SHOULD HAVE TAKEN THAT AEROBICS CLASS!
HEY, WAIT, ARE YOU GUYS ENGLISH? THAT'S REALLY COOL!
I'M SCOTTISH AND THAT'S EVEN COOLER. HE'S RORY, I'M AMY.
I'M RHODA HOFFMANN, THANKS FOR YOUR HELP!
WHY WAS THAT BLOKE CHASING YOU?
HE SPOTTED ME PUTTING UP POSTERS FOR THE RALLY. NOT BAD, HUH? IT'S MY OWN DESIGN!
UM...
PRAVDA VITEZI
DEMOKRACIE NYNÍ!
WAIT FOR THE TARDIS TRANSLATOR TO KICK IN...

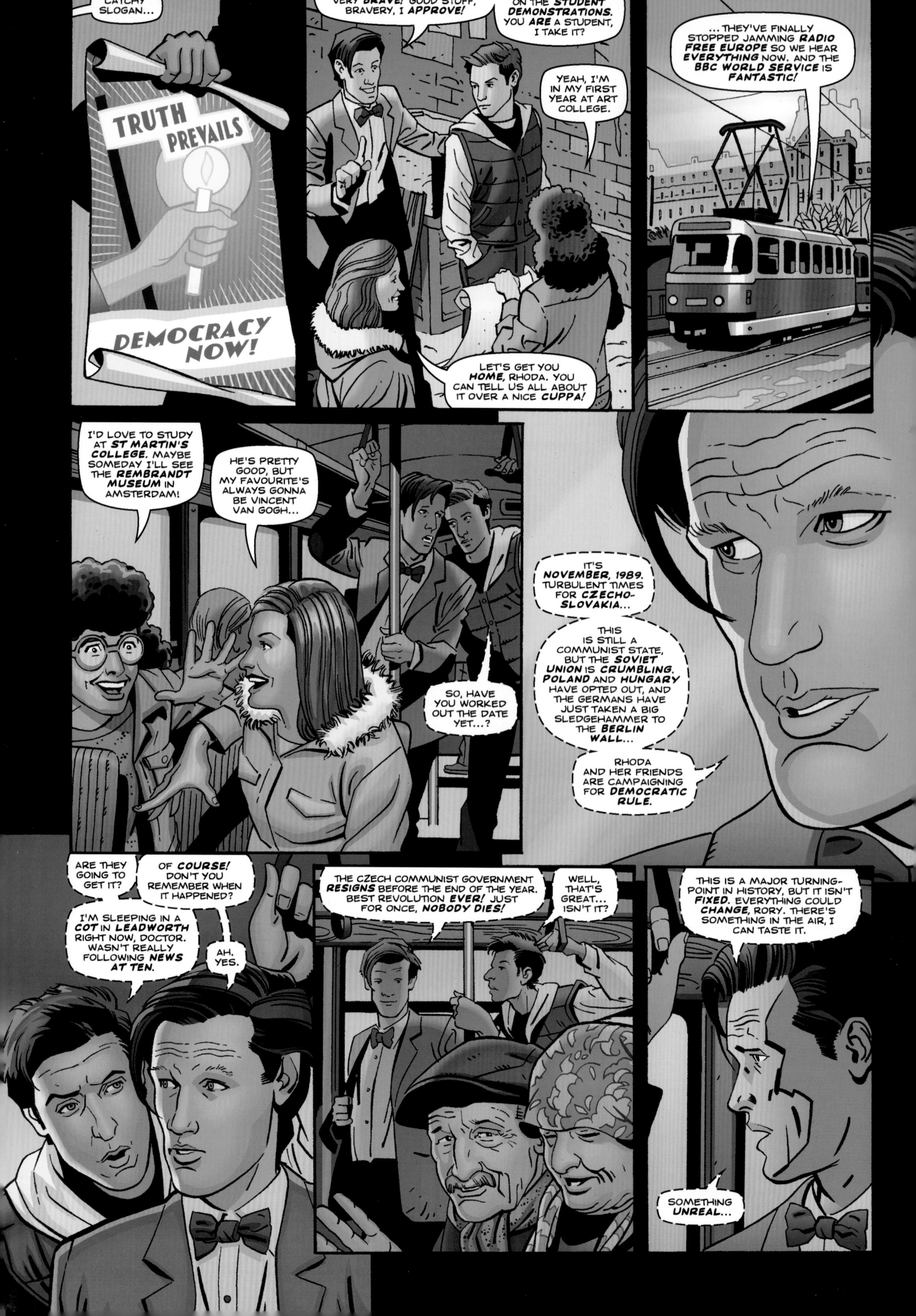
CATCHY SLOGAN...
TRUTH PREVAILS
DEMOCRACY NOW!
... BUT DANGEROUS, TOO. HELLO, RHODA, I'M THE DOCTOR, YOU'RE OBVIOUSLY VERY BRAVE! GOOD STUFF, BRAVERY, I APPROVE!
WE'RE FROM THE BBC, REPORTING ON THE STUDENT DEMONSTRATIONS. YOU ARE A STUDENT, I TAKE IT?
YEAH, I'M IN MY FIRST YEAR AT ART COLLEGE.
LET'S GET YOU HOME, RHODA. YOU CAN TELL US ALL ABOUT IT OVER A NICE CUPPA!
... THEY'VE FINALLY STOPPED JAMMING RADIO FREE EUROPE SO WE HEAR EVERYTHING NOW. AND THE BBC WORLD SERVICE IS FANTASTIC!
I'D LOVE TO STUDY AT ST MARTIN'S COLLEGE. MAYBE SOMEDAY I'LL SEE THE REMBRANDT MUSEUM IN AMSTERDAM!
HE'S PRETTY GOOD, BUT MY FAVOURITE'S ALWAYS GONNA BE VINCENT VAN GOGH...
SO, HAVE YOU WORKED OUT THE DATE YET...?
IT'S NOVEMBER, 1989. TURBULENT TIMES FOR CZECHO-SLOVAKIA...
THIS IS STILL A COMMUNIST STATE, BUT THE SOVIET UNION IS CRUMBLING. POLAND AND HUNGARY HAVE OPTED OUT, AND THE GERMANS HAVE JUST TAKEN A BIG SLEDGEHAMMER TO THE BERLIN WALL...
RHODA AND HER FRIENDS ARE CAMPAIGNING FOR DEMOCRATIC RULE.
ARE THEY GOING TO GET IT?
OF COURSE! DON'T YOU REMEMBER WHEN IT HAPPENED?
I'M SLEEPING IN A COT IN LEADWORTH RIGHT NOW, DOCTOR. WASN'T REALLY FOLLOWING NEWS AT TEN.
AH. YES.
THE CZECH COMMUNIST GOVERNMENT RESIGNS BEFORE THE END OF THE YEAR. BEST REVOLUTION EVER! JUST FOR ONCE, NOBODY DIES!
WELL, THAT'S GREAT... ISN'T IT?
THIS IS A MAJOR TURNING-POINT IN HISTORY, BUT IT ISN'T FIXED. EVERYTHING COULD CHANGE, RORY. THERE'S SOMETHING IN THE AIR, I CAN TASTE IT.
SOMETHING UNREAL...

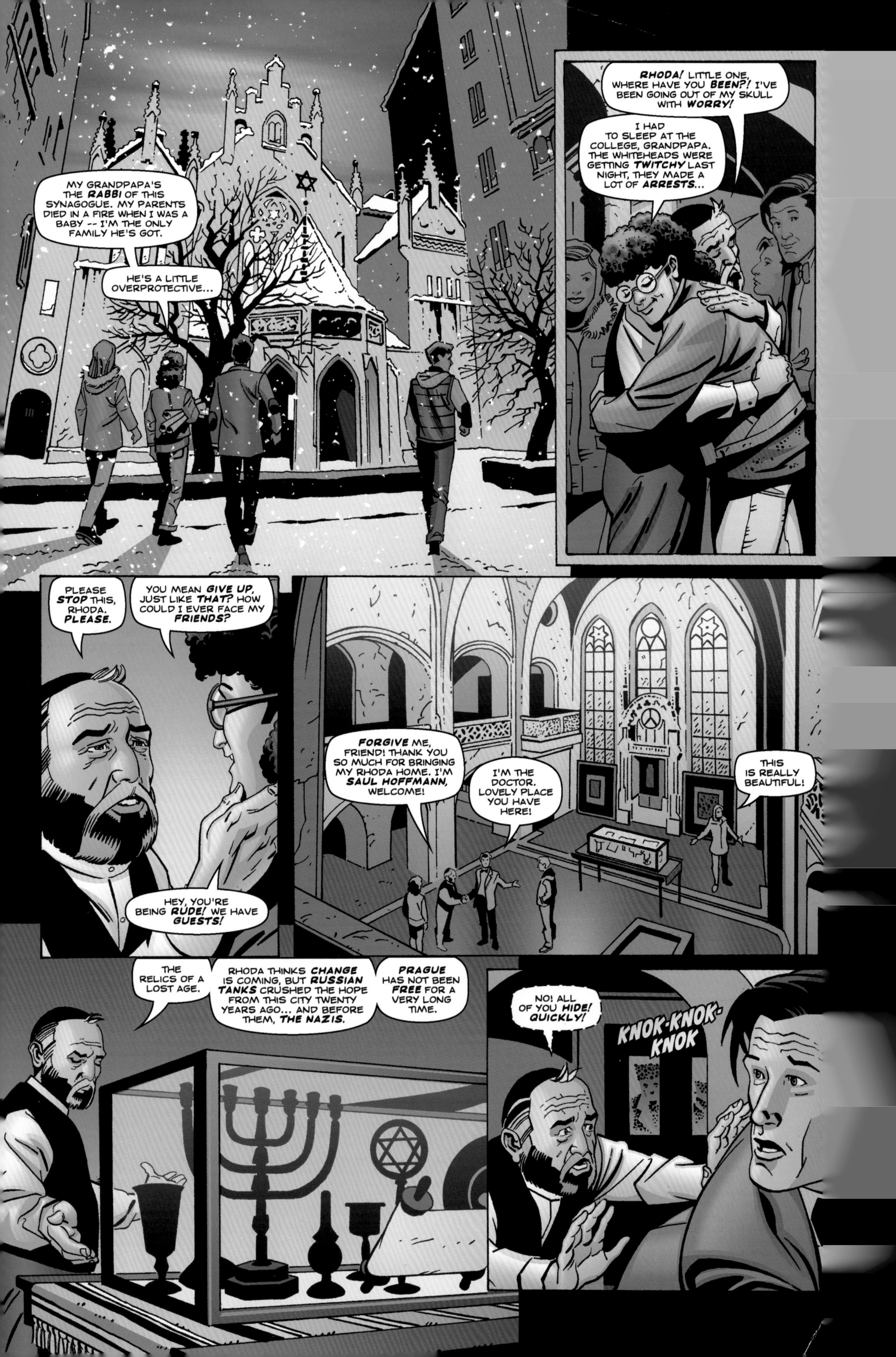
MY GRANDPAPA'S THE RABBI OF THIS SYNAGOGUE. MY PARENTS DIED IN A FIRE WHEN I WAS A BABY -- I'M THE ONLY FAMILY HE'S GOT.
HE'S A LITTLE OVERPROTECTIVE...
RHODA! LITTLE ONE, WHERE HAVE YOU BEEN?! I'VE BEEN GOING OUT OF MY SKULL WITH WORRY!
I HAD TO SLEEP AT THE COLLEGE, GRANDPAPA. THE WHITEHEADS WERE GETTING TWITCHY LAST NIGHT, THEY MADE A LOT OF ARRESTS...
PLEASE STOP THIS, RHODA. PLEASE.
YOU MEAN GIVE UP, JUST LIKE THAT? HOW COULD I EVER FACE MY FRIENDS?
HEY, YOU'RE BEING RUDE! WE HAVE GUESTS!
FORGIVE ME, FRIEND! THANK YOU SO MUCH FOR BRINGING MY RHODA HOME. I'M SAUL HOFFMANN, WELCOME!
I'M THE DOCTOR. LOVELY PLACE YOU HAVE HERE!
THIS IS REALLY BEAUTIFUL!
THE RELICS OF A LOST AGE.
RHODA THINKS CHANGE IS COMING, BUT RUSSIAN TANKS CRUSHED THE HOPE FROM THIS CITY TWENTY YEARS AGO... AND BEFORE THEM, THE NAZIS.
PRAGUE HAS NOT BEEN FREE FOR A VERY LONG TIME.
NO! ALL OF YOU HIDE! QUICKLY!
KNOK-KNOK-KNOK

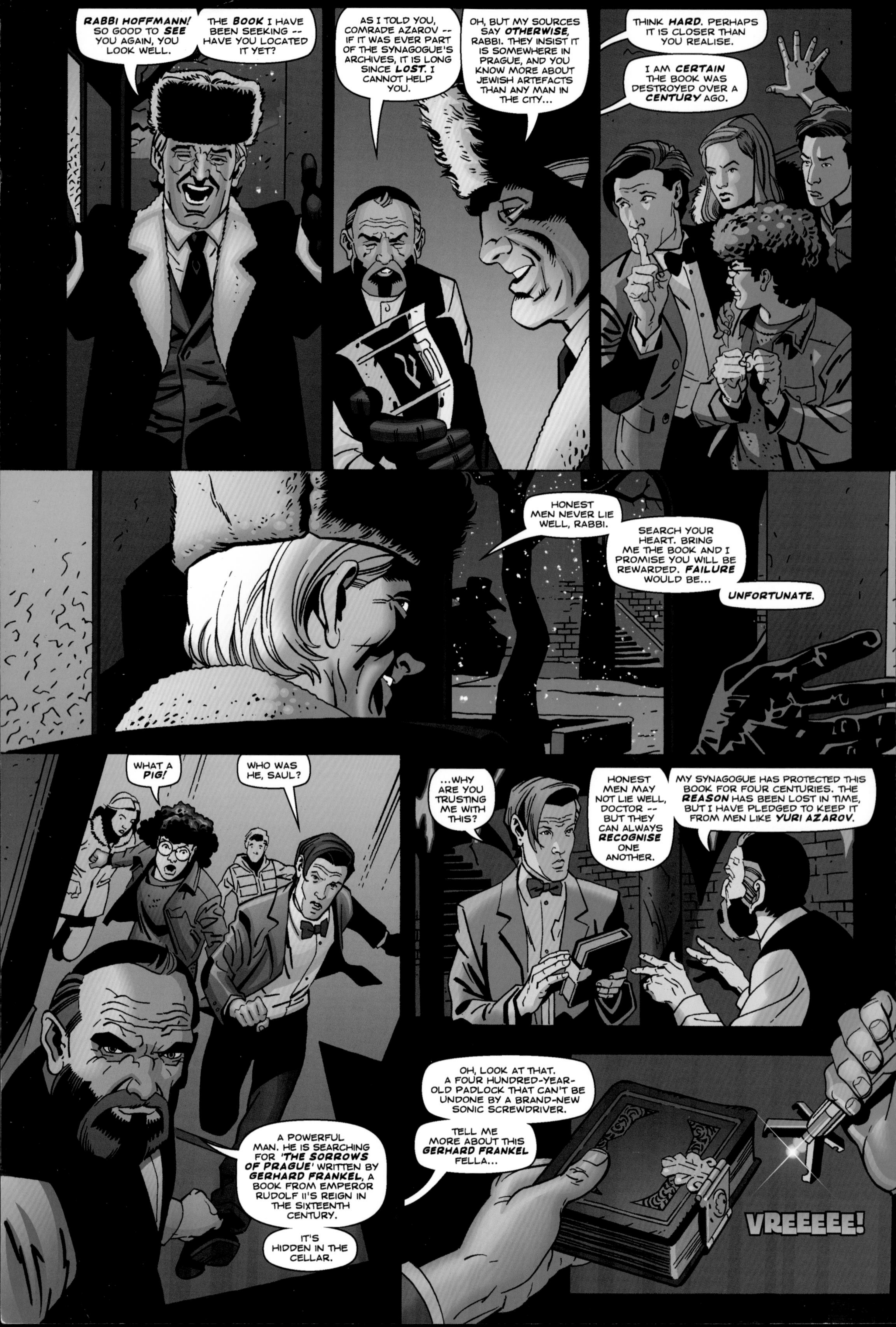
RABBI HOFFMANN! SO GOOD TO SEE YOU AGAIN, YOU LOOK WELL.
THE BOOK I HAVE BEEN SEEKING -- HAVE YOU LOCATED IT YET?
AS I TOLD YOU, COMRADE AZAROV -- IF IT WAS EVER PART OF THE SYNAGOGUE'S ARCHIVES, IT IS LONG SINCE LOST. I CANNOT HELP YOU.
OH, BUT MY SOURCES SAY OTHERWISE, RABBI. THEY INSIST IT IS SOMEWHERE IN PRAGUE, AND YOU KNOW MORE ABOUT JEWISH ARTEFACTS THAN ANY MAN IN THE CITY...
THINK HARD. PERHAPS IT IS CLOSER THAN YOU REALISE.
I AM CERTAIN THE BOOK WAS DESTROYED OVER A CENTURY AGO.
HONEST MEN NEVER LIE WELL, RABBI.
SEARCH YOUR HEART. BRING ME THE BOOK AND I PROMISE YOU WILL BE REWARDED. FAILURE WOULD BE...
UNFORTUNATE.
WHAT A PIG!
WHO WAS HE, SAUL?
A POWERFUL MAN. HE IS SEARCHING FOR 'THE SORROWS OF PRAGUE' WRITTEN BY GERHARD FRANKEL, A BOOK FROM EMPEROR RUDOLF II'S REIGN IN THE SIXTEENTH CENTURY.
IT'S HIDDEN IN THE CELLAR.
...WHY ARE YOU TRUSTING ME WITH THIS?
HONEST MEN MAY NOT LIE WELL, DOCTOR -- BUT THEY CAN ALWAYS RECOGNISE ONE ANOTHER.
MY SYNAGOGUE HAS PROTECTED THIS BOOK FOR FOUR CENTURIES. THE REASON HAS BEEN LOST IN TIME, BUT I HAVE PLEDGED TO KEEP IT FROM MEN LIKE YURI AZAROV.
OH, LOOK AT THAT. A FOUR HUNDRED-YEAR-OLD PADLOCK THAT CAN'T BE UNDONE BY A BRAND-NEW SONIC SCREWDRIVER.
TELL ME MORE ABOUT THIS GERHARD FRANKEL FELLA...
VREEEEE!

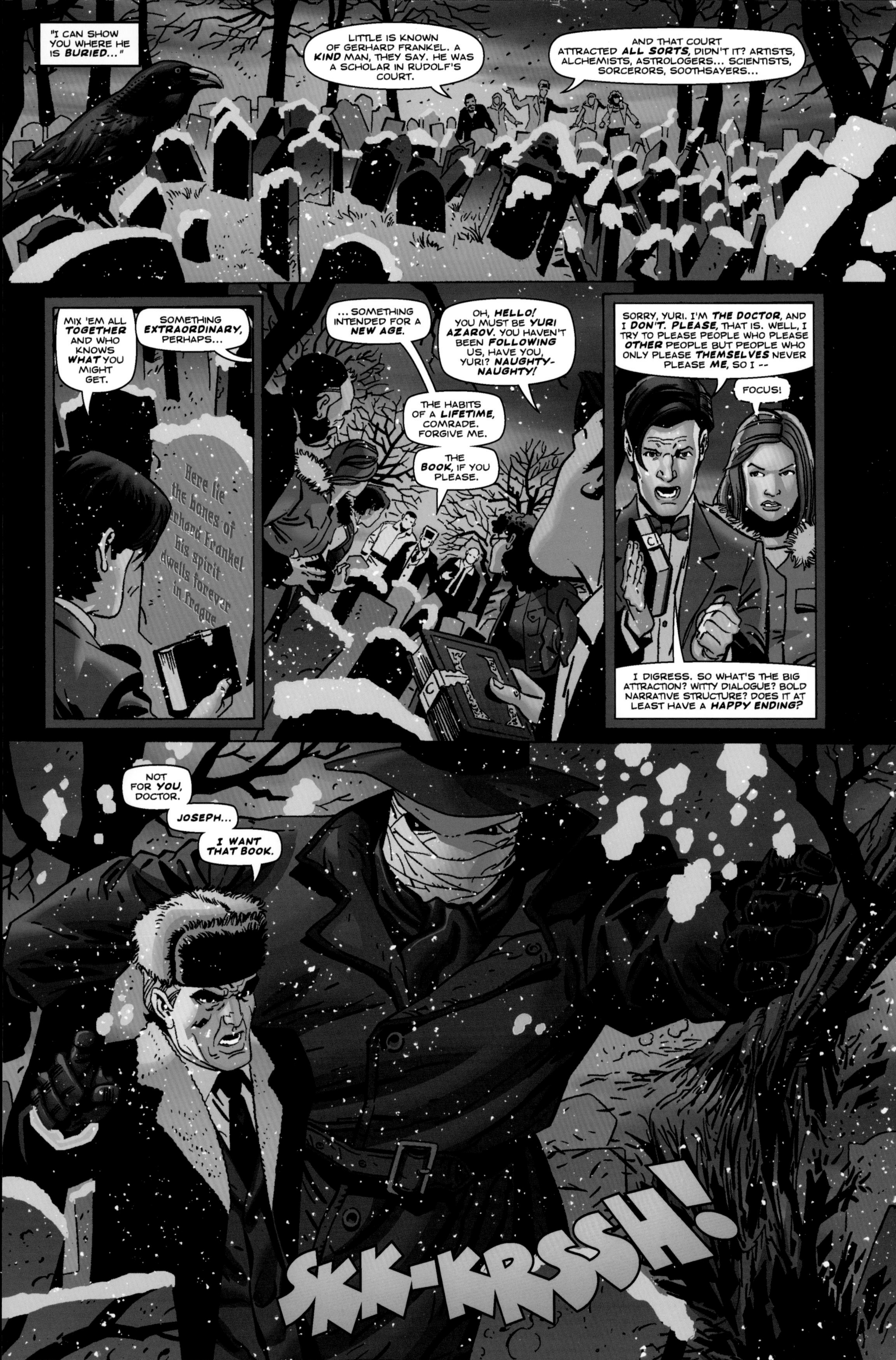
"I CAN SHOW YOU WHERE HE IS BURIED..."
LITTLE IS KNOWN OF GERHARD FRANKEL. A KIND MAN, THEY SAY. HE WAS A SCHOLAR IN RUDOLF'S COURT.
AND THAT COURT ATTRACTED ALL SORTS, DIDN'T IT? ARTISTS, ALCHEMISTS, ASTROLOGERS... SCIENTISTS, SORCERORS, SOOTHSAYERS...
MIX 'EM ALL TOGETHER AND WHO KNOWS WHAT YOU MIGHT GET.
SOMETHING EXTRAORDINARY, PERHAPS...
Here lie the bones of Gerhard Frankel His spirit dwells forever in Prague
...SOMETHING INTENDED FOR A NEW AGE.
OH, HELLO! YOU MUST BE YURI AZAROV. YOU HAVEN'T BEEN FOLLOWING US, HAVE YOU, YURI? NAUGHTY-NAUGHTY!
THE HABITS OF A LIFETIME, COMRADE. FORGIVE ME.
THE BOOK, IF YOU PLEASE.
SORRY, YURI. I'M THE DOCTOR, AND I DON'T. PLEASE, THAT IS. WELL, I TRY TO PLEASE PEOPLE WHO PLEASE OTHER PEOPLE BUT PEOPLE WHO ONLY PLEASE THEMSELVES NEVER PLEASE ME, SO I --
FOCUS!
I DIGRESS. SO WHAT'S THE BIG ATTRACTION? WITTY DIALOGUE? BOLD NARRATIVE STRUCTURE? DOES IT AT LEAST HAVE A HAPPY ENDING?
NOT FOR YOU, DOCTOR.
JOSEPH...
I WANT THAT BOOK.
SKK-KRSSH!

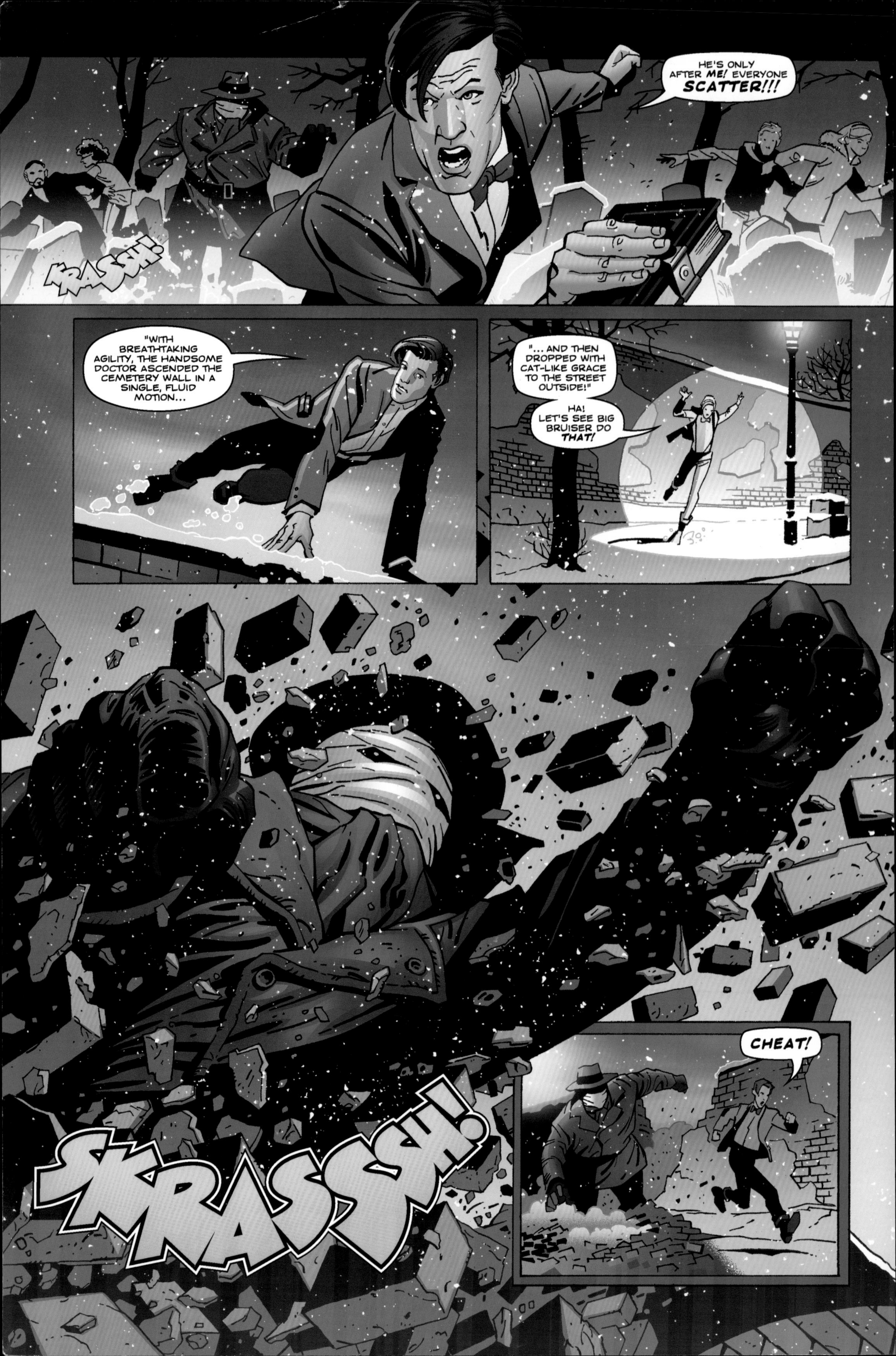

HE'S ONLY AFTER ME! EVERYONE SCATTER!!!
KRASSH!
"WITH BREATHTAKING AGILITY, THE HANDSOME DOCTOR ASCENDED THE CEMETERY WALL IN A SINGLE, FLUID MOTION...
"...AND THEN DROPPED WITH CAT-LIKE GRACE TO THE STREET OUTSIDE!"
HA! LET'S SEE BIG BRUISER DO THAT!
SKRASSH!
CHEAT!

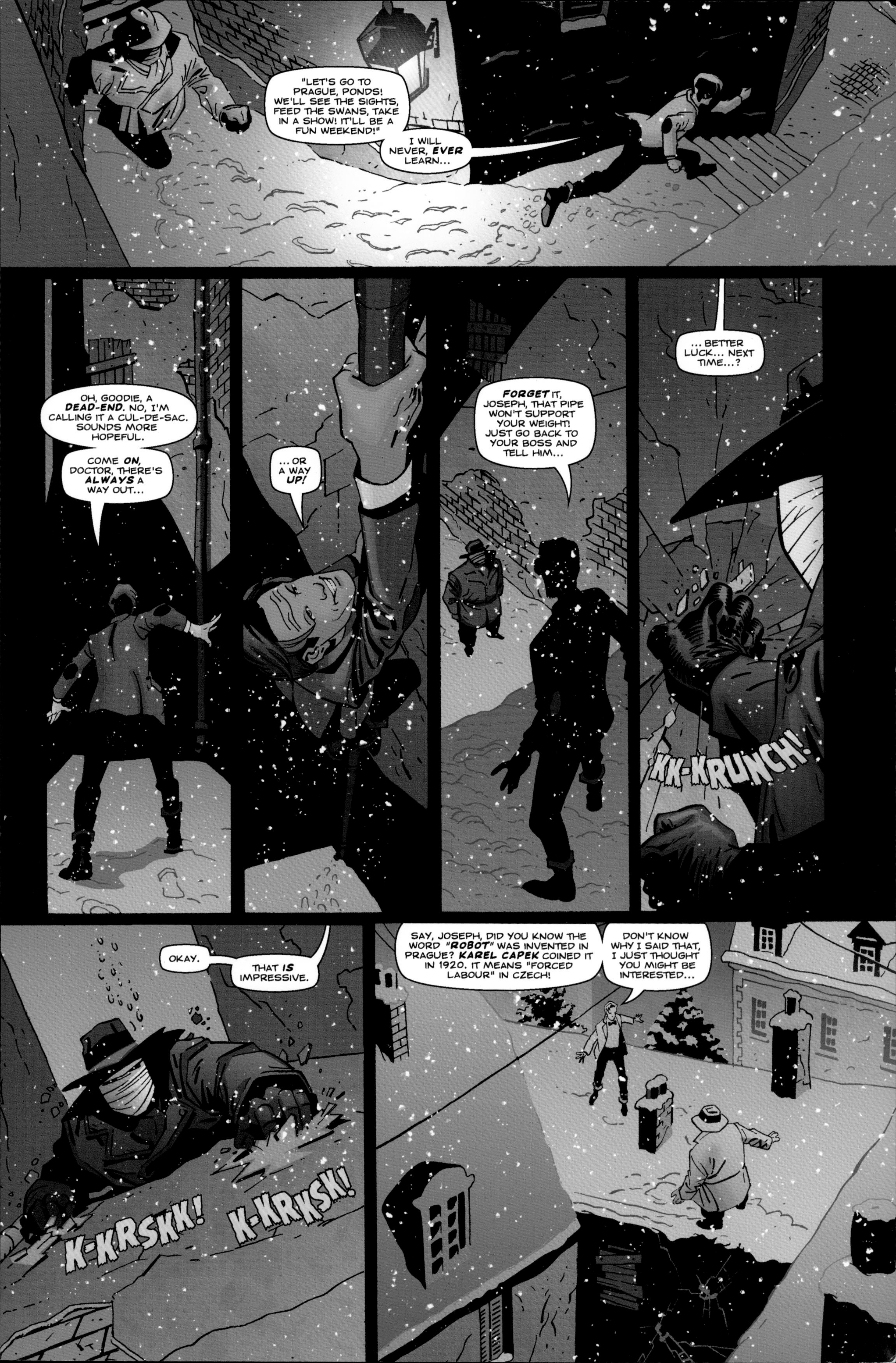
"LET'S GO TO PRAGUE, PONDS! WE'LL SEE THE SIGHTS, FEED THE SWANS, TAKE IN A SHOW! IT'LL BE A FUN WEEKEND!"
I WILL NEVER, EVER LEARN...
OH, GOODIE, A DEAD-END. NO, I'M CALLING IT A CUL-DE-SAC. SOUNDS MORE HOPEFUL.
COME ON, DOCTOR, THERE'S ALWAYS A WAY OUT...
...OR A WAY UP!
FORGET IT, JOSEPH, THAT PIPE WON'T SUPPORT YOUR WEIGHT! JUST GO BACK TO YOUR BOSS AND TELL HIM...
...BETTER LUCK... NEXT TIME...?
KK-KRUNCH!
OKAY.
THAT IS IMPRESSIVE.
K-KRSKK!
K-KRKSK!
SAY, JOSEPH, DID YOU KNOW THE WORD "ROBOT" WAS INVENTED IN PRAGUE? KAREL CAPEK COINED IT IN 1920. IT MEANS "FORCED LABOUR" IN CZECH!
DON'T KNOW WHY I SAID THAT, I JUST THOUGHT YOU MIGHT BE INTERESTED...

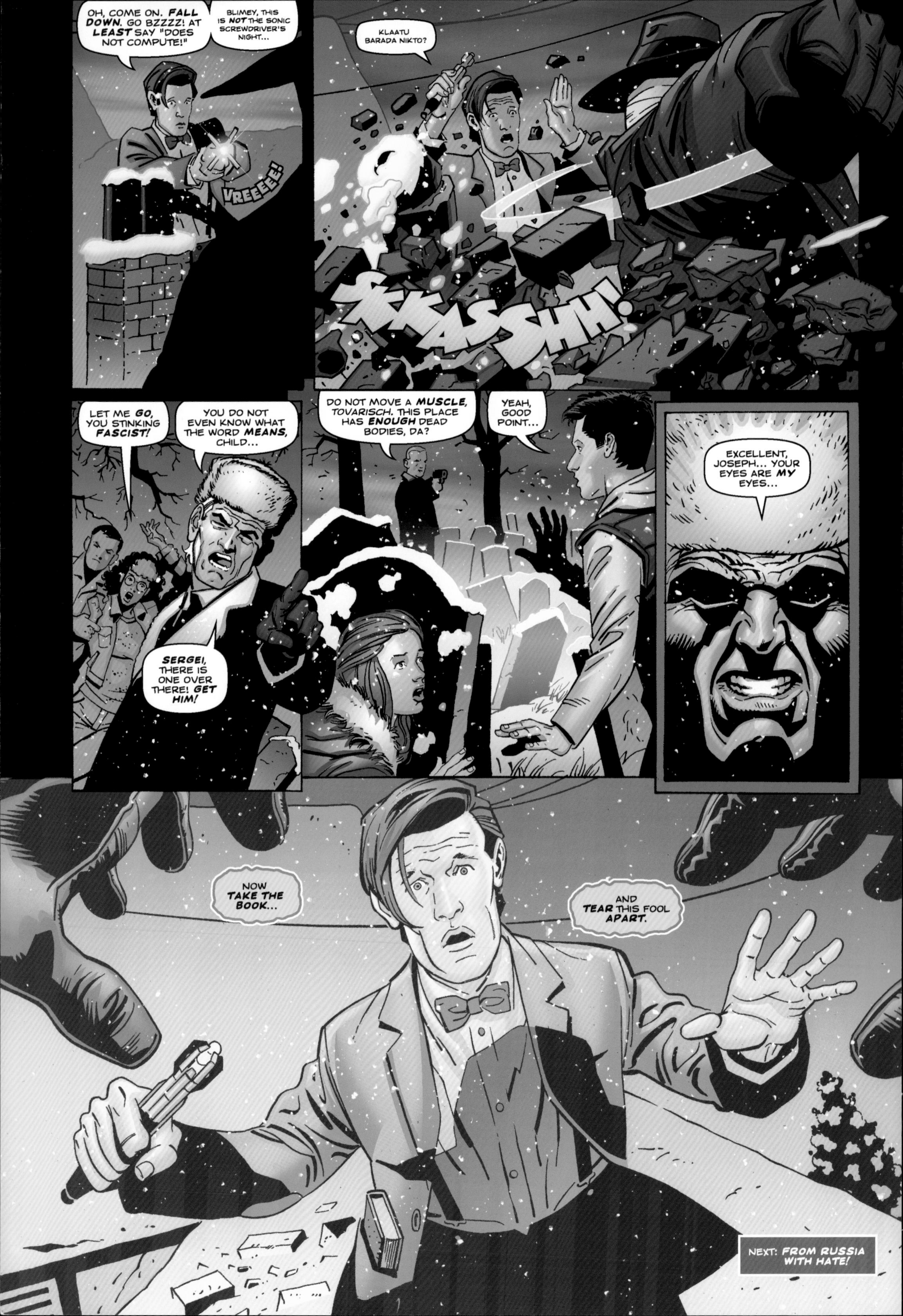
OH, COME ON. FALL DOWN. GO BZZZZ! AT LEAST SAY "DOES NOT COMPUTE!"
BLIMEY, THIS IS NOT THE SONIC SCREWDRIVER'S NIGHT...
VREEEEE!
KLAATU BARADA NIKTO?
SKKASSHH!
LET ME GO, YOU STINKING FASCIST!
YOU DO NOT EVEN KNOW WHAT THE WORD MEANS, CHILD...
SERGEI, THERE IS ONE OVER THERE! GET HIM!
DO NOT MOVE A MUSCLE, TOVARISCH. THIS PLACE HAS ENOUGH DEAD BODIES, DA?
YEAH, GOOD POINT...
EXCELLENT, JOSEPH... YOUR EYES ARE MY EYES...
NOW TAKE THE BOOK...
AND TEAR THIS FOOL APART.
NEXT: FROM RUSSIA WITH HATE!

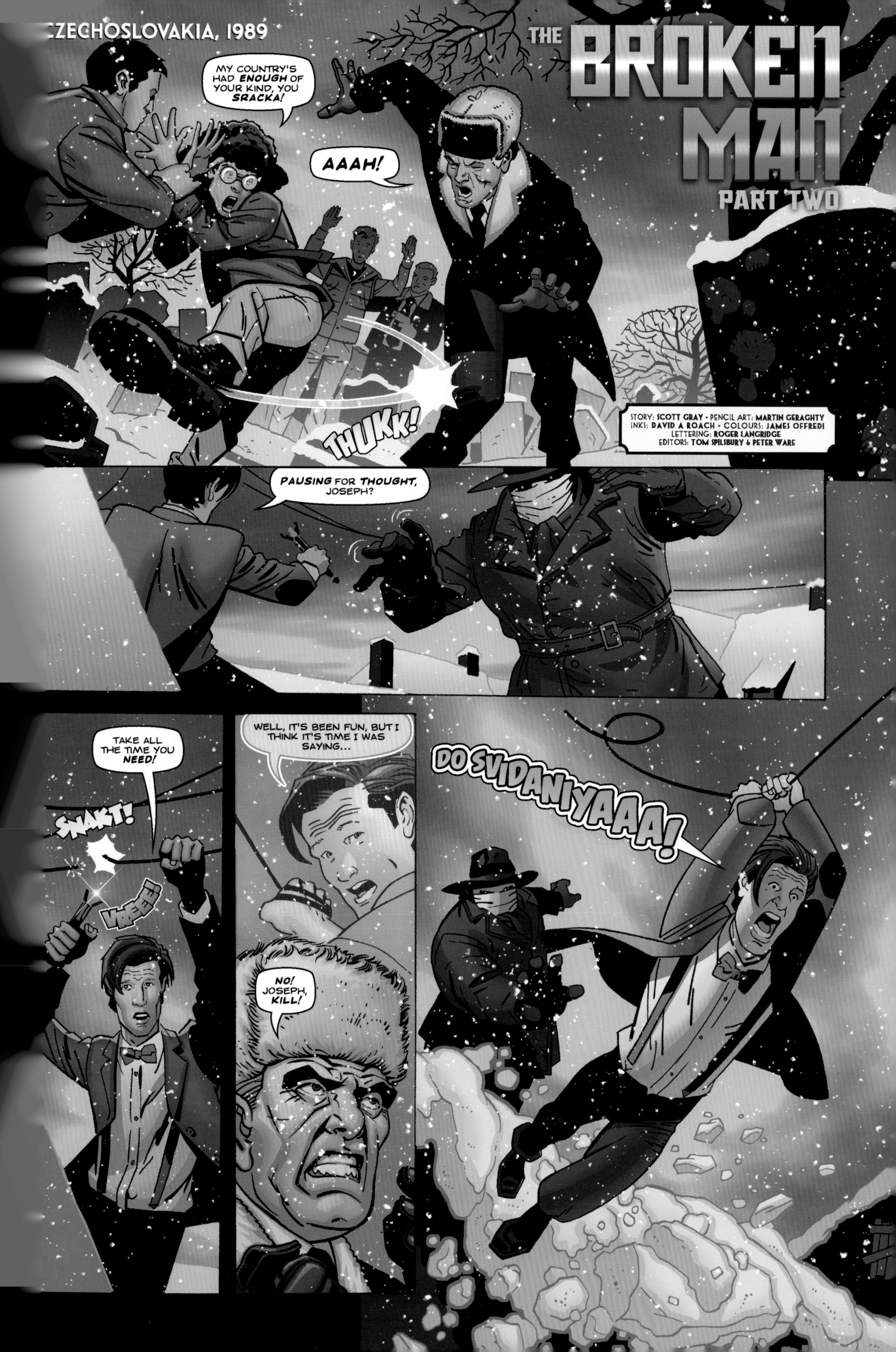
CZECHOSLOVAKIA, 1989
THE BROKEN MAN
PART TWO
MY COUNTRY'S HAD ENOUGH OF YOUR KIND, YOU SRACKA!
AAAH!
THUKK!
STORY: SCOTT GRAY • PENCIL ART: MARTIN GERAGHTY
INKS: DAVID A ROACH • COLOURS: JAMES OFFREDI
LETTERING: ROGER LANGRIDGE
EDITORS: TOM SPILSBURY & PETER WARE
PAUSING FOR THOUGHT, JOSEPH?
TAKE ALL THE TIME YOU NEED!
SNAKT!
VREEE!
WELL, IT'S BEEN FUN, BUT I THINK IT'S TIME I WAS SAYING...
NO! JOSEPH, KILL!
DO SVIDANIYAAAA!

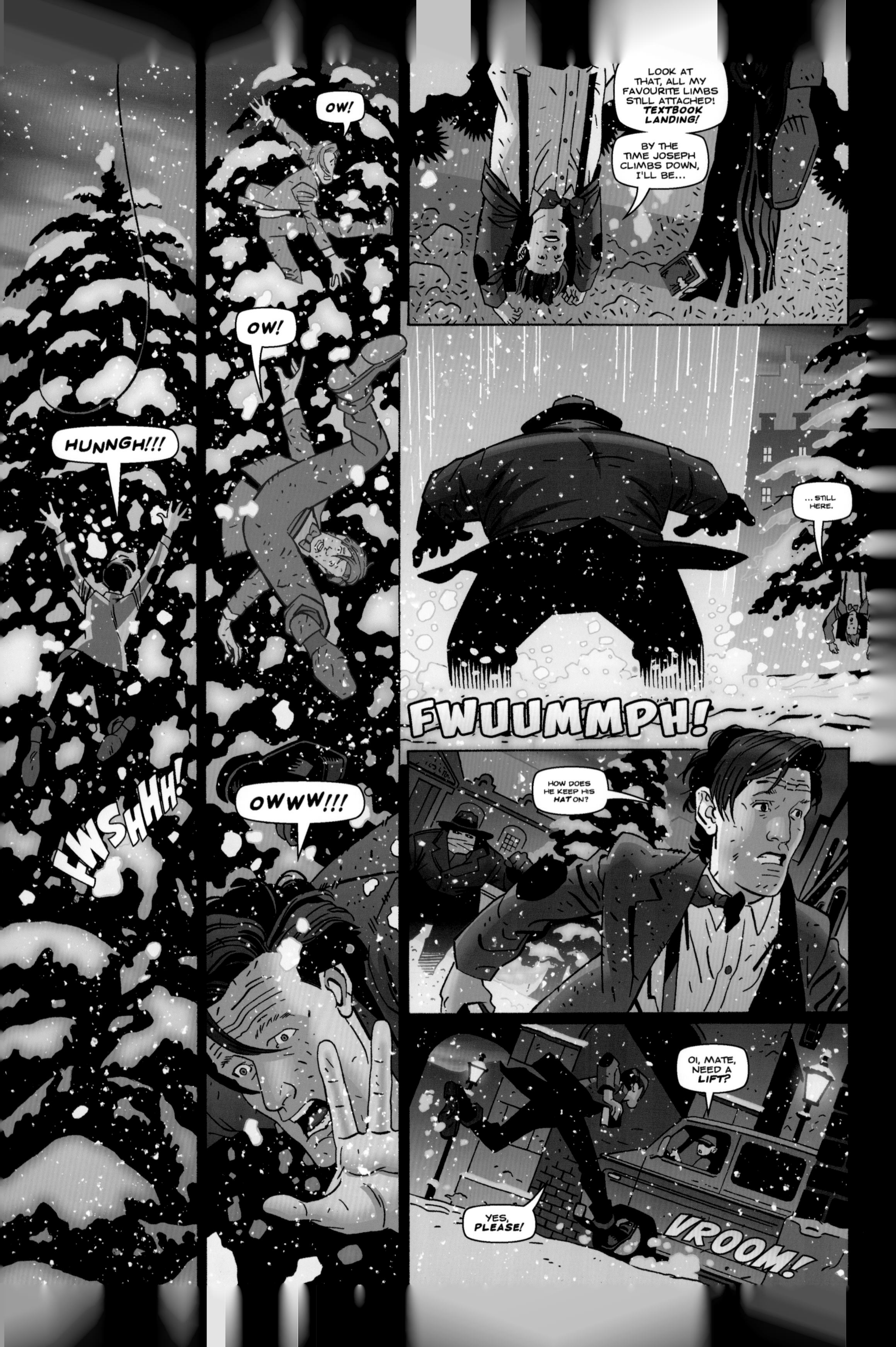
HUNNGH!!!
FWSHHH!
OW!
OW!
OWWW!!!
LOOK AT THAT, ALL MY FAVOURITE LIMBS STILL ATTACHED! TEXTBOOK LANDING!
BY THE TIME JOSEPH CLIMBS DOWN, I'LL BE...
...STILL HERE.
FWUUMMPH!
HOW DOES HE KEEP HIS HAT ON?
OI, MATE, NEED A LIFT?
YES, PLEASE!
VROOM!

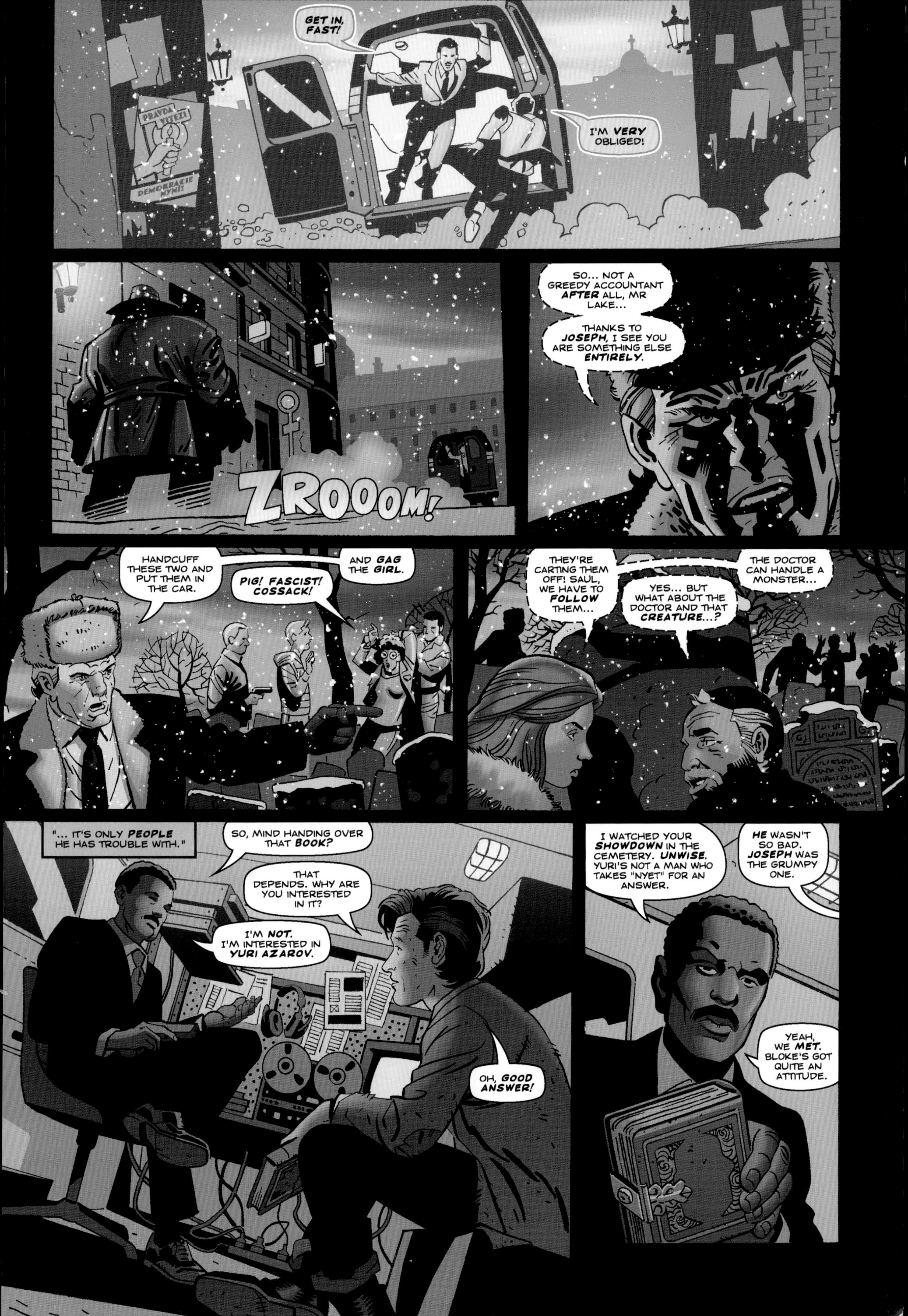
GET IN, FAST!
PRAVDA VITĚZÍ
DEMOKRACIE NYNÍ!
I'M VERY OBLIGED!
ZROOOM!
SO... NOT A GREEDY ACCOUNTANT AFTER ALL, MR LAKE...
THANKS TO JOSEPH, I SEE YOU ARE SOMETHING ELSE ENTIRELY.
HANDCUFF THESE TWO AND PUT THEM IN THE CAR.
AND GAG THE GIRL.
PIG! FASCIST! COSSACK!
THEY'RE CARTING THEM OFF! SAUL, WE HAVE TO FOLLOW THEM...
YES... BUT WHAT ABOUT THE DOCTOR AND THAT CREATURE...?
THE DOCTOR CAN HANDLE A MONSTER...
"... IT'S ONLY PEOPLE HE HAS TROUBLE WITH."
SO, MIND HANDING OVER THAT BOOK?
THAT DEPENDS. WHY ARE YOU INTERESTED IN IT?
I'M NOT. I'M INTERESTED IN YURI AZAROV.
OH, GOOD ANSWER!
I WATCHED YOUR SHOWDOWN IN THE CEMETERY. UNWISE. YURI'S NOT A MAN WHO TAKES "NYET" FOR AN ANSWER.
HE WASN'T SO BAD. JOSEPH WAS THE GRUMPY ONE.
YEAH, WE MET. BLOKE'S GOT QUITE AN ATTITUDE.

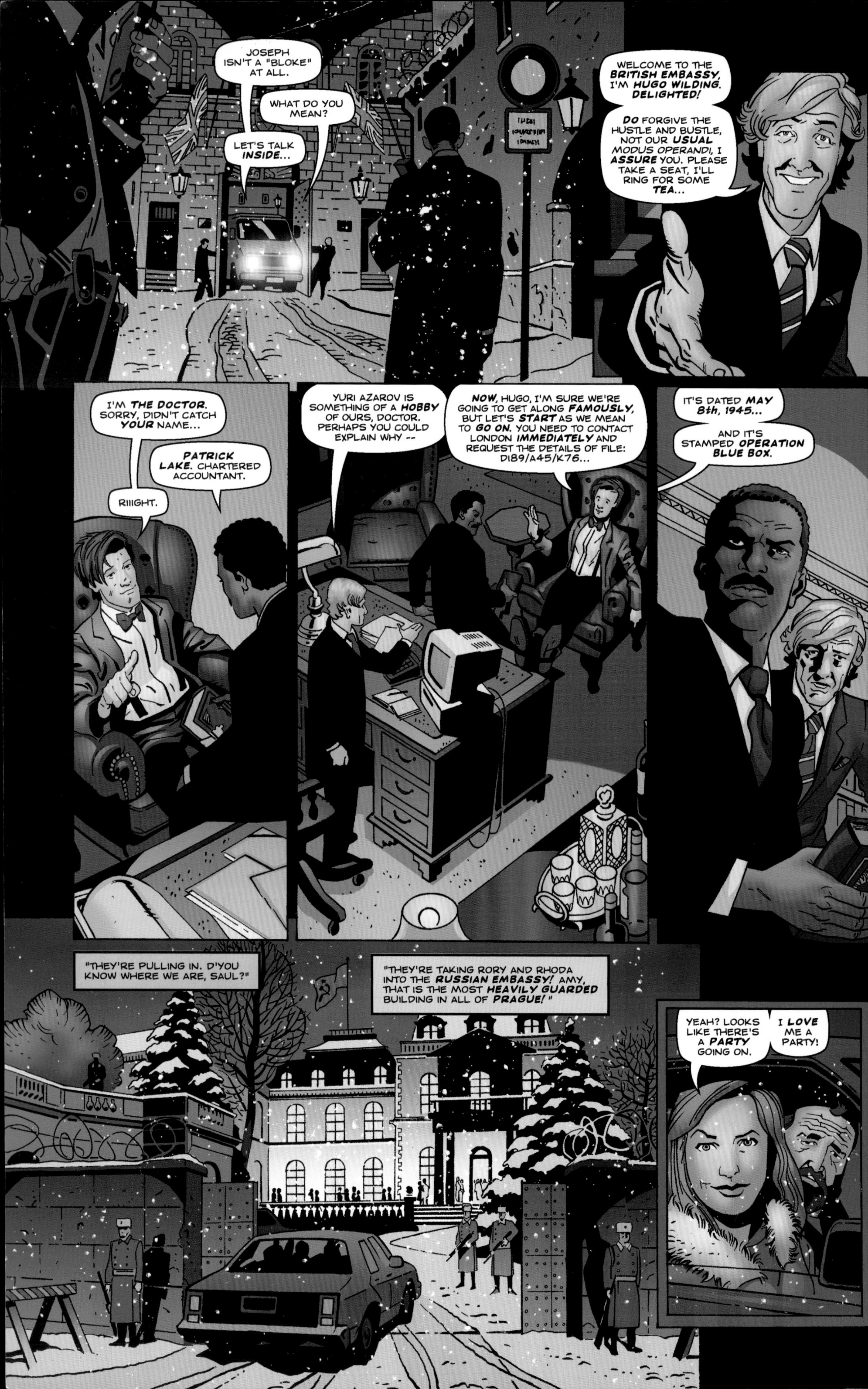
JOSEPH ISN'T A "BLOKE" AT ALL.
WHAT DO YOU MEAN?
LET'S TALK INSIDE...
WELCOME TO THE BRITISH EMBASSY, I'M HUGO WILDING. DELIGHTED!
DO FORGIVE THE HUSTLE AND BUSTLE, NOT OUR USUAL MODUS OPERANDI, I ASSURE YOU. PLEASE TAKE A SEAT, I'LL RING FOR SOME TEA...
I'M THE DOCTOR. SORRY, DIDN'T CATCH YOUR NAME...
PATRICK LAKE. CHARTERED ACCOUNTANT.
RIIIGHT.
YURI AZAROV IS SOMETHING OF A HOBBY OF OURS, DOCTOR. PERHAPS YOU COULD EXPLAIN WHY --
NOW, HUGO, I'M SURE WE'RE GOING TO GET ALONG FAMOUSLY, BUT LET'S START AS WE MEAN TO GO ON. YOU NEED TO CONTACT LONDON IMMEDIATELY AND REQUEST THE DETAILS OF FILE: D189/A45/K76...
IT'S DATED MAY 8th, 1945...
AND IT'S STAMPED OPERATION BLUE BOX.
"THEY'RE PULLING IN. D'YOU KNOW WHERE WE ARE, SAUL?"
"THEY'RE TAKING RORY AND RHODA INTO THE RUSSIAN EMBASSY! AMY, THAT IS THE MOST HEAVILY GUARDED BUILDING IN ALL OF PRAGUE!"
YEAH? LOOKS LIKE THERE'S A PARTY GOING ON.
I LOVE ME A PARTY!

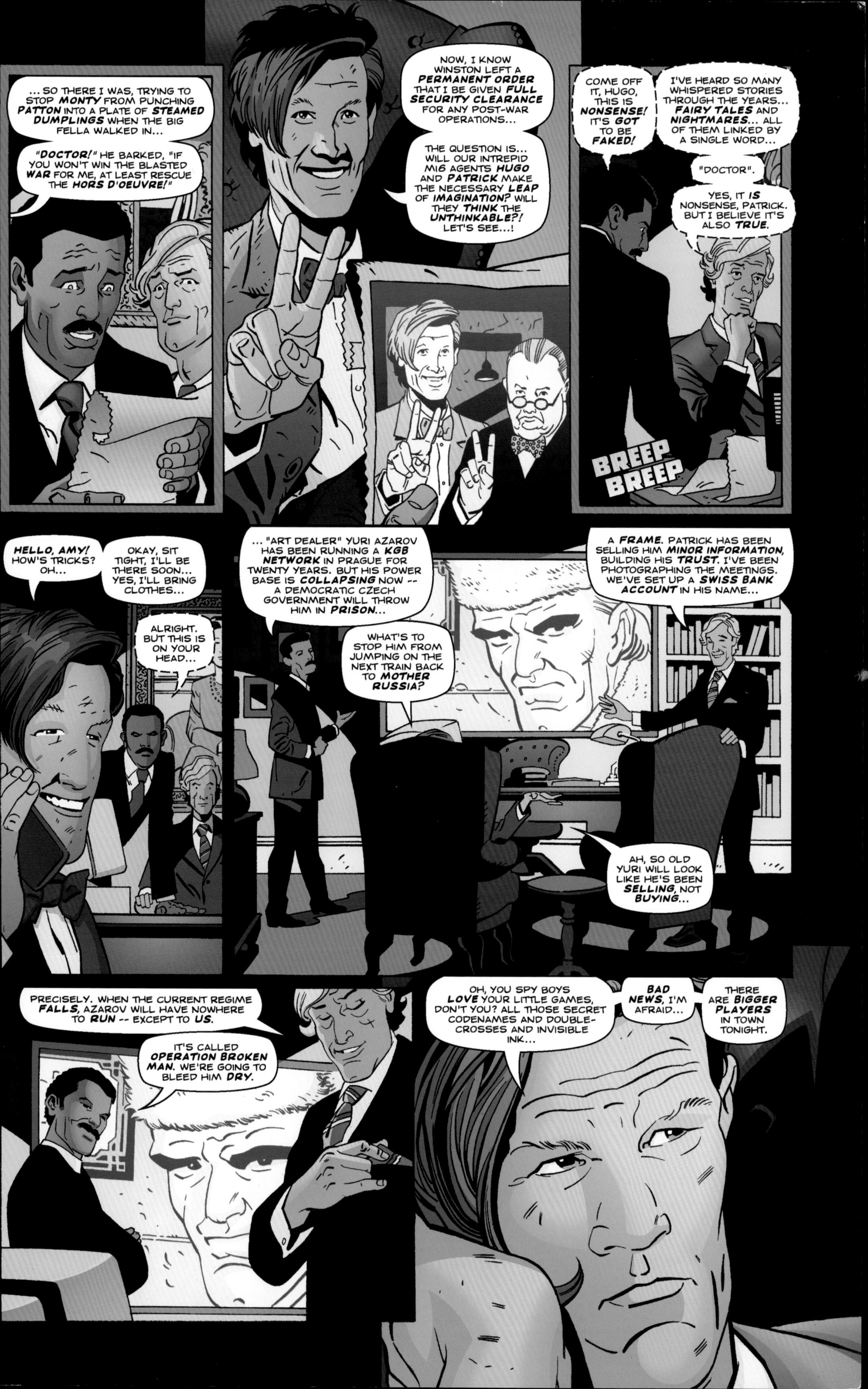

... SO THERE I WAS, TRYING TO STOP MONTY FROM PUNCHING PATTON INTO A PLATE OF STEAMED DUMPLINGS WHEN THE BIG FELLA WALKED IN...
"DOCTOR!" HE BARKED, "IF YOU WON'T WIN THE BLASTED WAR FOR ME, AT LEAST RESCUE THE HORS D'OEUVRE!"
NOW, I KNOW WINSTON LEFT A PERMANENT ORDER THAT I BE GIVEN FULL SECURITY CLEARANCE FOR ANY POST-WAR OPERATIONS...
THE QUESTION IS... WILL OUR INTREPID MI6 AGENTS HUGO AND PATRICK MAKE THE NECESSARY LEAP OF IMAGINATION? WILL THEY THINK THE UNTHINKABLE?! LET'S SEE...!
COME OFF IT, HUGO, THIS IS NONSENSE! IT'S GOT TO BE FAKED!
I'VE HEARD SO MANY WHISPERED STORIES THROUGH THE YEARS... FAIRY TALES AND NIGHTMARES... ALL OF THEM LINKED BY A SINGLE WORD...
"DOCTOR".
YES, IT IS NONSENSE, PATRICK. BUT I BELIEVE IT'S ALSO TRUE.
BREEP BREEP
HELLO, AMY! HOW'S TRICKS? OH...
OKAY, SIT TIGHT, I'LL BE THERE SOON... YES, I'LL BRING CLOTHES...
ALRIGHT. BUT THIS IS ON YOUR HEAD...
... "ART DEALER" YURI AZAROV HAS BEEN RUNNING A KGB NETWORK IN PRAGUE FOR TWENTY YEARS. BUT HIS POWER BASE IS COLLAPSING NOW -- A DEMOCRATIC CZECH GOVERNMENT WILL THROW HIM IN PRISON...
WHAT'S TO STOP HIM FROM JUMPING ON THE NEXT TRAIN BACK TO MOTHER RUSSIA?
A FRAME. PATRICK HAS BEEN SELLING HIM MINOR INFORMATION, BUILDING HIS TRUST. I'VE BEEN PHOTOGRAPHING THE MEETINGS. WE'VE SET UP A SWISS BANK ACCOUNT IN HIS NAME...
AH, SO OLD YURI WILL LOOK LIKE HE'S BEEN SELLING, NOT BUYING...
PRECISELY. WHEN THE CURRENT REGIME FALLS, AZAROV WILL HAVE NOWHERE TO RUN -- EXCEPT TO US.
IT'S CALLED OPERATION BROKEN MAN. WE'RE GOING TO BLEED HIM DRY.
OH, YOU SPY BOYS LOVE YOUR LITTLE GAMES, DON'T YOU? ALL THOSE SECRET CODENAMES AND DOUBLE-CROSSES AND INVISIBLE INK...
BAD NEWS, I'M AFRAID...
THERE ARE BIGGER PLAYERS IN TOWN TONIGHT.

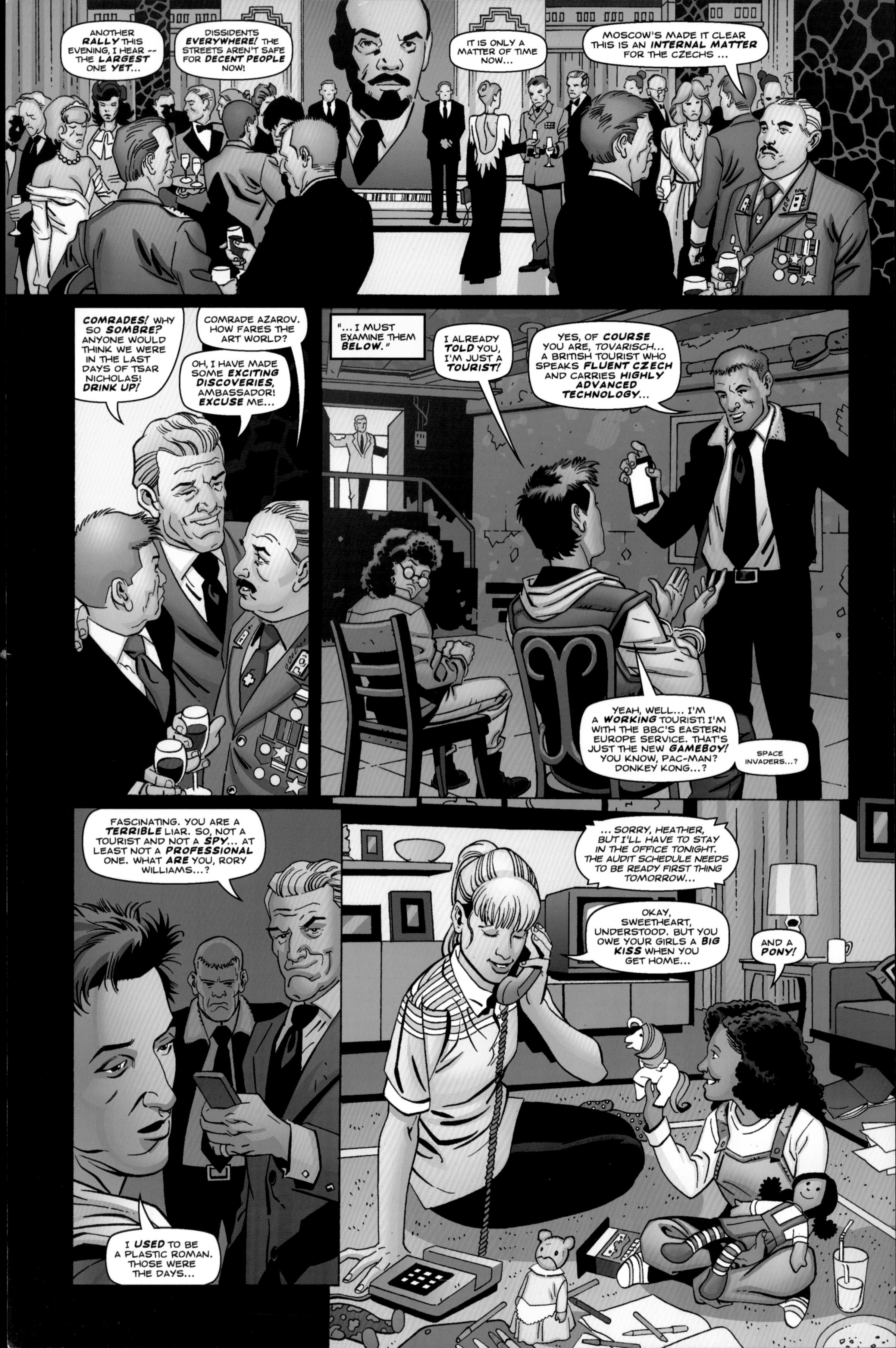
ANOTHER RALLY THIS EVENING, I HEAR -- THE LARGEST ONE YET...
DISSIDENTS EVERYWHERE! THE STREETS AREN'T SAFE FOR DECENT PEOPLE NOW!
IT IS ONLY A MATTER OF TIME NOW...
MOSCOW'S MADE IT CLEAR THIS IS AN INTERNAL MATTER FOR THE CZECHS ...
COMRADES! WHY SO SOMBRE? ANYONE WOULD THINK WE WERE IN THE LAST DAYS OF TSAR NICHOLAS! DRINK UP!
COMRADE AZAROV. HOW FARES THE ART WORLD?
OH, I HAVE MADE SOME EXCITING DISCOVERIES, AMBASSADOR! EXCUSE ME...
"... I MUST EXAMINE THEM BELOW."
I ALREADY TOLD YOU, I'M JUST A TOURIST!
YES, OF COURSE YOU ARE, TOVARISCH... A BRITISH TOURIST WHO SPEAKS FLUENT CZECH AND CARRIES HIGHLY ADVANCED TECHNOLOGY...
YEAH, WELL... I'M A WORKING TOURIST! I'M WITH THE BBC'S EASTERN EUROPE SERVICE. THAT'S JUST THE NEW GAMEBOY! YOU KNOW, PAC-MAN? DONKEY KONG...?
SPACE INVADERS...?
FASCINATING. YOU ARE A TERRIBLE LIAR. SO, NOT A TOURIST AND NOT A SPY... AT LEAST NOT A PROFESSIONAL ONE. WHAT ARE YOU, RORY WILLIAMS...?
I USED TO BE A PLASTIC ROMAN. THOSE WERE THE DAYS...
... SORRY, HEATHER, BUT I'LL HAVE TO STAY IN THE OFFICE TONIGHT. THE AUDIT SCHEDULE NEEDS TO BE READY FIRST THING TOMORROW...
OKAY, SWEETHEART, UNDERSTOOD. BUT YOU OWE YOUR GIRLS A BIG KISS WHEN YOU GET HOME...
AND A PONY!

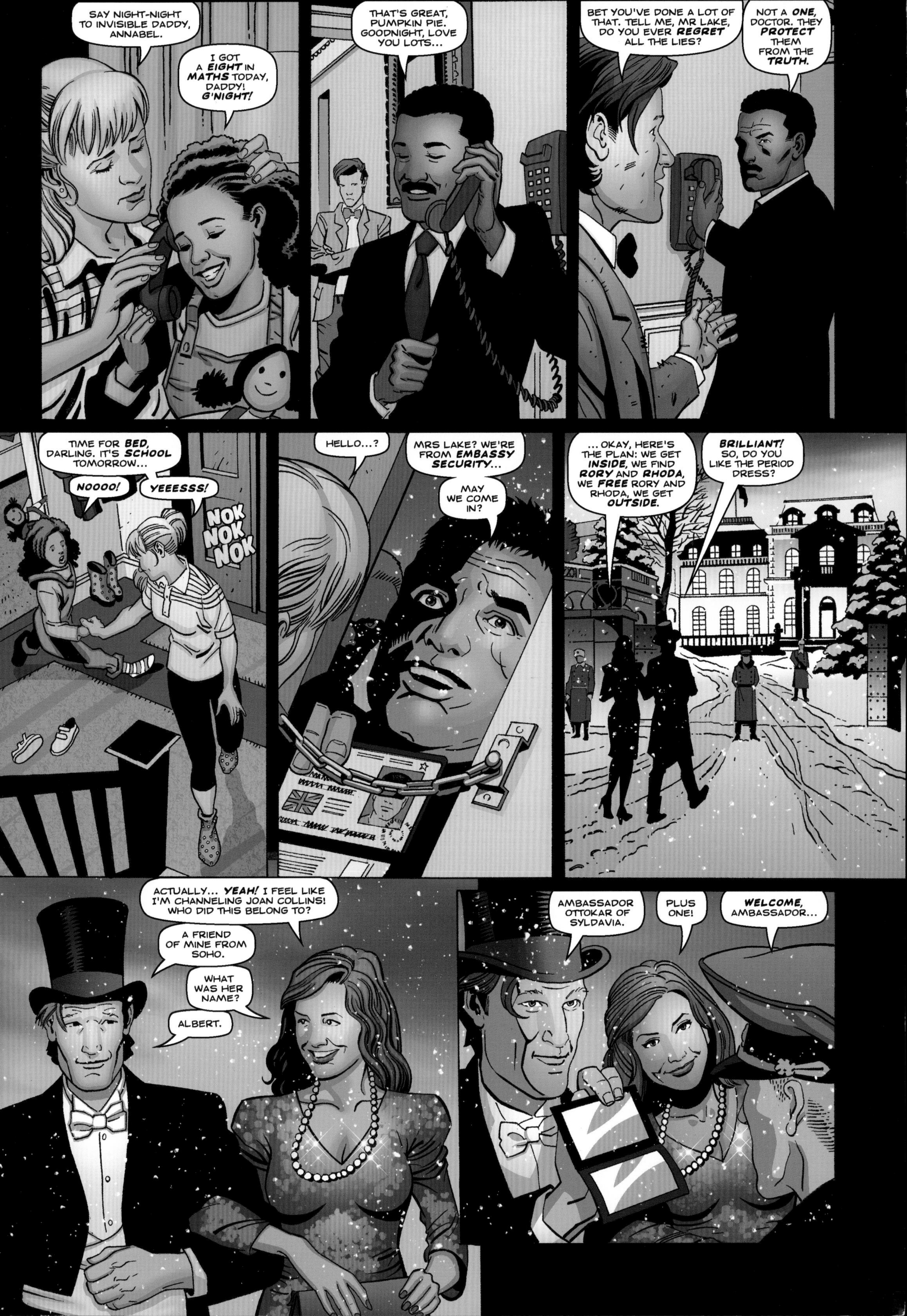
SAY NIGHT-NIGHT TO INVISIBLE DADDY, ANNABEL.
I GOT A EIGHT IN MATHS TODAY, DADDY! G'NIGHT!
THAT'S GREAT, PUMPKIN PIE. GOODNIGHT, LOVE YOU LOTS...
BET YOU'VE DONE A LOT OF THAT. TELL ME, MR LAKE, DO YOU EVER REGRET ALL THE LIES?
NOT A ONE, DOCTOR. THEY PROTECT THEM FROM THE TRUTH.
TIME FOR BED, DARLING. IT'S SCHOOL TOMORROW...
NOOOO!
YEEESSS!
NOK NOK NOK
HELLO...?
MRS LAKE? WE'RE FROM EMBASSY SECURITY...
MAY WE COME IN?
...OKAY, HERE'S THE PLAN: WE GET INSIDE, WE FIND RORY AND RHODA, WE FREE RORY AND RHODA, WE GET OUTSIDE.
BRILLIANT! SO, DO YOU LIKE THE PERIOD DRESS?
ACTUALLY... YEAH! I FEEL LIKE I'M CHANNELING JOAN COLLINS! WHO DID THIS BELONG TO?
A FRIEND OF MINE FROM SOHO.
WHAT WAS HER NAME?
ALBERT.
AMBASSADOR OTTOKAR OF SYLDAVIA.
PLUS ONE!
WELCOME, AMBASSADOR...

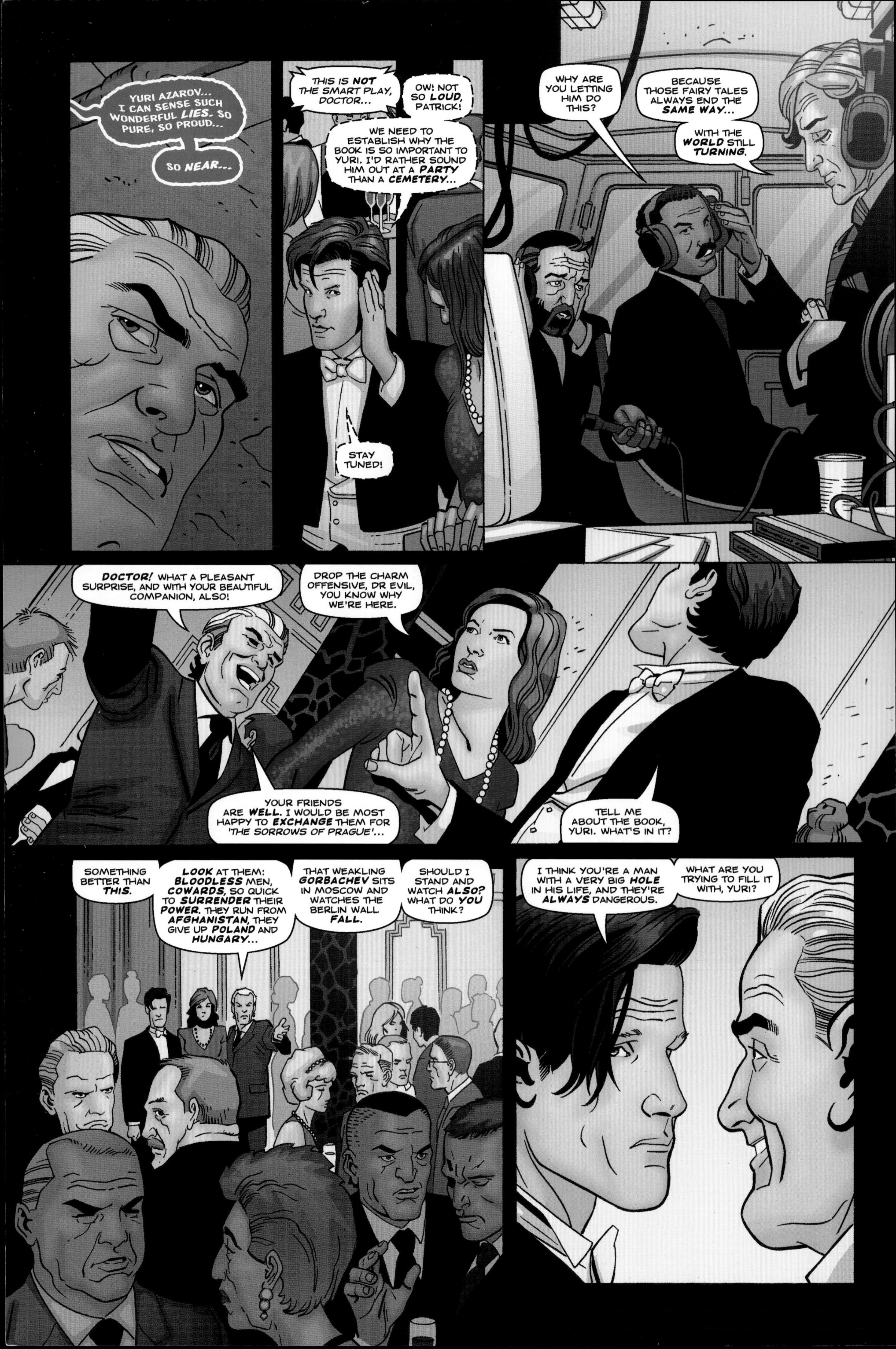
YURI AZAROV... I CAN SENSE SUCH WONDERFUL LIES. SO PURE, SO PROUD...
SO NEAR...
THIS IS NOT THE SMART PLAY, DOCTOR...
OW! NOT SO LOUD, PATRICK!
WE NEED TO ESTABLISH WHY THE BOOK IS SO IMPORTANT TO YURI. I'D RATHER SOUND HIM OUT AT A PARTY THAN A CEMETERY...
STAY TUNED!
WHY ARE YOU LETTING HIM DO THIS?
BECAUSE THOSE FAIRY TALES ALWAYS END THE SAME WAY...
WITH THE WORLD STILL TURNING.
DOCTOR! WHAT A PLEASANT SURPRISE, AND WITH YOUR BEAUTIFUL COMPANION, ALSO!
DROP THE CHARM OFFENSIVE, DR EVIL, YOU KNOW WHY WE'RE HERE.
YOUR FRIENDS ARE WELL. I WOULD BE MOST HAPPY TO EXCHANGE THEM FOR 'THE SORROWS OF PRAGUE'...
TELL ME ABOUT THE BOOK, YURI. WHAT'S IN IT?
SOMETHING BETTER THAN THIS.
LOOK AT THEM: BLOODLESS MEN, COWARDS, SO QUICK TO SURRENDER THEIR POWER. THEY RUN FROM AFGHANISTAN, THEY GIVE UP POLAND AND HUNGARY...
THAT WEAKLING GORBACHEV SITS IN MOSCOW AND WATCHES THE BERLIN WALL FALL.
SHOULD I STAND AND WATCH ALSO? WHAT DO YOU THINK?
I THINK YOU'RE A MAN WITH A VERY BIG HOLE IN HIS LIFE, AND THEY'RE ALWAYS DANGEROUS.
WHAT ARE YOU TRYING TO FILL IT WITH, YURI?

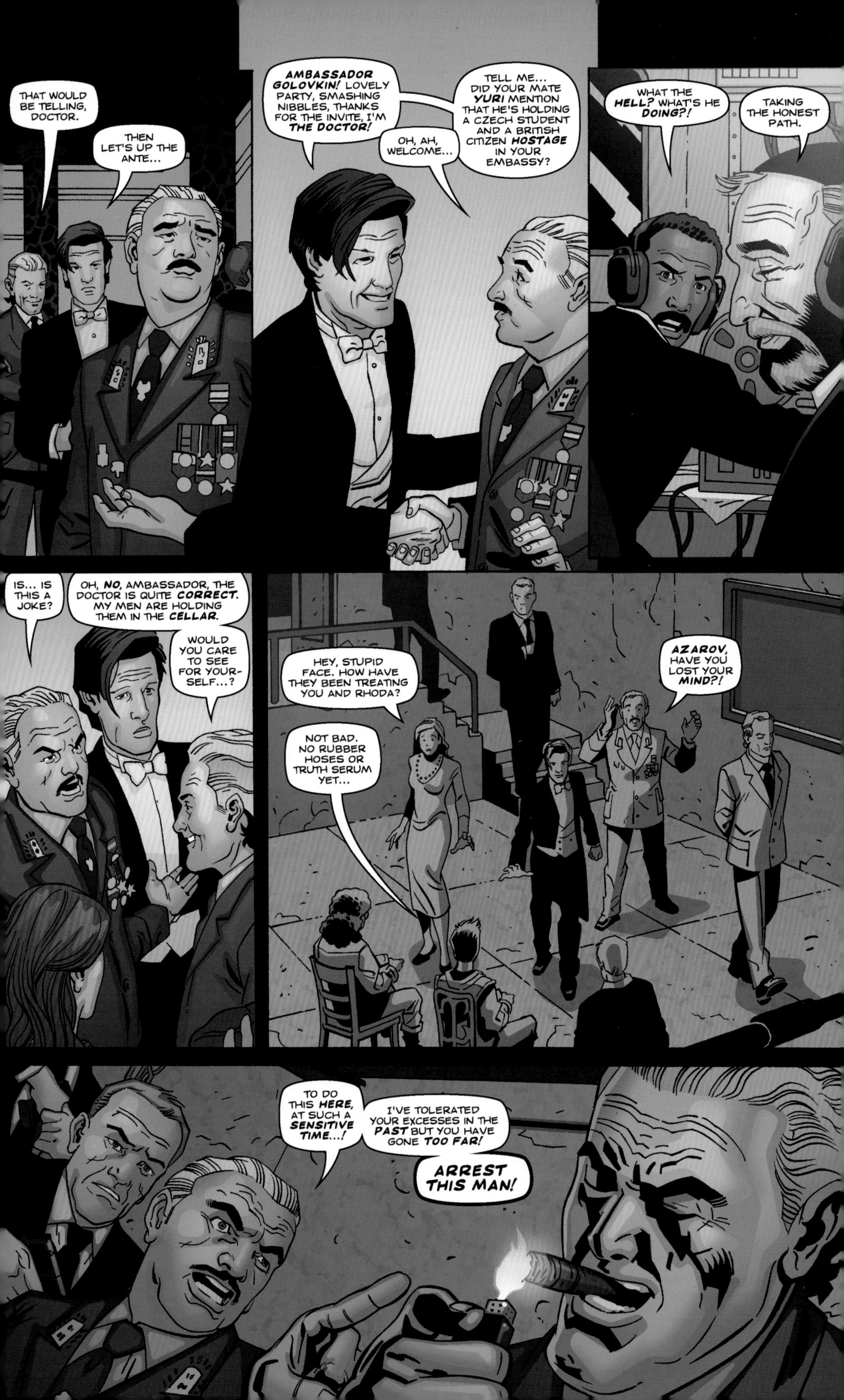
THAT WOULD BE TELLING, DOCTOR.
THEN LET'S UP THE ANTE...
AMBASSADOR GOLOVKIN! LOVELY PARTY, SMASHING NIBBLES, THANKS FOR THE INVITE, I'M THE DOCTOR!
OH, AH, WELCOME...
TELL ME... DID YOUR MATE YURI MENTION THAT HE'S HOLDING A CZECH STUDENT AND A BRITISH CITIZEN HOSTAGE IN YOUR EMBASSY?
WHAT THE HELL? WHAT'S HE DOING?!
TAKING THE HONEST PATH.
IS... IS THIS A JOKE?
OH, NO, AMBASSADOR, THE DOCTOR IS QUITE CORRECT. MY MEN ARE HOLDING THEM IN THE CELLAR.
WOULD YOU CARE TO SEE FOR YOUR-SELF...?
HEY, STUPID FACE. HOW HAVE THEY BEEN TREATING YOU AND RHODA?
NOT BAD. NO RUBBER HOSES OR TRUTH SERUM YET...
AZAROV, HAVE YOU LOST YOUR MIND?!
TO DO THIS HERE, AT SUCH A SENSITIVE TIME...!
I'VE TOLERATED YOUR EXCESSES IN THE PAST BUT YOU HAVE GONE TOO FAR!
ARREST THIS MAN!

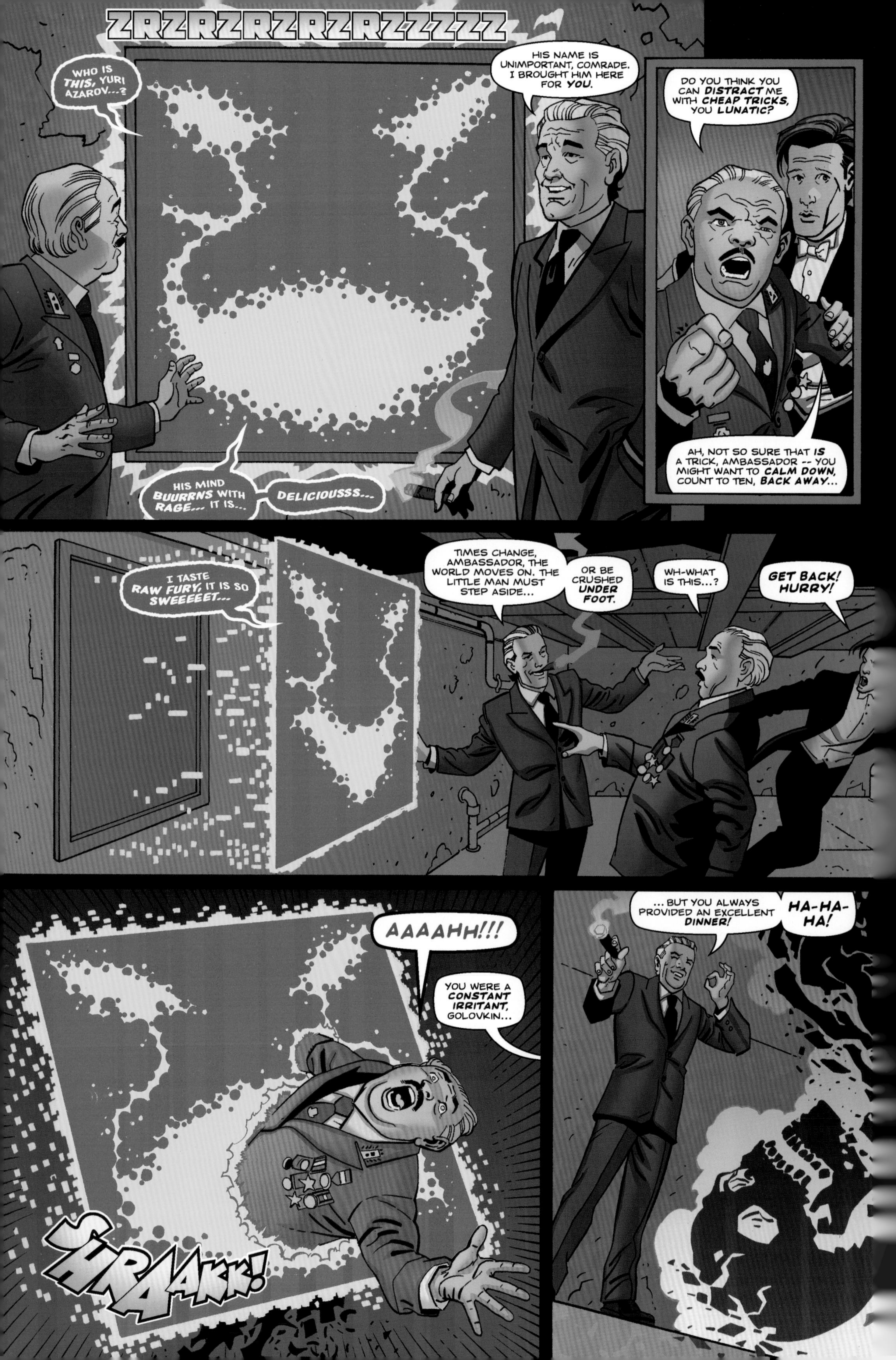
ZRZRZRZRZRZRZZZZZ
WHO IS THIS, YURI AZAROV...?
HIS NAME IS UNIMPORTANT, COMRADE. I BROUGHT HIM HERE FOR YOU.
HIS MIND BUURRNS WITH RAGE... IT IS...
DELICIOUSSS...
DO YOU THINK YOU CAN DISTRACT ME WITH CHEAP TRICKS, YOU LUNATIC?
AH, NOT SO SURE THAT IS A TRICK, AMBASSADOR -- YOU MIGHT WANT TO CALM DOWN, COUNT TO TEN, BACK AWAY...
I TASTE RAW FURY, IT IS SO SWEEEEET...
TIMES CHANGE, AMBASSADOR, THE WORLD MOVES ON. THE LITTLE MAN MUST STEP ASIDE...
OR BE CRUSHED UNDER FOOT.
WH-WHAT IS THIS...?
GET BACK! HURRY!
AAAAHH!!!
YOU WERE A CONSTANT IRRITANT, GOLOVKIN...
SHRAAKK!
... BUT YOU ALWAYS PROVIDED AN EXCELLENT DINNER!
HA-HA-HA!

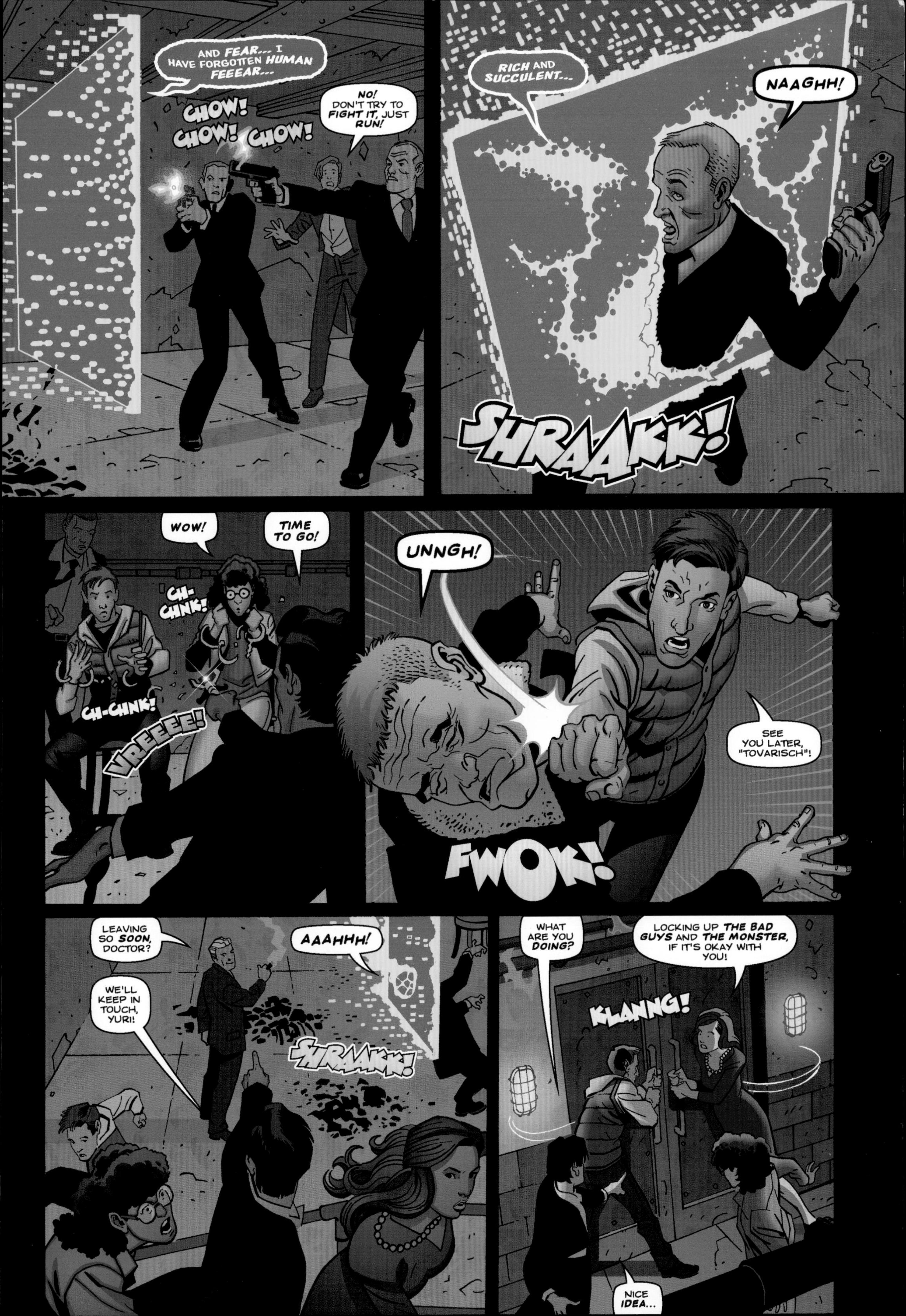
AND FEAR... I HAVE FORGOTTEN HUMAN FEEEAR...
CHOW! CHOW! CHOW!
NO! DON'T TRY TO FIGHT IT, JUST RUN!
RICH AND SUCCULENT...
NAAGHH!
SHRAAKK!
WOW!
TIME TO GO!
CH-CHNK!
CH-CHNK!
VREEEEE!
UNNGH!
SEE YOU LATER, "TOVARISCH"!
FWOK!
LEAVING SO SOON, DOCTOR?
AAAHHH!
WE'LL KEEP IN TOUCH, YURI!
SHRAAKK!
WHAT ARE YOU DOING?
LOCKING UP THE BAD GUYS AND THE MONSTER, IF IT'S OKAY WITH YOU!
KLANNG!
NICE IDEA...

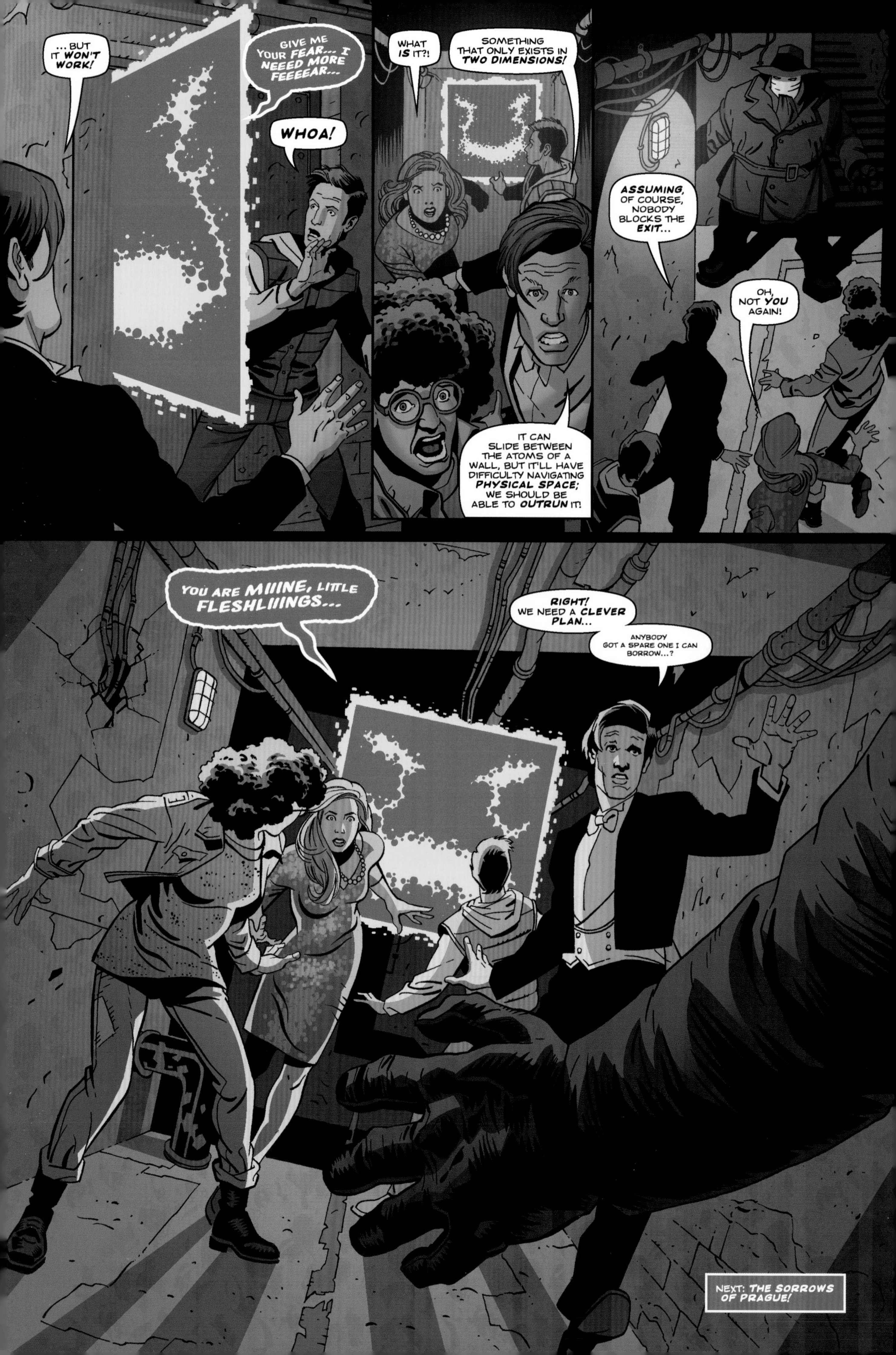

... BUT IT WON'T WORK!
GIVE ME YOUR FEAR... I NEED MORE FEEEEAR...
WHOA!
WHAT IS IT?!
SOMETHING THAT ONLY EXISTS IN TWO DIMENSIONS!
IT CAN SLIDE BETWEEN THE ATOMS OF A WALL, BUT IT'LL HAVE DIFFICULTY NAVIGATING PHYSICAL SPACE; WE SHOULD BE ABLE TO OUTRUN IT!
ASSUMING, OF COURSE, NOBODY BLOCKS THE EXIT...
OH, NOT YOU AGAIN!
YOU ARE MIIINE, LITTLE FLESHLIIINGS...
RIGHT! WE NEED A CLEVER PLAN...
ANYBODY GOT A SPARE ONE I CAN BORROW...?
NEXT: THE SORROWS OF PRAGUE!

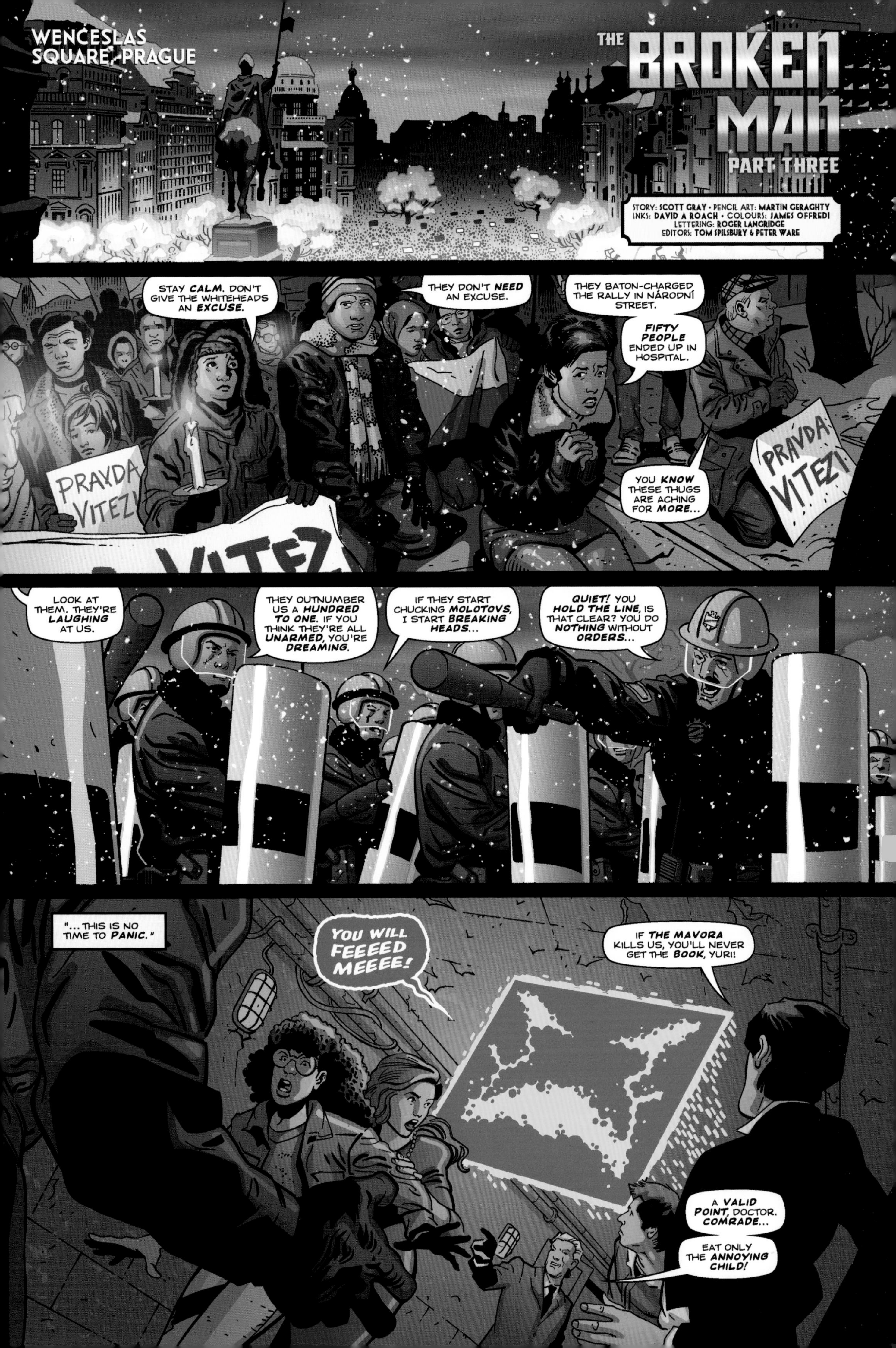

WENCESLAS SQUARE, PRAGUE
THE BROKEN MAN
PART THREE
STORY: SCOTT GRAY • PENCIL ART: MARTIN GERAGHTY
INKS: DAVID A ROACH • COLOURS: JAMES OFFREDI
LETTERING: ROGER LANGRIDGE
EDITORS: TOM SPILSBURY & PETER WARE
STAY CALM. DON'T GIVE THE WHITEHEADS AN EXCUSE.
THEY DON'T NEED AN EXCUSE.
THEY BATON-CHARGED THE RALLY IN NÁRODNÍ STREET.
FIFTY PEOPLE ENDED UP IN HOSPITAL.
YOU KNOW THESE THUGS ARE ACHING FOR MORE...
PRAVDA VITEZI
PRAVDA VITEZI
VITEZ
LOOK AT THEM. THEY'RE LAUGHING AT US.
THEY OUTNUMBER US A HUNDRED TO ONE. IF YOU THINK THEY'RE ALL UNARMED, YOU'RE DREAMING.
IF THEY START CHUCKING MOLOTOVS, I START BREAKING HEADS...
QUIET! YOU HOLD THE LINE, IS THAT CLEAR? YOU DO NOTHING WITHOUT ORDERS...
"...THIS IS NO TIME TO PANIC."
YOU WILL FEEEED MEEEE!
IF THE MAVORA KILLS US, YOU'LL NEVER GET THE BOOK, YURI!
A VALID POINT, DOCTOR. COMRADE...
EAT ONLY THE ANNOYING CHILD!

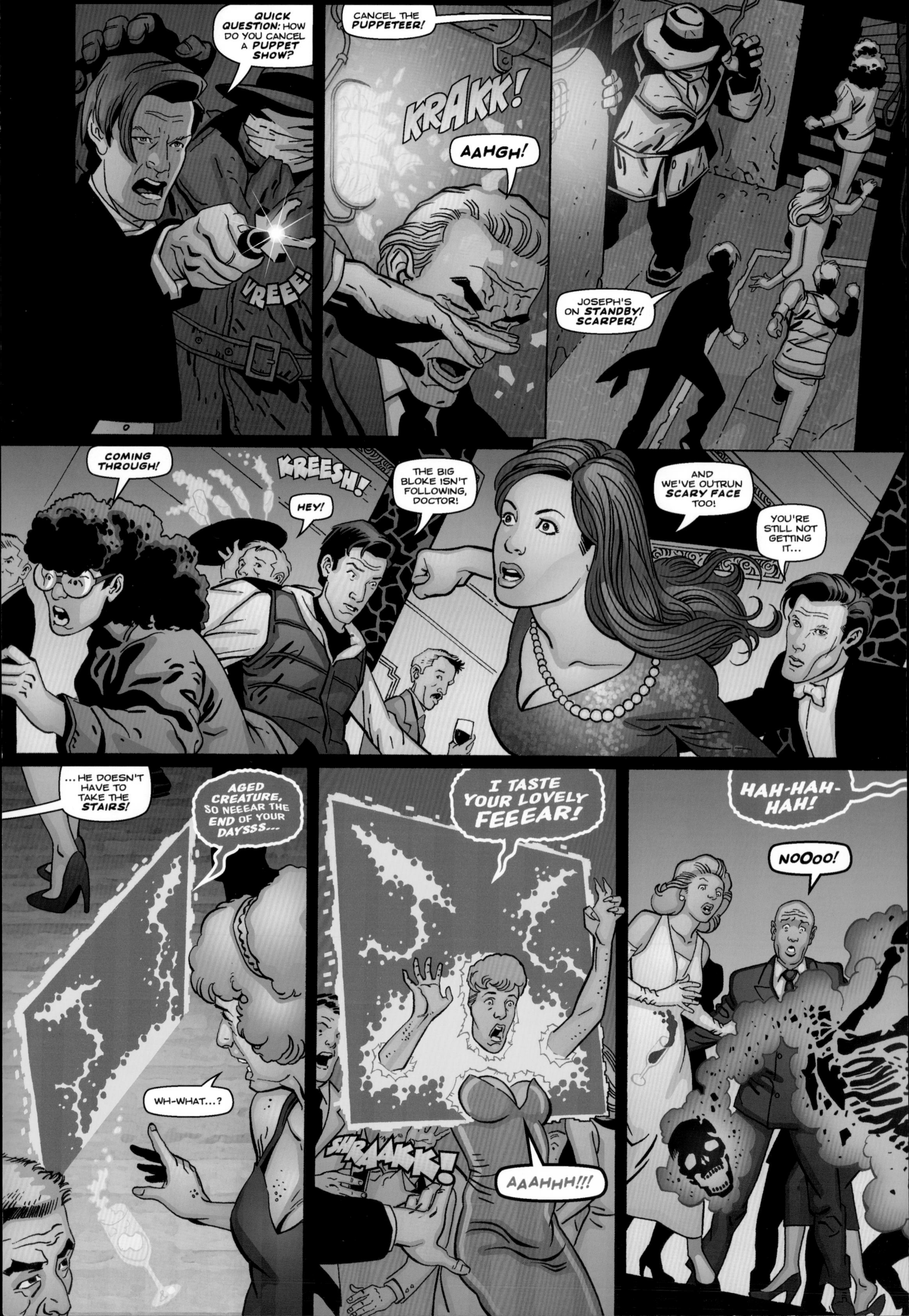
QUICK QUESTION: HOW DO YOU CANCEL A PUPPET SHOW?
VREEE!
CANCEL THE PUPPETEER!
KRAKK!
AAHGH!
JOSEPH'S ON STANDBY! SCARPER!
COMING THROUGH!
KREESH!
HEY!
THE BIG BLOKE ISN'T FOLLOWING, DOCTOR!
AND WE'VE OUTRUN SCARY FACE TOO!
YOU'RE STILL NOT GETTING IT...
...HE DOESN'T HAVE TO TAKE THE STAIRS!
AGED CREATURE, SO NEEEAR THE END OF YOUR DAYSSS...
WH-WHAT...?
I TASTE YOUR LOVELY FEEEAR!
SHRAAKK!
AAAHHH!!!
HAH-HAH-HAH!
NOOOO!

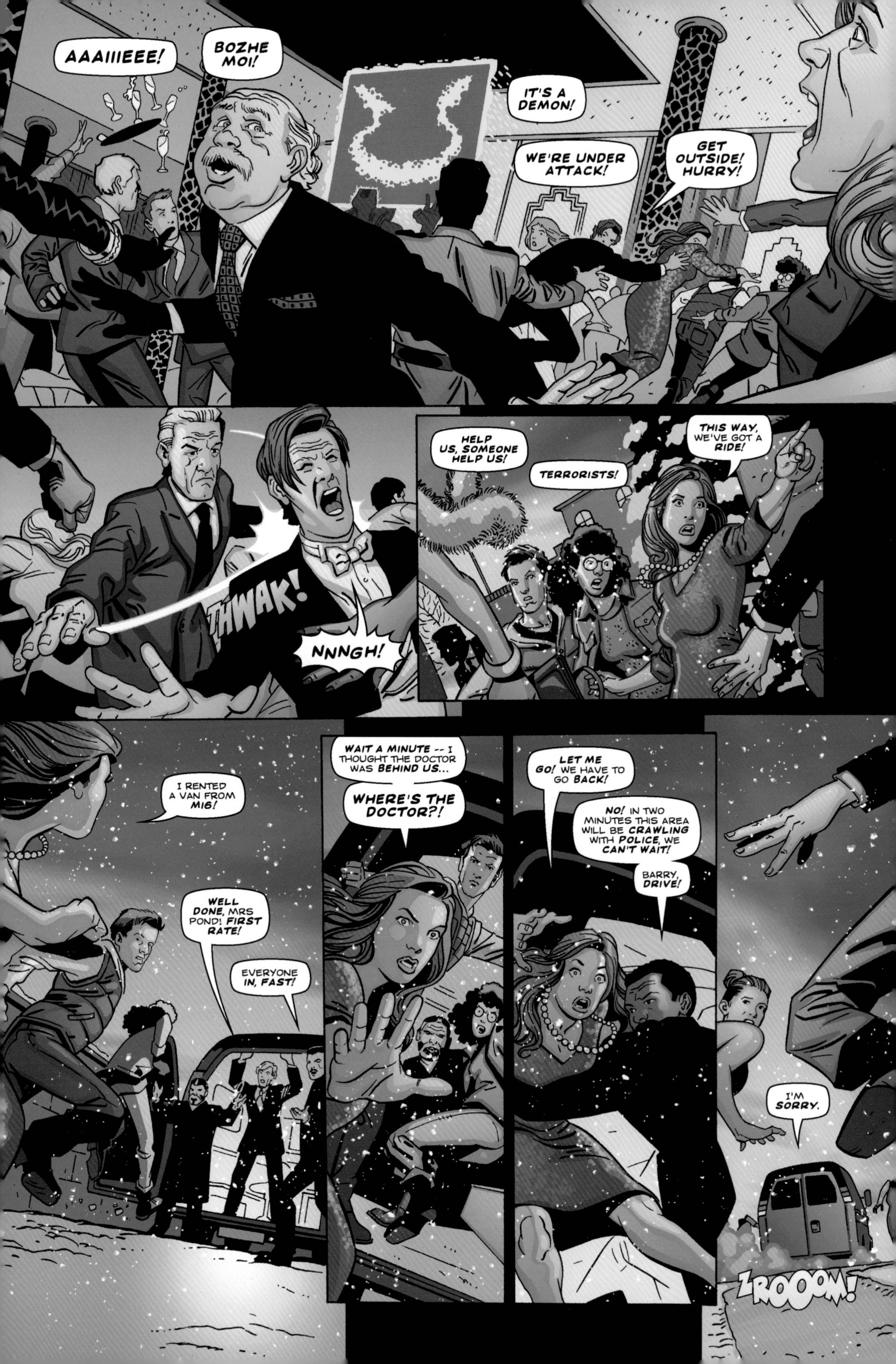
AAAIIIEEE!
BOZHE MOI!
IT'S A DEMON!
WE'RE UNDER ATTACK!
GET OUTSIDE! HURRY!
THWAK!
NNNGH!
HELP US, SOMEONE HELP US!
TERRORISTS!
THIS WAY, WE'VE GOT A RIDE!
I RENTED A VAN FROM MI6!
WELL DONE, MRS POND! FIRST RATE!
EVERYONE IN, FAST!
WAIT A MINUTE -- I THOUGHT THE DOCTOR WAS BEHIND US...
WHERE'S THE DOCTOR?!
LET ME GO! WE HAVE TO GO BACK!
NO! IN TWO MINUTES THIS AREA WILL BE CRAWLING WITH POLICE, WE CAN'T WAIT!
BARRY, DRIVE!
I'M SORRY.
ZROOOM!

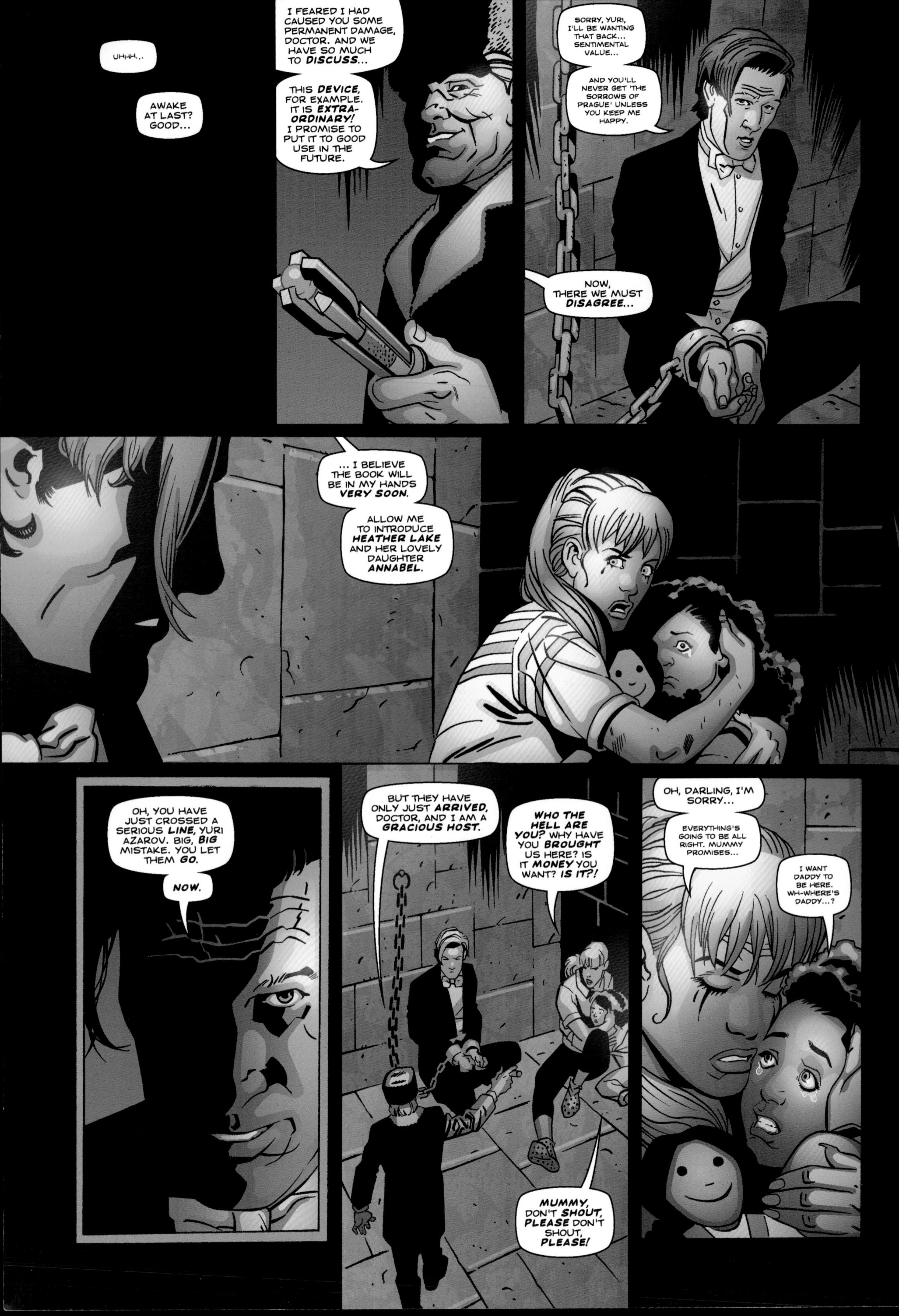
UHHH...
AWAKE AT LAST? GOOD...
I FEARED I HAD CAUSED YOU SOME PERMANENT DAMAGE, DOCTOR. AND WE HAVE SO MUCH TO DISCUSS...
THIS DEVICE, FOR EXAMPLE. IT IS EXTRA-ORDINARY! I PROMISE TO PUT IT TO GOOD USE IN THE FUTURE.
SORRY, YURI, I'LL BE WANTING THAT BACK... SENTIMENTAL VALUE...
AND YOU'LL NEVER GET 'THE SORROWS OF PRAGUE' UNLESS YOU KEEP ME HAPPY.
NOW, THERE WE MUST DISAGREE...
... I BELIEVE THE BOOK WILL BE IN MY HANDS VERY SOON.
ALLOW ME TO INTRODUCE HEATHER LAKE AND HER LOVELY DAUGHTER ANNABEL.
OH, YOU HAVE JUST CROSSED A SERIOUS LINE, YURI AZAROV. BIG, BIG MISTAKE. YOU LET THEM GO.
NOW.
BUT THEY HAVE ONLY JUST ARRIVED, DOCTOR, AND I AM A GRACIOUS HOST.
WHO THE HELL ARE YOU? WHY HAVE YOU BROUGHT US HERE? IS IT MONEY YOU WANT? IS IT?!
MUMMY, DON'T SHOUT, PLEASE DON'T SHOUT, PLEASE!
OH, DARLING, I'M SORRY...
EVERYTHING'S GOING TO BE ALL RIGHT. MUMMY PROMISES...
I WANT DADDY TO BE HERE. WH-WHERE'S DADDY...?

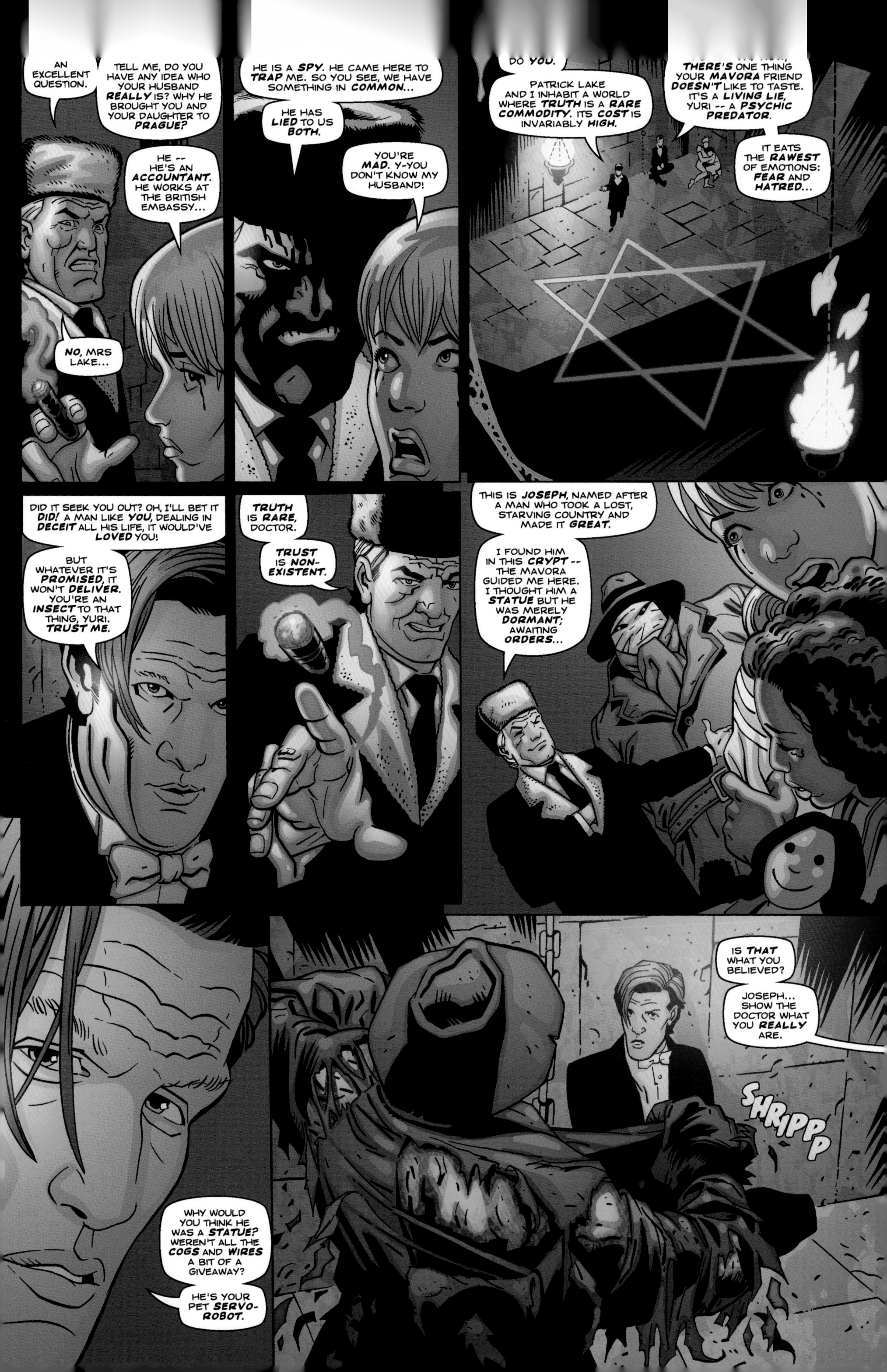
AN EXCELLENT QUESTION.
TELL ME, DO YOU HAVE ANY IDEA WHO YOUR HUSBAND REALLY IS? WHY HE BROUGHT YOU AND YOUR DAUGHTER TO PRAGUE?
HE -- HE'S AN ACCOUNTANT. HE WORKS AT THE BRITISH EMBASSY...
NO, MRS LAKE...
HE IS A SPY. HE CAME HERE TO TRAP ME. SO YOU SEE, WE HAVE SOMETHING IN COMMON...
HE HAS LIED TO US BOTH.
YOU'RE MAD. Y-YOU DON'T KNOW MY HUSBAND!
DO YOU.
PATRICK LAKE AND I INHABIT A WORLD WHERE TRUTH IS A RARE COMMODITY. ITS COST IS INVARIABLY HIGH.
THERE'S ONE THING YOUR MAVORA FRIEND DOESN'T LIKE TO TASTE. IT'S A LIVING LIE, YURI -- A PSYCHIC PREDATOR.
IT EATS THE RAWEST OF EMOTIONS: FEAR AND HATRED...
DID IT SEEK YOU OUT? OH, I'LL BET IT DID! A MAN LIKE YOU, DEALING IN DECEIT ALL HIS LIFE, IT WOULD'VE LOVED YOU!
BUT WHATEVER IT'S PROMISED, IT WON'T DELIVER. YOU'RE AN INSECT TO THAT THING, YURI. TRUST ME.
TRUTH IS RARE, DOCTOR.
TRUST IS NON-EXISTENT.
THIS IS JOSEPH, NAMED AFTER A MAN WHO TOOK A LOST, STARVING COUNTRY AND MADE IT GREAT.
I FOUND HIM IN THIS CRYPT -- THE MAVORA GUIDED ME HERE. I THOUGHT HIM A STATUE BUT HE WAS MERELY DORMANT; AWAITING ORDERS...
WHY WOULD YOU THINK HE WAS A STATUE? WEREN'T ALL THE COGS AND WIRES A BIT OF A GIVEAWAY?
HE'S YOUR PET SERVO-ROBOT.
IS THAT WHAT YOU BELIEVED?
JOSEPH... SHOW THE DOCTOR WHAT YOU REALLY ARE.
SHRIPPP

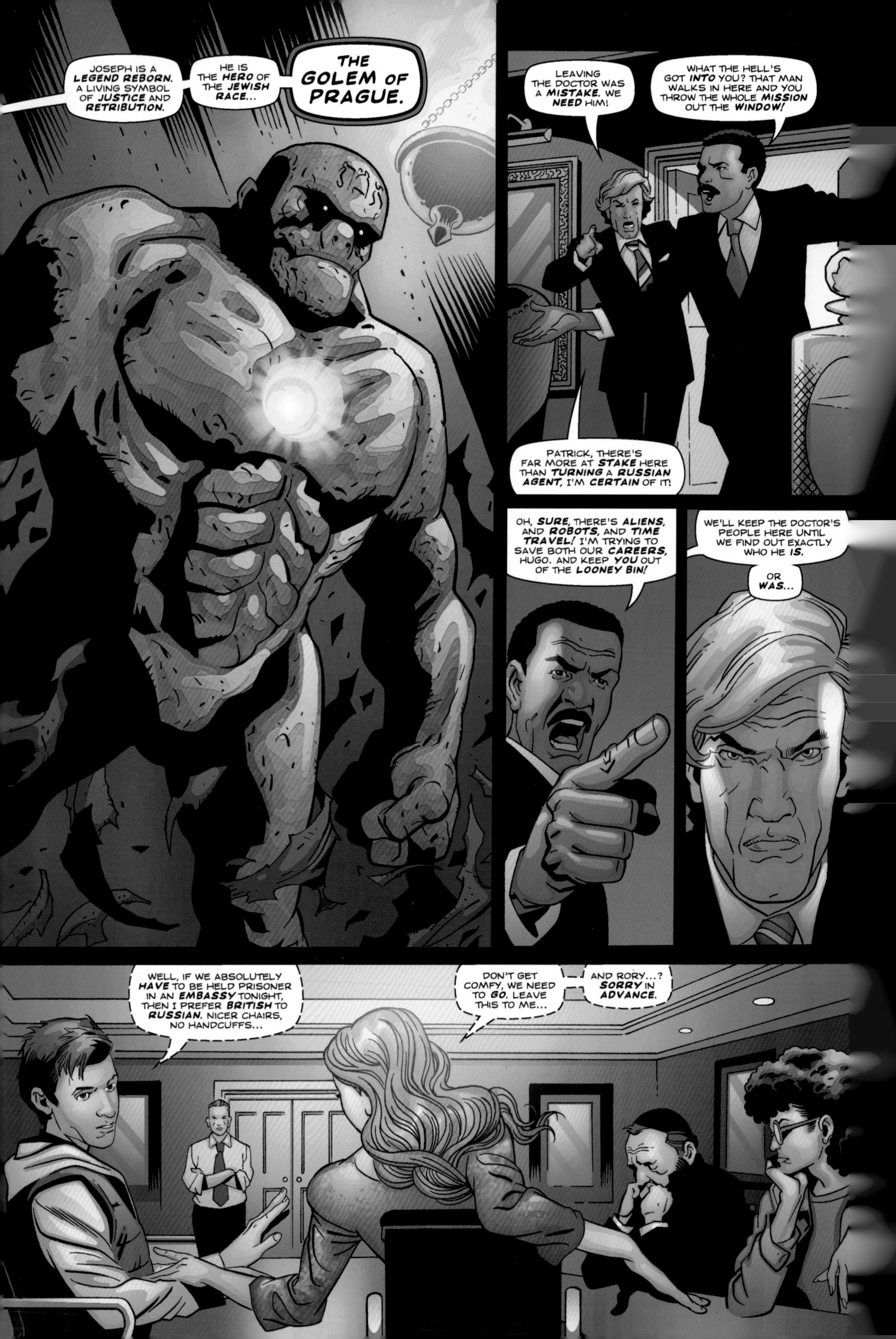
JOSEPH IS A LEGEND REBORN. A LIVING SYMBOL OF JUSTICE AND RETRIBUTION.
HE IS THE HERO OF THE JEWISH RACE...
THE GOLEM OF PRAGUE.
LEAVING THE DOCTOR WAS A MISTAKE. WE NEED HIM!
WHAT THE HELL'S GOT INTO YOU? THAT MAN WALKS IN HERE AND YOU THROW THE WHOLE MISSION OUT THE WINDOW!
PATRICK, THERE'S FAR MORE AT STAKE HERE THAN TURNING A RUSSIAN AGENT, I'M CERTAIN OF IT!
OH, SURE, THERE'S ALIENS, AND ROBOTS, AND TIME TRAVEL! I'M TRYING TO SAVE BOTH OUR CAREERS, HUGO. AND KEEP YOU OUT OF THE LOONEY BIN!
WE'LL KEEP THE DOCTOR'S PEOPLE HERE UNTIL WE FIND OUT EXACTLY WHO HE IS.
OR WAS...
WELL, IF WE ABSOLUTELY HAVE TO BE HELD PRISONER IN AN EMBASSY TONIGHT, THEN I PREFER BRITISH TO RUSSIAN. NICER CHAIRS, NO HANDCUFFS...
DON'T GET COMFY, WE NEED TO GO. LEAVE THIS TO ME...
AND RORY...? SORRY IN ADVANCE.

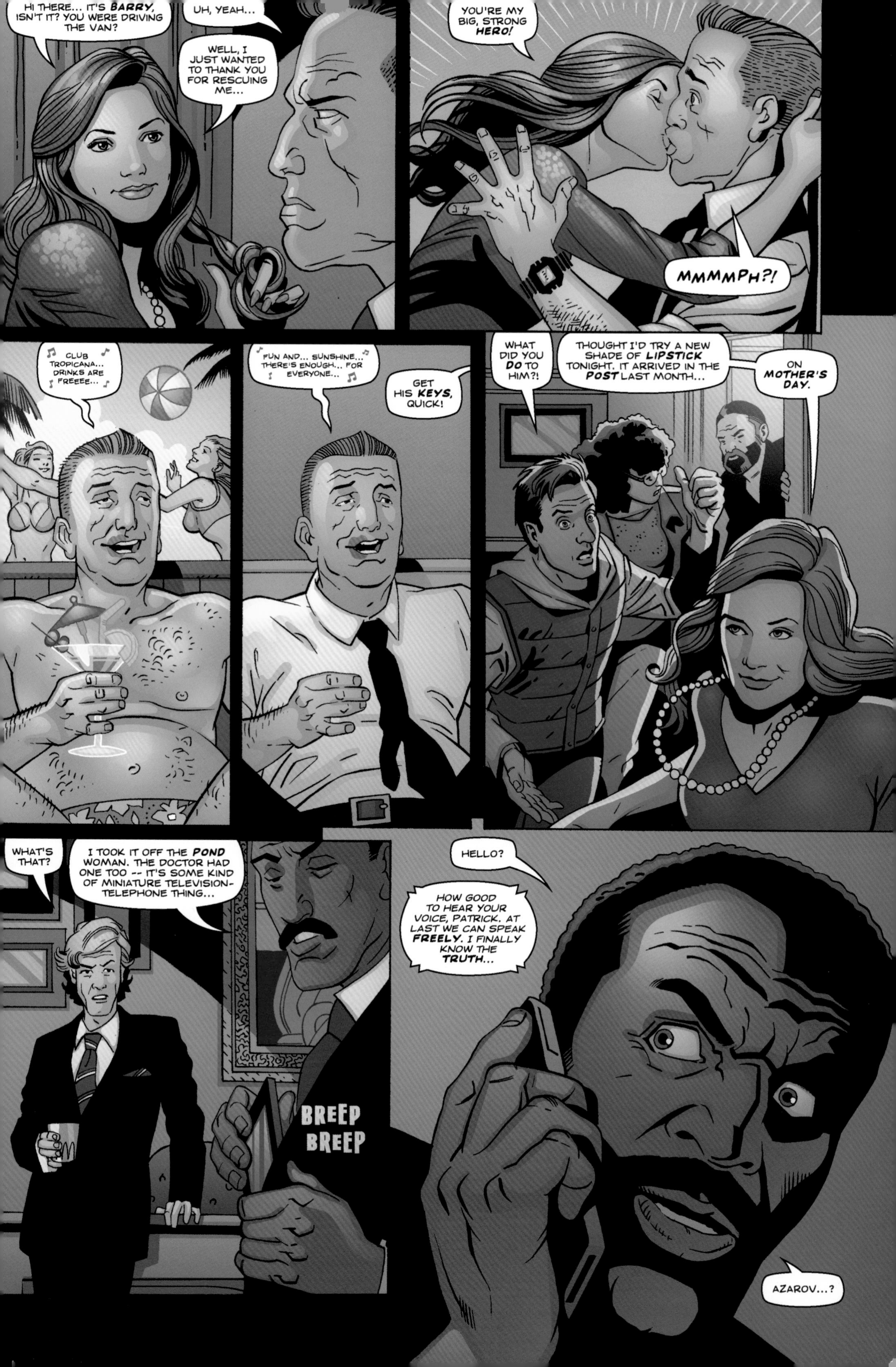
HI THERE... IT'S BARRY, ISN'T IT? YOU WERE DRIVING THE VAN?
UH, YEAH...
WELL, I JUST WANTED TO THANK YOU FOR RESCUING ME...
YOU'RE MY BIG, STRONG HERO!
MMMMPH?!
CLUB TROPICANA... DRINKS ARE FREEEE...
FUN AND... SUNSHINE... THERE'S ENOUGH... FOR EVERYONE...
GET HIS KEYS, QUICK!
WHAT DID YOU DO TO HIM?!
THOUGHT I'D TRY A NEW SHADE OF LIPSTICK TONIGHT. IT ARRIVED IN THE POST LAST MONTH...
ON MOTHER'S DAY.
WHAT'S THAT?
I TOOK IT OFF THE POND WOMAN. THE DOCTOR HAD ONE TOO -- IT'S SOME KIND OF MINIATURE TELEVISION-TELEPHONE THING...
BREEP BREEP
HELLO?
HOW GOOD TO HEAR YOUR VOICE, PATRICK. AT LAST WE CAN SPEAK FREELY. I FINALLY KNOW THE TRUTH...
AZAROV...?

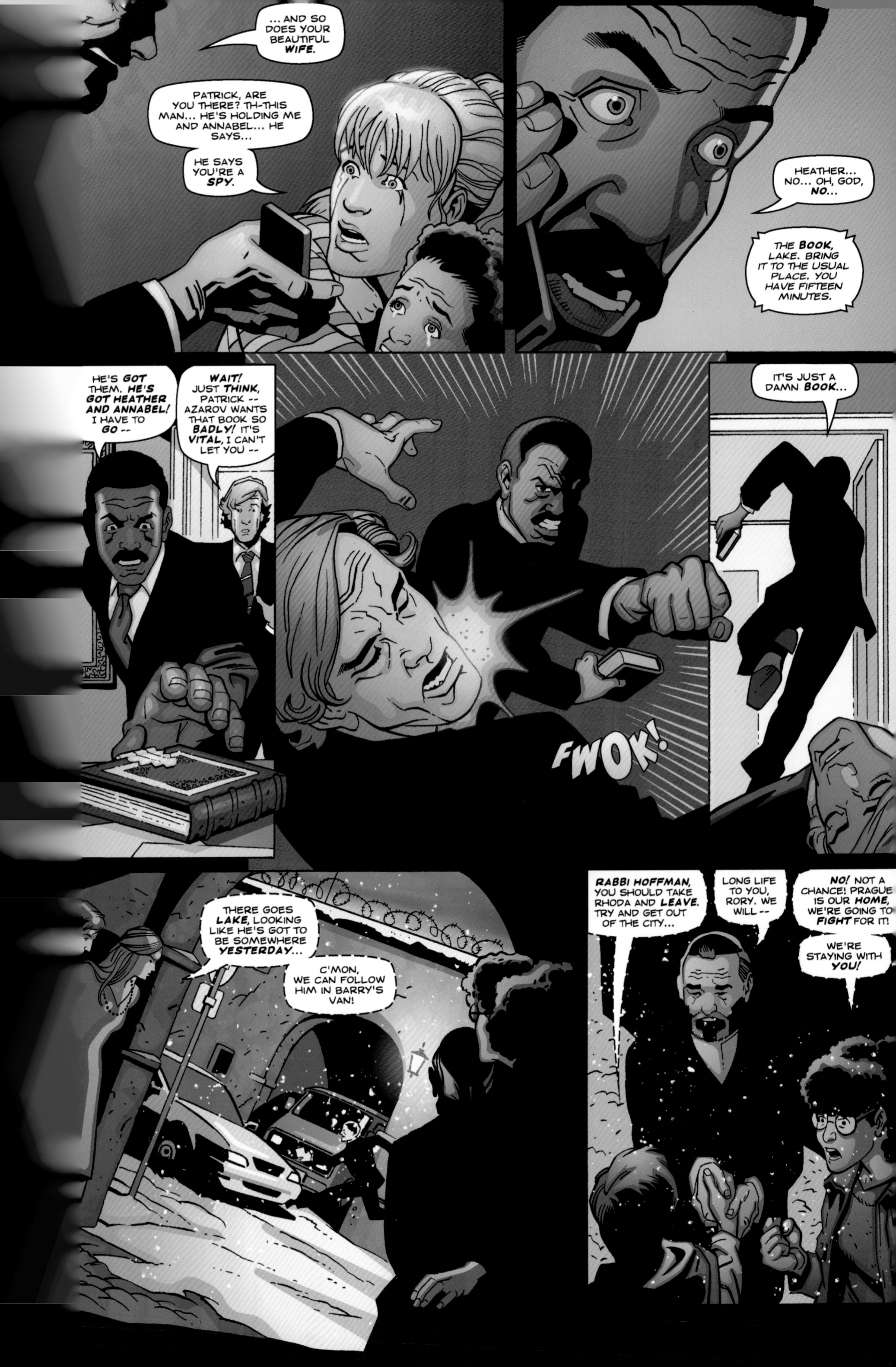
...AND SO DOES YOUR BEAUTIFUL WIFE.
PATRICK, ARE YOU THERE? TH-THIS MAN... HE'S HOLDING ME AND ANNABEL... HE SAYS...
HE SAYS YOU'RE A SPY.
HEATHER... NO... OH, GOD, NO...
THE BOOK, LAKE. BRING IT TO THE USUAL PLACE. YOU HAVE FIFTEEN MINUTES.
HE'S GOT THEM. HE'S GOT HEATHER AND ANNABEL! I HAVE TO GO --
WAIT! JUST THINK, PATRICK -- AZAROV WANTS THAT BOOK SO BADLY! IT'S VITAL, I CAN'T LET YOU --
FWOK!
IT'S JUST A DAMN BOOK...
THERE GOES LAKE, LOOKING LIKE HE'S GOT TO BE SOMEWHERE YESTERDAY...
C'MON, WE CAN FOLLOW HIM IN BARRY'S VAN!
RABBI HOFFMAN, YOU SHOULD TAKE RHODA AND LEAVE. TRY AND GET OUT OF THE CITY...
LONG LIFE TO YOU, RORY. WE WILL --
NO! NOT A CHANCE! PRAGUE IS OUR HOME, WE'RE GOING TO FIGHT FOR IT!
WE'RE STAYING WITH YOU!

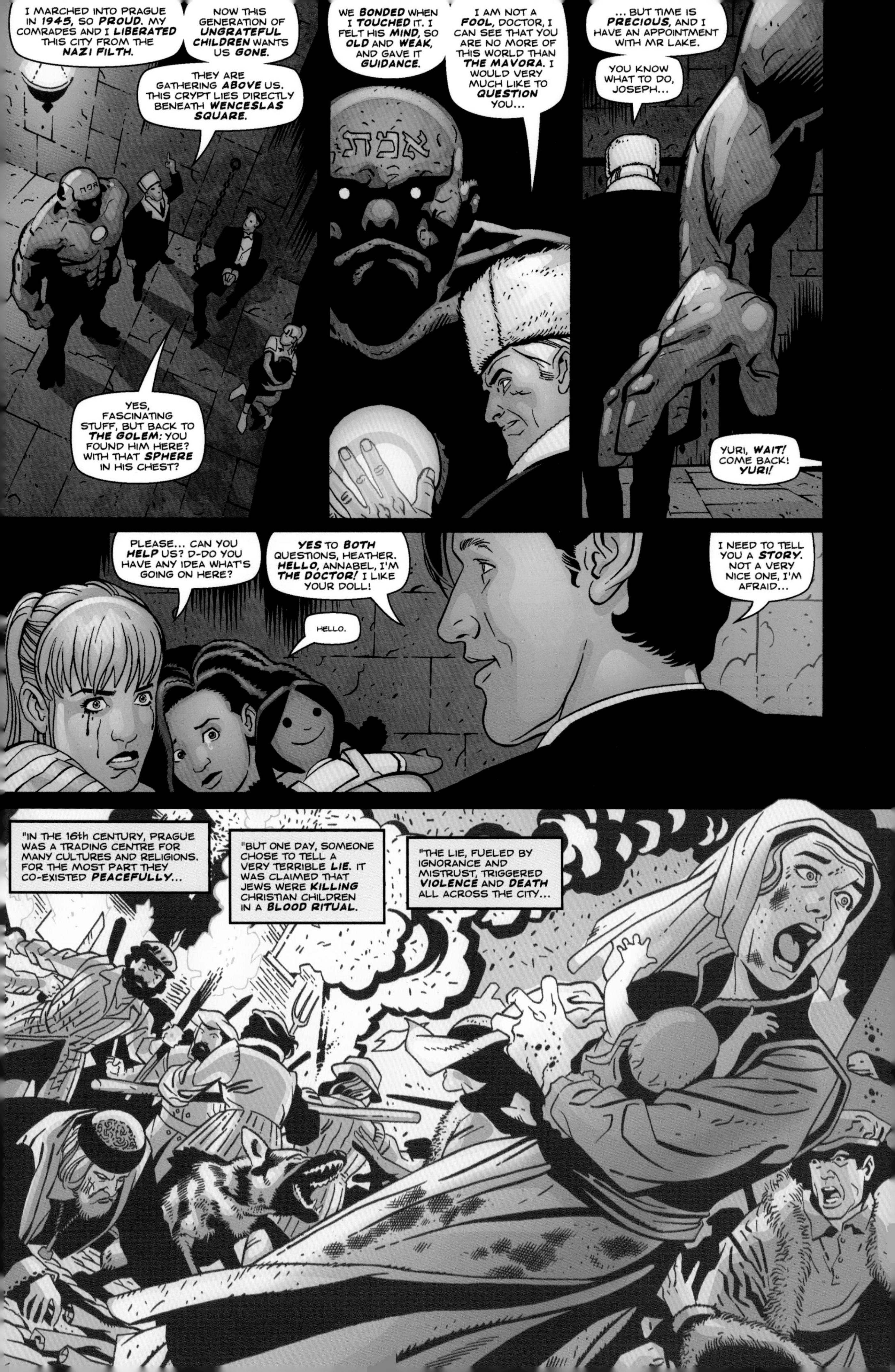

I MARCHED INTO PRAGUE IN 1945, SO PROUD. MY COMRADES AND I LIBERATED THIS CITY FROM THE NAZI FILTH.
NOW THIS GENERATION OF UNGRATEFUL CHILDREN WANTS US GONE.
THEY ARE GATHERING ABOVE US. THIS CRYPT LIES DIRECTLY BENEATH WENCESLAS SQUARE.
YES, FASCINATING STUFF, BUT BACK TO THE GOLEM: YOU FOUND HIM HERE? WITH THAT SPHERE IN HIS CHEST?
WE BONDED WHEN I TOUCHED IT. I FELT HIS MIND, SO OLD AND WEAK, AND GAVE IT GUIDANCE.
I AM NOT A FOOL, DOCTOR, I CAN SEE THAT YOU ARE NO MORE OF THIS WORLD THAN THE MAVORA. I WOULD VERY MUCH LIKE TO QUESTION YOU...
אמת
... BUT TIME IS PRECIOUS, AND I HAVE AN APPOINTMENT WITH MR LAKE.
YOU KNOW WHAT TO DO, JOSEPH...
YURI, WAIT! COME BACK! YURI!
PLEASE... CAN YOU HELP US? D-DO YOU HAVE ANY IDEA WHAT'S GOING ON HERE?
YES TO BOTH QUESTIONS, HEATHER. HELLO, ANNABEL, I'M THE DOCTOR! I LIKE YOUR DOLL!
HELLO.
I NEED TO TELL YOU A STORY. NOT A VERY NICE ONE, I'M AFRAID...
"IN THE 16th CENTURY, PRAGUE WAS A TRADING CENTRE FOR MANY CULTURES AND RELIGIONS. FOR THE MOST PART THEY CO-EXISTED PEACEFULLY...
"BUT ONE DAY, SOMEONE CHOSE TO TELL A VERY TERRIBLE LIE. IT WAS CLAIMED THAT JEWS WERE KILLING CHRISTIAN CHILDREN IN A BLOOD RITUAL.
"THE LIE, FUELED BY IGNORANCE AND MISTRUST, TRIGGERED VIOLENCE AND DEATH ALL ACROSS THE CITY...

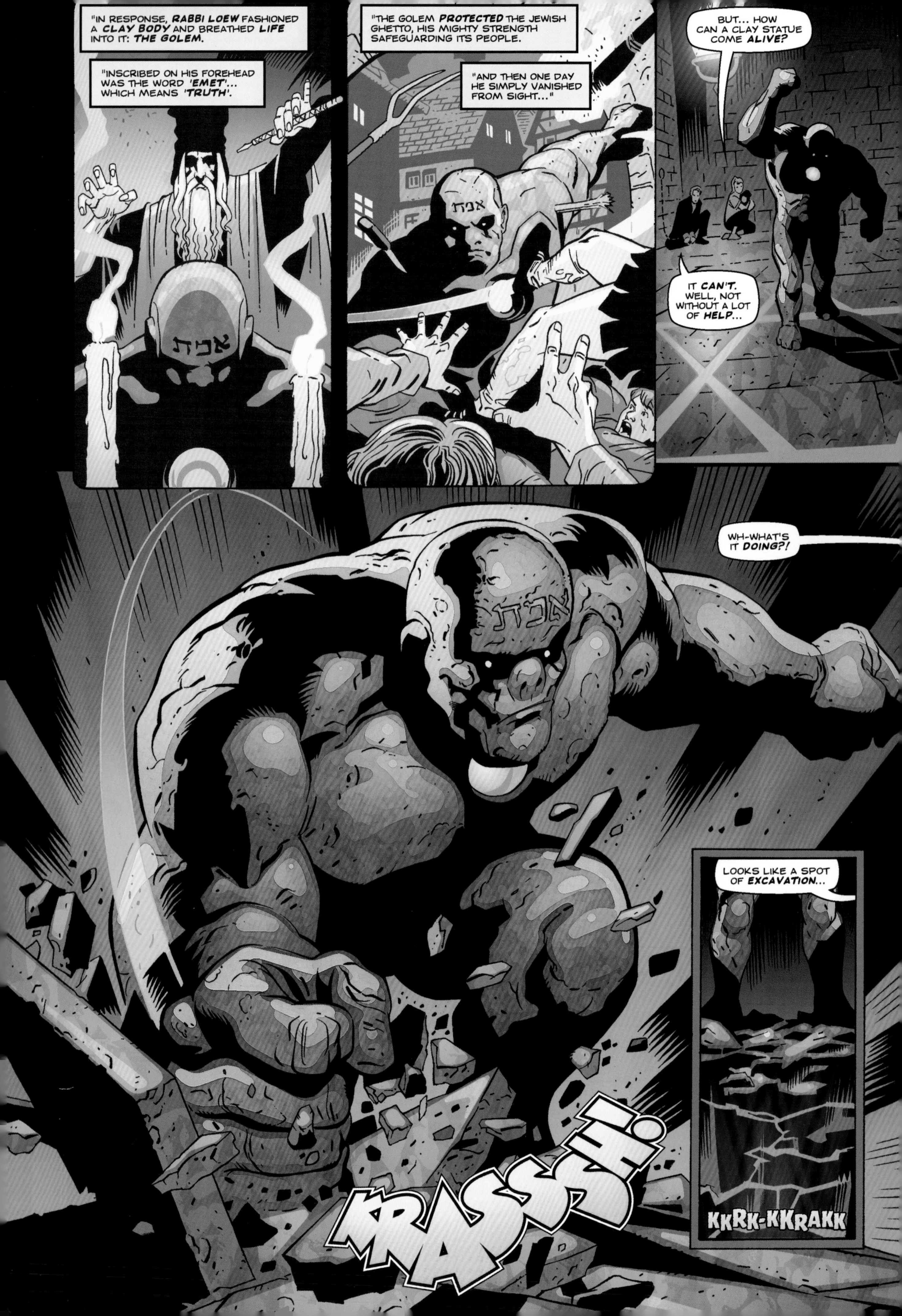
"IN RESPONSE, RABBI LOEW FASHIONED A CLAY BODY AND BREATHED LIFE INTO IT: THE GOLEM.
"INSCRIBED ON HIS FOREHEAD WAS THE WORD 'EMET'... WHICH MEANS 'TRUTH'.
אמת
"THE GOLEM PROTECTED THE JEWISH GHETTO, HIS MIGHTY STRENGTH SAFEGUARDING ITS PEOPLE.
"AND THEN ONE DAY HE SIMPLY VANISHED FROM SIGHT..."
אמת
BUT... HOW CAN A CLAY STATUE COME ALIVE?
IT CAN'T. WELL, NOT WITHOUT A LOT OF HELP...
WH-WHAT'S IT DOING?!
אמת
KRASSSH!
LOOKS LIKE A SPOT OF EXCAVATION...
KKRK-KKRAKK

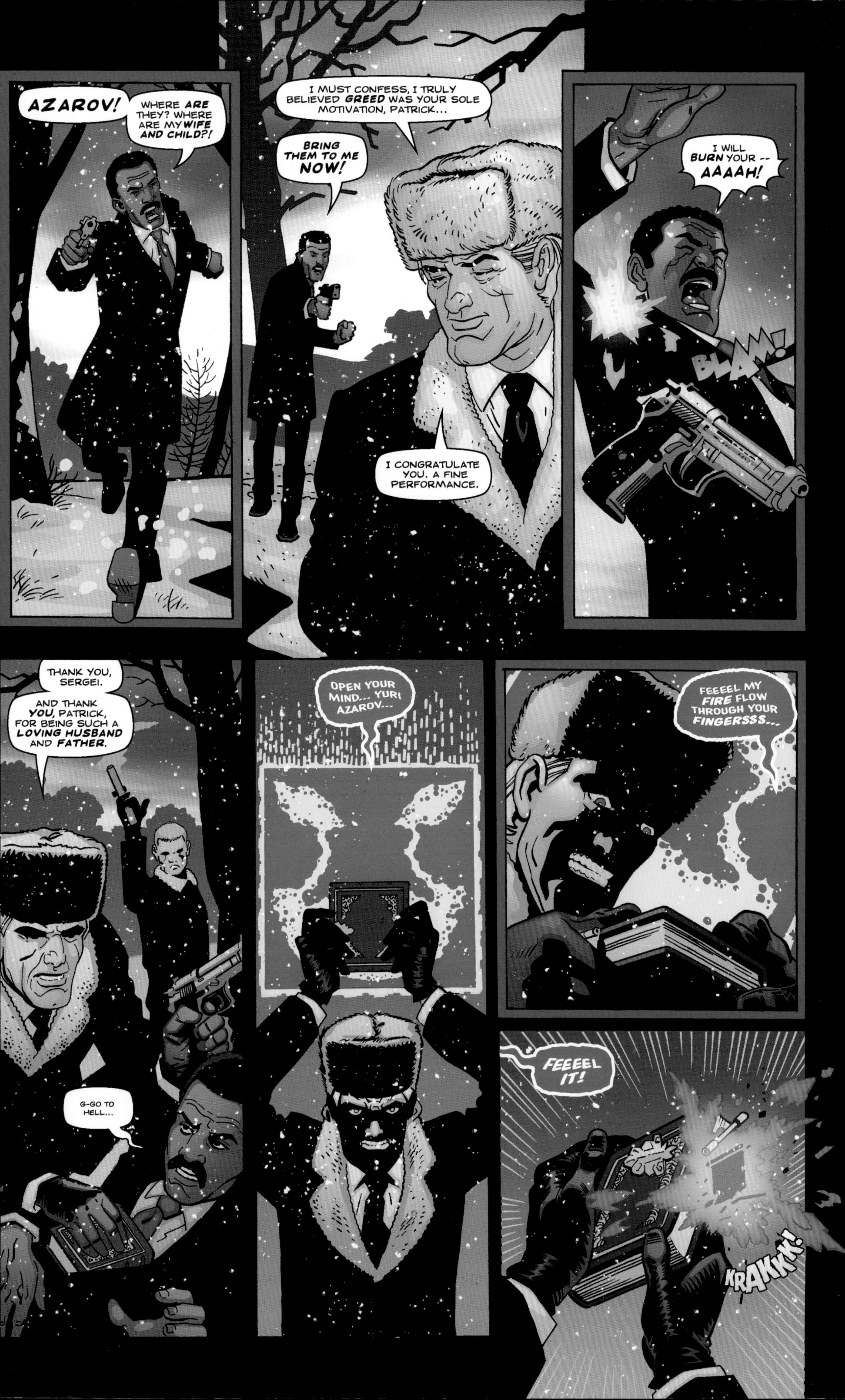
AZAROV!
WHERE ARE THEY? WHERE ARE MY WIFE AND CHILD?!
I MUST CONFESS, I TRULY BELIEVED GREED WAS YOUR SOLE MOTIVATION, PATRICK...
BRING THEM TO ME NOW!
I CONGRATULATE YOU. A FINE PERFORMANCE.
I WILL BURN YOUR -- AAAAH!
BLAM!
THANK YOU, SERGEI.
AND THANK YOU, PATRICK, FOR BEING SUCH A LOVING HUSBAND AND FATHER.
G-GO TO HELL...
OPEN YOUR MIND... YURI AZAROV...
FEEEEL MY FIRE FLOW THROUGH YOUR FINGERSSS...
FEEEEL IT!
KRAKKK!

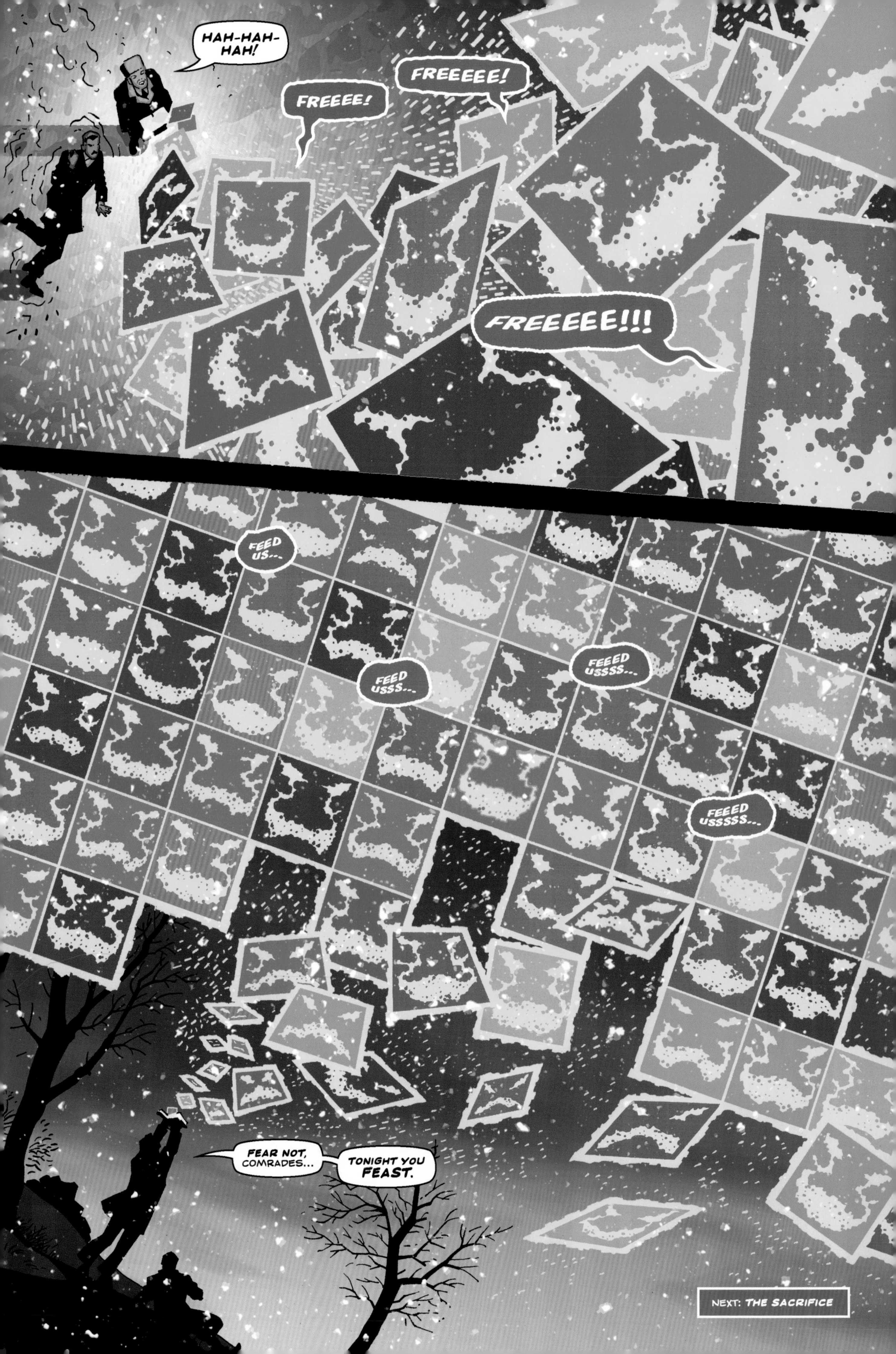
HAH-HAH-HAH!
FREEEE!
FREEEEEE!
FREEEEEE!!!
FEED US...
FEED USSS...
FEEED USSSS...
FEEED USSSSS...
FEAR NOT, COMRADES...
TONIGHT YOU FEAST.
NEXT: THE SACRIFICE

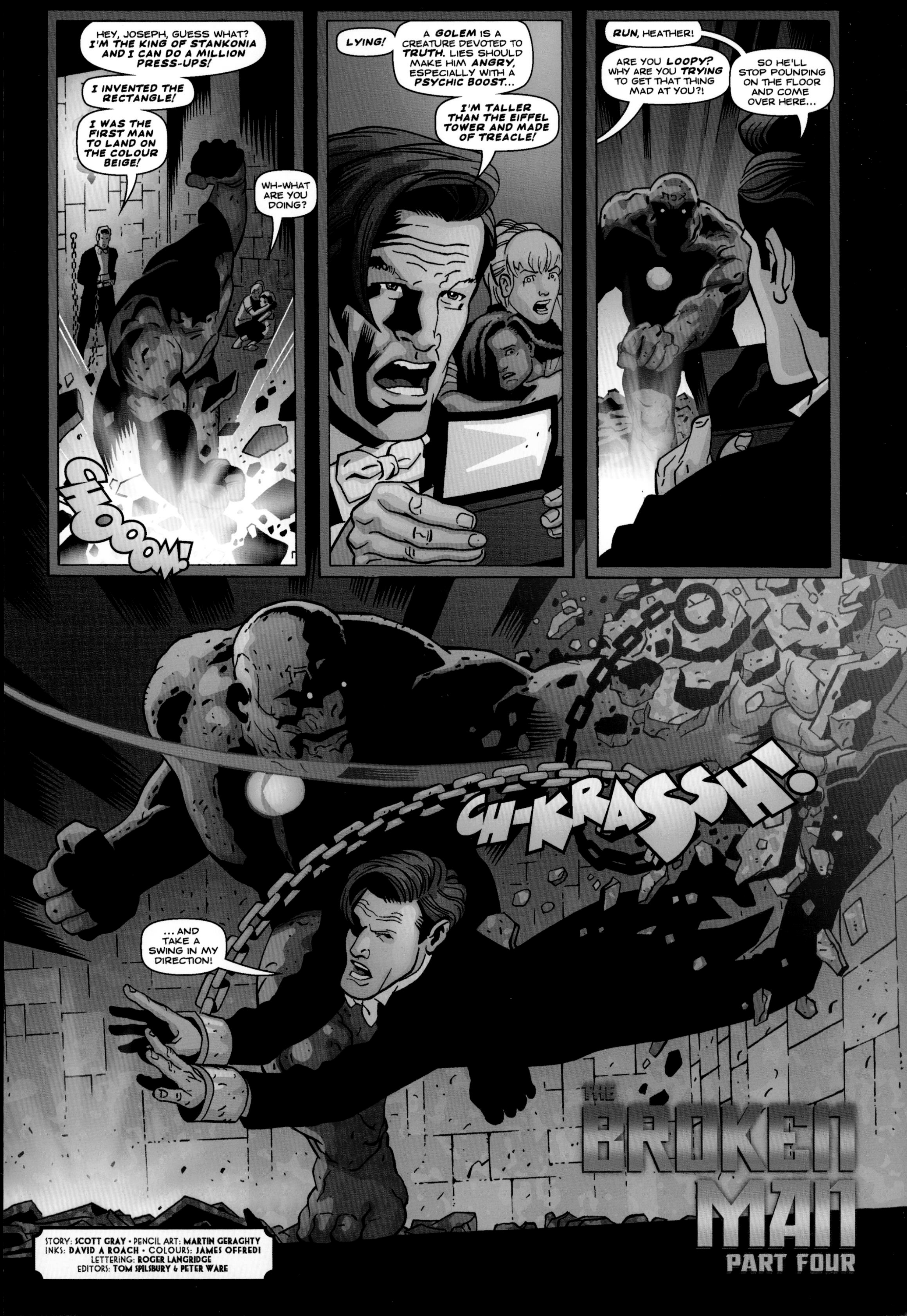
HEY, JOSEPH, GUESS WHAT? I'M THE KING OF STANKONIA AND I CAN DO A MILLION PRESS-UPS!
I INVENTED THE RECTANGLE!
I WAS THE FIRST MAN TO LAND ON THE COLOUR BEIGE!
WH-WHAT ARE YOU DOING?
CHOOOOM!
LYING!
A GOLEM IS A CREATURE DEVOTED TO TRUTH. LIES SHOULD MAKE HIM ANGRY, ESPECIALLY WITH A PSYCHIC BOOST...
I'M TALLER THAN THE EIFFEL TOWER AND MADE OF TREACLE!
RUN, HEATHER!
ARE YOU LOOPY? WHY ARE YOU TRYING TO GET THAT THING MAD AT YOU?!
SO HE'LL STOP POUNDING ON THE FLOOR AND COME OVER HERE...
CH-KRASSH!
...AND TAKE A SWING IN MY DIRECTION!
THE BROKEN MAN
PART FOUR
STORY: SCOTT GRAY • PENCIL ART: MARTIN GERAGHTY
INKS: DAVID A ROACH • COLOURS: JAMES OFFREDI
LETTERING: ROGER LANGRIDGE
EDITORS: TOM SPILSBURY & PETER WARE

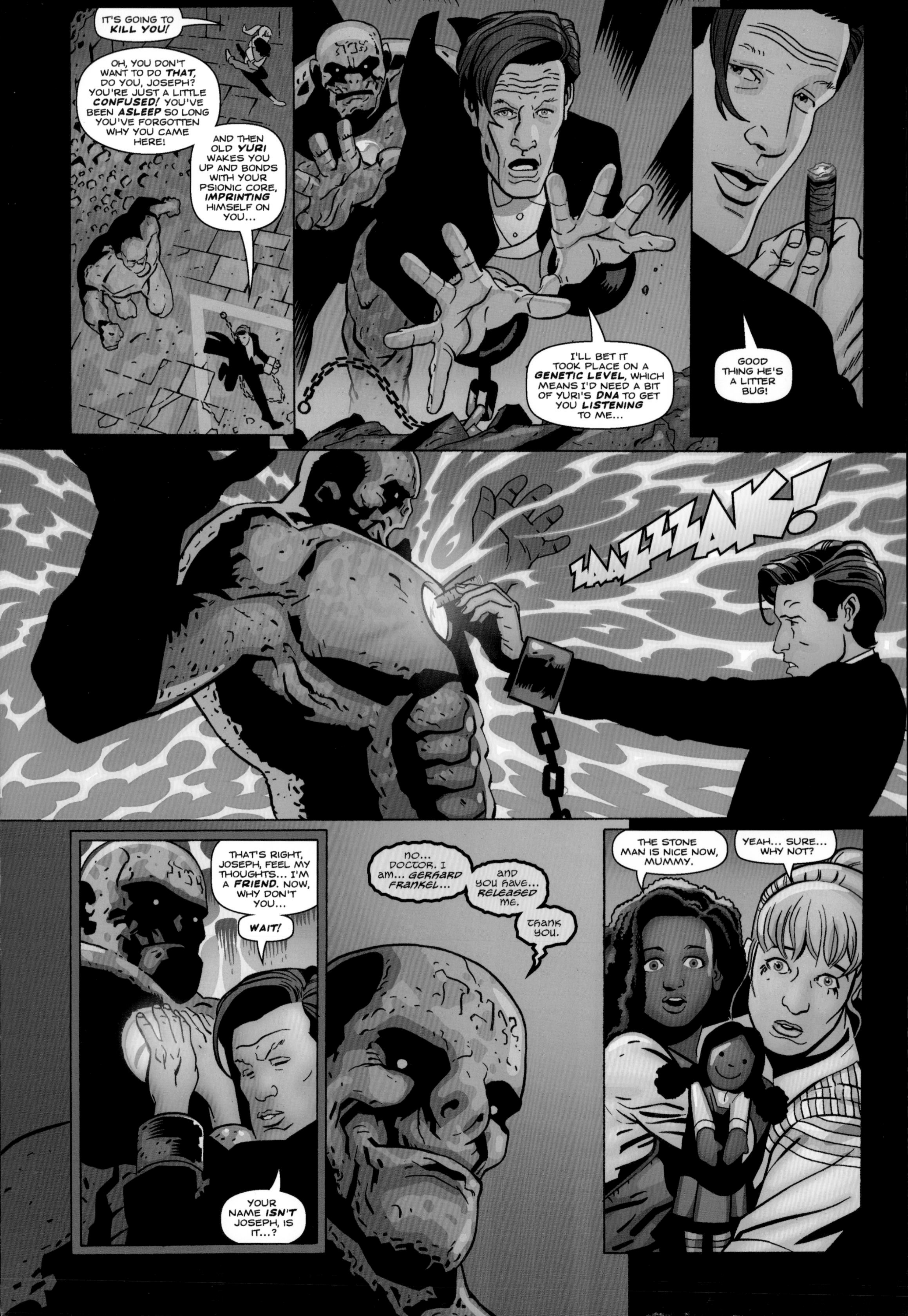

IT'S GOING TO KILL YOU!
OH, YOU DON'T WANT TO DO THAT, DO YOU, JOSEPH? YOU'RE JUST A LITTLE CONFUSED! YOU'VE BEEN ASLEEP SO LONG YOU'VE FORGOTTEN WHY YOU CAME HERE!
AND THEN OLD YURI WAKES YOU UP AND BONDS WITH YOUR PSIONIC CORE, IMPRINTING HIMSELF ON YOU...
I'LL BET IT TOOK PLACE ON A GENETIC LEVEL, WHICH MEANS I'D NEED A BIT OF YURI'S DNA TO GET YOU LISTENING TO ME...
GOOD THING HE'S A LITTER BUG!
ZAAZZZAK!
THAT'S RIGHT, JOSEPH, FEEL MY THOUGHTS... I'M A FRIEND. NOW, WHY DON'T YOU...
WAIT!
YOUR NAME ISN'T JOSEPH, IS IT...?
NO... DOCTOR. I AM... GERHARD FRANKEL...
AND YOU HAVE... RELEASED ME.
THANK YOU.
THE STONE MAN IS NICE NOW, MUMMY.
YEAH... SURE... WHY NOT?

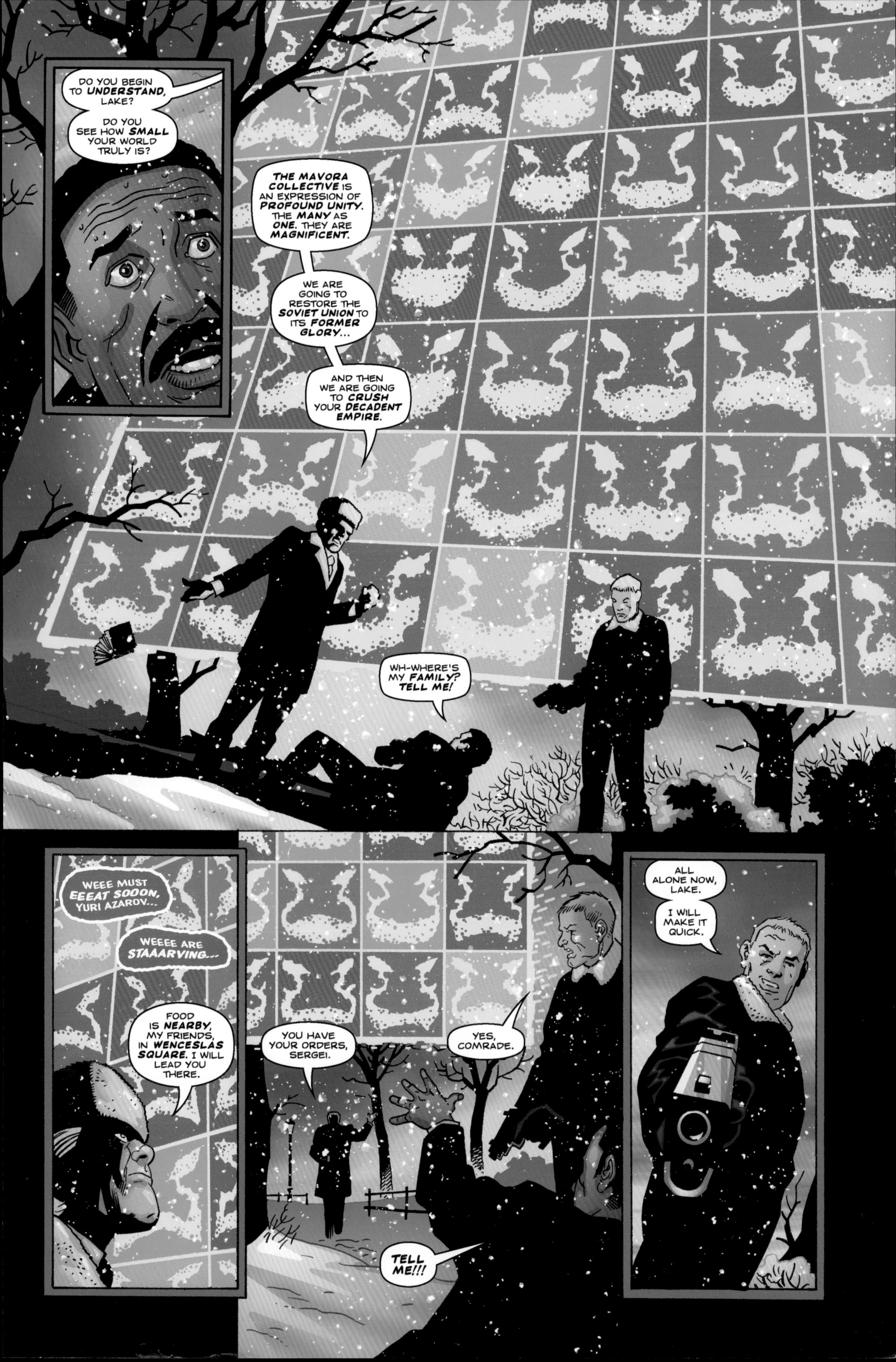
DO YOU BEGIN TO UNDERSTAND, LAKE?
DO YOU SEE HOW SMALL YOUR WORLD TRULY IS?
THE MAVORA COLLECTIVE IS AN EXPRESSION OF PROFOUND UNITY. THE MANY AS ONE. THEY ARE MAGNIFICENT.
WE ARE GOING TO RESTORE THE SOVIET UNION TO ITS FORMER GLORY...
AND THEN WE ARE GOING TO CRUSH YOUR DECADENT EMPIRE.
WH-WHERE'S MY FAMILY? TELL ME!
WEEE MUST EEEAT SOOON, YURI AZAROV...
WEEEE ARE STAAARVING...
FOOD IS NEARBY, MY FRIENDS, IN WENCESLAS SQUARE. I WILL LEAD YOU THERE.
YOU HAVE YOUR ORDERS, SERGEI.
YES, COMRADE.
TELL ME!!!
ALL ALONE NOW, LAKE.
I WILL MAKE IT QUICK.

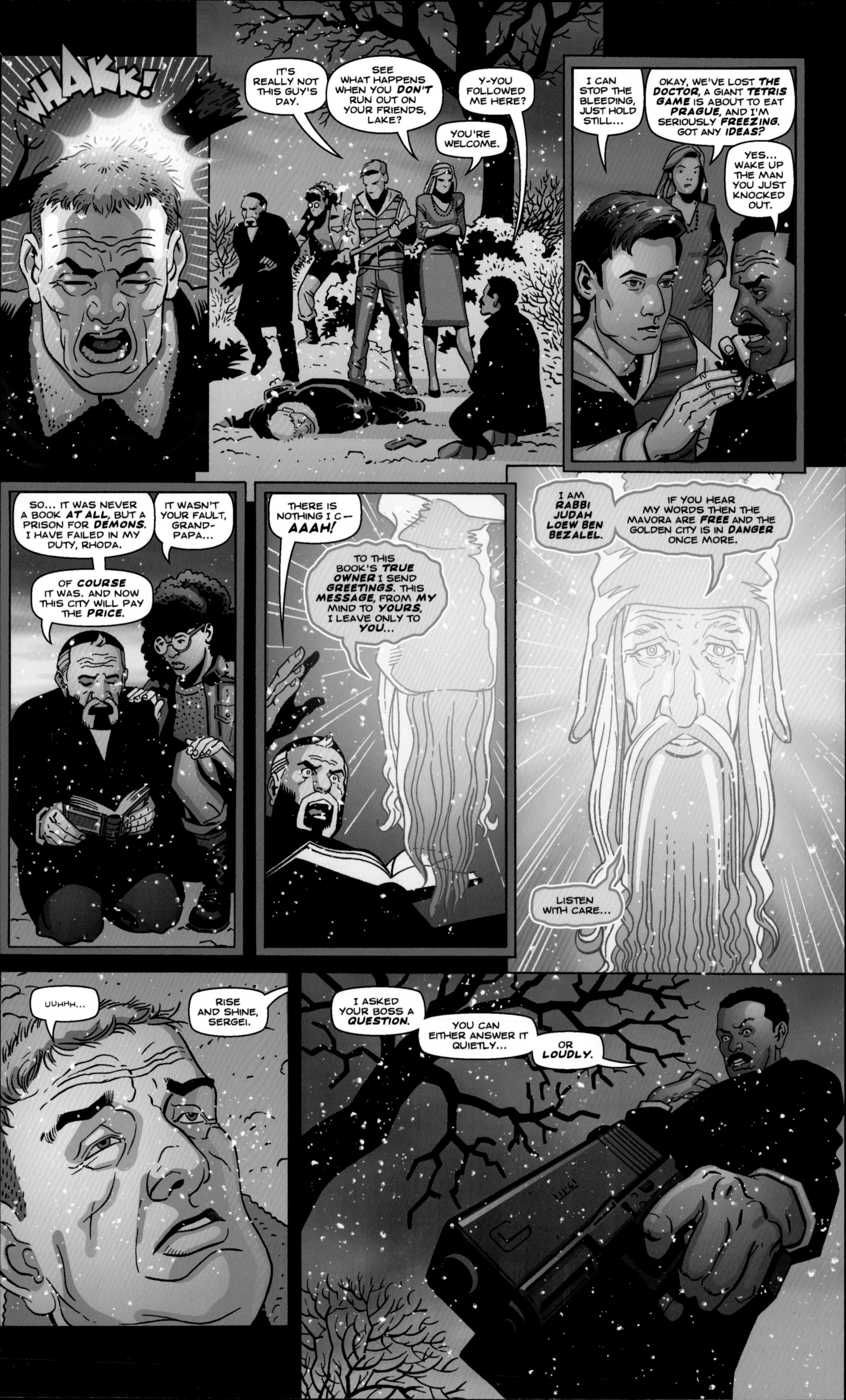

WHAKK!
IT'S REALLY NOT THIS GUY'S DAY.
SEE WHAT HAPPENS WHEN YOU DON'T RUN OUT ON YOUR FRIENDS, LAKE?
Y-YOU FOLLOWED ME HERE?
YOU'RE WELCOME.
I CAN STOP THE BLEEDING, JUST HOLD STILL...
OKAY, WE'VE LOST THE DOCTOR, A GIANT TETRIS GAME IS ABOUT TO EAT PRAGUE, AND I'M SERIOUSLY FREEZING. GOT ANY IDEAS?
YES... WAKE UP THE MAN YOU JUST KNOCKED OUT.
SO... IT WAS NEVER A BOOK AT ALL, BUT A PRISON FOR DEMONS. I HAVE FAILED IN MY DUTY, RHODA.
IT WASN'T YOUR FAULT, GRAND-PAPA...
OF COURSE IT WAS. AND NOW THIS CITY WILL PAY THE PRICE.
THERE IS NOTHING I C— AAAH!
TO THIS BOOK'S TRUE OWNER I SEND GREETINGS. THIS MESSAGE, FROM MY MIND TO YOURS, I LEAVE ONLY TO YOU...
I AM RABBI JUDAH LOEW BEN BEZALEL.
IF YOU HEAR MY WORDS THEN THE MAVORA ARE FREE AND THE GOLDEN CITY IS IN DANGER ONCE MORE.
LISTEN WITH CARE...
UUHHH...
RISE AND SHINE, SERGEI.
I ASKED YOUR BOSS A QUESTION.
YOU CAN EITHER ANSWER IT QUIETLY...
OR LOUDLY.

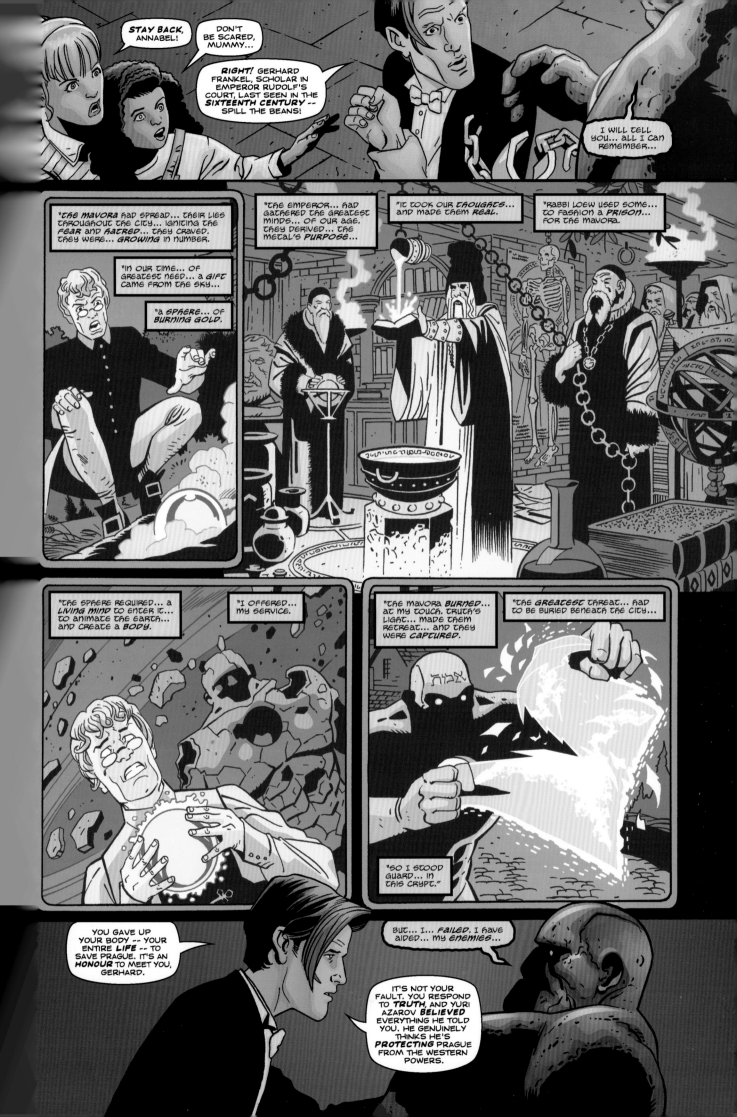

STAY BACK, ANNABEL!

DON'T BE SCARED, MUMMY...

RIGHT! GERHARD FRANKEL, SCHOLAR IN EMPEROR RUDOLF'S COURT, LAST SEEN IN THE SIXTEENTH CENTURY -- SPILL THE BEANS!

I WILL TELL YOU... ALL I CAN REMEMBER...

"THE MAVORA HAD SPREAD... THEIR LIES THROUGHOUT THE CITY... IGNITING THE FEAR AND HATRED... THEY CRAVED. THEY WERE... GROWING IN NUMBER.

"IN OUR TIME... OF GREATEST NEED... A GIFT CAME FROM THE SKY...

"A SPHERE... OF BURNING GOLD.

"THE EMPEROR... HAD GATHERED THE GREATEST MINDS... OF OUR AGE. THEY DERIVED... THE METAL'S PURPOSE...

"IT TOOK OUR THOUGHTS... AND MADE THEM REAL.

"RABBI LOEW USED SOME... TO FASHION A PRISON... FOR THE MAVORA.

"THE SPHERE REQUIRED... A LIVING MIND TO ENTER IT... TO ANIMATE THE EARTH... AND CREATE A BODY.

"I OFFERED... MY SERVICE.

"THE MAVORA BURNED... AT MY TOUCH. TRUTH'S LIGHT... MADE THEM RETREAT... AND THEY WERE CAPTURED.

"THE GREATEST THREAT... HAD TO BE BURIED BENEATH THE CITY...

"SO I STOOD GUARD... IN THIS CRYPT."

YOU GAVE UP YOUR BODY -- YOUR ENTIRE LIFE -- TO SAVE PRAGUE. IT'S AN HONOUR TO MEET YOU, GERHARD.

BUT... I... FAILED. I HAVE AIDED... MY ENEMIES...

IT'S NOT YOUR FAULT. YOU RESPOND TO TRUTH, AND YURI AZAROV BELIEVED EVERYTHING HE TOLD YOU. HE GENUINELY THINKS HE'S PROTECTING PRAGUE FROM THE WESTERN POWERS.

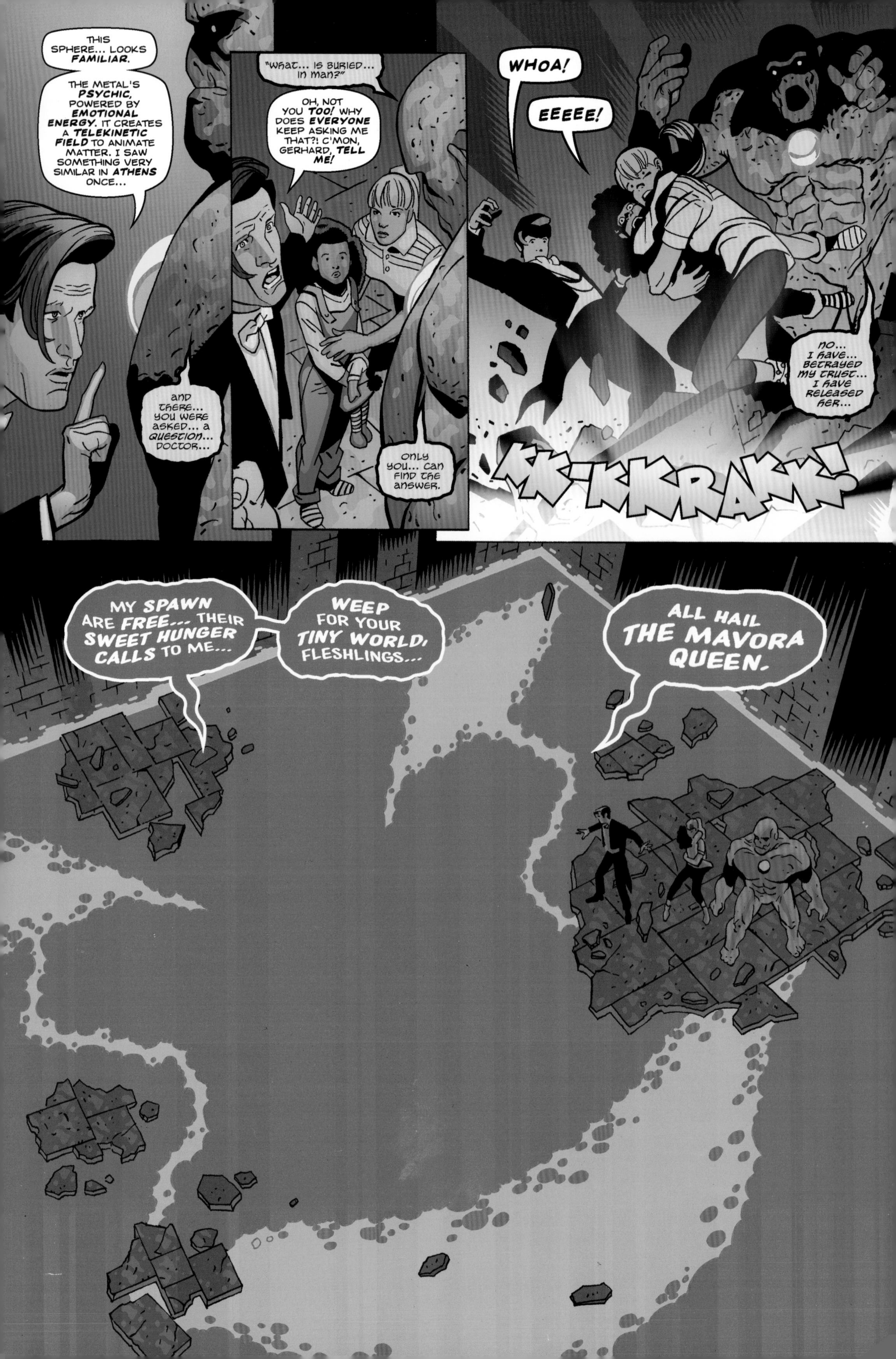
THIS SPHERE... LOOKS FAMILIAR.
THE METAL'S PSYCHIC, POWERED BY EMOTIONAL ENERGY. IT CREATES A TELEKINETIC FIELD TO ANIMATE MATTER. I SAW SOMETHING VERY SIMILAR IN ATHENS ONCE...
AND THERE... YOU WERE ASKED... A QUESTION... DOCTOR...
"WHAT... IS BURIED... IN MAN?"
OH, NOT YOU TOO! WHY DOES EVERYONE KEEP ASKING ME THAT?! C'MON, GERHARD, TELL ME!
ONLY YOU... CAN FIND THE ANSWER.
WHOA!
EEEEE!
NO... I HAVE... BETRAYED MY TRUST... I HAVE RELEASED HER...
KK-KKRANK!
MY SPAWN ARE FREE... THEIR SWEET HUNGER CALLS TO ME...
WEEP FOR YOUR TINY WORLD, FLESHLINGS...
ALL HAIL THE MAVORA QUEEN.

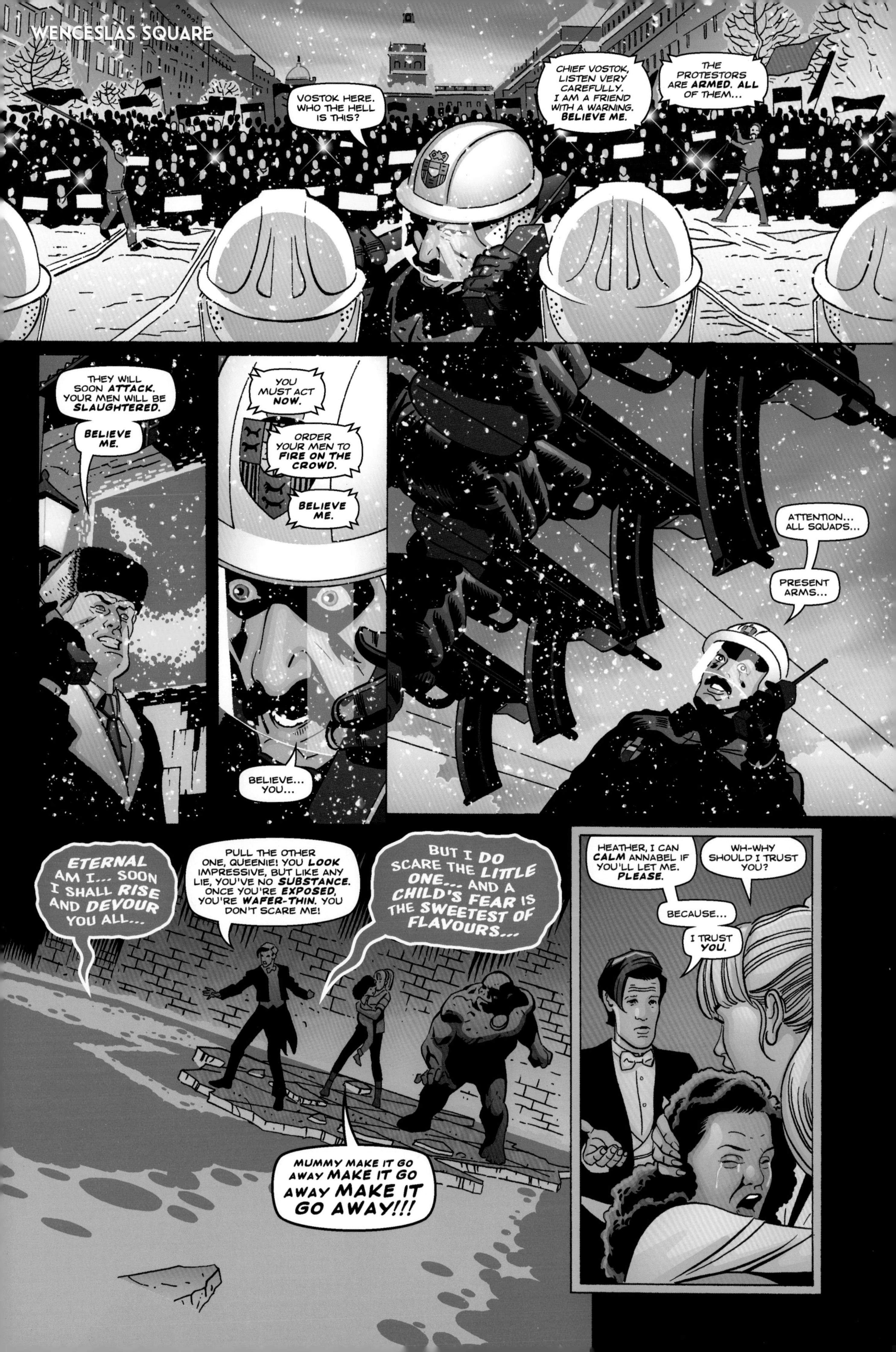
WENCESLAS SQUARE
VOSTOK HERE. WHO THE HELL IS THIS?
CHIEF VOSTOK, LISTEN VERY CAREFULLY. I AM A FRIEND WITH A WARNING. BELIEVE ME.
THE PROTESTORS ARE ARMED. ALL OF THEM...
THEY WILL SOON ATTACK. YOUR MEN WILL BE SLAUGHTERED.
BELIEVE ME.
YOU MUST ACT NOW.
ORDER YOUR MEN TO FIRE ON THE CROWD.
BELIEVE ME.
BELIEVE... YOU...
ATTENTION... ALL SQUADS...
PRESENT ARMS...
ETERNAL AM I... SOON I SHALL RISE AND DEVOUR YOU ALL...
PULL THE OTHER ONE, QUEENIE! YOU LOOK IMPRESSIVE, BUT LIKE ANY LIE, YOU'VE NO SUBSTANCE. ONCE YOU'RE EXPOSED, YOU'RE WAFER-THIN. YOU DON'T SCARE ME!
BUT I DO SCARE THE LITTLE ONE... AND A CHILD'S FEAR IS THE SWEETEST OF FLAVOURS...
MUMMY MAKE IT GO AWAY MAKE IT GO AWAY MAKE IT GO AWAY!!!
HEATHER, I CAN CALM ANNABEL IF YOU'LL LET ME. PLEASE.
WH-WHY SHOULD I TRUST YOU?
BECAUSE...
I TRUST YOU.

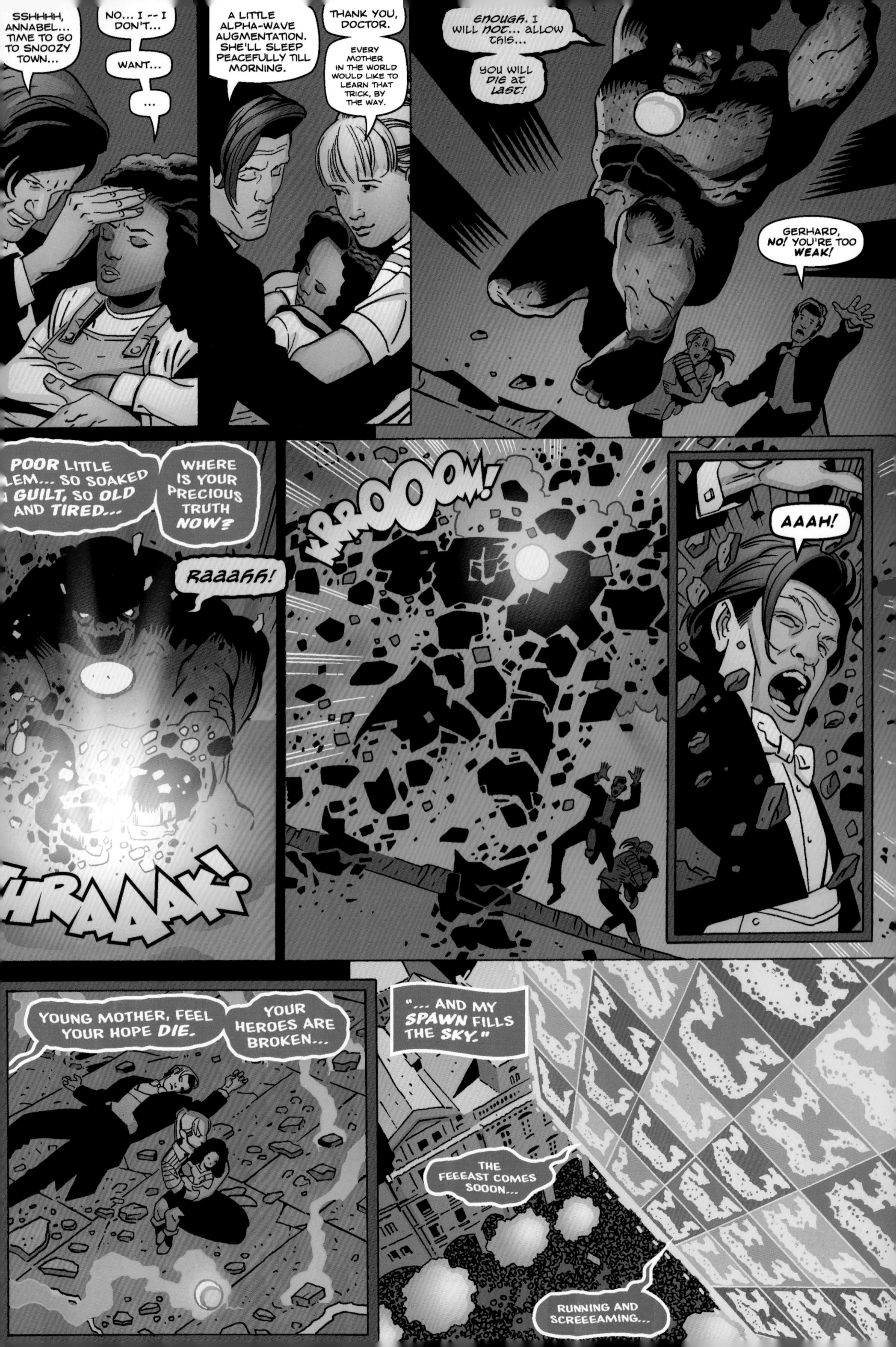
SSHHHH, ANNABEL... TIME TO GO TO SNOOZY TOWN...
NO... I -- I DON'T...
WANT...
...
A LITTLE ALPHA-WAVE AUGMENTATION. SHE'LL SLEEP PEACEFULLY TILL MORNING.
THANK YOU, DOCTOR.
EVERY MOTHER IN THE WORLD WOULD LIKE TO LEARN THAT TRICK, BY THE WAY.
ENOUGH. I WILL NOT... ALLOW THIS...
YOU WILL DIE AT LAST!
GERHARD, NO! YOU'RE TOO WEAK!
POOR LITTLE LEM... SO SOAKED IN GUILT, SO OLD AND TIRED...
WHERE IS YOUR PRECIOUS TRUTH NOW?
RAAAHH!
THRAAAK!
KRROOOOM!
AAAH!
YOUNG MOTHER, FEEL YOUR HOPE DIE.
YOUR HEROES ARE BROKEN...
"... AND MY SPAWN FILLS THE SKY."
THE FEEEAST COMES SOOON...
RUNNING AND SCREEEAMING...

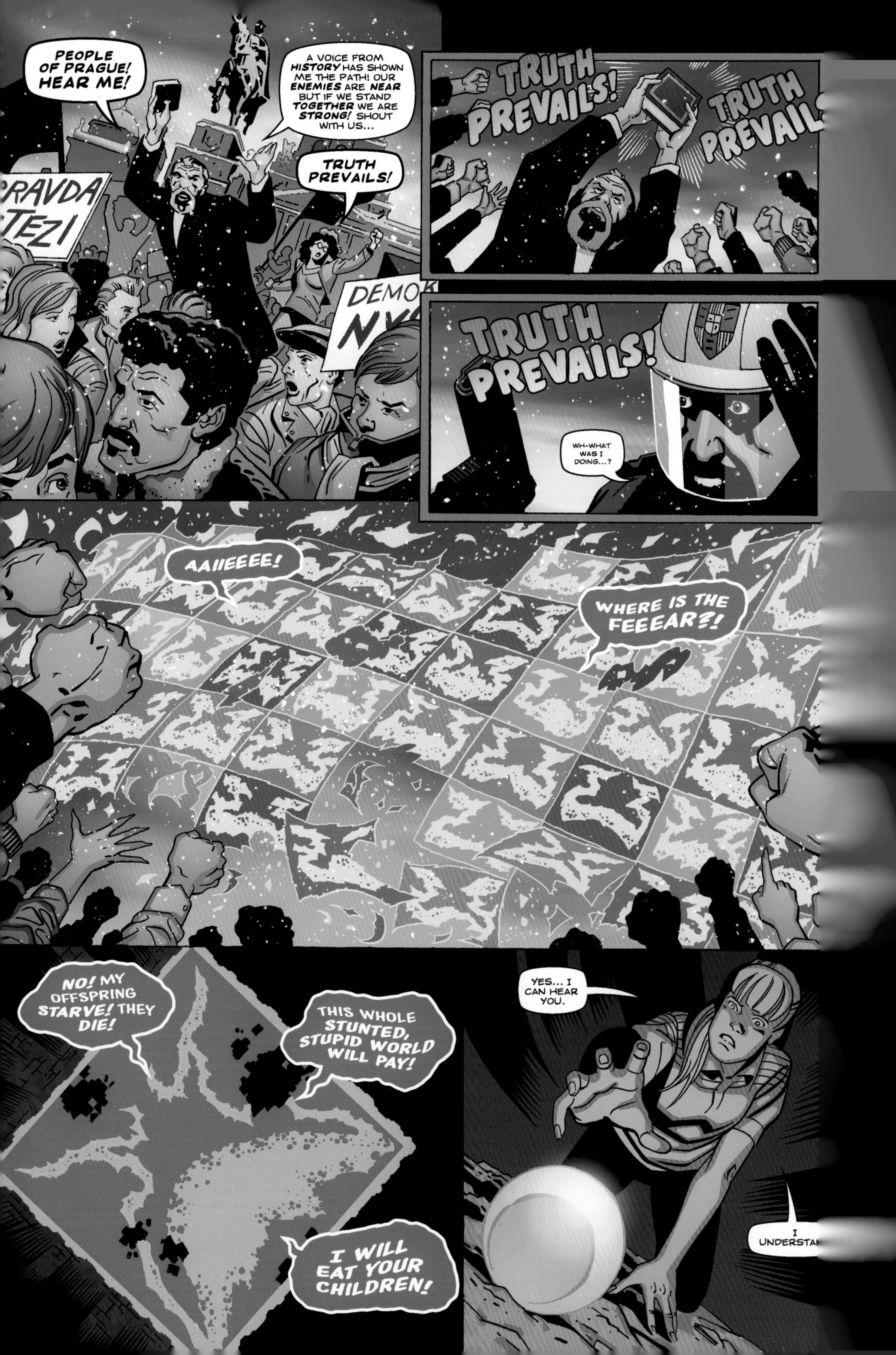
PEOPLE OF PRAGUE! HEAR ME!
A VOICE FROM HISTORY HAS SHOWN ME THE PATH! OUR ENEMIES ARE NEAR BUT IF WE STAND TOGETHER WE ARE STRONG! SHOUT WITH US...
TRUTH PREVAILS!
PRAVDA
TEZI
DEMOK
NY
TRUTH PREVAILS!
TRUTH PREVAILS
TRUTH PREVAILS!
WH-WHAT WAS I DOING...?
AAIIEEEE!
WHERE IS THE FEEEAR?!
NO! MY OFFSPRING STARVE! THEY DIE!
THIS WHOLE STUNTED, STUPID WORLD WILL PAY!
I WILL EAT YOUR CHILDREN!
YES... I CAN HEAR YOU.
I UNDERSTA

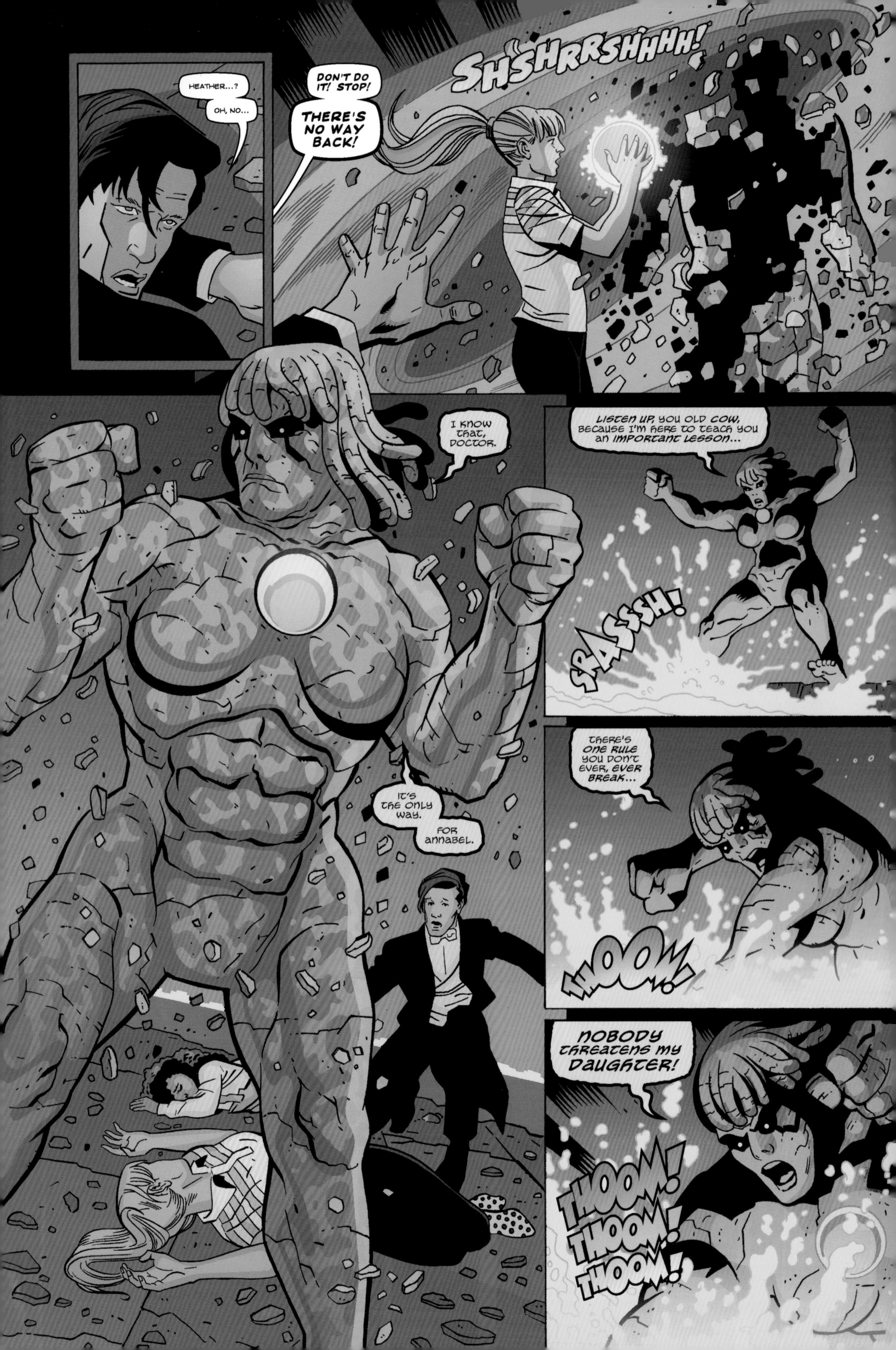
HEATHER...?
OH, NO...
DON'T DO IT! STOP!
THERE'S NO WAY BACK!
SHSHRRSHHHH!
I KNOW THAT, DOCTOR.
IT'S THE ONLY WAY.
FOR ANNABEL.
LISTEN UP, YOU OLD COW, BECAUSE I'M HERE TO TEACH YOU AN IMPORTANT LESSON...
SPLASSSH!
THERE'S ONE RULE YOU DON'T EVER, EVER BREAK...
THOOOM!
NOBODY THREATENS MY DAUGHTER!
THOOM! THOOM! THOOM!

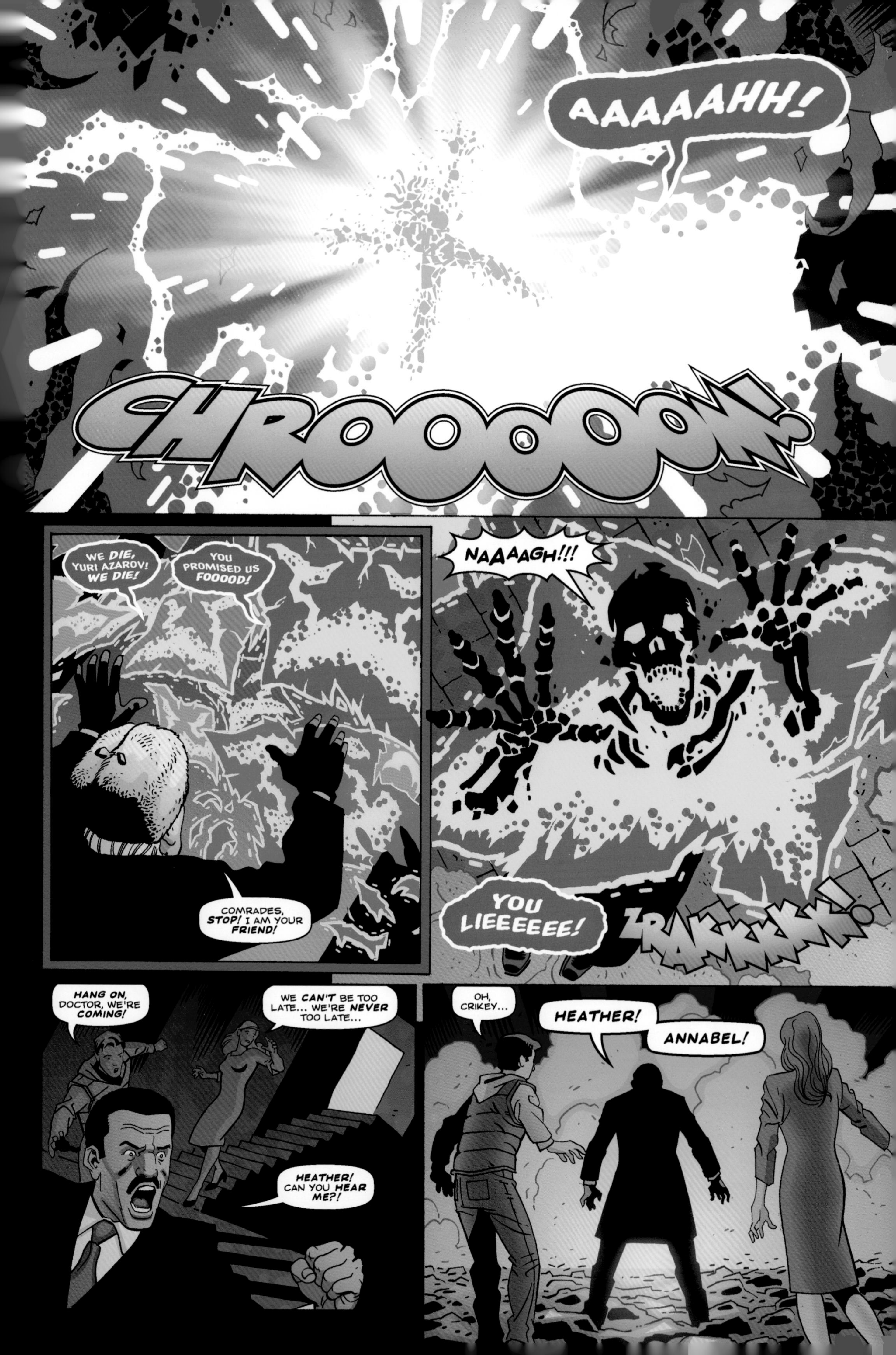
AAAAAHH!
CHROOOOOM!
WE DIE, YURI AZAROV! WE DIE!
YOU PROMISED US FOOOOD!
COMRADES, STOP! I AM YOUR FRIEND!
NAAAAGH!!!
YOU LIEEEEEE!
ZRAKKKKK!
HANG ON, DOCTOR, WE'RE COMING!
WE CAN'T BE TOO LATE... WE'RE NEVER TOO LATE...
HEATHER! CAN YOU HEAR ME?!
OH, CRIKEY...
HEATHER!
ANNABEL!

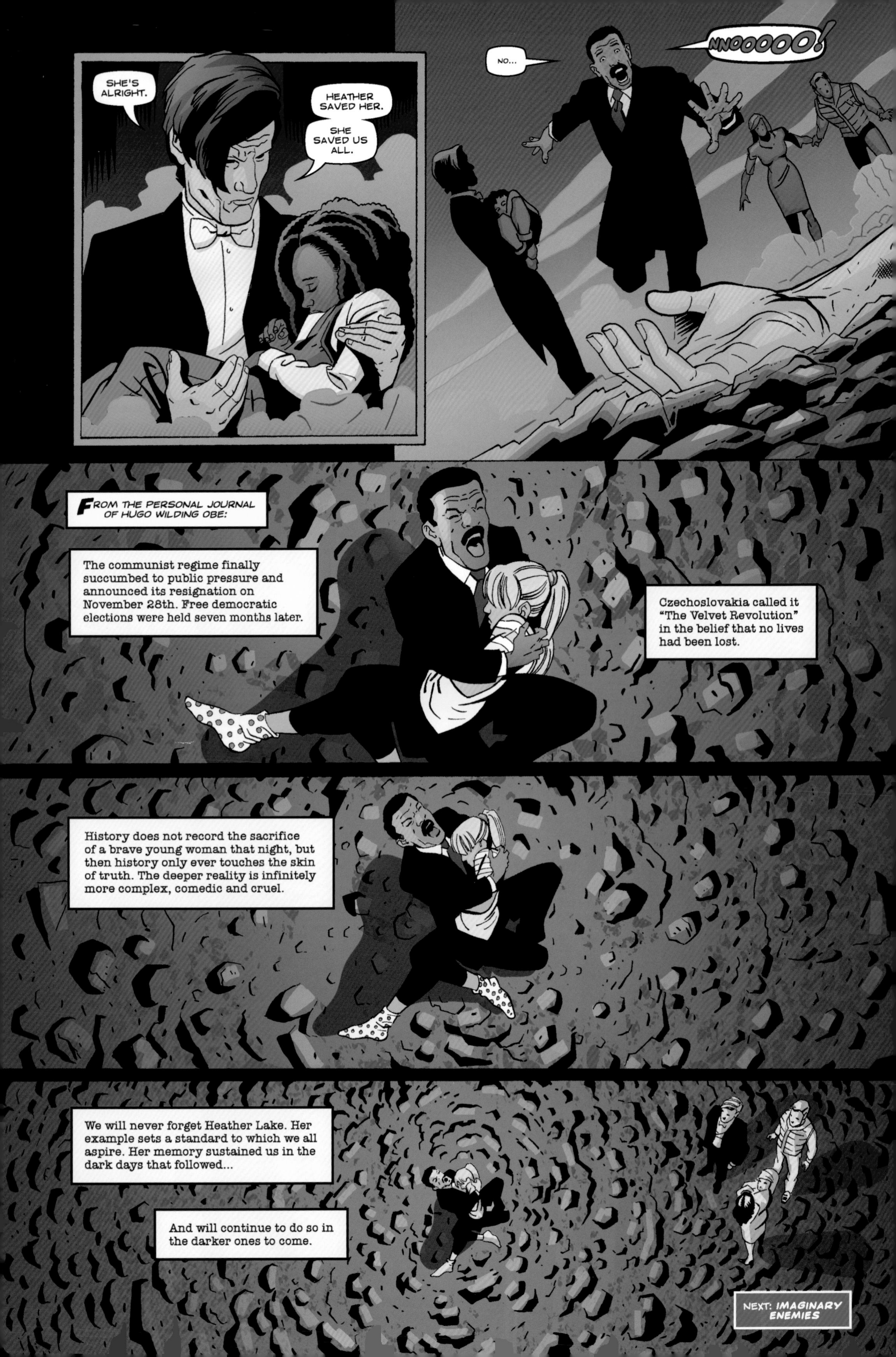
SHE'S ALRIGHT.
HEATHER SAVED HER.
SHE SAVED US ALL.
NO...
NNOOOOO!
FROM THE PERSONAL JOURNAL OF HUGO WILDING OBE:
The communist regime finally succumbed to public pressure and announced its resignation on November 28th. Free democratic elections were held seven months later.
Czechoslovakia called it "The Velvet Revolution" in the belief that no lives had been lost.
History does not record the sacrifice of a brave young woman that night, but then history only ever touches the skin of truth. The deeper reality is infinitely more complex, comedic and cruel.
We will never forget Heather Lake. Her example sets a standard to which we all aspire. Her memory sustained us in the dark days that followed...
And will continue to do so in the darker ones to come.
NEXT: IMAGINARY ENEMIES

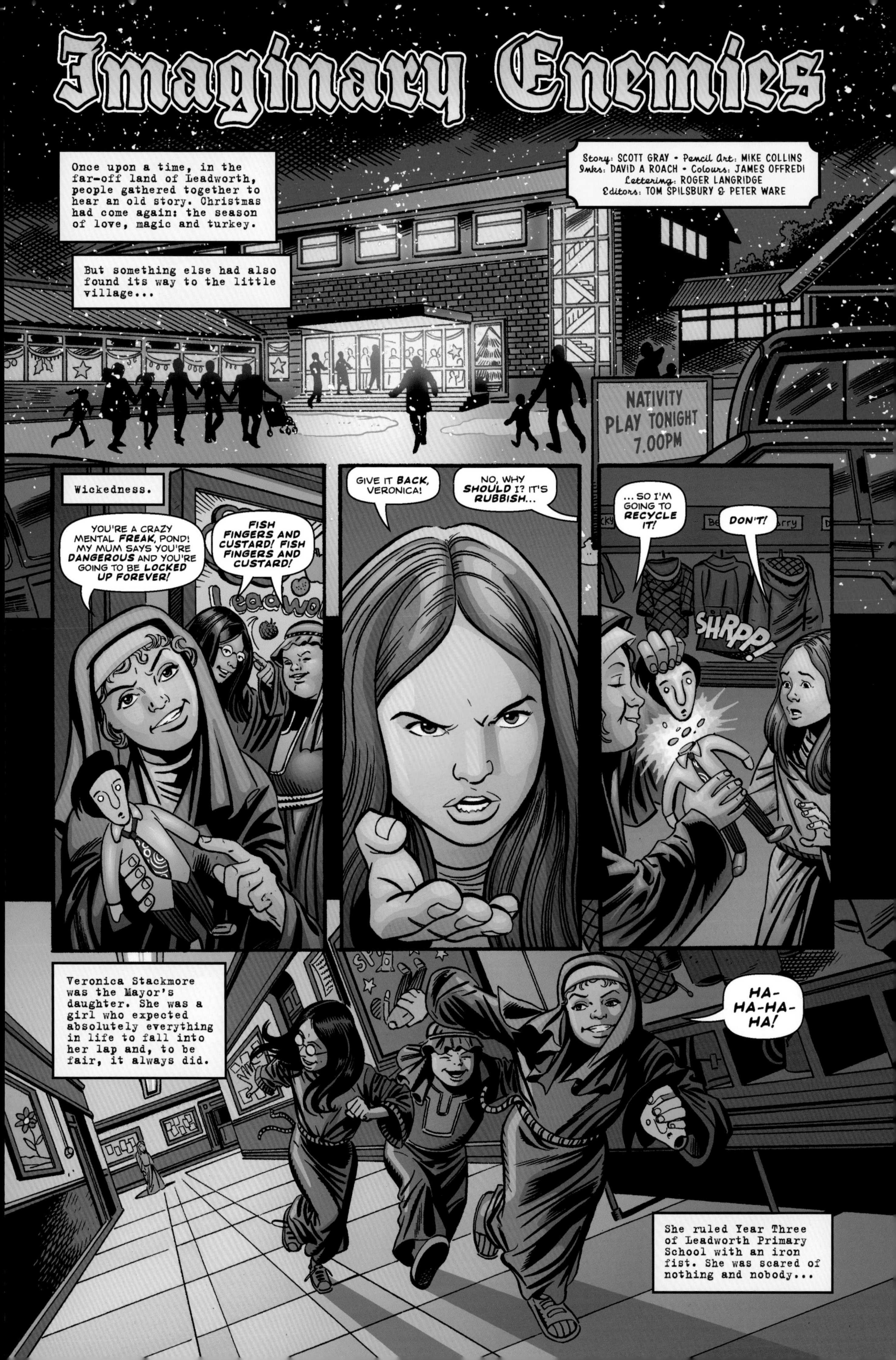
Imaginary Enemies
Once upon a time, in the far-off land of Leadworth, people gathered together to hear an old story. Christmas had come again: the season of love, magic and turkey.
Story: SCOTT GRAY • Pencil Art: MIKE COLLINS
Inks: DAVID A ROACH • Colours: JAMES OFFREDI
Lettering: ROGER LANGRIDGE
Editors: TOM SPILSBURY & PETER WARE
But something else had also found its way to the little village...
NATIVITY PLAY TONIGHT 7.00PM
Wickedness.
YOU'RE A CRAZY MENTAL FREAK, POND! MY MUM SAYS YOU'RE DANGEROUS AND YOU'RE GOING TO BE LOCKED UP FOREVER!
FISH FINGERS AND CUSTARD! FISH FINGERS AND CUSTARD!
GIVE IT BACK, VERONICA!
NO, WHY SHOULD I? IT'S RUBBISH...
...SO I'M GOING TO RECYCLE IT!
DON'T!
SHRPP!
Veronica Stackmore was the Mayor's daughter. She was a girl who expected absolutely everything in life to fall into her lap and, to be fair, it always did.
HA-HA-HA-HA!
She ruled Year Three of Leadworth Primary School with an iron fist. She was scared of nothing and nobody...

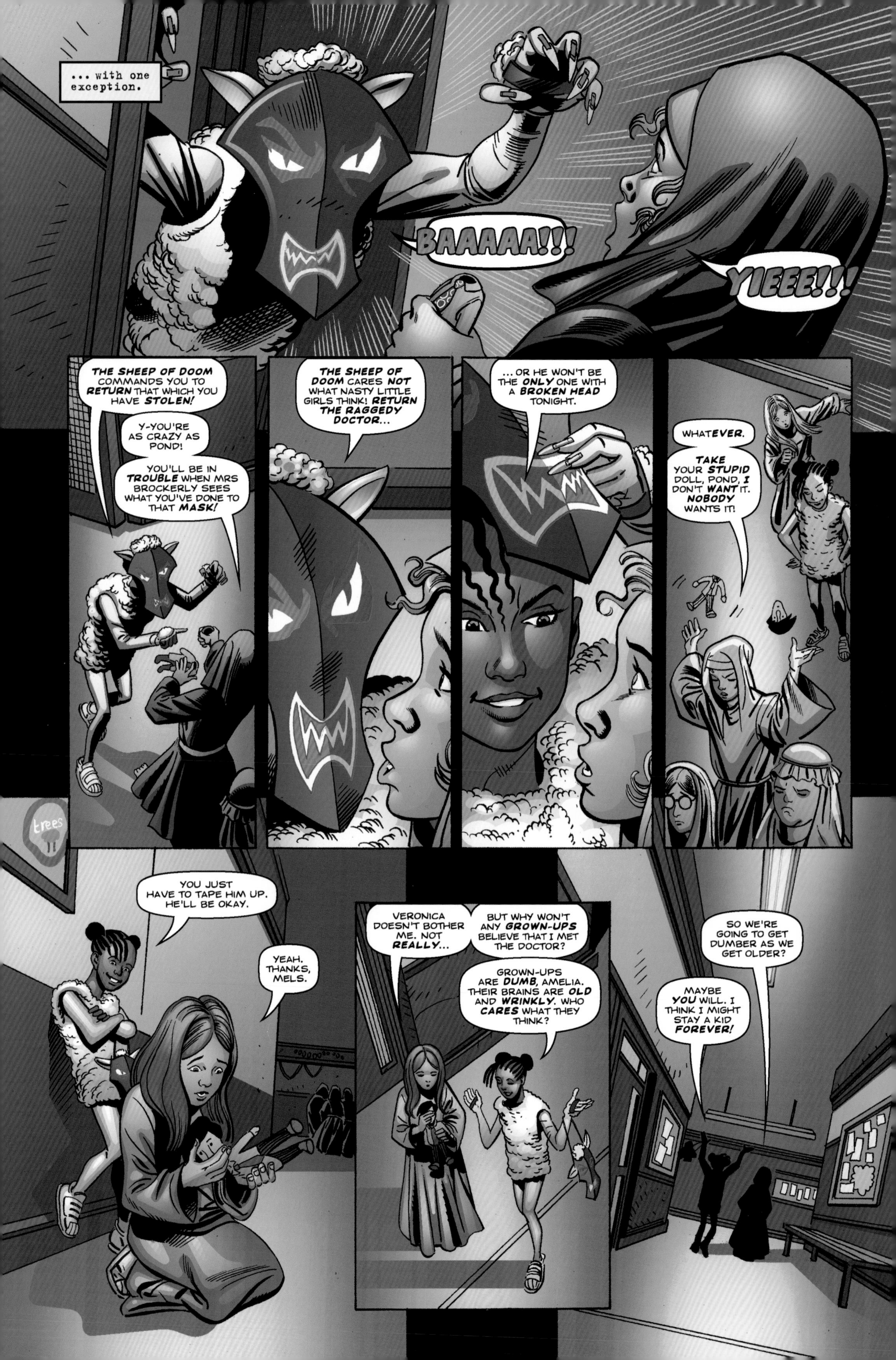
... with one exception.
BAAAAA!!!
YIEEE!!!
THE SHEEP OF DOOM COMMANDS YOU TO RETURN THAT WHICH YOU HAVE STOLEN!
Y-YOU'RE AS CRAZY AS POND!
YOU'LL BE IN TROUBLE WHEN MRS BROCKERLY SEES WHAT YOU'VE DONE TO THAT MASK!
THE SHEEP OF DOOM CARES NOT WHAT NASTY LITTLE GIRLS THINK! RETURN THE RAGGEDY DOCTOR...
...OR HE WON'T BE THE ONLY ONE WITH A BROKEN HEAD TONIGHT.
WHATEVER.
TAKE YOUR STUPID DOLL, POND, I DON'T WANT IT. NOBODY WANTS IT!
trees
YOU JUST HAVE TO TAPE HIM UP. HE'LL BE OKAY.
YEAH. THANKS, MELS.
VERONICA DOESN'T BOTHER ME. NOT REALLY...
BUT WHY WON'T ANY GROWN-UPS BELIEVE THAT I MET THE DOCTOR?
GROWN-UPS ARE DUMB, AMELIA. THEIR BRAINS ARE OLD AND WRINKLY. WHO CARES WHAT THEY THINK?
SO WE'RE GOING TO GET DUMBER AS WE GET OLDER?
MAYBE YOU WILL. I THINK I MIGHT STAY A KID FOREVER!

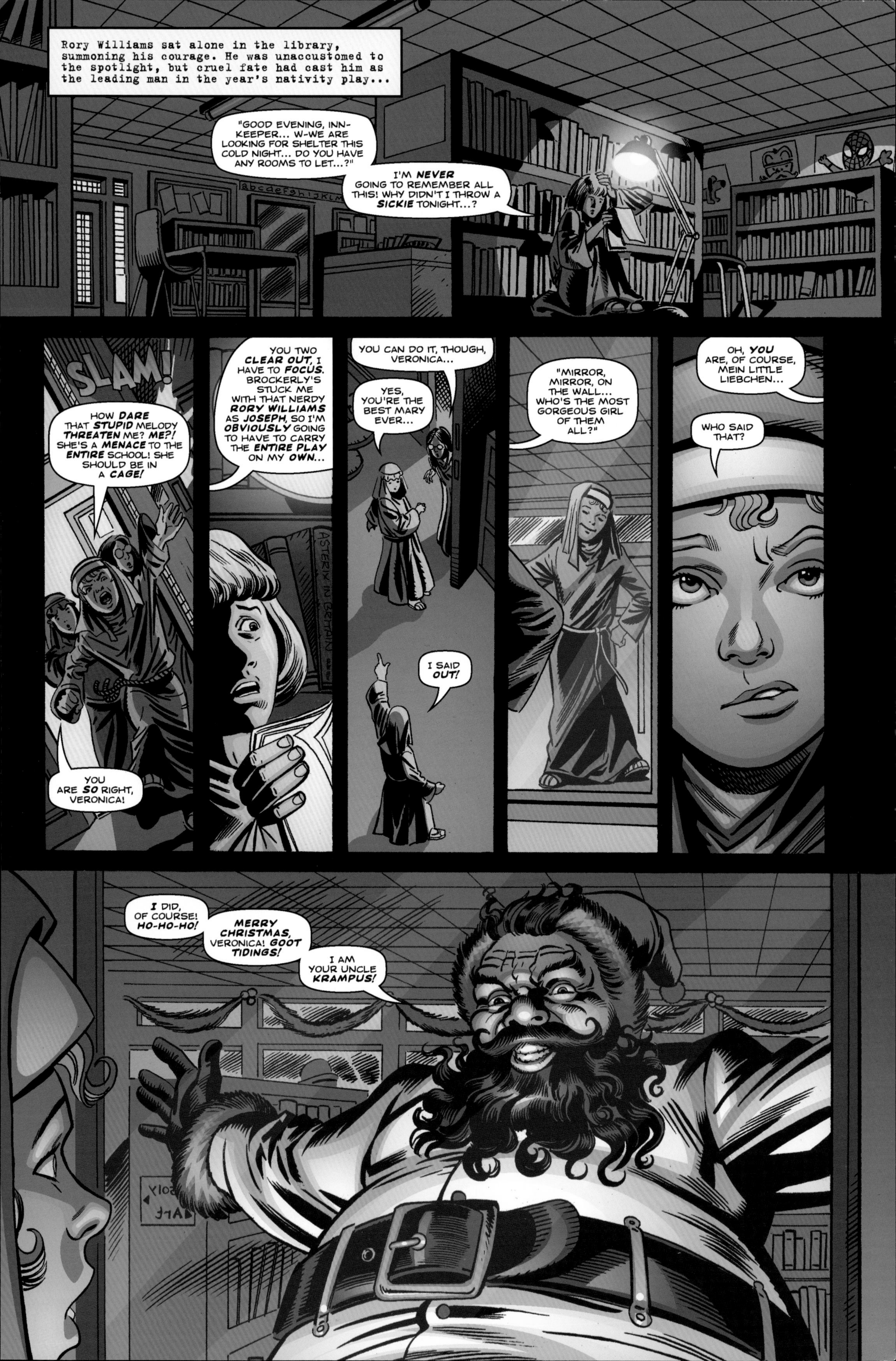

Rory Williams sat alone in the library, summoning his courage. He was unaccustomed to the spotlight, but cruel fate had cast him as the leading man in the year's nativity play...
"GOOD EVENING, INN-KEEPER... W-WE ARE LOOKING FOR SHELTER THIS COLD NIGHT... DO YOU HAVE ANY ROOMS TO LET...?"
I'M NEVER GOING TO REMEMBER ALL THIS! WHY DIDN'T I THROW A SICKIE TONIGHT...?
SLAM!
HOW DARE THAT STUPID MELODY THREATEN ME? ME?! SHE'S A MENACE TO THE ENTIRE SCHOOL! SHE SHOULD BE IN A CAGE!
YOU ARE SO RIGHT, VERONICA!
YOU TWO CLEAR OUT, I HAVE TO FOCUS. BROCKERLY'S STUCK ME WITH THAT NERDY RORY WILLIAMS AS JOSEPH, SO I'M OBVIOUSLY GOING TO HAVE TO CARRY THE ENTIRE PLAY ON MY OWN...
ASTERIX IN BRITAIN
YOU CAN DO IT, THOUGH, VERONICA...
YES, YOU'RE THE BEST MARY EVER...
I SAID OUT!
"MIRROR, MIRROR, ON THE WALL... WHO'S THE MOST GORGEOUS GIRL OF THEM ALL?"
OH, YOU ARE, OF COURSE, MEIN LITTLE LIEBCHEN...
WHO SAID THAT?
I DID, OF COURSE! HO-HO-HO!
MERRY CHRISTMAS, VERONICA! GOOT TIDINGS!
I AM YOUR UNCLE KRAMPUS!

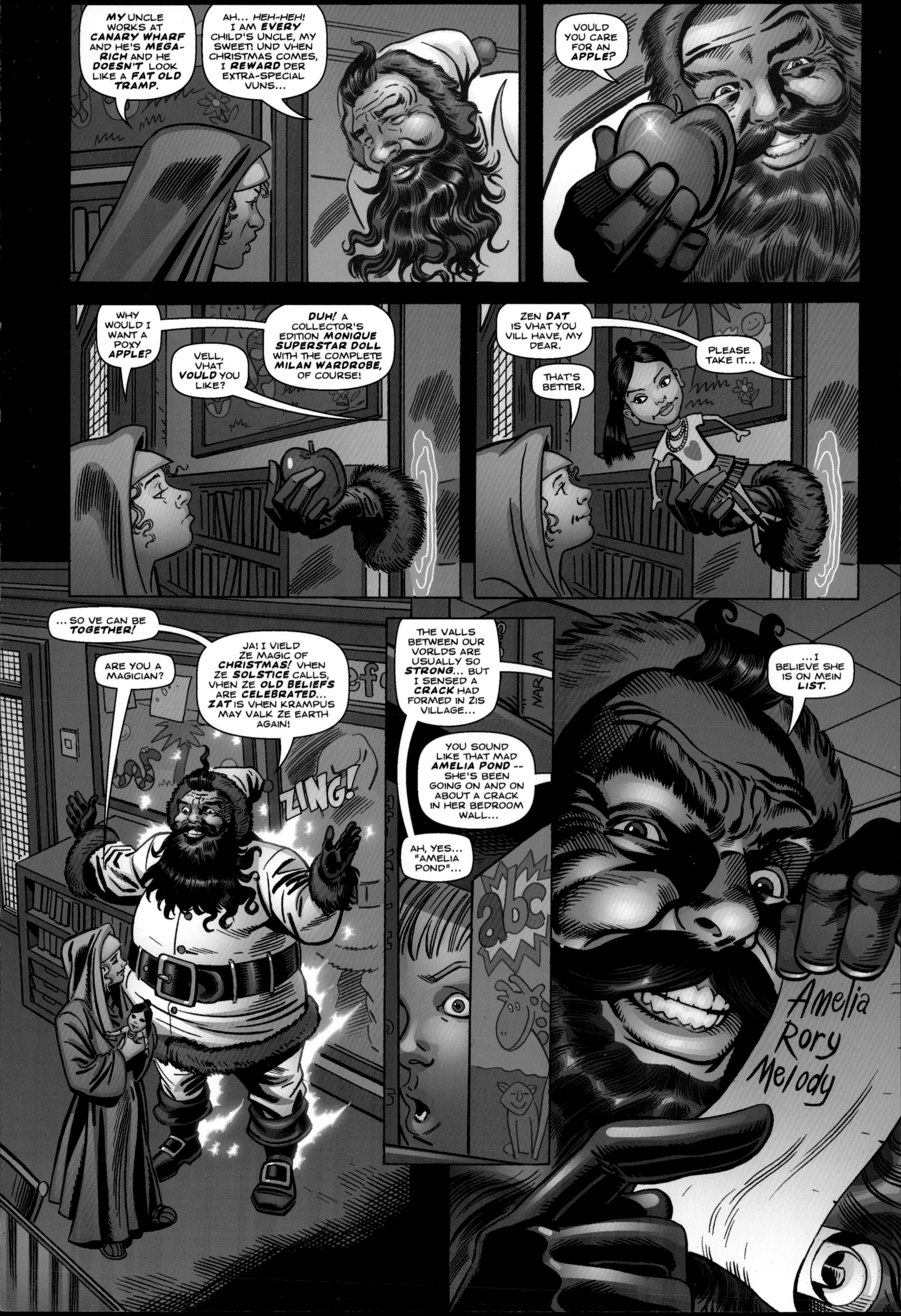
MY UNCLE WORKS AT CANARY WHARF AND HE'S MEGA-RICH AND HE DOESN'T LOOK LIKE A FAT OLD TRAMP.
AH... HEH-HEH! I AM EVERY CHILD'S UNCLE, MY SWEET! UND VHEN CHRISTMAS COMES, I REWARD DER EXTRA-SPECIAL VUNS...
VOULD YOU CARE FOR AN APPLE?
WHY WOULD I WANT A POXY APPLE?
VELL, VHAT VOULD YOU LIKE?
DUH! A COLLECTOR'S EDITION MONIQUE SUPERSTAR DOLL WITH THE COMPLETE MILAN WARDROBE, OF COURSE!
ZEN DAT IS VHAT YOU VILL HAVE, MY DEAR.
PLEASE TAKE IT...
THAT'S BETTER.
ARE YOU A MAGICIAN?
...SO VE CAN BE TOGETHER!
JA! I VIELD ZE MAGIC OF CHRISTMAS! VHEN ZE SOLSTICE CALLS, VHEN ZE OLD BELIEFS ARE CELEBRATED... ZAT IS VHEN KRAMPUS MAY VALK ZE EARTH AGAIN!
ZING!
THE VALLS BETWEEN OUR VORLDS ARE USUALLY SO STRONG... BUT I SENSED A CRACK HAD FORMED IN ZIS VILLAGE...
YOU SOUND LIKE THAT MAD AMELIA POND -- SHE'S BEEN GOING ON AND ON ABOUT A CRACK IN HER BEDROOM WALL...
AH, YES... "AMELIA POND"...
...I BELIEVE SHE IS ON MEIN LIST.
Amelia
Rory
Melody

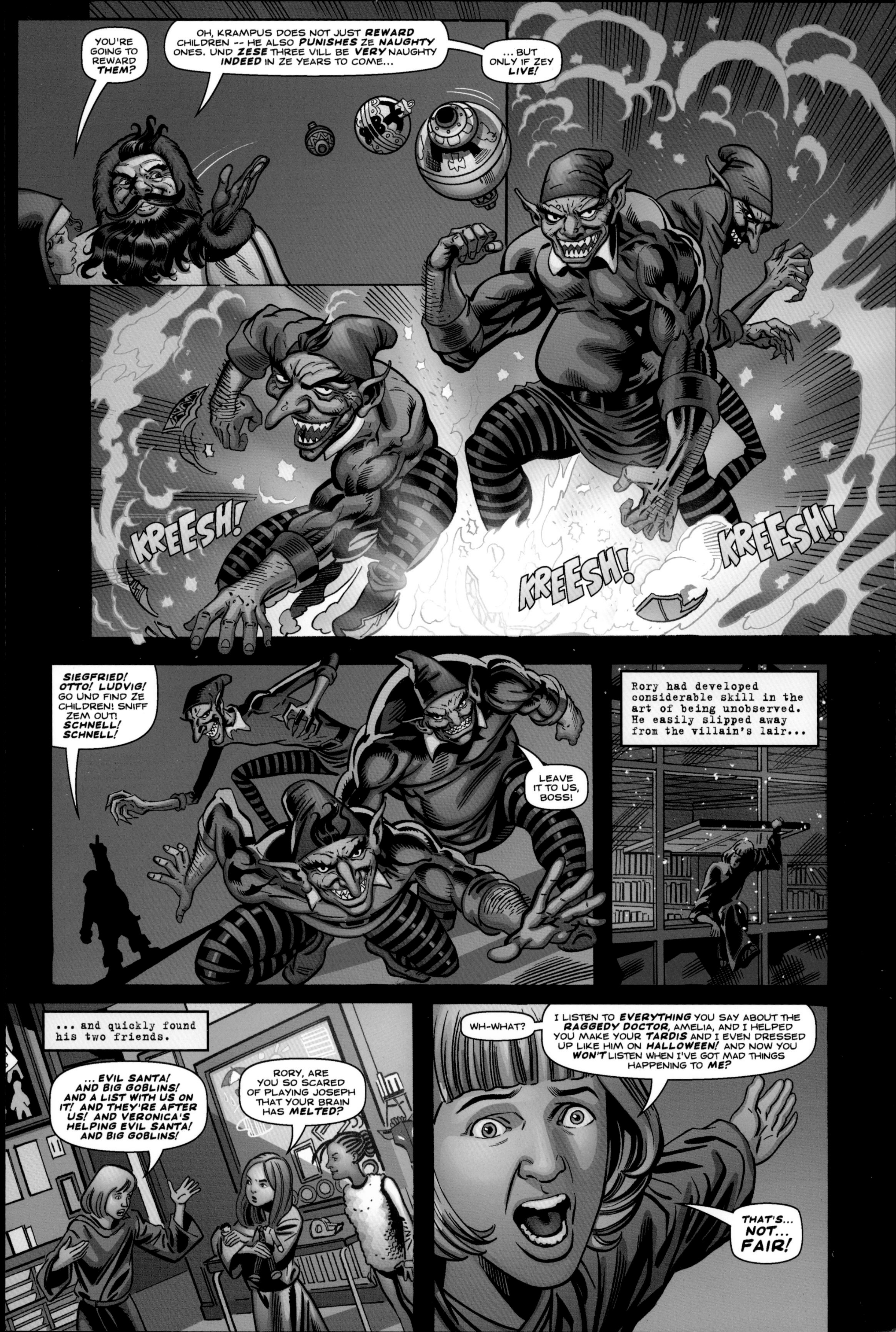

YOU'RE GOING TO REWARD THEM?
OH, KRAMPUS DOES NOT JUST REWARD CHILDREN -- HE ALSO PUNISHES ZE NAUGHTY ONES. UND ZESE THREE VILL BE VERY NAUGHTY INDEED IN ZE YEARS TO COME...
... BUT ONLY IF ZEY LIVE!
KREESH!
KREESH!
KREESH!
SIEGFRIED! OTTO! LUDVIG! GO UND FIND ZE CHILDREN! SNIFF ZEM OUT! SCHNELL! SCHNELL!
LEAVE IT TO US, BOSS!
Rory had developed considerable skill in the art of being unobserved. He easily slipped away from the villain's lair...
... and quickly found his two friends.
... EVIL SANTA! AND BIG GOBLINS! AND A LIST WITH US ON IT! AND THEY'RE AFTER US! AND VERONICA'S HELPING EVIL SANTA! AND BIG GOBLINS!
RORY, ARE YOU SO SCARED OF PLAYING JOSEPH THAT YOUR BRAIN HAS MELTED?
WH-WHAT?
I LISTEN TO EVERYTHING YOU SAY ABOUT THE RAGGEDY DOCTOR, AMELIA, AND I HELPED YOU MAKE YOUR TARDIS AND I EVEN DRESSED UP LIKE HIM ON HALLOWEEN! AND NOW YOU WON'T LISTEN WHEN I'VE GOT MAD THINGS HAPPENING TO ME?
THAT'S... NOT... FAIR!

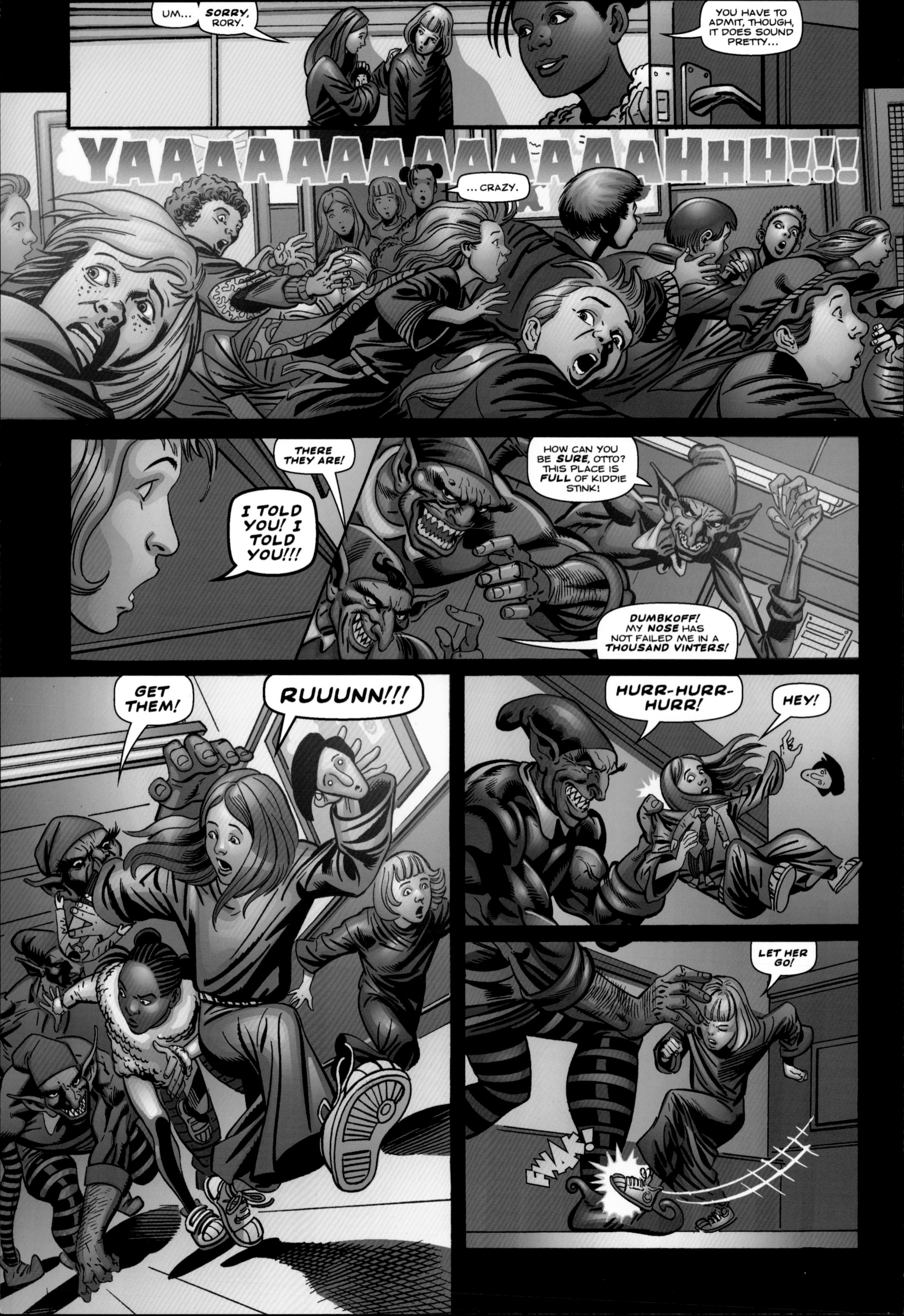
UM... SORRY, RORY.
YOU HAVE TO ADMIT, THOUGH, IT DOES SOUND PRETTY...
YAAAAAAAAAAAAAHHH!!!
...CRAZY.
I TOLD YOU! I TOLD YOU!!!
THERE THEY ARE!
HOW CAN YOU BE SURE, OTTO? THIS PLACE IS FULL OF KIDDIE STINK!
DUMBKOFF! MY NOSE HAS NOT FAILED ME IN A THOUSAND VINTERS!
GET THEM!
RUUUNN!!!
HURR-HURR-HURR!
HEY!
LET HER GO!
FWAK!

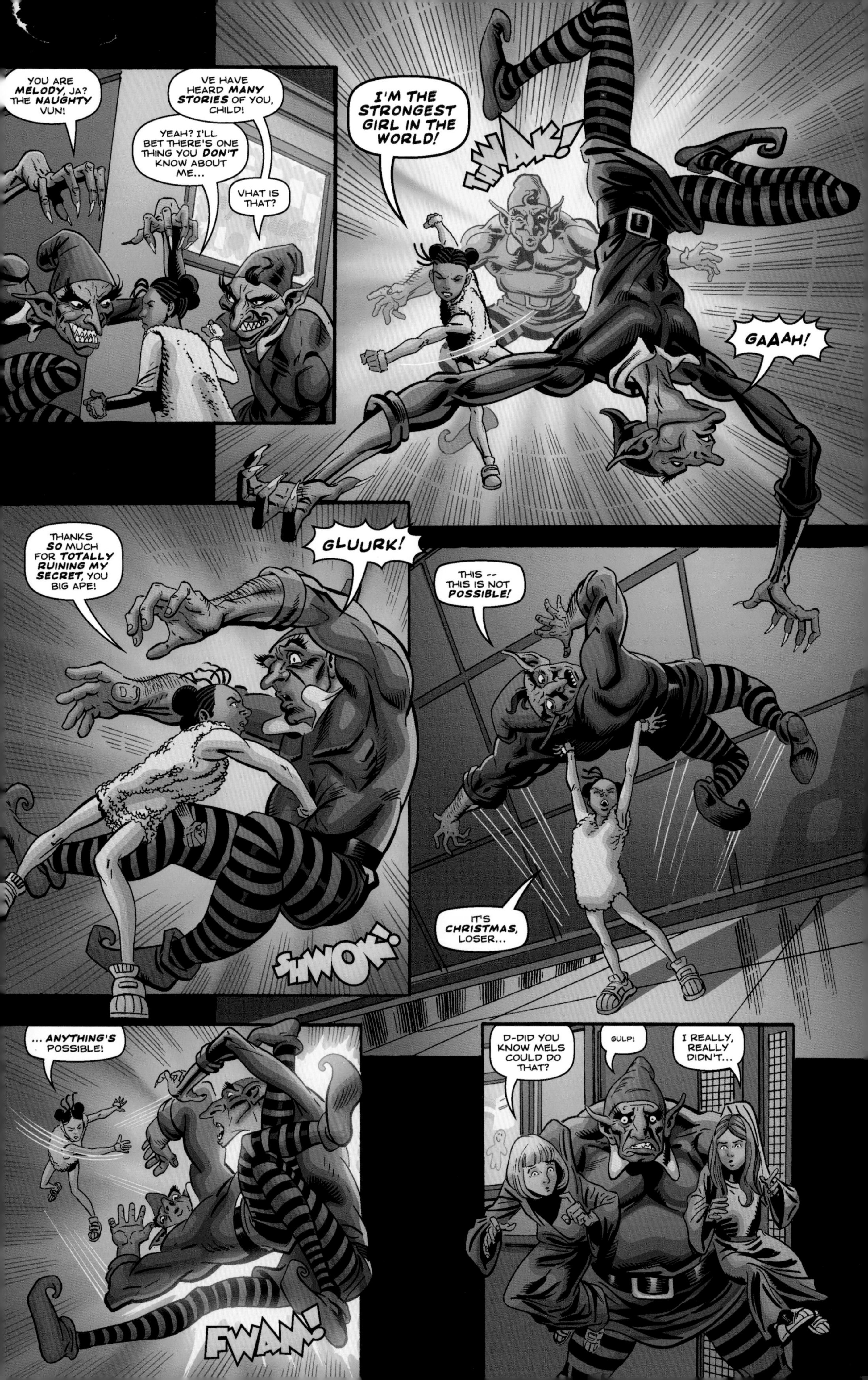
YOU ARE MELODY, JA? THE NAUGHTY VUN!
VE HAVE HEARD MANY STORIES OF YOU, CHILD!
YEAH? I'LL BET THERE'S ONE THING YOU DON'T KNOW ABOUT ME...
VHAT IS THAT?
I'M THE STRONGEST GIRL IN THE WORLD!
THWAK!
GAAAH!
THANKS SO MUCH FOR TOTALLY RUINING MY SECRET, YOU BIG APE!
GLUURK!
SHWOK!
THIS -- THIS IS NOT POSSIBLE!
IT'S CHRISTMAS, LOSER...
... ANYTHING'S POSSIBLE!
FWAM!
D-DID YOU KNOW MELS COULD DO THAT?
GULP!
I REALLY, REALLY DIDN'T...

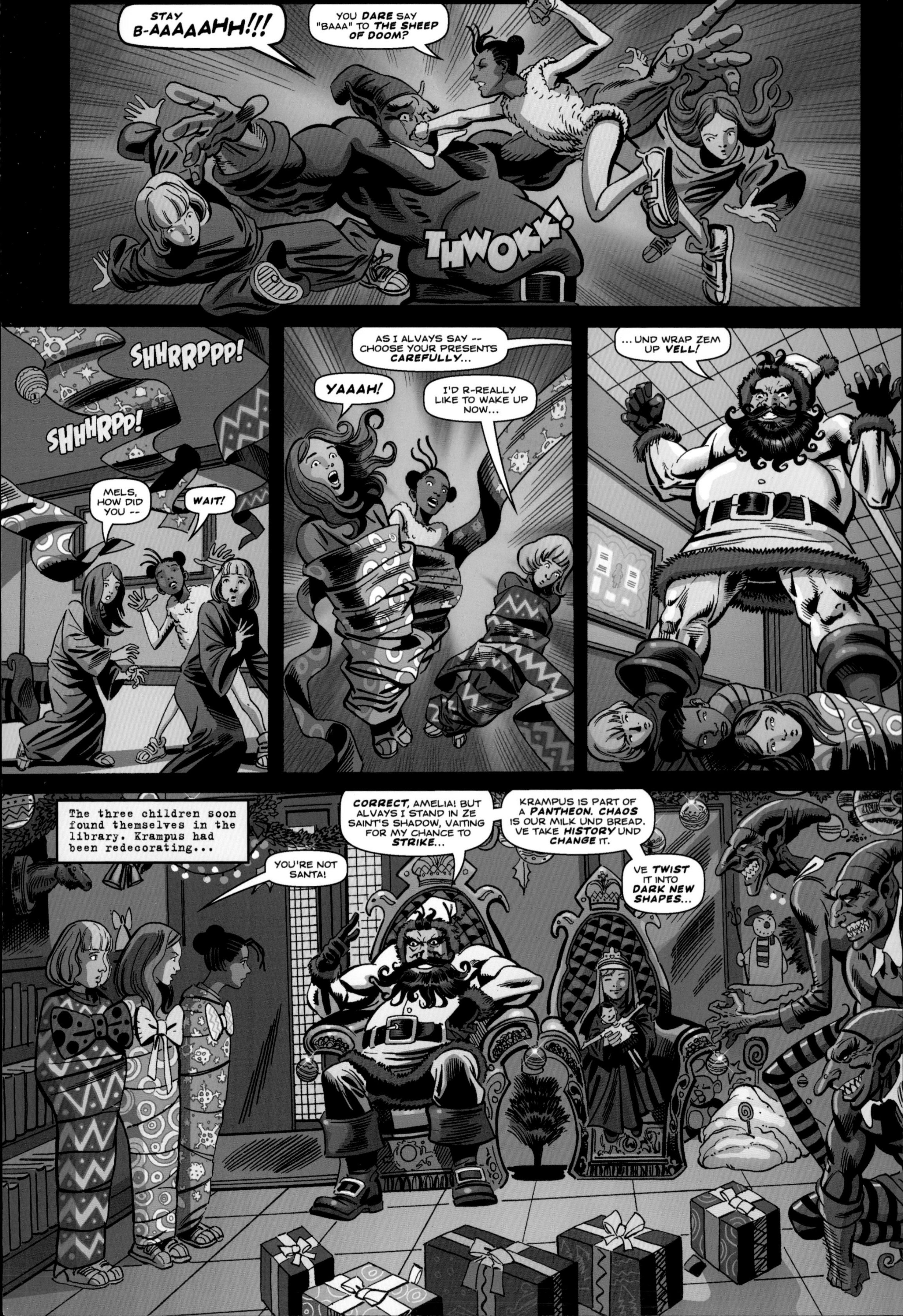

STAY B-AAAAAHH!!!
YOU DARE SAY "BAAA" TO THE SHEEP OF DOOM?
THWOKK!
SHHRRPPP!
SHHHRPP!
MELS, HOW DID YOU --
WAIT!
AS I ALWAYS SAY -- CHOOSE YOUR PRESENTS CAREFULLY...
YAAAH!
I'D R-REALLY LIKE TO WAKE UP NOW...
... UND WRAP ZEM UP VELL!
The three children soon found themselves in the library. Krampus had been redecorating...
YOU'RE NOT SANTA!
CORRECT, AMELIA! BUT ALVAYS I STAND IN ZE SAINT'S SHADOW, VAITING FOR MY CHANCE TO STRIKE...
KRAMPUS IS PART OF A PANTHEON. CHAOS IS OUR MILK UND BREAD. VE TAKE HISTORY UND CHANGE IT.
VE TWIST IT INTO DARK NEW SHAPES...

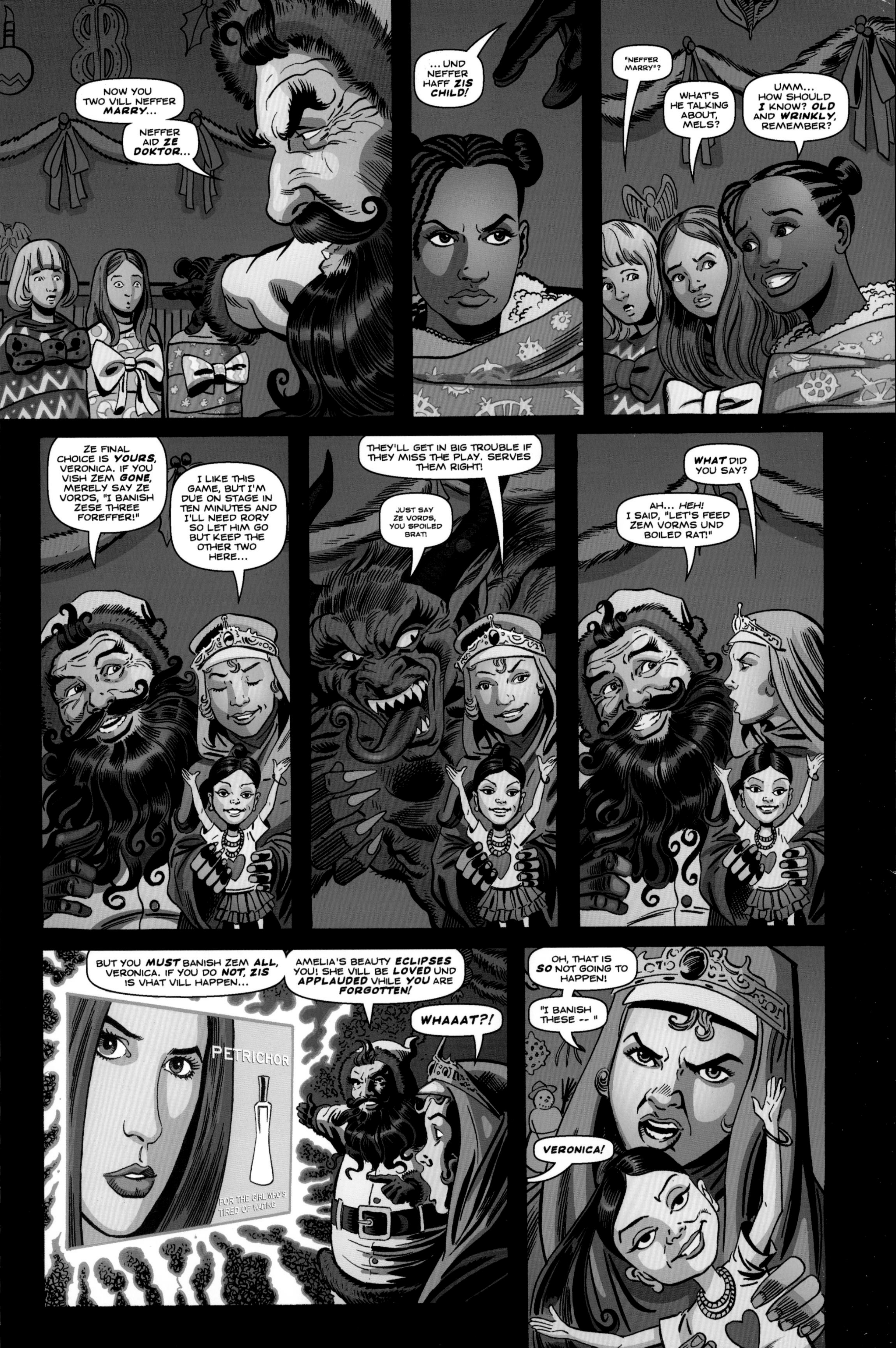
NOW YOU TWO VILL NEFFER MARRY...
NEFFER AID ZE DOKTOR...
...UND NEFFER HAFF ZIS CHILD!
"NEFFER MARRY"?
WHAT'S HE TALKING ABOUT, MELS?
UMM... HOW SHOULD I KNOW? OLD AND WRINKLY, REMEMBER?
ZE FINAL CHOICE IS YOURS, VERONICA. IF YOU VISH ZEM GONE, MERELY SAY ZE VORDS, "I BANISH ZESE THREE FOREFFER!"
I LIKE THIS GAME, BUT I'M DUE ON STAGE IN TEN MINUTES AND I'LL NEED RORY SO LET HIM GO BUT KEEP THE OTHER TWO HERE...
THEY'LL GET IN BIG TROUBLE IF THEY MISS THE PLAY. SERVES THEM RIGHT!
JUST SAY ZE VORDS, YOU SPOILED BRAT!
WHAT DID YOU SAY?
AH... HEH! I SAID, "LET'S FEED ZEM VORMS UND BOILED RAT!"
BUT YOU MUST BANISH ZEM ALL, VERONICA. IF YOU DO NOT, ZIS IS VHAT VILL HAPPEN...
AMELIA'S BEAUTY ECLIPSES YOU! SHE VILL BE LOVED UND APPLAUDED VHILE YOU ARE FORGOTTEN!
PETRICHOR
FOR THE GIRL WHO'S TIRED OF WAITING
WHAAAT?!
OH, THAT IS SO NOT GOING TO HAPPEN!
"I BANISH THESE -- "
VERONICA!

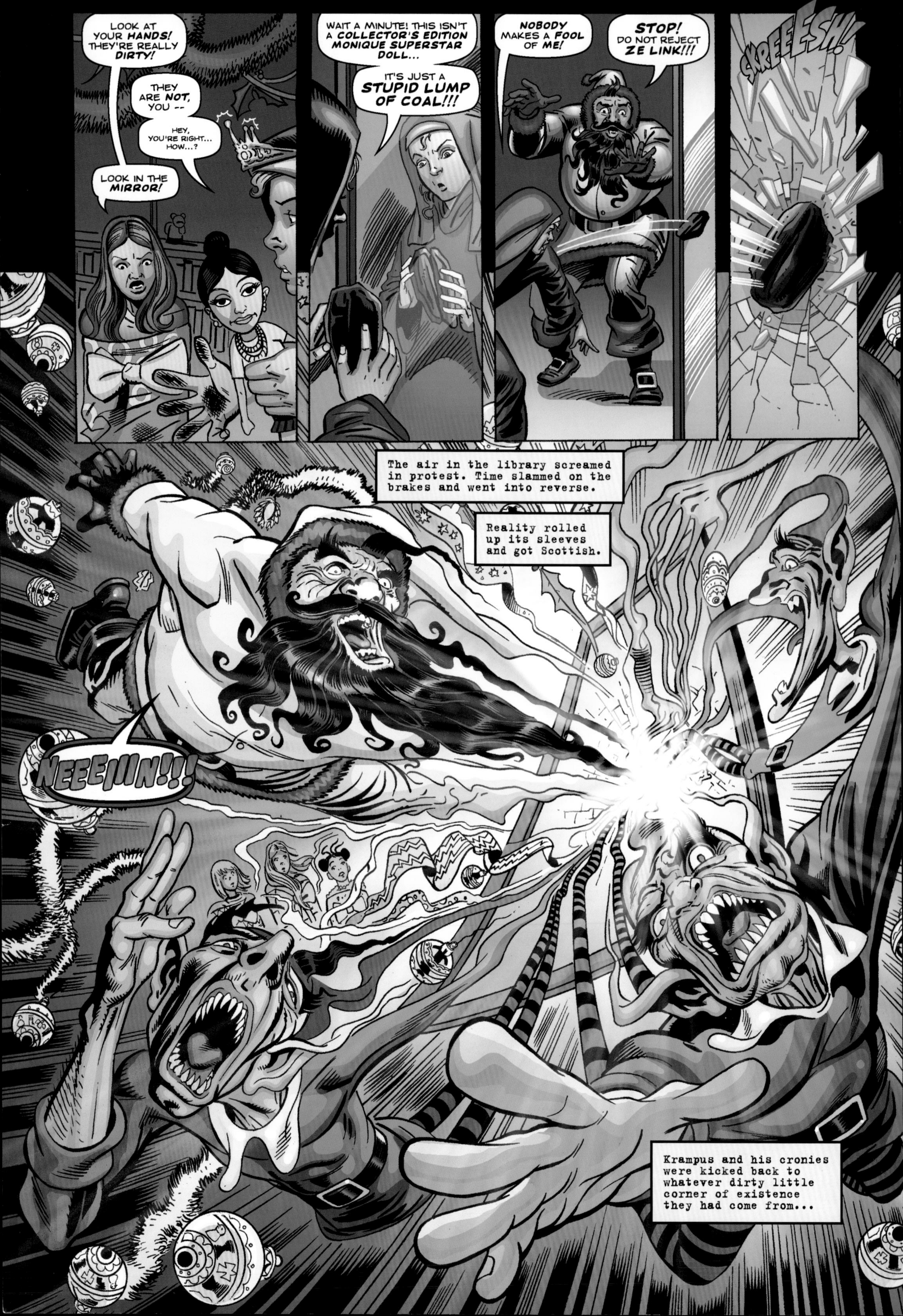
LOOK AT YOUR HANDS! THEY'RE REALLY DIRTY!
THEY ARE NOT, YOU --
HEY, YOU'RE RIGHT... HOW...?
LOOK IN THE MIRROR!
WAIT A MINUTE! THIS ISN'T A COLLECTOR'S EDITION MONIQUE SUPERSTAR DOLL...
IT'S JUST A STUPID LUMP OF COAL!!!
NOBODY MAKES A FOOL OF ME!
STOP! DO NOT REJECT ZE LINK!!!
SKREEESH!
The air in the library screamed in protest. Time slammed on the brakes and went into reverse.
Reality rolled up its sleeves and got Scottish.
NEEEIIIN!!!
Krampus and his cronies were kicked back to whatever dirty little corner of existence they had come from...

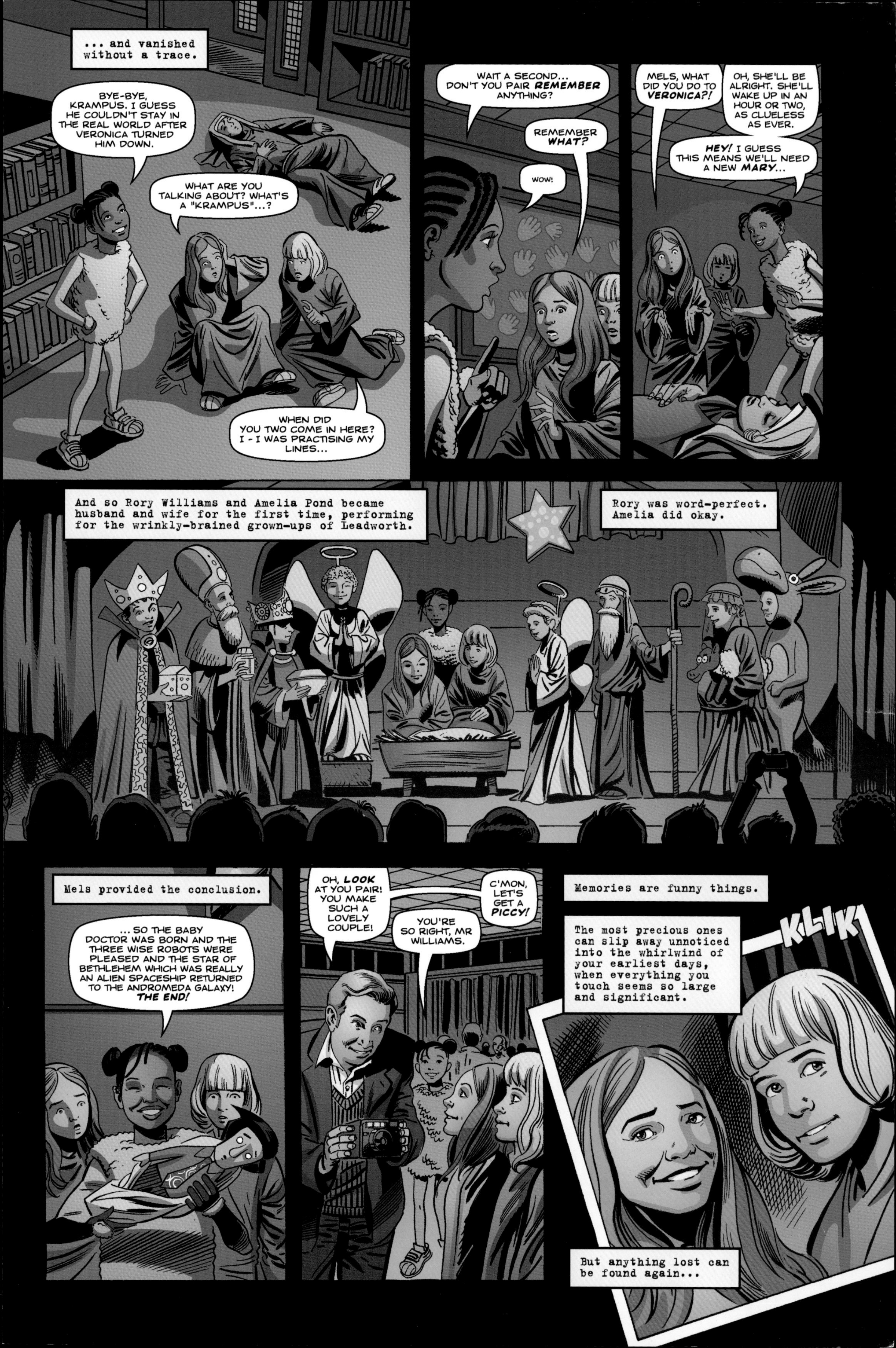
... and vanished without a trace.
BYE-BYE, KRAMPUS. I GUESS HE COULDN'T STAY IN THE REAL WORLD AFTER VERONICA TURNED HIM DOWN.
WHAT ARE YOU TALKING ABOUT? WHAT'S A "KRAMPUS"...?
WHEN DID YOU TWO COME IN HERE? I - I WAS PRACTISING MY LINES...
WAIT A SECOND... DON'T YOU PAIR REMEMBER ANYTHING?
REMEMBER WHAT?
WOW!
MELS, WHAT DID YOU DO TO VERONICA?!
OH, SHE'LL BE ALRIGHT. SHE'LL WAKE UP IN AN HOUR OR TWO, AS CLUELESS AS EVER.
HEY! I GUESS THIS MEANS WE'LL NEED A NEW MARY...
And so Rory Williams and Amelia Pond became husband and wife for the first time, performing for the wrinkly-brained grown-ups of Leadworth.
Rory was word-perfect. Amelia did okay.
Mels provided the conclusion.
... SO THE BABY DOCTOR WAS BORN AND THE THREE WISE ROBOTS WERE PLEASED AND THE STAR OF BETHLEHEM WHICH WAS REALLY AN ALIEN SPACESHIP RETURNED TO THE ANDROMEDA GALAXY! THE END!
OH, LOOK AT YOU PAIR! YOU MAKE SUCH A LOVELY COUPLE!
C'MON, LET'S GET A PICCY!
YOU'RE SO RIGHT, MR WILLIAMS.
Memories are funny things.
KLIK
The most precious ones can slip away unnoticed into the whirlwind of your earliest days, when everything you touch seems so large and significant.
But anything lost can be found again...

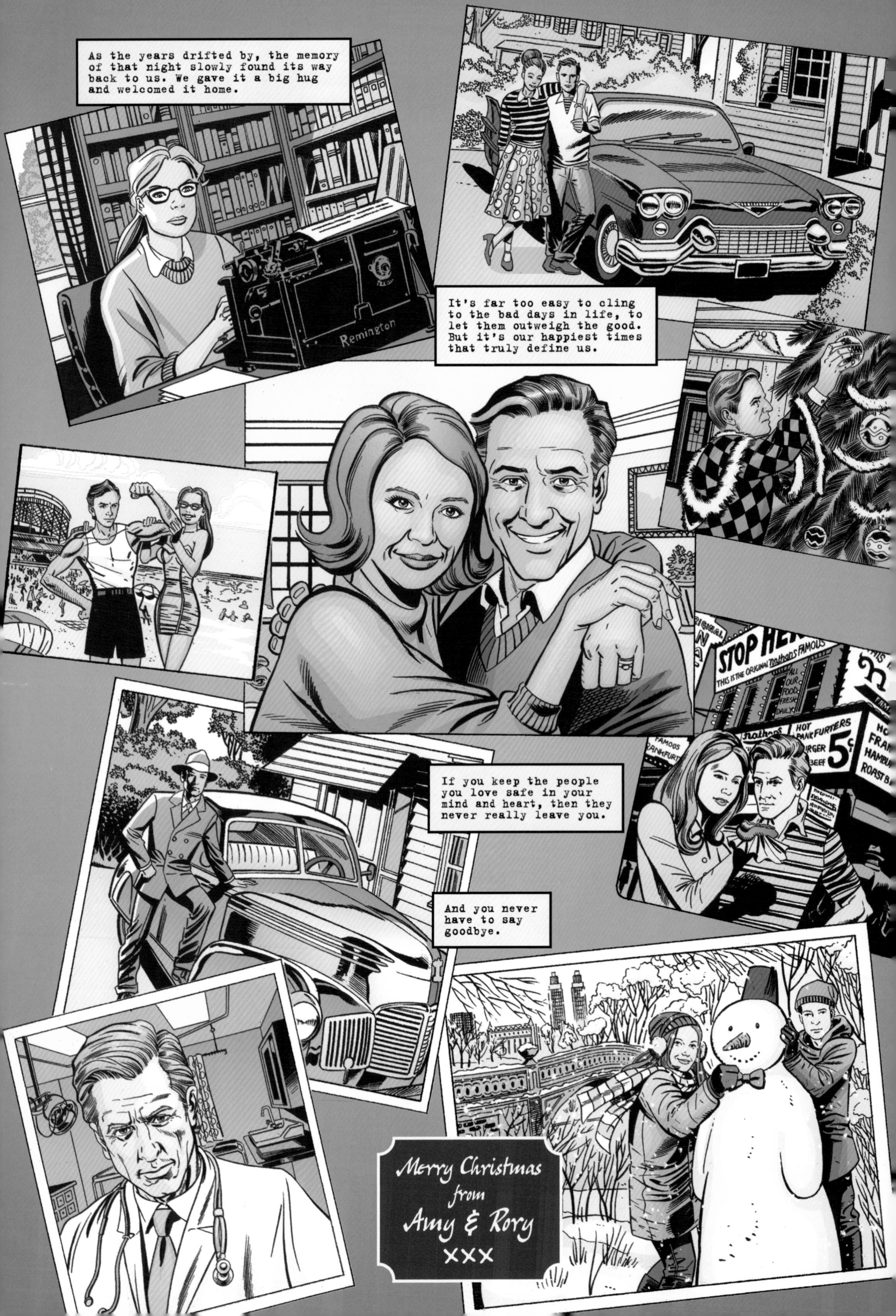
As the years drifted by, the memory of that night slowly found its way back to us. We gave it a big hug and welcomed it home.
Remington
It's far too easy to cling to the bad days in life, to let them outweigh the good. But it's our happiest times that truly define us.
STOP HERE
THIS IS THE ORIGINAL Nathan's FAMOUS
ALL OUR FOOD FRESH DAILY
HOT FRANKFURTERS
5¢
If you keep the people you love safe in your mind and heart, then they never really leave you.
And you never have to say goodbye.
Merry Christmas from Amy & Rory XXX

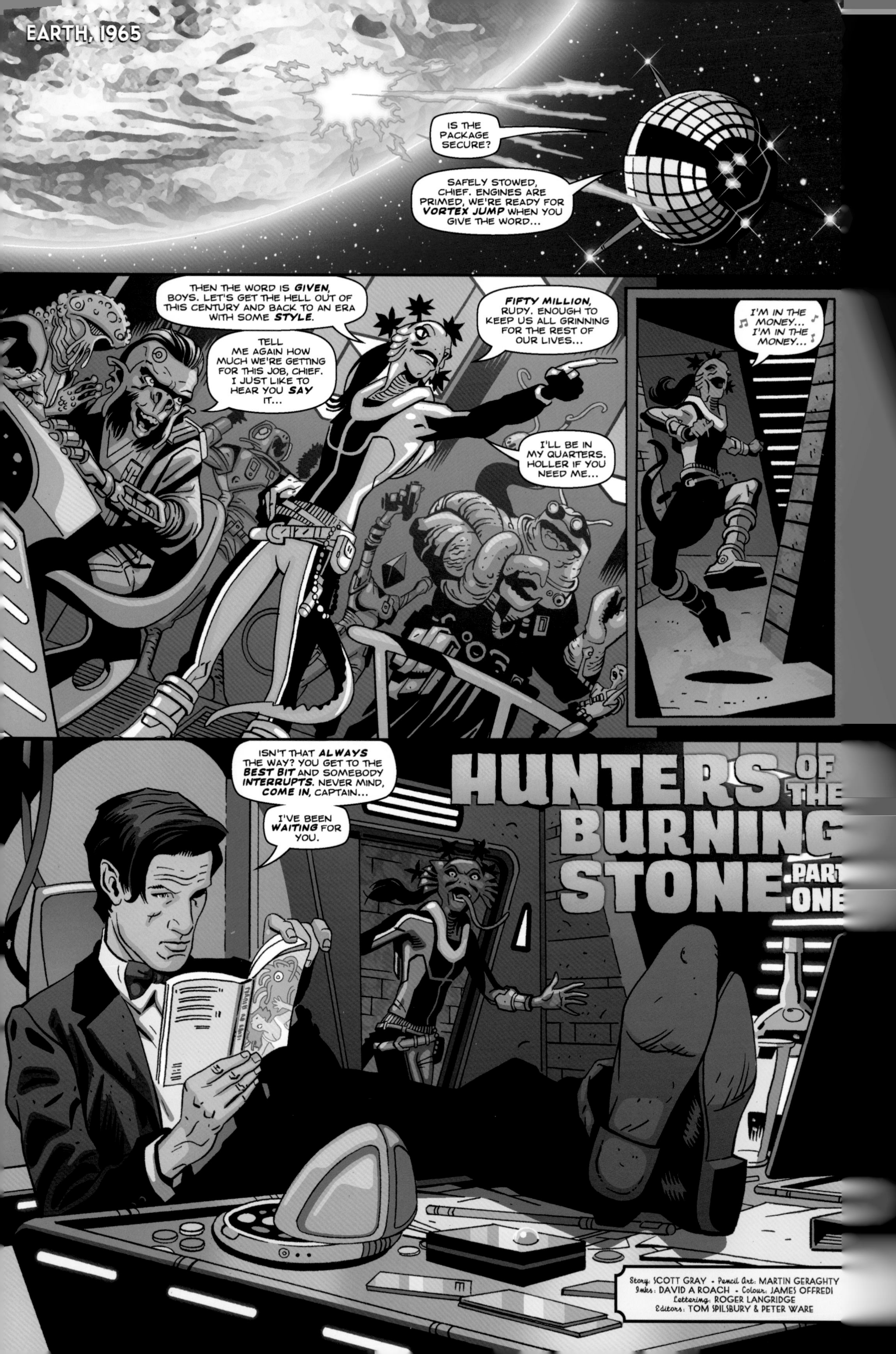

EARTH, 1965
IS THE PACKAGE SECURE?
SAFELY STOWED, CHIEF. ENGINES ARE PRIMED, WE'RE READY FOR VORTEX JUMP WHEN YOU GIVE THE WORD...
THEN THE WORD IS GIVEN, BOYS. LET'S GET THE HELL OUT OF THIS CENTURY AND BACK TO AN ERA WITH SOME STYLE.
TELL ME AGAIN HOW MUCH WE'RE GETTING FOR THIS JOB, CHIEF. I JUST LIKE TO HEAR YOU SAY IT...
FIFTY MILLION, RUDY. ENOUGH TO KEEP US ALL GRINNING FOR THE REST OF OUR LIVES...
I'LL BE IN MY QUARTERS. HOLLER IF YOU NEED ME...
I'M IN THE MONEY... I'M IN THE MONEY...
ISN'T THAT ALWAYS THE WAY? YOU GET TO THE BEST BIT AND SOMEBODY INTERRUPTS. NEVER MIND, COME IN, CAPTAIN...
I'VE BEEN WAITING FOR YOU.
HUNTERS OF THE BURNING STONE PART ONE
Story: SCOTT GRAY • Pencil Art: MARTIN GERAGHTY
Inks: DAVID A ROACH • Colour: JAMES OFFREDI
Lettering: ROGER LANGRIDGE
Editors: TOM SPILSBURY & PETER WARE

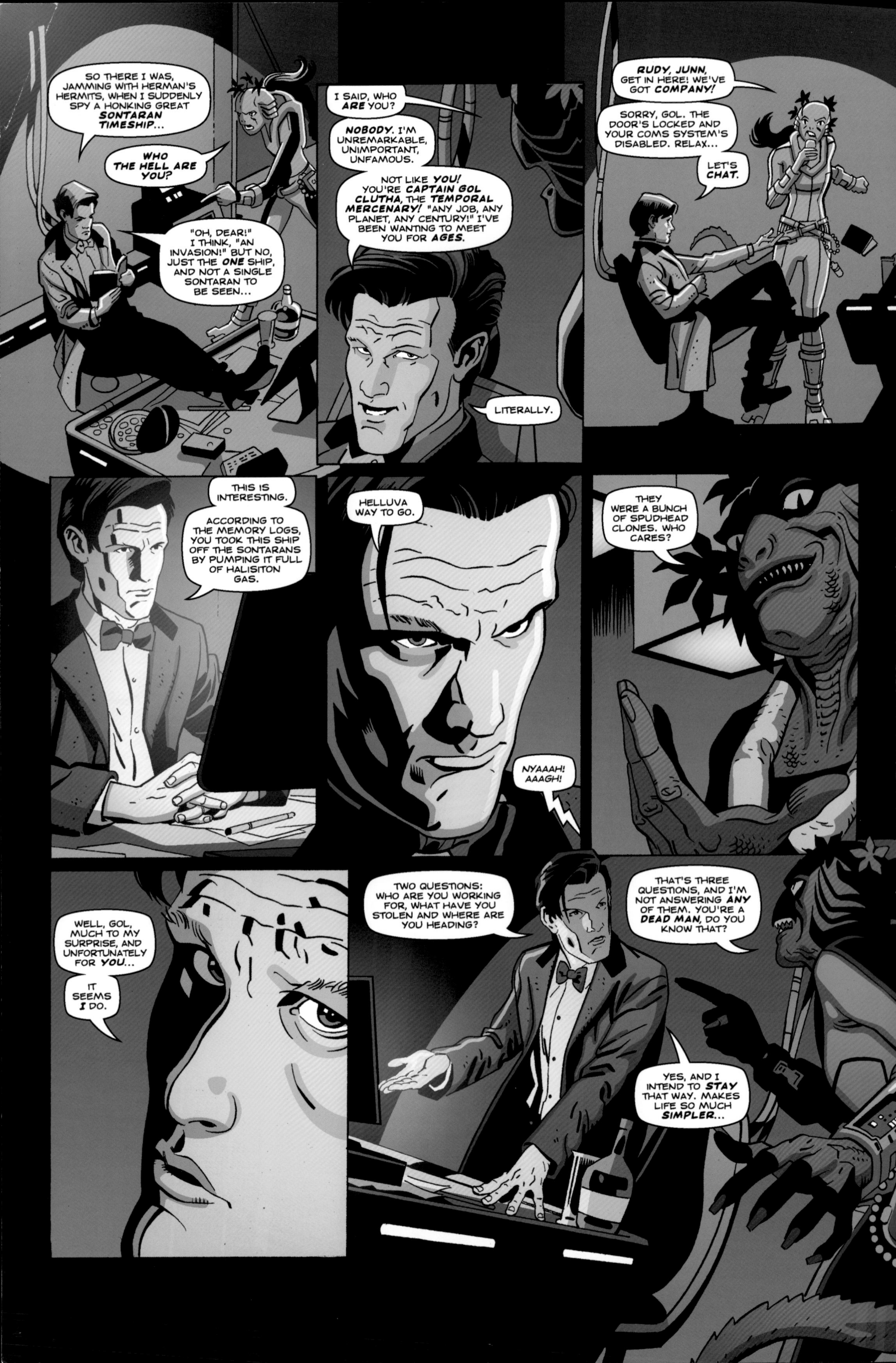
SO THERE I WAS, JAMMING WITH HERMAN'S HERMITS, WHEN I SUDDENLY SPY A HONKING GREAT SONTARAN TIMESHIP...
WHO THE HELL ARE YOU?
"OH, DEAR!" I THINK, "AN INVASION!" BUT NO, JUST THE ONE SHIP, AND NOT A SINGLE SONTARAN TO BE SEEN...
I SAID, WHO ARE YOU?
NOBODY. I'M UNREMARKABLE, UNIMPORTANT, UNFAMOUS.
NOT LIKE YOU! YOU'RE CAPTAIN GOL CLUTHA, THE TEMPORAL MERCENARY! "ANY JOB, ANY PLANET, ANY CENTURY!" I'VE BEEN WANTING TO MEET YOU FOR AGES.
LITERALLY.
RUDY, JUNN, GET IN HERE! WE'VE GOT COMPANY!
SORRY, GOL. THE DOOR'S LOCKED AND YOUR COMS SYSTEM'S DISABLED. RELAX...
LET'S CHAT.
THIS IS INTERESTING.
ACCORDING TO THE MEMORY LOGS, YOU TOOK THIS SHIP OFF THE SONTARANS BY PUMPING IT FULL OF HALISITON GAS.
HELLUVA WAY TO GO.
NYAAAH! AAAGH!
THEY WERE A BUNCH OF SPUDHEAD CLONES. WHO CARES?
WELL, GOL, MUCH TO MY SURPRISE, AND UNFORTUNATELY FOR YOU...
IT SEEMS I DO.
TWO QUESTIONS: WHO ARE YOU WORKING FOR, WHAT HAVE YOU STOLEN AND WHERE ARE YOU HEADING?
THAT'S THREE QUESTIONS, AND I'M NOT ANSWERING ANY OF THEM. YOU'RE A DEAD MAN, DO YOU KNOW THAT?
YES, AND I INTEND TO STAY THAT WAY. MAKES LIFE SO MUCH SIMPLER...

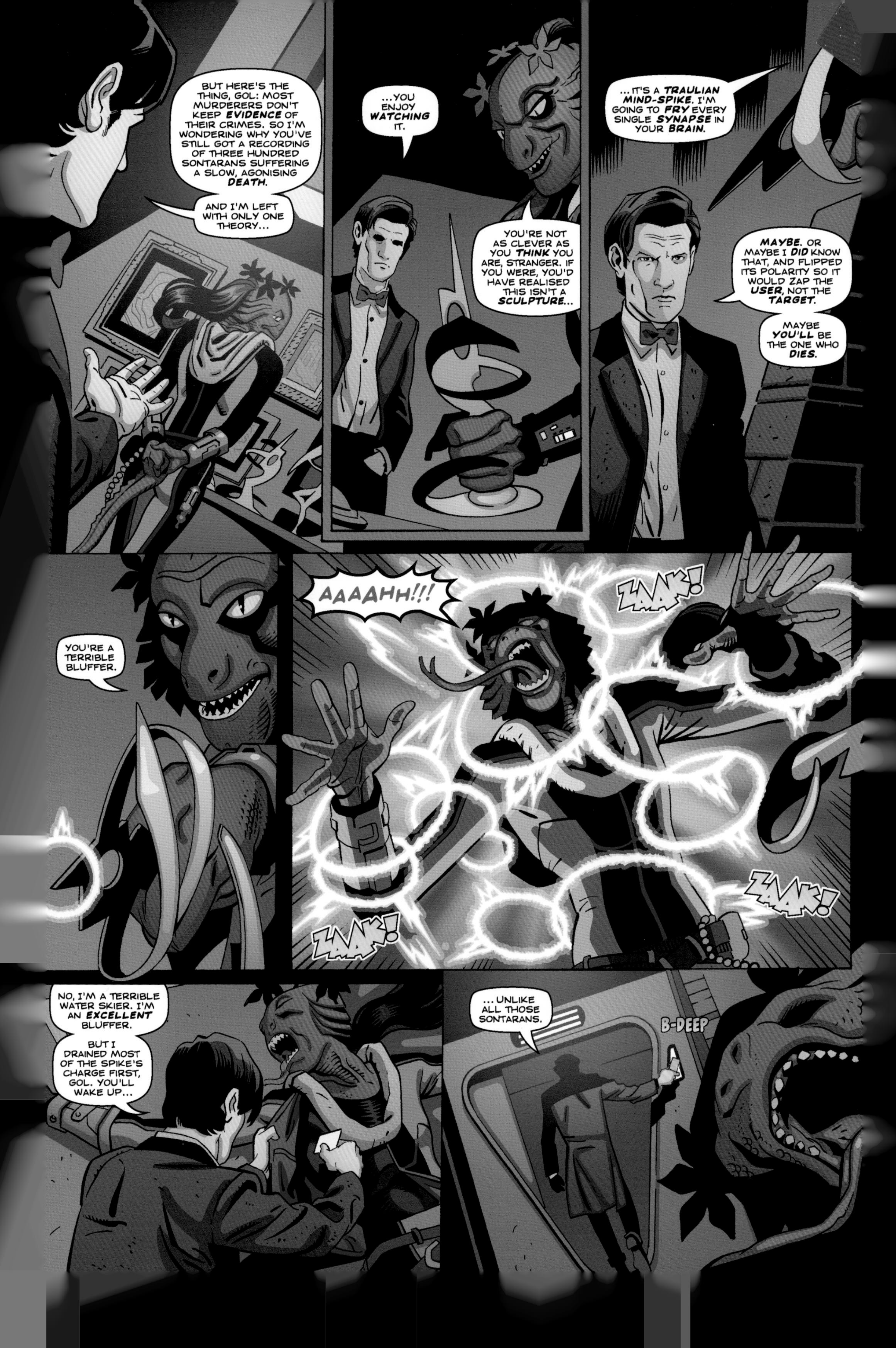
BUT HERE'S THE THING, GOL: MOST MURDERERS DON'T KEEP EVIDENCE OF THEIR CRIMES. SO I'M WONDERING WHY YOU'VE STILL GOT A RECORDING OF THREE HUNDRED SONTARANS SUFFERING A SLOW, AGONISING DEATH.
AND I'M LEFT WITH ONLY ONE THEORY...
...YOU ENJOY WATCHING IT.
YOU'RE NOT AS CLEVER AS YOU THINK YOU ARE, STRANGER. IF YOU WERE, YOU'D HAVE REALISED THIS ISN'T A SCULPTURE...
...IT'S A TRAULIAN MIND-SPIKE. I'M GOING TO FRY EVERY SINGLE SYNAPSE IN YOUR BRAIN.
MAYBE. OR MAYBE I DID KNOW THAT, AND FLIPPED ITS POLARITY SO IT WOULD ZAP THE USER, NOT THE TARGET.
MAYBE YOU'LL BE THE ONE WHO DIES.
YOU'RE A TERRIBLE BLUFFER.
AAAAHH!!!
ZAAK!
ZAAK!
ZAAK!
NO, I'M A TERRIBLE WATER SKIER. I'M AN EXCELLENT BLUFFER.
BUT I DRAINED MOST OF THE SPIKE'S CHARGE FIRST, GOL. YOU'LL WAKE UP...
...UNLIKE ALL THOSE SONTARANS.
B-DEEP

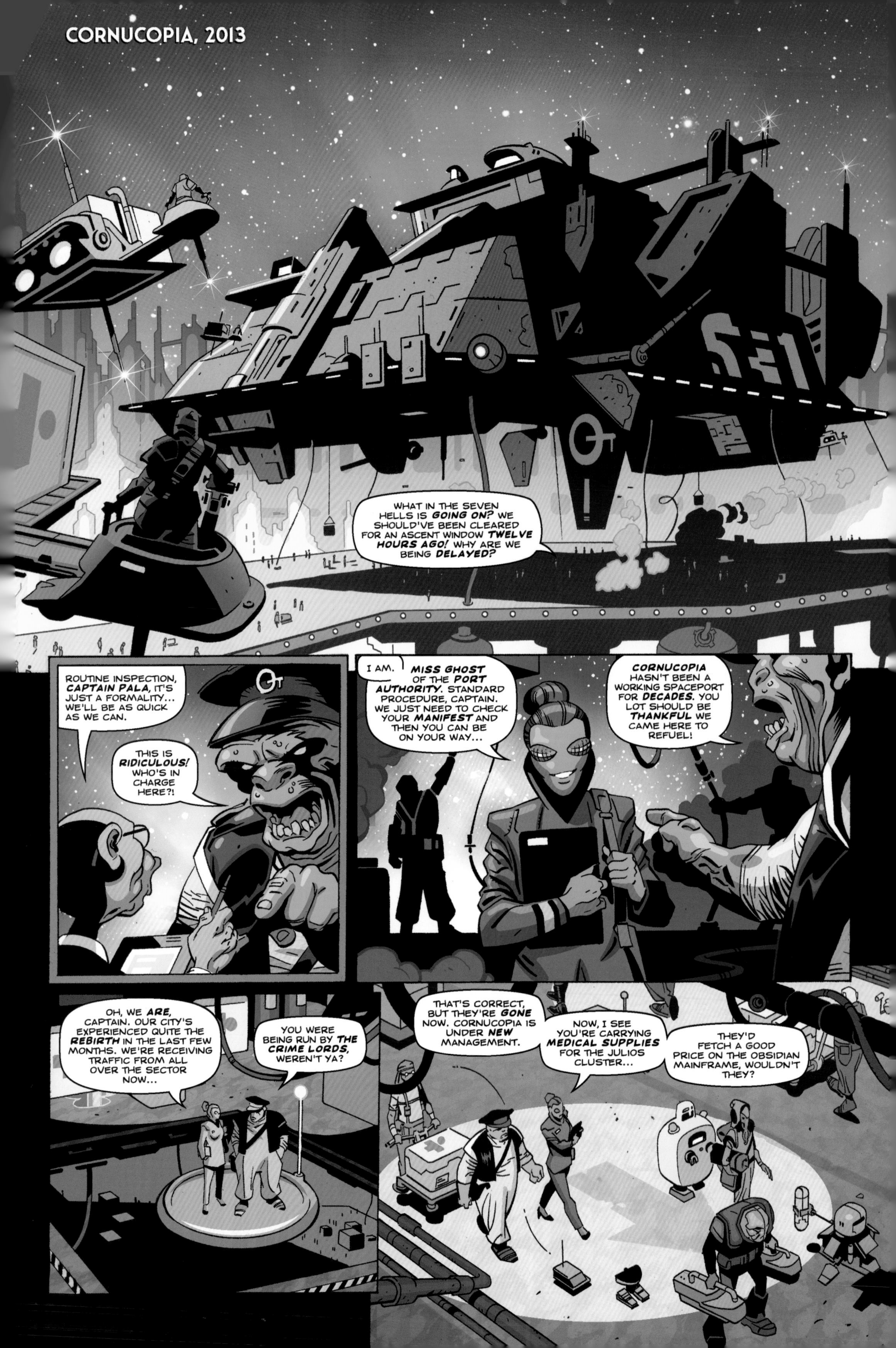
CORNUCOPIA, 2013
WHAT IN THE SEVEN HELLS IS GOING ON? WE SHOULD'VE BEEN CLEARED FOR AN ASCENT WINDOW TWELVE HOURS AGO! WHY ARE WE BEING DELAYED?
ROUTINE INSPECTION, CAPTAIN PALA, IT'S JUST A FORMALITY... WE'LL BE AS QUICK AS WE CAN.
THIS IS RIDICULOUS! WHO'S IN CHARGE HERE?!
I AM.
MISS GHOST OF THE PORT AUTHORITY. STANDARD PROCEDURE, CAPTAIN. WE JUST NEED TO CHECK YOUR MANIFEST AND THEN YOU CAN BE ON YOUR WAY...
CORNUCOPIA HASN'T BEEN A WORKING SPACEPORT FOR DECADES. YOU LOT SHOULD BE THANKFUL WE CAME HERE TO REFUEL!
OH, WE ARE, CAPTAIN. OUR CITY'S EXPERIENCED QUITE THE REBIRTH IN THE LAST FEW MONTHS. WE'RE RECEIVING TRAFFIC FROM ALL OVER THE SECTOR NOW...
YOU WERE BEING RUN BY THE CRIME LORDS, WEREN'T YA?
THAT'S CORRECT, BUT THEY'RE GONE NOW. CORNUCOPIA IS UNDER NEW MANAGEMENT.
NOW, I SEE YOU'RE CARRYING MEDICAL SUPPLIES FOR THE JULIOS CLUSTER...
THEY'D FETCH A GOOD PRICE ON THE OBSIDIAN MAINFRAME, WOULDN'T THEY?

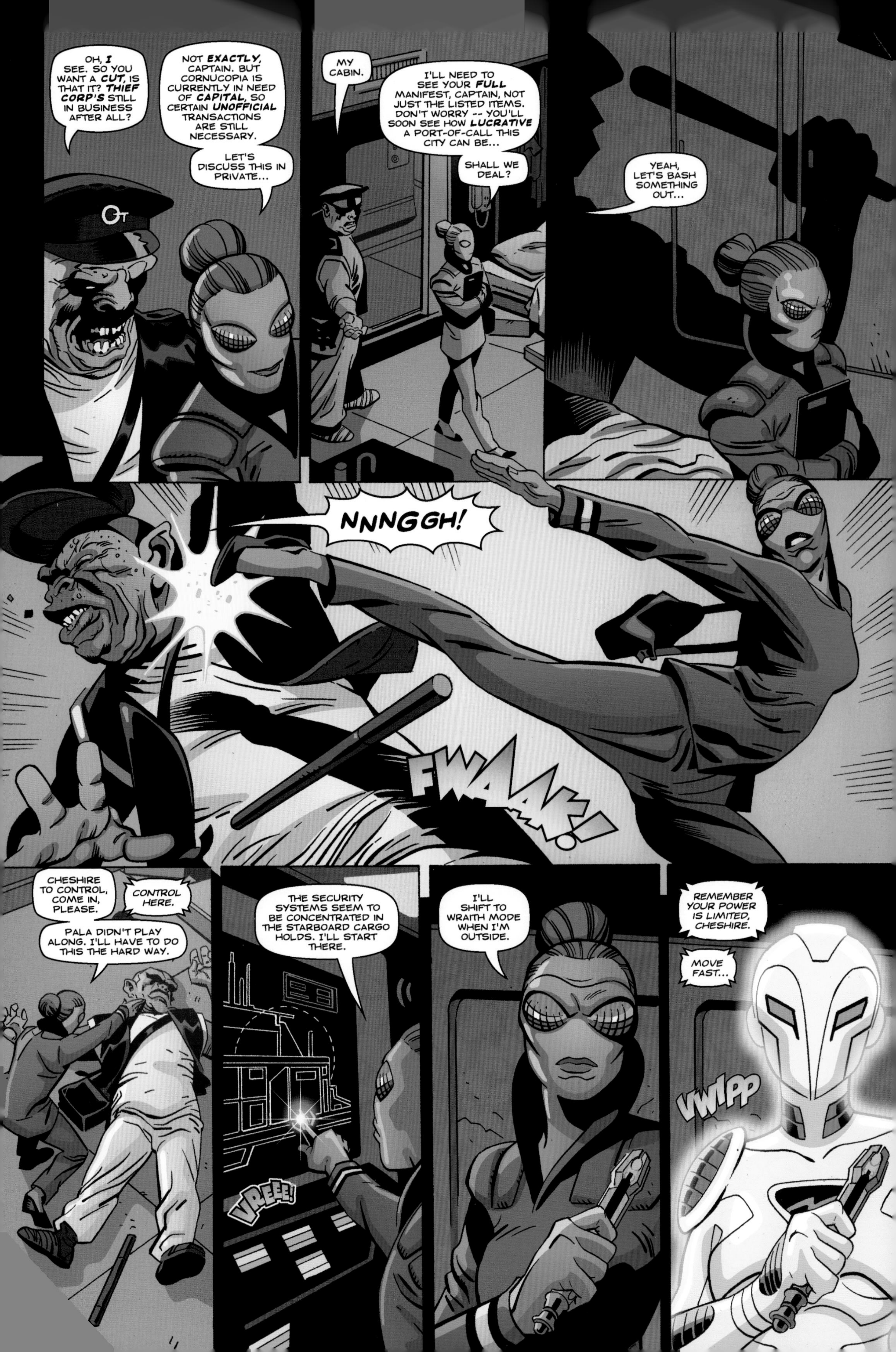
OH, I SEE. SO YOU WANT A CUT, IS THAT IT? THIEF CORP'S STILL IN BUSINESS AFTER ALL?
NOT EXACTLY, CAPTAIN. BUT CORNUCOPIA IS CURRENTLY IN NEED OF CAPITAL, SO CERTAIN UNOFFICIAL TRANSACTIONS ARE STILL NECESSARY.
LET'S DISCUSS THIS IN PRIVATE...
MY CABIN.
I'LL NEED TO SEE YOUR FULL MANIFEST, CAPTAIN, NOT JUST THE LISTED ITEMS. DON'T WORRY -- YOU'LL SOON SEE HOW LUCRATIVE A PORT-OF-CALL THIS CITY CAN BE...
SHALL WE DEAL?
YEAH, LET'S BASH SOMETHING OUT...
NNNGGH!
FWAAK!
CHESHIRE TO CONTROL, COME IN, PLEASE.
CONTROL HERE.
PALA DIDN'T PLAY ALONG. I'LL HAVE TO DO THIS THE HARD WAY.
THE SECURITY SYSTEMS SEEM TO BE CONCENTRATED IN THE STARBOARD CARGO HOLDS. I'LL START THERE.
VREEE!
I'LL SHIFT TO WRAITH MODE WHEN I'M OUTSIDE.
REMEMBER YOUR POWER IS LIMITED, CHESHIRE.
MOVE FAST...
VWIPP

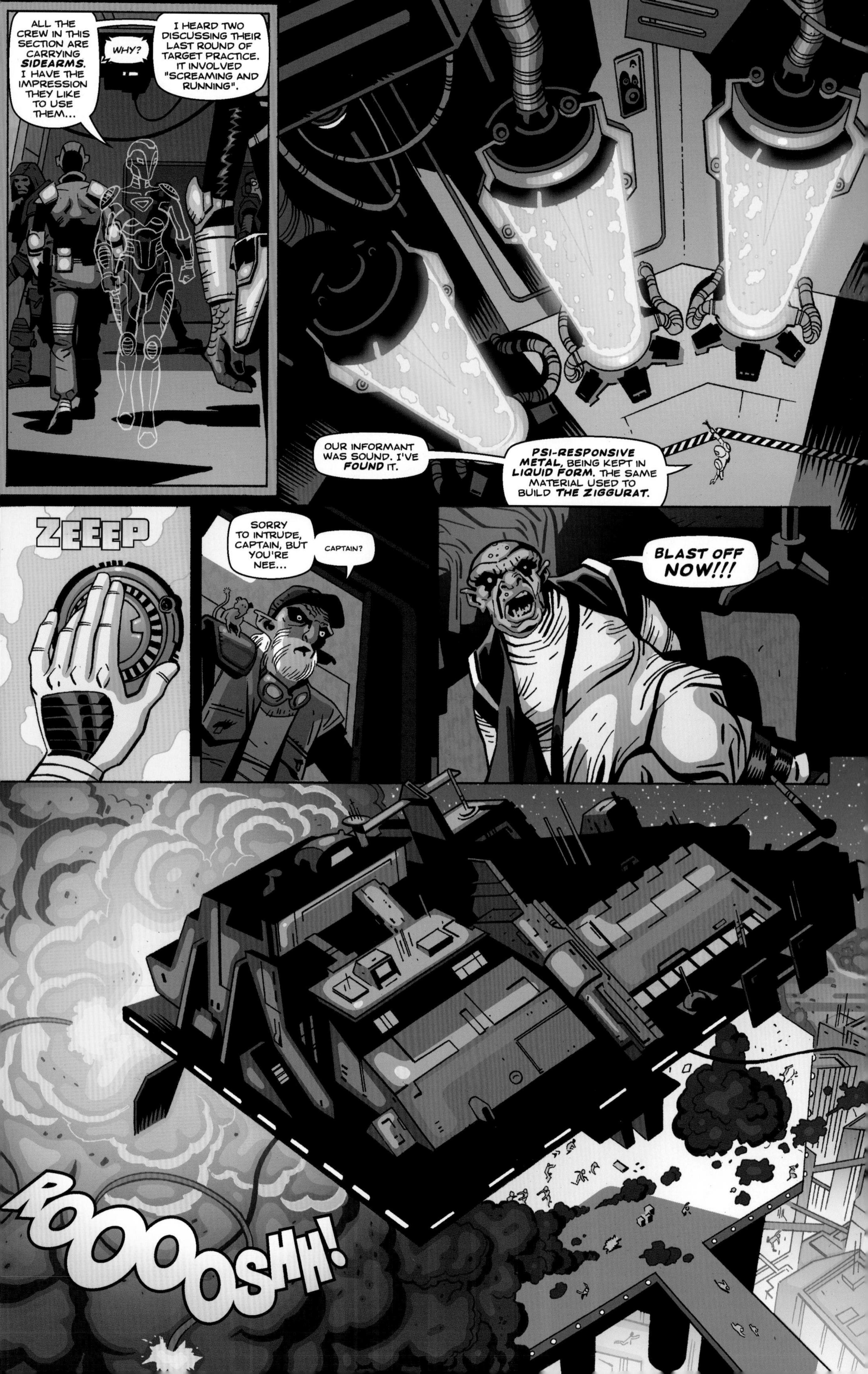

ALL THE CREW IN THIS SECTION ARE CARRYING SIDEARMS. I HAVE THE IMPRESSION THEY LIKE TO USE THEM...
WHY?
I HEARD TWO DISCUSSING THEIR LAST ROUND OF TARGET PRACTICE. IT INVOLVED "SCREAMING AND RUNNING".
OUR INFORMANT WAS SOUND. I'VE FOUND IT.
PSI-RESPONSIVE METAL, BEING KEPT IN LIQUID FORM. THE SAME MATERIAL USED TO BUILD THE ZIGGURAT.
ZEEEP
SORRY TO INTRUDE, CAPTAIN, BUT YOU'RE NEE...
CAPTAIN?
BLAST OFF NOW!!!
ROOOOSHH!

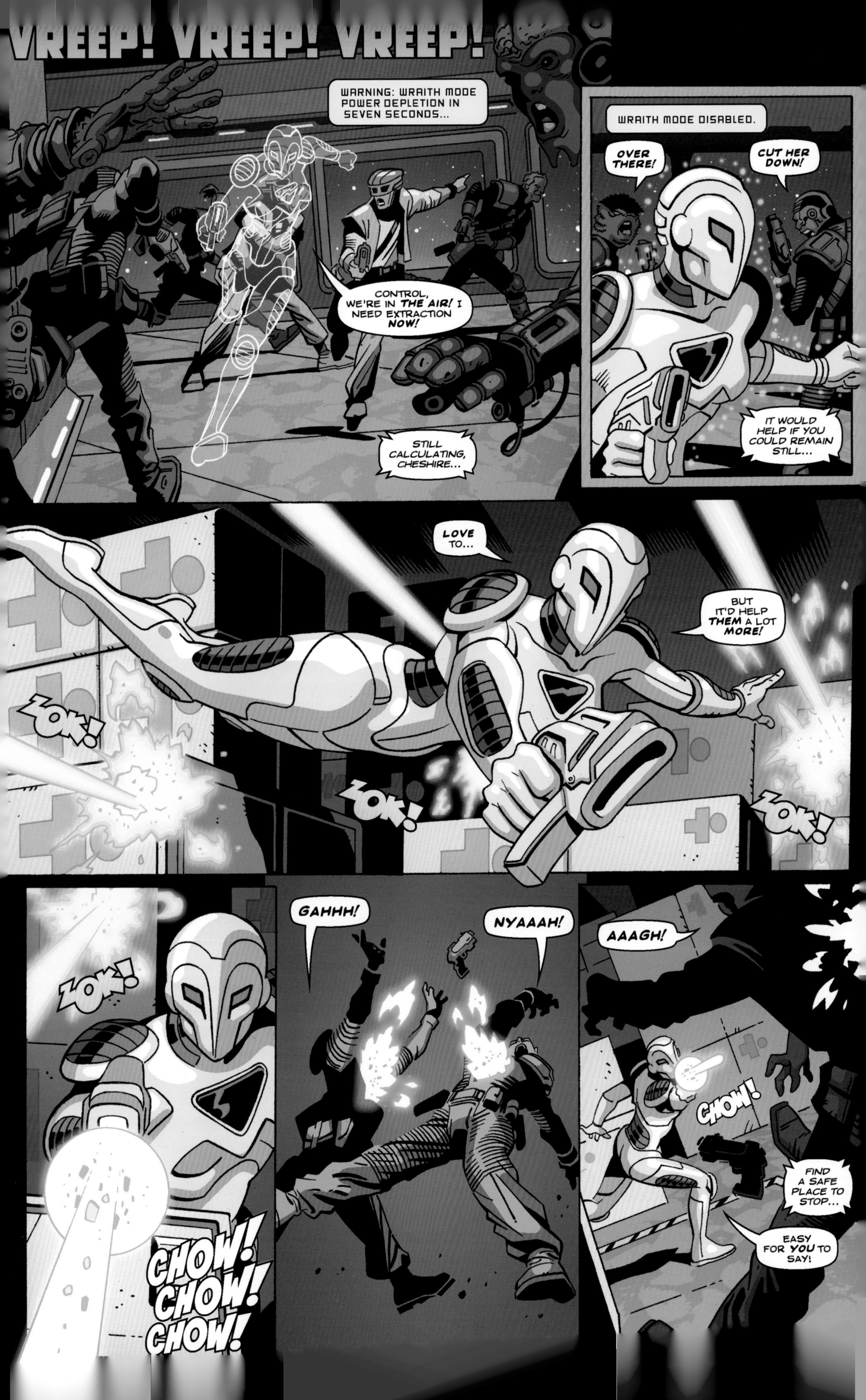
VREEP! VREEP! VREEP!
WARNING: WRAITH MODE POWER DEPLETION IN SEVEN SECONDS...
CONTROL, WE'RE IN THE AIR! I NEED EXTRACTION NOW!
STILL CALCULATING, CHESHIRE...
WRAITH MODE DISABLED.
OVER THERE!
CUT HER DOWN!
IT WOULD HELP IF YOU COULD REMAIN STILL...
LOVE TO...
BUT IT'D HELP THEM A LOT MORE!
ZOK!
ZOK!
ZOK!
ZOK!
CHOW! CHOW! CHOW!
GAHHH!
NYAAAH!
AAAGH!
CHOW!
FIND A SAFE PLACE TO STOP...
EASY FOR YOU TO SAY!

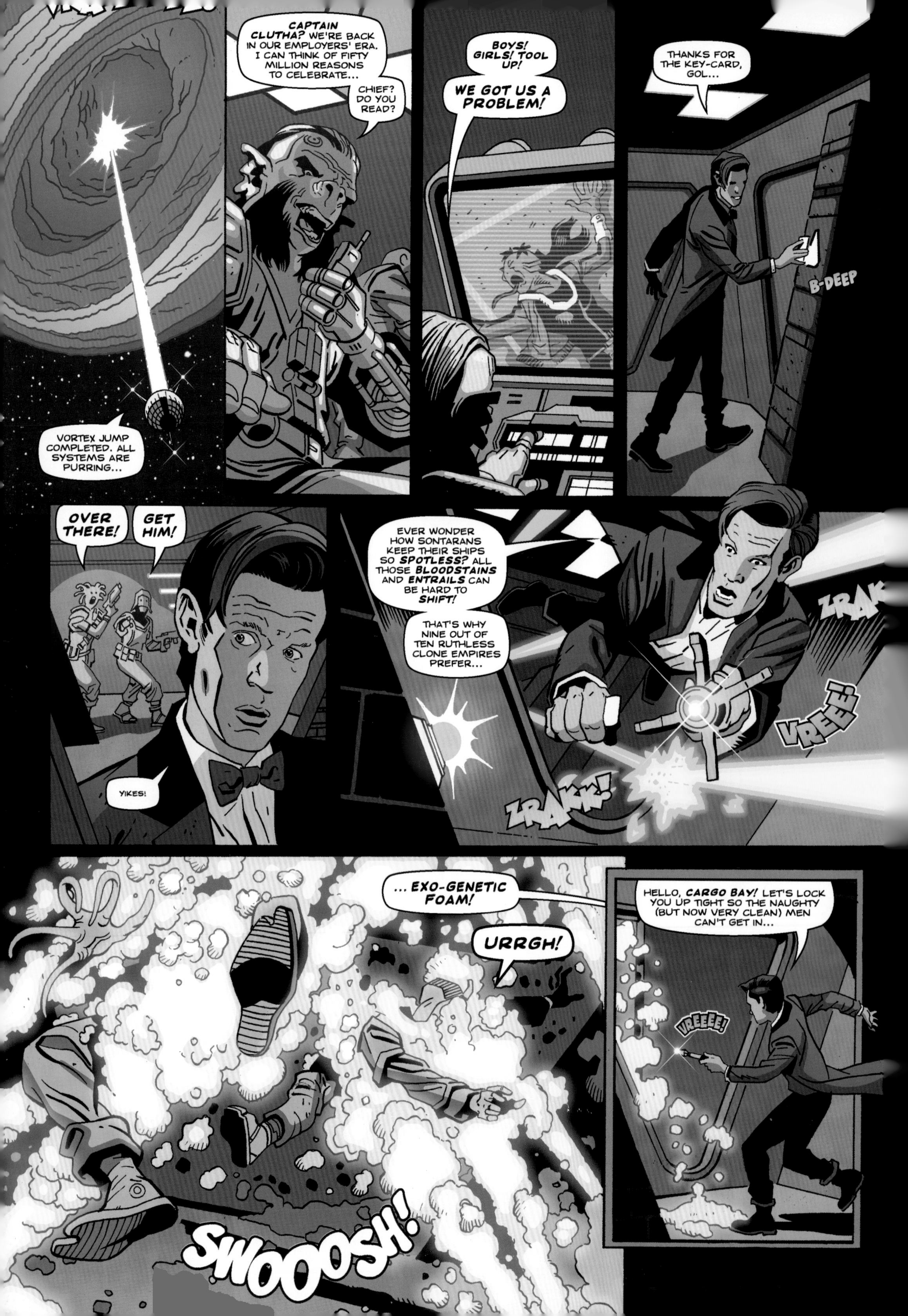
VORTEX JUMP COMPLETED. ALL SYSTEMS ARE PURRING...
CAPTAIN CLUTHA? WE'RE BACK IN OUR EMPLOYERS' ERA. I CAN THINK OF FIFTY MILLION REASONS TO CELEBRATE...
CHIEF? DO YOU READ?
BOYS! GIRLS! TOOL UP!
WE GOT US A PROBLEM!
THANKS FOR THE KEY-CARD, GOL...
B-DEEP
OVER THERE!
GET HIM!
YIKES!
EVER WONDER HOW SONTARANS KEEP THEIR SHIPS SO SPOTLESS? ALL THOSE BLOODSTAINS AND ENTRAILS CAN BE HARD TO SHIFT!
THAT'S WHY NINE OUT OF TEN RUTHLESS CLONE EMPIRES PREFER...
ZRAK
VREEE!
ZRAKK!
... EXO-GENETIC FOAM!
URRGH!
SWOOOSH!
HELLO, CARGO BAY! LET'S LOCK YOU UP TIGHT SO THE NAUGHTY (BUT NOW VERY CLEAN) MEN CAN'T GET IN...
VREEEE!

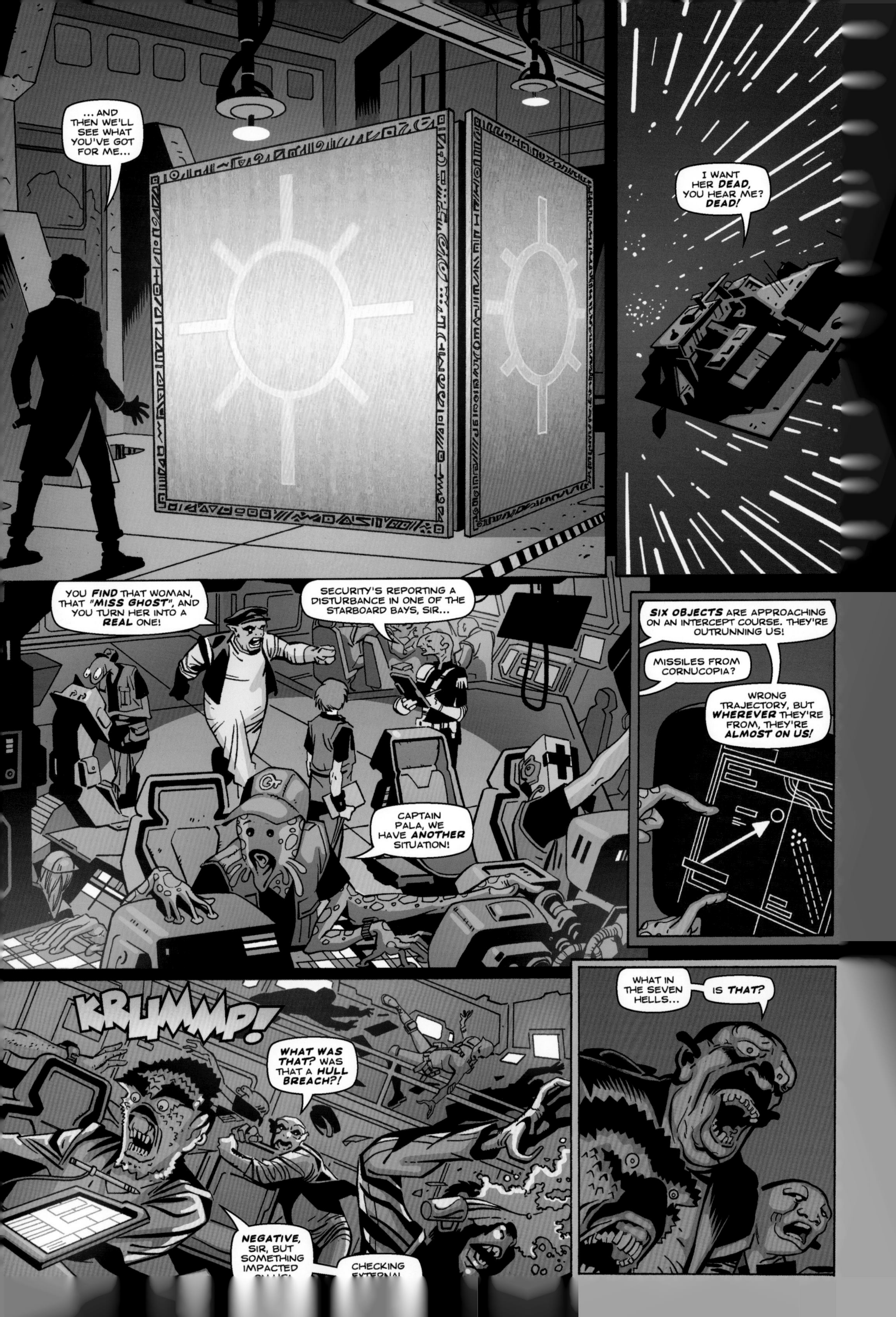

... AND THEN WE'LL SEE WHAT YOU'VE GOT FOR ME...
I WANT HER DEAD, YOU HEAR ME? DEAD!
YOU FIND THAT WOMAN, THAT "MISS GHOST", AND YOU TURN HER INTO A REAL ONE!
SECURITY'S REPORTING A DISTURBANCE IN ONE OF THE STARBOARD BAYS, SIR...
CAPTAIN PALA, WE HAVE ANOTHER SITUATION!
SIX OBJECTS ARE APPROACHING ON AN INTERCEPT COURSE. THEY'RE OUTRUNNING US!
MISSILES FROM CORNUCOPIA?
WRONG TRAJECTORY, BUT WHEREVER THEY'RE FROM, THEY'RE ALMOST ON US!
KRUMMP!
WHAT WAS THAT? WAS THAT A HULL BREACH?!
NEGATIVE, SIR, BUT SOMETHING IMPACTED
CHECKING
WHAT IN THE SEVEN HELLS...
IS THAT?

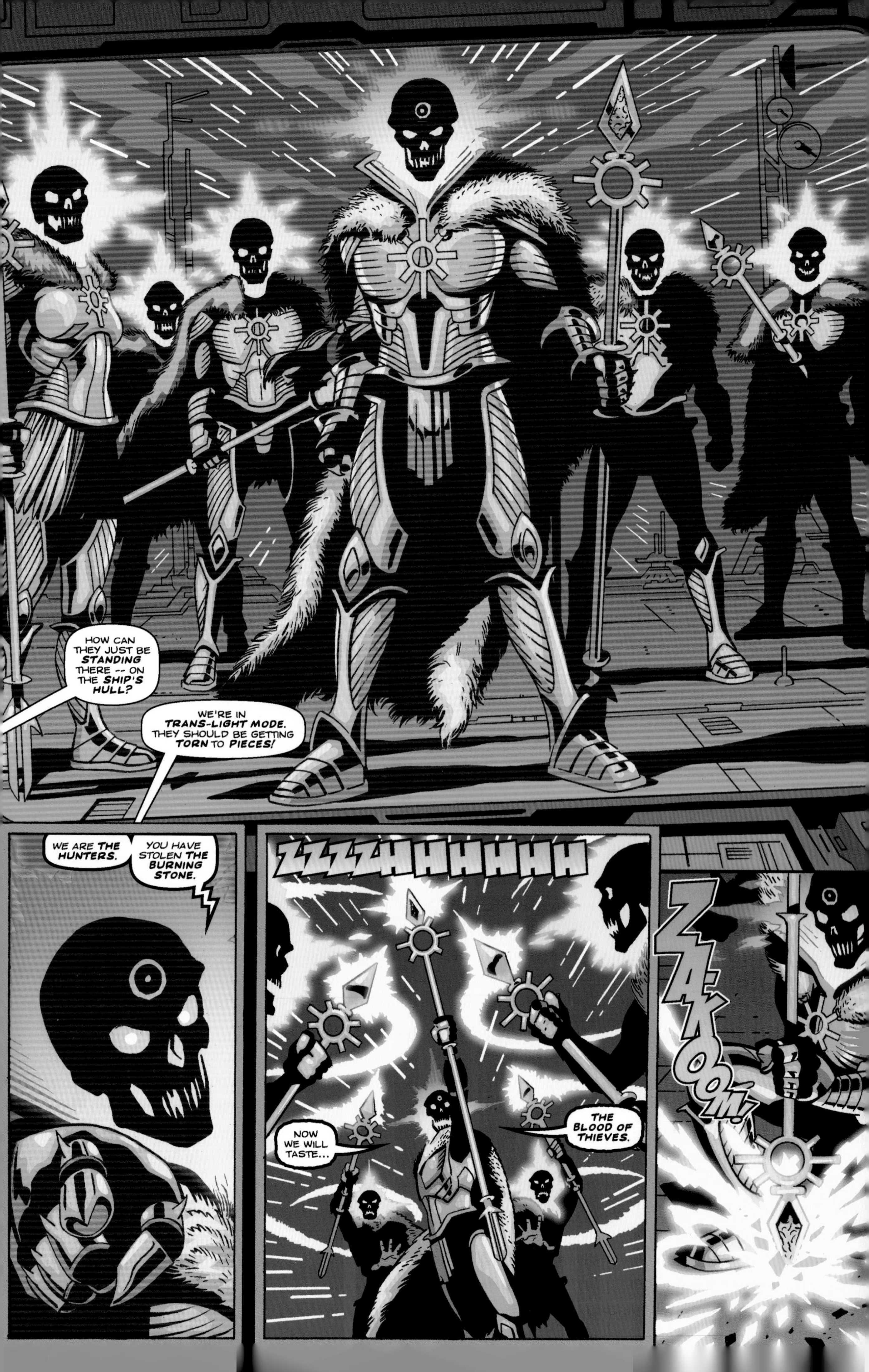
HOW CAN THEY JUST BE STANDING THERE -- ON THE SHIP'S HULL?
WE'RE IN TRANS-LIGHT MODE. THEY SHOULD BE GETTING TORN TO PIECES!
WE ARE THE HUNTERS.
YOU HAVE STOLEN THE BURNING STONE.
ZZZZHHHHHHH
NOW WE WILL TASTE...
THE BLOOD OF THIEVES.
ZAKOOM!

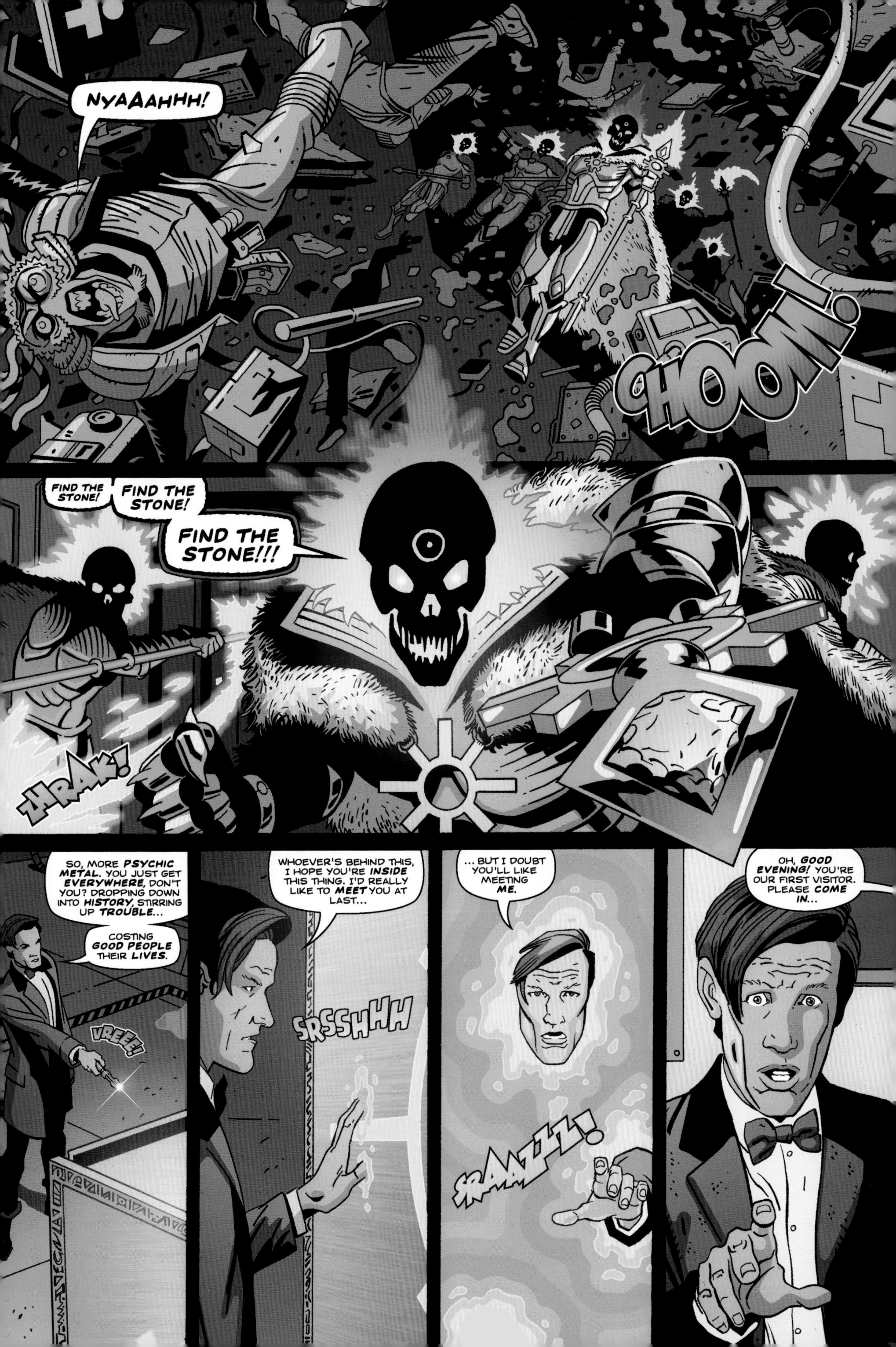
NYAAAHHH!
CHOOM!
FIND THE STONE!
FIND THE STONE!
FIND THE STONE!!!
ZHRAK!
SO, MORE PSYCHIC METAL. YOU JUST GET EVERYWHERE, DON'T YOU? DROPPING DOWN INTO HISTORY, STIRRING UP TROUBLE...
COSTING GOOD PEOPLE THEIR LIVES.
VREEE!
WHOEVER'S BEHIND THIS, I HOPE YOU'RE INSIDE THIS THING. I'D REALLY LIKE TO MEET YOU AT LAST...
SRSSHHH
... BUT I DOUBT YOU'LL LIKE MEETING ME.
SRAAZZZ!
OH, GOOD EVENING! YOU'RE OUR FIRST VISITOR. PLEASE COME IN...

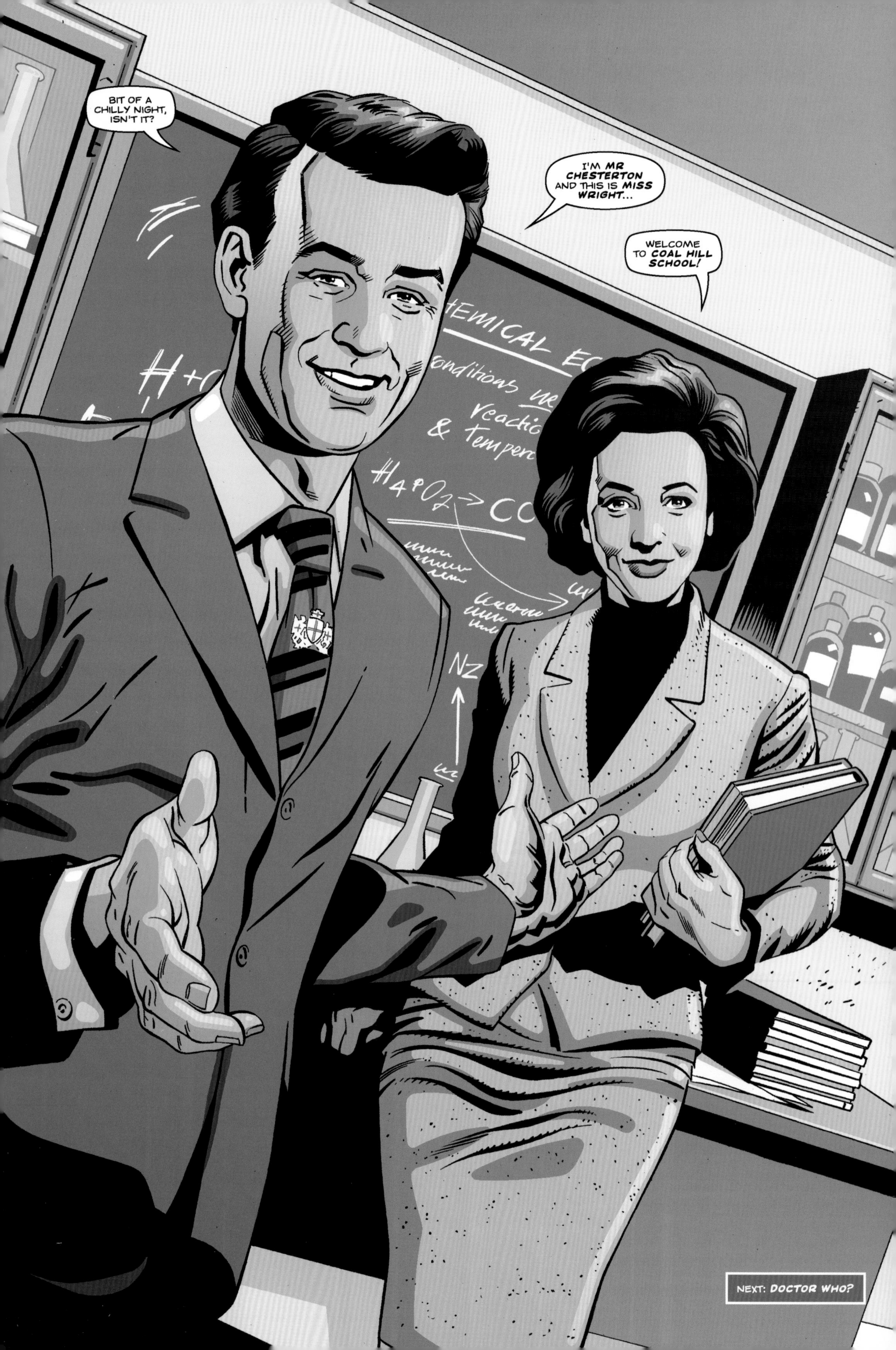
BIT OF A CHILLY NIGHT, ISN'T IT?
I'M MR CHESTERTON AND THIS IS MISS WRIGHT...
WELCOME TO COAL HILL SCHOOL!
NEXT: DOCTOR WHO?

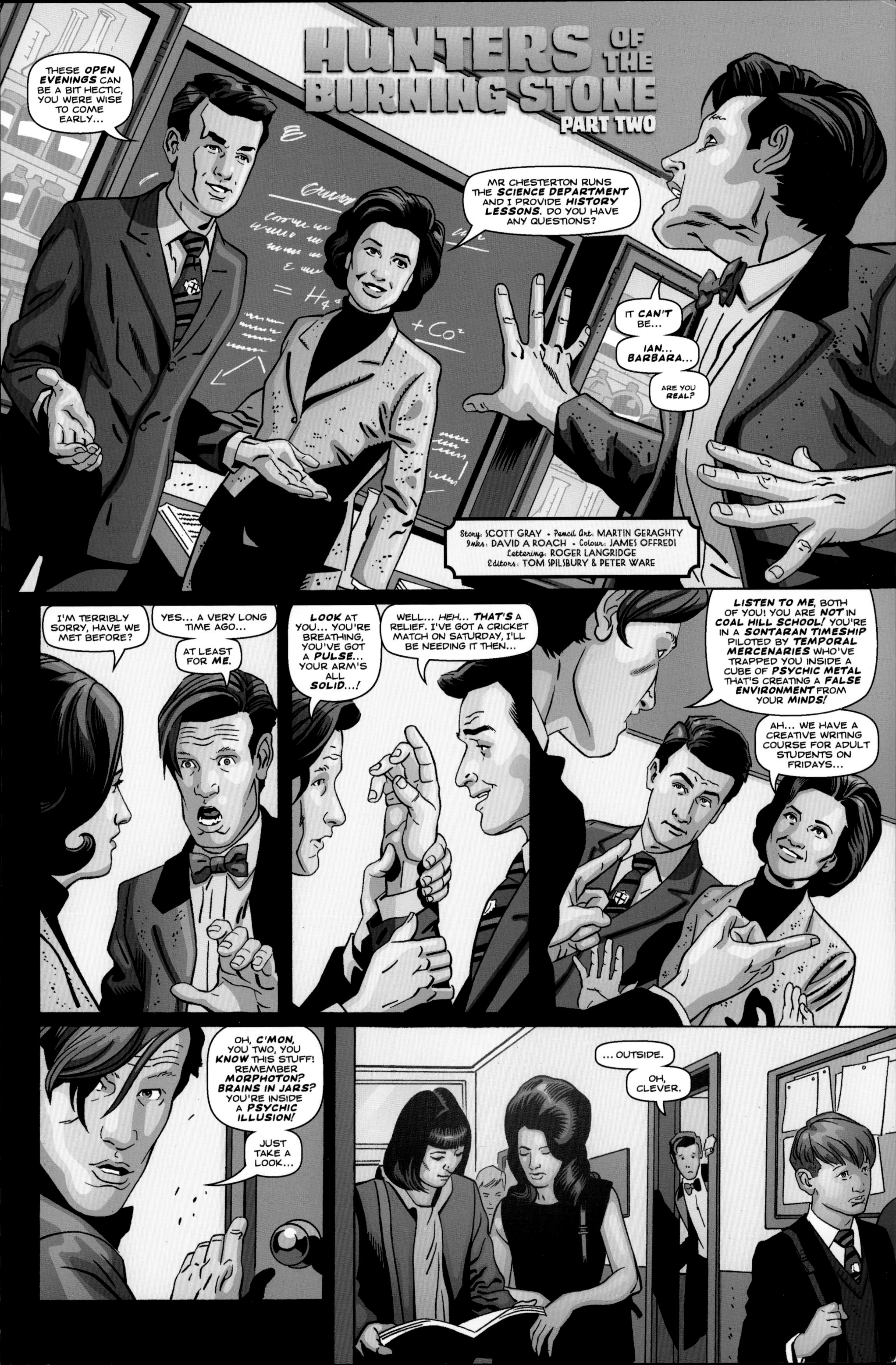
HUNTERS OF THE BURNING STONE
PART TWO
THESE OPEN EVENINGS CAN BE A BIT HECTIC, YOU WERE WISE TO COME EARLY...
MR CHESTERTON RUNS THE SCIENCE DEPARTMENT AND I PROVIDE HISTORY LESSONS. DO YOU HAVE ANY QUESTIONS?
IT CAN'T BE...
IAN... BARBARA...
ARE YOU REAL?
Story: SCOTT GRAY • Pencil Art: MARTIN GERAGHTY
Inks: DAVID A ROACH • Colour: JAMES OFFREDI
Lettering: ROGER LANGRIDGE
Editors: TOM SPILSBURY & PETER WARE
I'M TERRIBLY SORRY, HAVE WE MET BEFORE?
YES... A VERY LONG TIME AGO...
AT LEAST FOR ME.
LOOK AT YOU... YOU'RE BREATHING, YOU'VE GOT A PULSE... YOUR ARM'S ALL SOLID...!
WELL... HEH... THAT'S A RELIEF. I'VE GOT A CRICKET MATCH ON SATURDAY, I'LL BE NEEDING IT THEN...
LISTEN TO ME, BOTH OF YOU! YOU ARE NOT IN COAL HILL SCHOOL! YOU'RE IN A SONTARAN TIMESHIP PILOTED BY TEMPORAL MERCENARIES WHO'VE TRAPPED YOU INSIDE A CUBE OF PSYCHIC METAL THAT'S CREATING A FALSE ENVIRONMENT FROM YOUR MINDS!
AH... WE HAVE A CREATIVE WRITING COURSE FOR ADULT STUDENTS ON FRIDAYS...
OH, C'MON, YOU TWO, YOU KNOW THIS STUFF! REMEMBER MORPHOTON? BRAINS IN JARS? YOU'RE INSIDE A PSYCHIC ILLUSION!
JUST TAKE A LOOK...
... OUTSIDE.
OH, CLEVER.

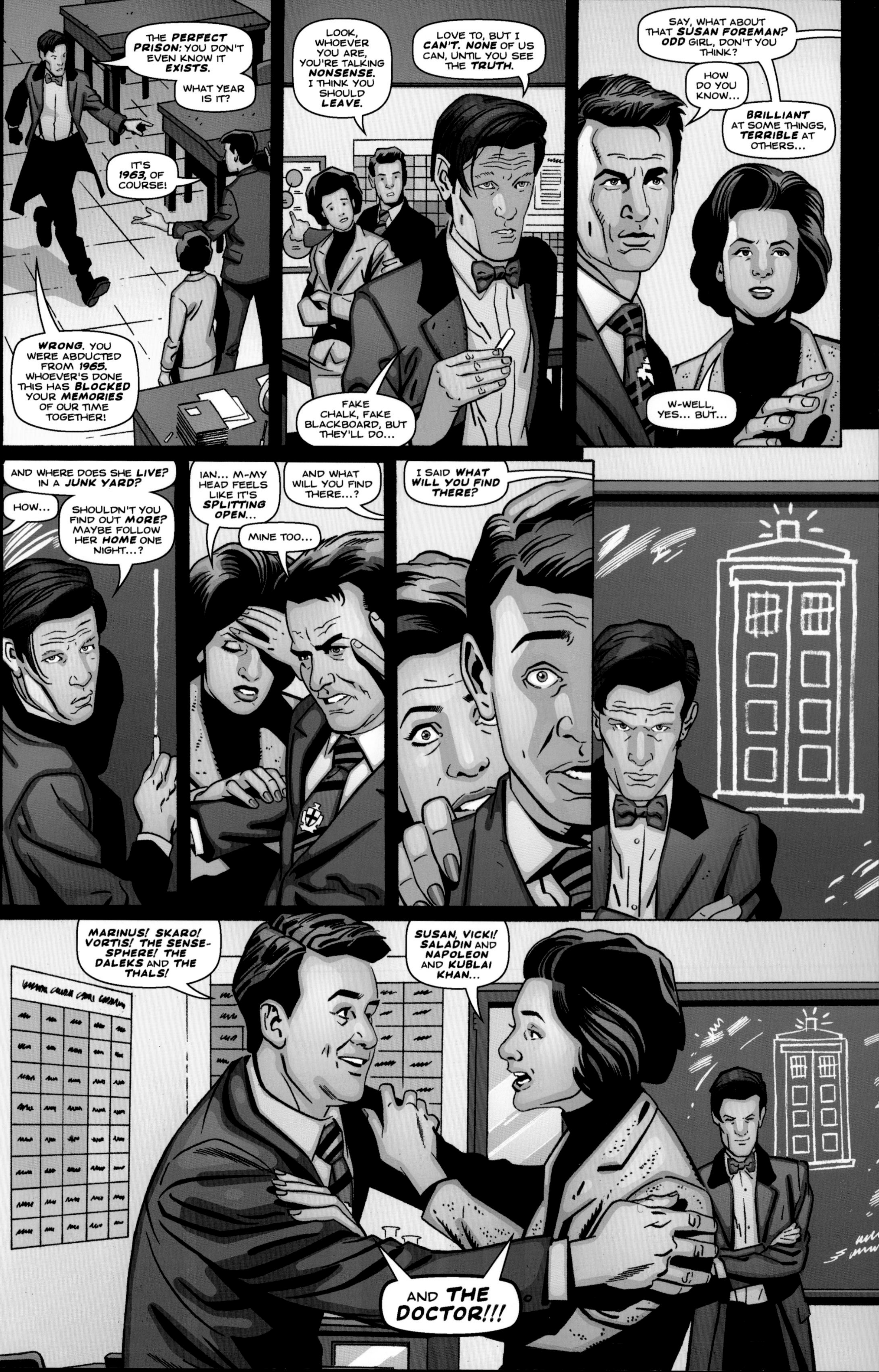
THE PERFECT PRISON: YOU DON'T EVEN KNOW IT EXISTS.
WHAT YEAR IS IT?
IT'S 1963, OF COURSE!
WRONG. YOU WERE ABDUCTED FROM 1965. WHOEVER'S DONE THIS HAS BLOCKED YOUR MEMORIES OF OUR TIME TOGETHER!
LOOK, WHOEVER YOU ARE, YOU'RE TALKING NONSENSE. I THINK YOU SHOULD LEAVE.
LOVE TO, BUT I CAN'T. NONE OF US CAN, UNTIL YOU SEE THE TRUTH.
FAKE CHALK, FAKE BLACKBOARD, BUT THEY'LL DO...
SAY, WHAT ABOUT THAT SUSAN FOREMAN? ODD GIRL, DON'T YOU THINK?
HOW DO YOU KNOW...
BRILLIANT AT SOME THINGS, TERRIBLE AT OTHERS...
W-WELL, YES... BUT...
AND WHERE DOES SHE LIVE? IN A JUNK YARD?
HOW...
SHOULDN'T YOU FIND OUT MORE? MAYBE FOLLOW HER HOME ONE NIGHT...?
IAN... M-MY HEAD FEELS LIKE IT'S SPLITTING OPEN...
AND WHAT WILL YOU FIND THERE...?
MINE TOO...
I SAID WHAT WILL YOU FIND THERE?
MARINUS! SKARO! VORTIS! THE SENSE-SPHERE! THE DALEKS AND THE THALS!
SUSAN, VICKI! SALADIN AND NAPOLEON AND KUBLAI KHAN...
AND THE DOCTOR!!!

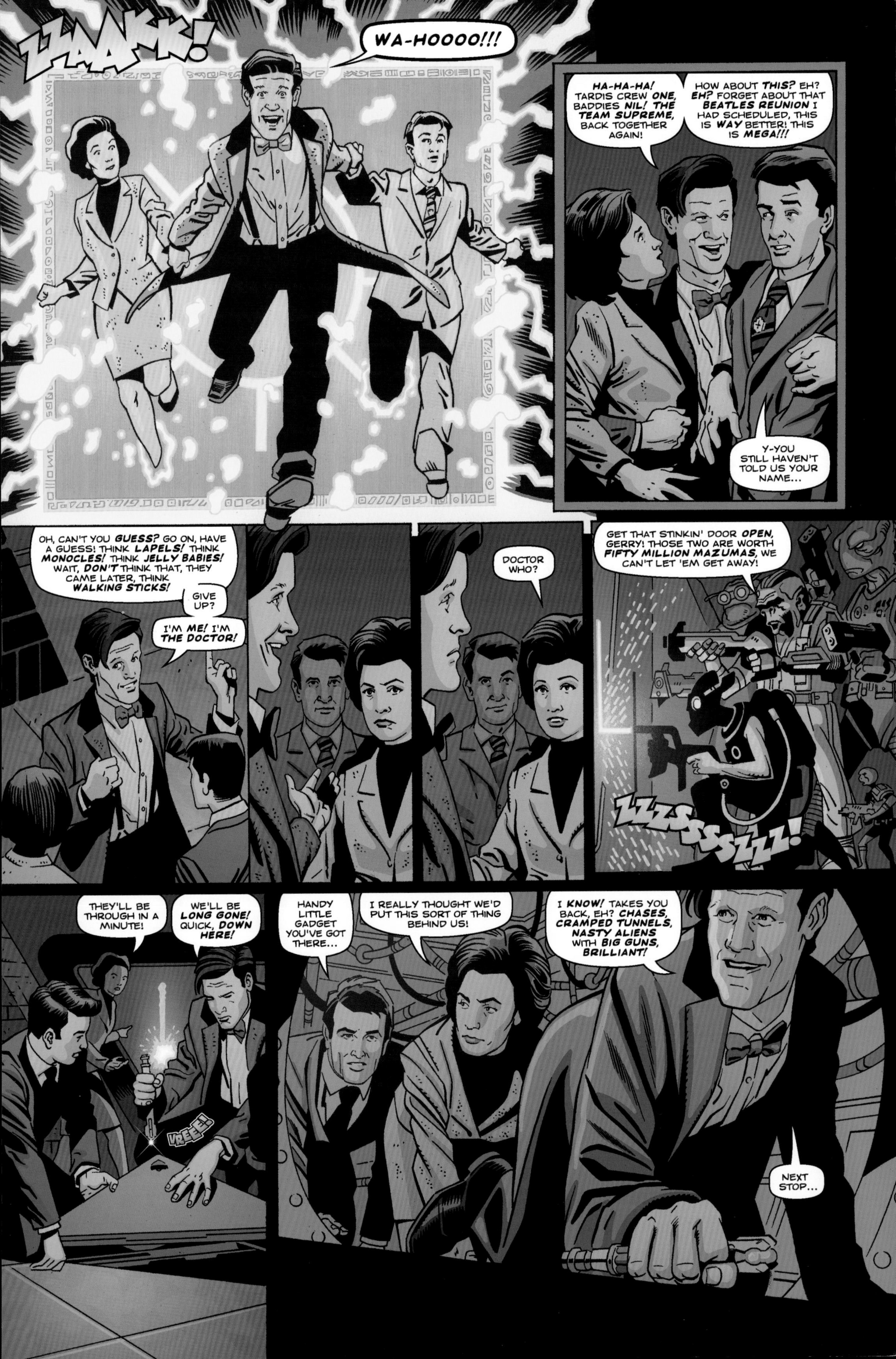
ZZAAK!
WA-HOOOO!!!
HA-HA-HA! TARDIS CREW ONE, BADDIES NIL! THE TEAM SUPREME, BACK TOGETHER AGAIN!
HOW ABOUT THIS? EH? EH? FORGET ABOUT THAT BEATLES REUNION I HAD SCHEDULED, THIS IS WAY BETTER! THIS IS MEGA!!!
Y-YOU STILL HAVEN'T TOLD US YOUR NAME...
OH, CAN'T YOU GUESS? GO ON, HAVE A GUESS! THINK LAPELS! THINK MONOCLES! THINK JELLY BABIES! WAIT, DON'T THINK THAT, THEY CAME LATER, THINK WALKING STICKS!
GIVE UP?
I'M ME! I'M THE DOCTOR!
DOCTOR WHO?
GET THAT STINKIN' DOOR OPEN, GERRY! THOSE TWO ARE WORTH FIFTY MILLION MAZUMAS, WE CAN'T LET 'EM GET AWAY!
ZZZSSSSSZZZ!
THEY'LL BE THROUGH IN A MINUTE!
WE'LL BE LONG GONE! QUICK, DOWN HERE!
VREEE!
HANDY LITTLE GADGET YOU'VE GOT THERE...
I REALLY THOUGHT WE'D PUT THIS SORT OF THING BEHIND US!
I KNOW! TAKES YOU BACK, EH? CHASES, CRAMPED TUNNELS, NASTY ALIENS WITH BIG GUNS, BRILLIANT!
NEXT STOP...

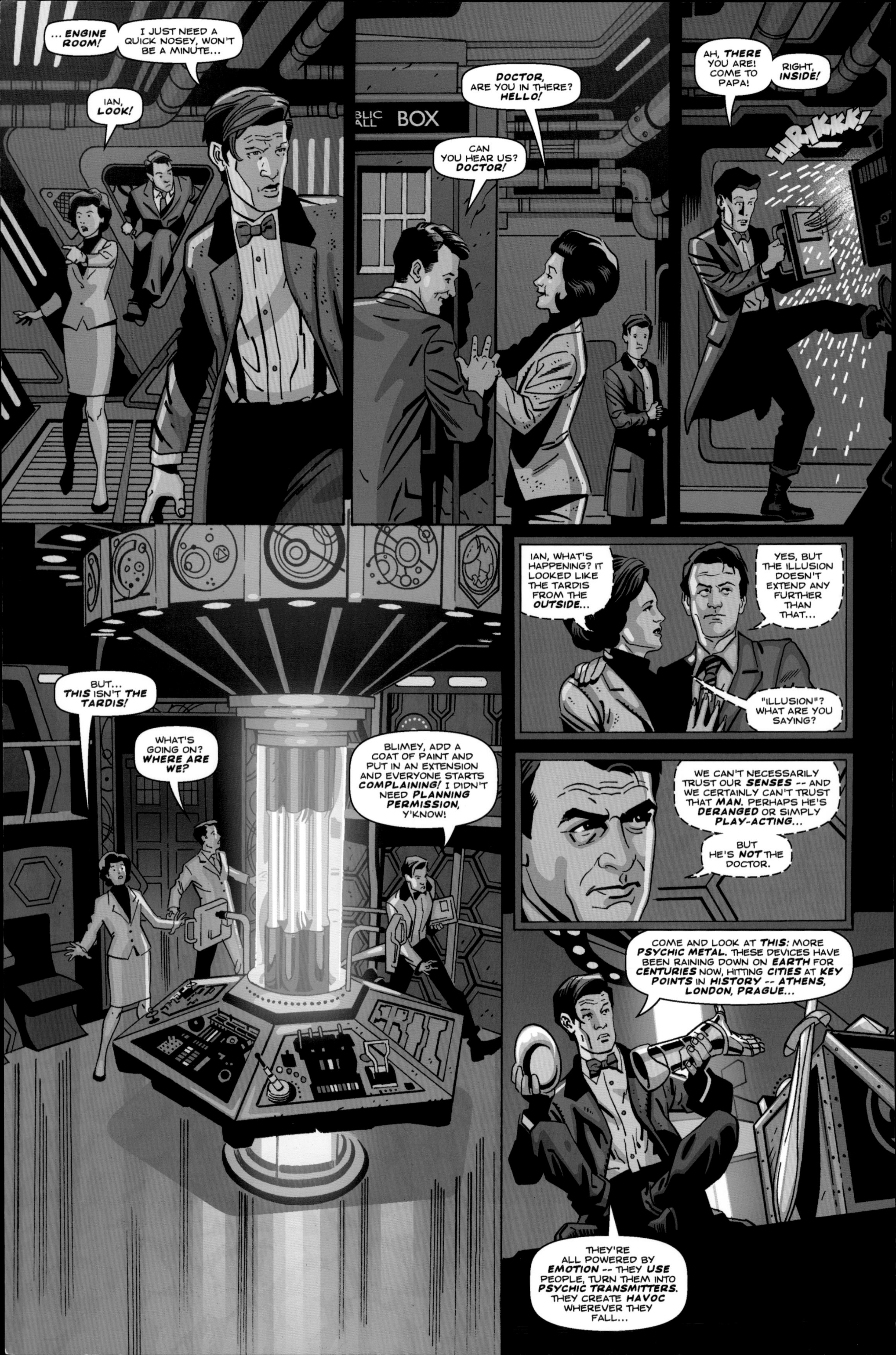

... ENGINE ROOM!
I JUST NEED A QUICK NOSEY, WON'T BE A MINUTE...
IAN, LOOK!
DOCTOR, ARE YOU IN THERE? HELLO!
CAN YOU HEAR US? DOCTOR!
BLIC ALL BOX
AH, THERE YOU ARE! COME TO PAPA!
RIGHT, INSIDE!
WHRIKKK!
BUT... THIS ISN'T THE TARDIS!
WHAT'S GOING ON? WHERE ARE WE?
BLIMEY, ADD A COAT OF PAINT AND PUT IN AN EXTENSION AND EVERYONE STARTS COMPLAINING! I DIDN'T NEED PLANNING PERMISSION, Y'KNOW!
IAN, WHAT'S HAPPENING? IT LOOKED LIKE THE TARDIS FROM THE OUTSIDE...
YES, BUT THE ILLUSION DOESN'T EXTEND ANY FURTHER THAN THAT...
"ILLUSION"? WHAT ARE YOU SAYING?
WE CAN'T NECESSARILY TRUST OUR SENSES -- AND WE CERTAINLY CAN'T TRUST THAT MAN. PERHAPS HE'S DERANGED OR SIMPLY PLAY-ACTING...
BUT HE'S NOT THE DOCTOR.
COME AND LOOK AT THIS: MORE PSYCHIC METAL. THESE DEVICES HAVE BEEN RAINING DOWN ON EARTH FOR CENTURIES NOW, HITTING CITIES AT KEY POINTS IN HISTORY -- ATHENS, LONDON, PRAGUE...
THEY'RE ALL POWERED BY EMOTION -- THEY USE PEOPLE, TURN THEM INTO PSYCHIC TRANSMITTERS. THEY CREATE HAVOC WHEREVER THEY FALL...

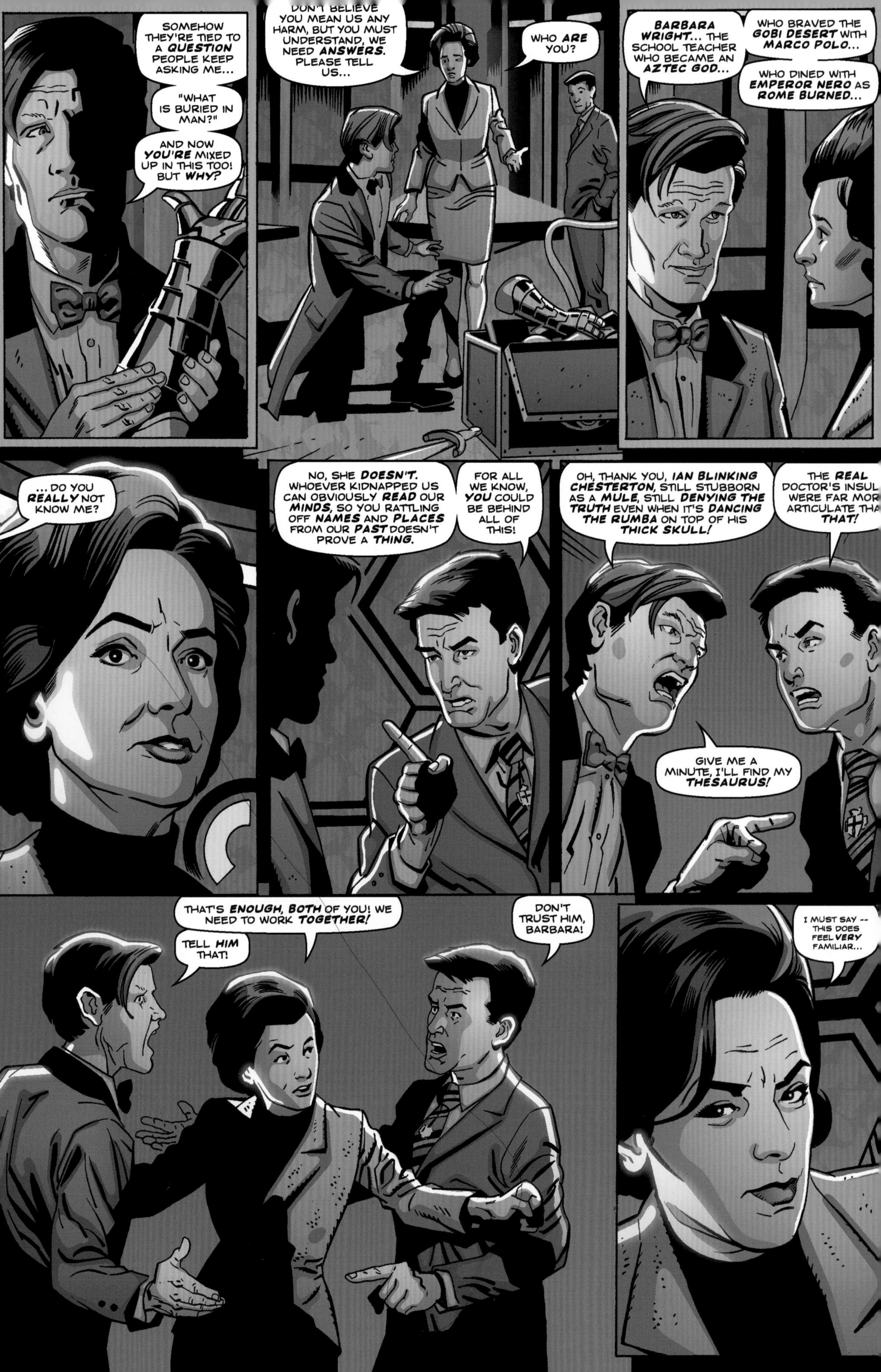

SOMEHOW THEY'RE TIED TO A QUESTION PEOPLE KEEP ASKING ME...
"WHAT IS BURIED IN MAN?"
AND NOW YOU'RE MIXED UP IN THIS TOO! BUT WHY?
DON'T BELIEVE YOU MEAN US ANY HARM, BUT YOU MUST UNDERSTAND, WE NEED ANSWERS. PLEASE TELL US...
WHO ARE YOU?
BARBARA WRIGHT... THE SCHOOL TEACHER WHO BECAME AN AZTEC GOD...
WHO BRAVED THE GOBI DESERT WITH MARCO POLO...
WHO DINED WITH EMPEROR NERO AS ROME BURNED...
...DO YOU REALLY NOT KNOW ME?
NO, SHE DOESN'T. WHOEVER KIDNAPPED US CAN OBVIOUSLY READ OUR MINDS, SO YOU RATTLING OFF NAMES AND PLACES FROM OUR PAST DOESN'T PROVE A THING.
FOR ALL WE KNOW, YOU COULD BE BEHIND ALL OF THIS!
OH, THANK YOU, IAN BLINKING CHESTERTON, STILL STUBBORN AS A MULE, STILL DENYING THE TRUTH EVEN WHEN IT'S DANCING THE RUMBA ON TOP OF HIS THICK SKULL!
THE REAL DOCTOR'S INSUL WERE FAR MOR ARTICULATE THA THAT!
GIVE ME A MINUTE, I'LL FIND MY THESAURUS!
THAT'S ENOUGH, BOTH OF YOU! WE NEED TO WORK TOGETHER!
TELL HIM THAT!
DON'T TRUST HIM, BARBARA!
I MUST SAY -- THIS DOES FEEL VERY FAMILIAR...

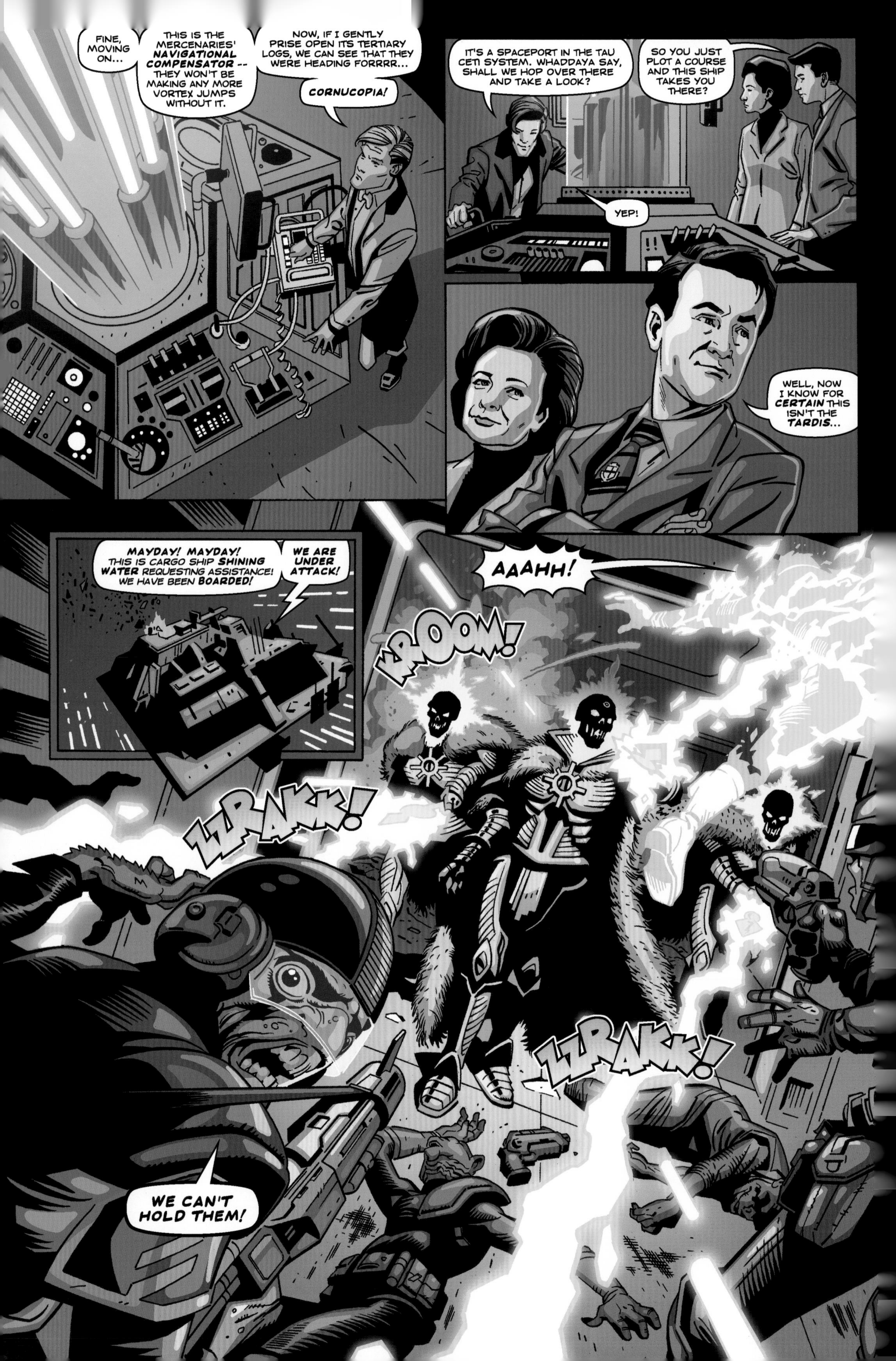
FINE, MOVING ON...
THIS IS THE MERCENARIES' NAVIGATIONAL COMPENSATOR -- THEY WON'T BE MAKING ANY MORE VORTEX JUMPS WITHOUT IT.
NOW, IF I GENTLY PRISE OPEN ITS TERTIARY LOGS, WE CAN SEE THAT THEY WERE HEADING FORRRR...
CORNUCOPIA!
IT'S A SPACEPORT IN THE TAU CETI SYSTEM. WHADDAYA SAY, SHALL WE HOP OVER THERE AND TAKE A LOOK?
SO YOU JUST PLOT A COURSE AND THIS SHIP TAKES YOU THERE?
YEP!
WELL, NOW I KNOW FOR CERTAIN THIS ISN'T THE TARDIS...
MAYDAY! MAYDAY! THIS IS CARGO SHIP SHINING WATER REQUESTING ASSISTANCE! WE HAVE BEEN BOARDED!
WE ARE UNDER ATTACK!
AAAHH!
KROOOM!
ZZRAKK!
ZZRAKK!
WE CAN'T HOLD THEM!

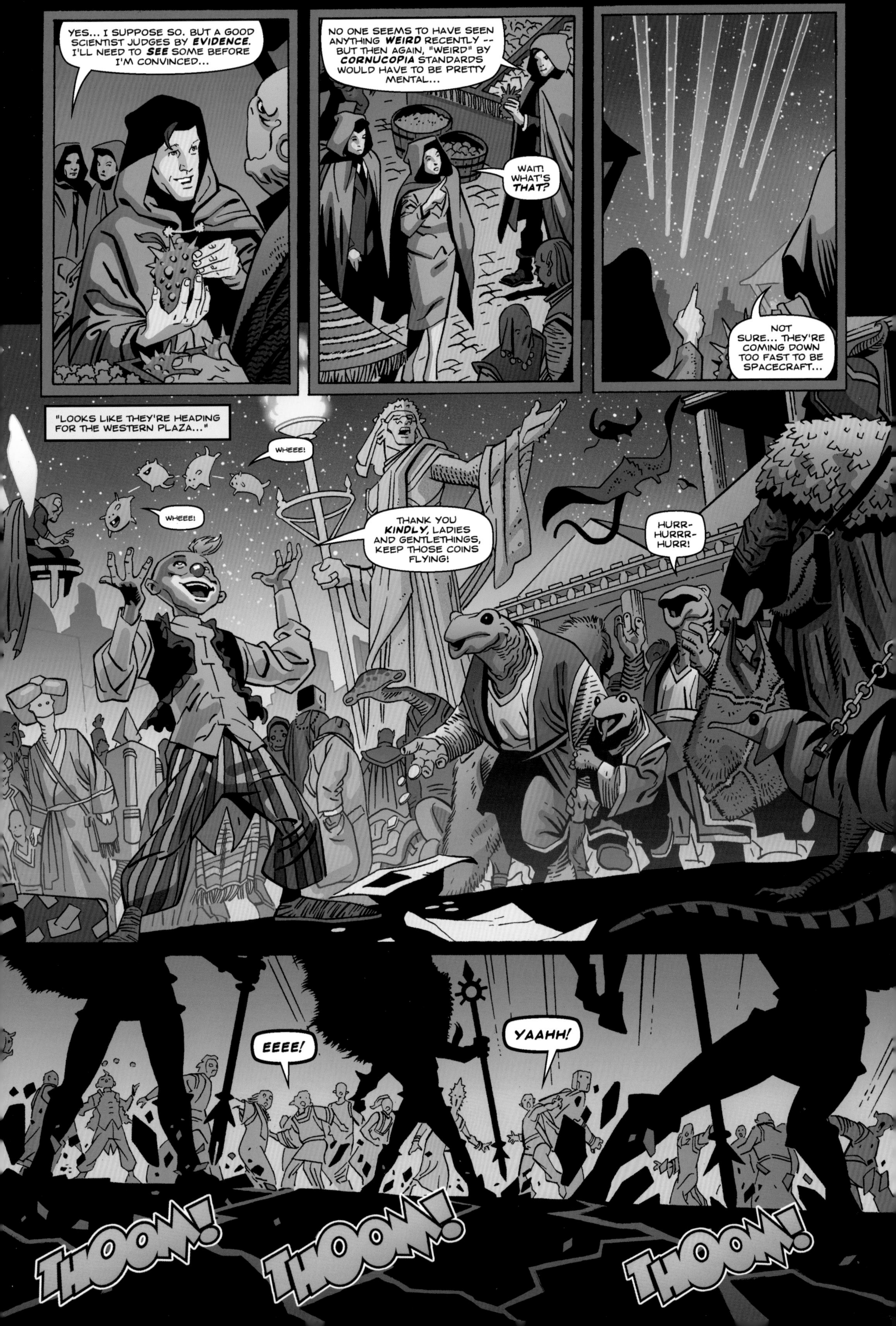
YES... I SUPPOSE SO. BUT A GOOD SCIENTIST JUDGES BY EVIDENCE. I'LL NEED TO SEE SOME BEFORE I'M CONVINCED...
NO ONE SEEMS TO HAVE SEEN ANYTHING WEIRD RECENTLY -- BUT THEN AGAIN, "WEIRD" BY CORNUCOPIA STANDARDS WOULD HAVE TO BE PRETTY MENTAL...
WAIT! WHAT'S THAT?
NOT SURE... THEY'RE COMING DOWN TOO FAST TO BE SPACECRAFT...
"LOOKS LIKE THEY'RE HEADING FOR THE WESTERN PLAZA..."
WHEEE!
WHEEE!
THANK YOU KINDLY, LADIES AND GENTLETHINGS, KEEP THOSE COINS FLYING!
HURR-HURRR-HURR!
EEEE!
YAAHH!
THOOM!
THOOM!
THOOM!

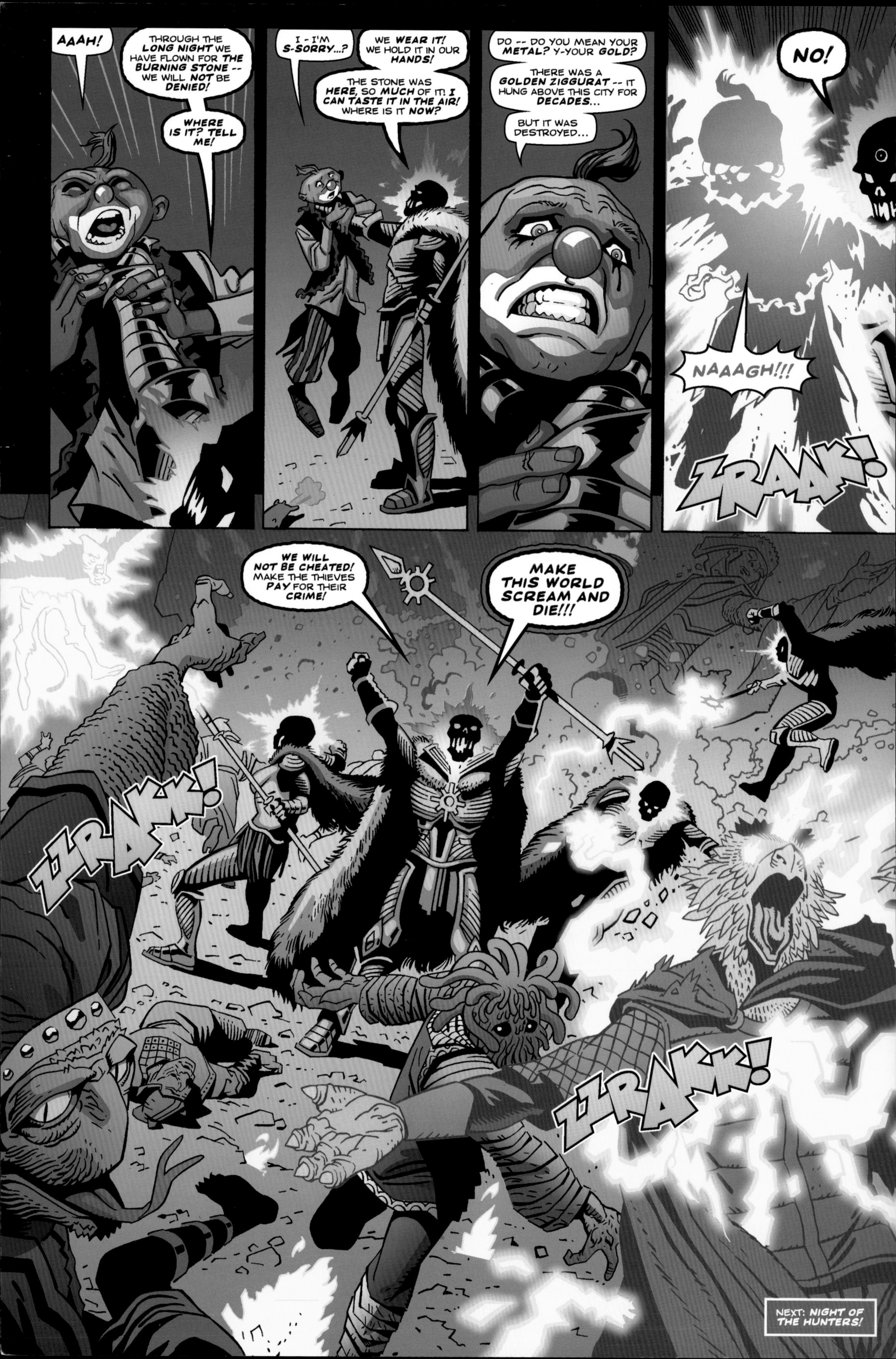

AAAH!
THROUGH THE LONG NIGHT WE HAVE FLOWN FOR THE BURNING STONE -- WE WILL NOT BE DENIED!
WHERE IS IT? TELL ME!
I - I'M S-SORRY...?
WE WEAR IT! WE HOLD IT IN OUR HANDS!
THE STONE WAS HERE, SO MUCH OF IT! I CAN TASTE IT IN THE AIR! WHERE IS IT NOW?
DO -- DO YOU MEAN YOUR METAL? Y-YOUR GOLD?
THERE WAS A GOLDEN ZIGGURAT -- IT HUNG ABOVE THIS CITY FOR DECADES...
BUT IT WAS DESTROYED...
NO!
NAAAGH!!!
ZRAAK!
WE WILL NOT BE CHEATED! MAKE THE THIEVES PAY FOR THEIR CRIME!
MAKE THIS WORLD SCREAM AND DIE!!!
ZZRAKK!
ZZRAKK!
NEXT: NIGHT OF THE HUNTERS!

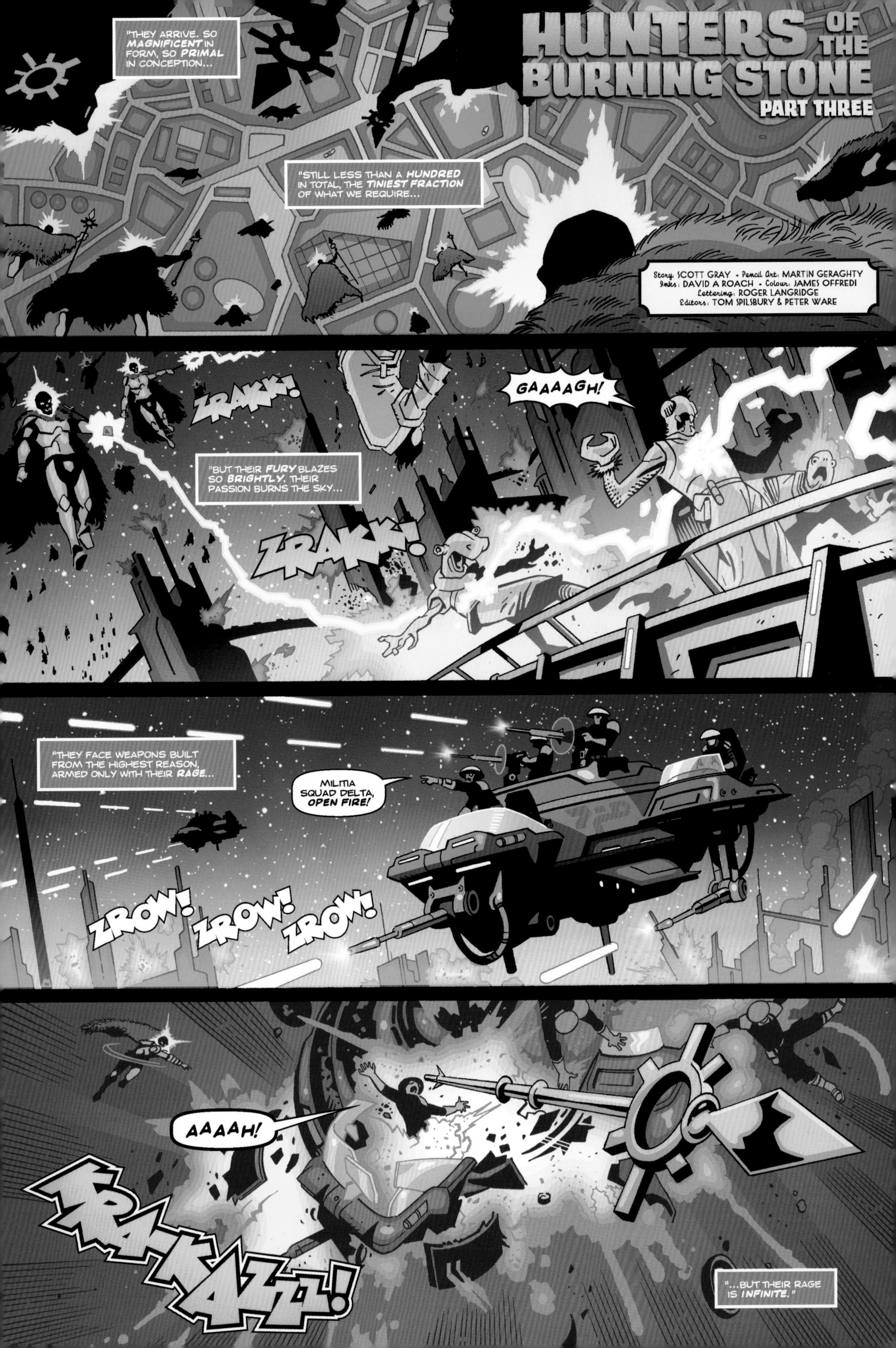
HUNTERS OF THE BURNING STONE
PART THREE
"THEY ARRIVE. SO MAGNIFICENT IN FORM, SO PRIMAL IN CONCEPTION...
"STILL LESS THAN A HUNDRED IN TOTAL, THE TINIEST FRACTION OF WHAT WE REQUIRE...
Story: SCOTT GRAY • Pencil Art: MARTIN GERAGHTY
Inks: DAVID A ROACH • Colour: JAMES OFFREDI
Lettering: ROGER LANGRIDGE
Editors: TOM SPILSBURY & PETER WARE
ZRAKK!
GAAAAGH!
"BUT THEIR FURY BLAZES SO BRIGHTLY. THEIR PASSION BURNS THE SKY...
ZRAKK!
"THEY FACE WEAPONS BUILT FROM THE HIGHEST REASON, ARMED ONLY WITH THEIR RAGE...
MILITIA SQUAD DELTA, OPEN FIRE!
ZROW! ZROW! ZROW!
AAAAH!
KRA-KA-ZZZ!
"...BUT THEIR RAGE IS INFINITE."

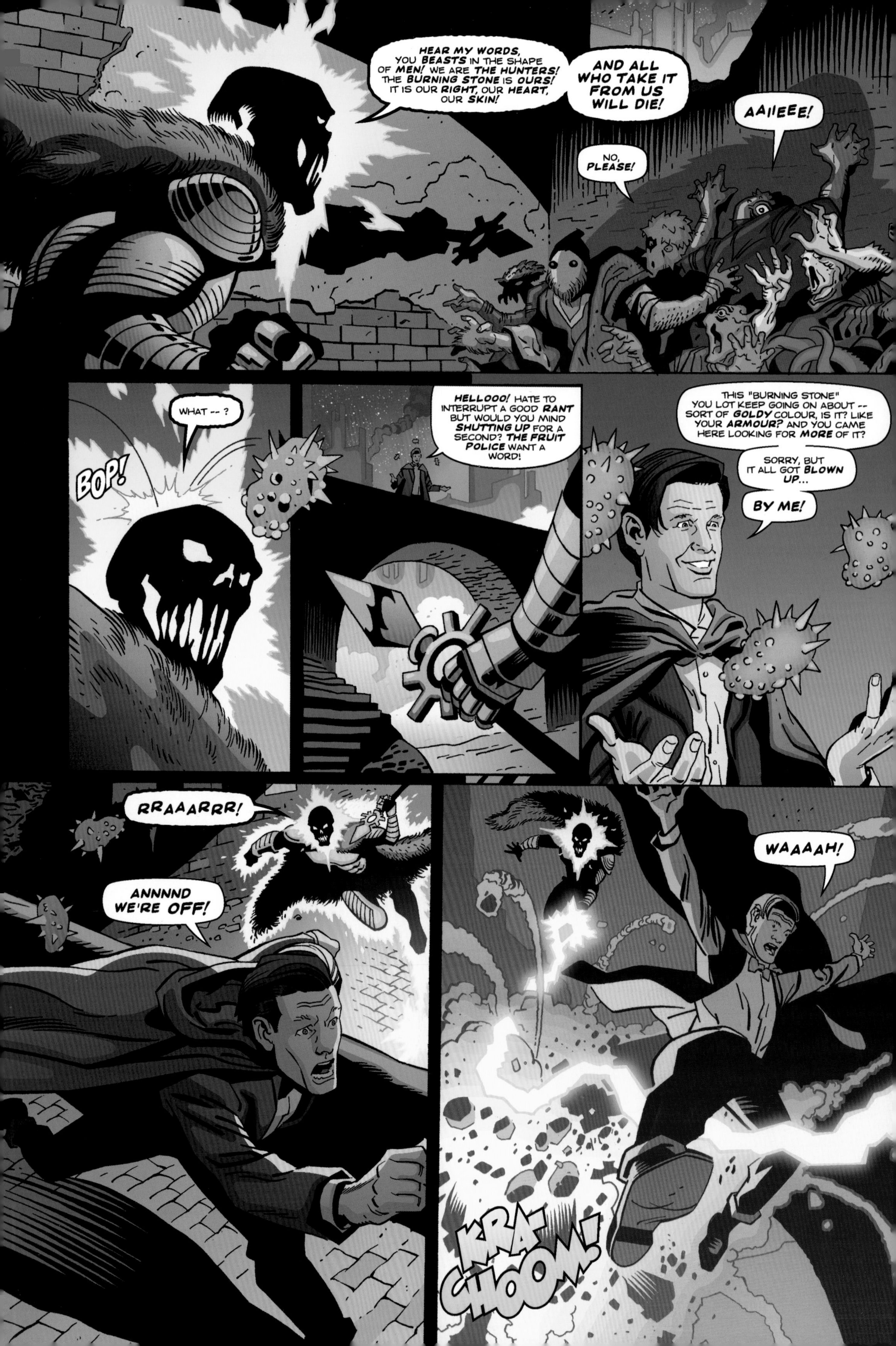
HEAR MY WORDS, YOU BEASTS IN THE SHAPE OF MEN! WE ARE THE HUNTERS! THE BURNING STONE IS OURS! IT IS OUR RIGHT, OUR HEART, OUR SKIN!
AND ALL WHO TAKE IT FROM US WILL DIE!
AAIIEEE!
NO, PLEASE!
WHAT -- ?
BOP!
HELLOOO! HATE TO INTERRUPT A GOOD RANT BUT WOULD YOU MIND SHUTTING UP FOR A SECOND? THE FRUIT POLICE WANT A WORD!
THIS "BURNING STONE" YOU LOT KEEP GOING ON ABOUT -- SORT OF GOLDY COLOUR, IS IT? LIKE YOUR ARMOUR? AND YOU CAME HERE LOOKING FOR MORE OF IT?
SORRY, BUT IT ALL GOT BLOWN UP...
BY ME!
RRAAARRR!
ANNNND WE'RE OFF!
WAAAAH!
KRA-CHOOM!

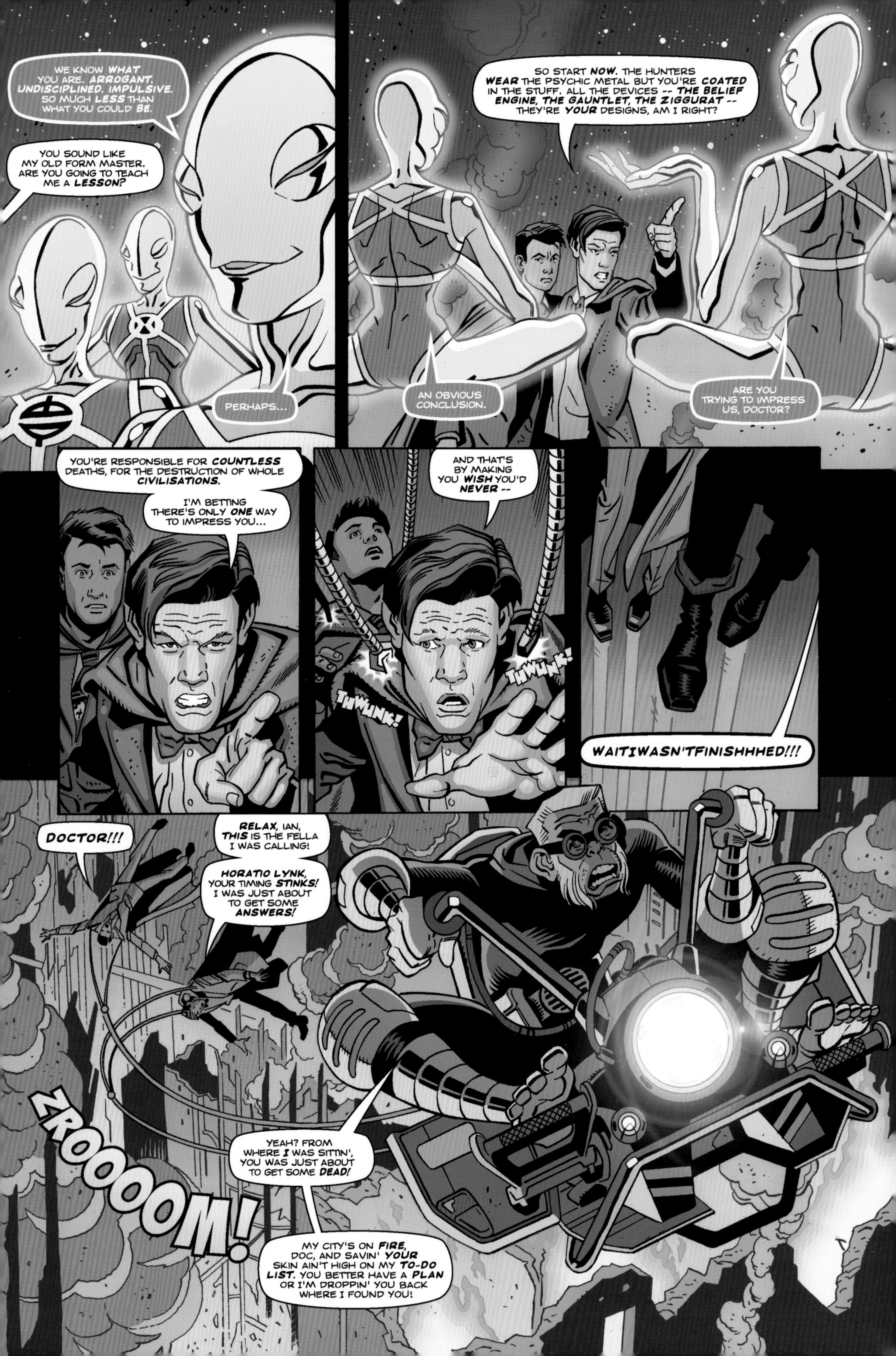
WE KNOW WHAT YOU ARE. ARROGANT. UNDISCIPLINED. IMPULSIVE. SO MUCH LESS THAN WHAT YOU COULD BE.
YOU SOUND LIKE MY OLD FORM MASTER. ARE YOU GOING TO TEACH ME A LESSON?
PERHAPS...
SO START NOW. THE HUNTERS WEAR THE PSYCHIC METAL BUT YOU'RE COATED IN THE STUFF. ALL THE DEVICES -- THE BELIEF ENGINE, THE GAUNTLET, THE ZIGGURAT -- THEY'RE YOUR DESIGNS, AM I RIGHT?
AN OBVIOUS CONCLUSION.
ARE YOU TRYING TO IMPRESS US, DOCTOR?
YOU'RE RESPONSIBLE FOR COUNTLESS DEATHS, FOR THE DESTRUCTION OF WHOLE CIVILISATIONS.
I'M BETTING THERE'S ONLY ONE WAY TO IMPRESS YOU...
AND THAT'S BY MAKING YOU WISH YOU'D NEVER --
THWUNK!
THWUNK!
WAITIWASN'TFINISHHHED!!!
DOCTOR!!!
RELAX, IAN, THIS IS THE FELLA I WAS CALLING!
HORATIO LYNK, YOUR TIMING STINKS! I WAS JUST ABOUT TO GET SOME ANSWERS!
ZROOOOOM!
YEAH? FROM WHERE I WAS SITTIN', YOU WAS JUST ABOUT TO GET SOME DEAD!
MY CITY'S ON FIRE, DOC, AND SAVIN' YOUR SKIN AIN'T HIGH ON MY TO-DO LIST. YOU BETTER HAVE A PLAN OR I'M DROPPIN' YOU BACK WHERE I FOUND YOU!

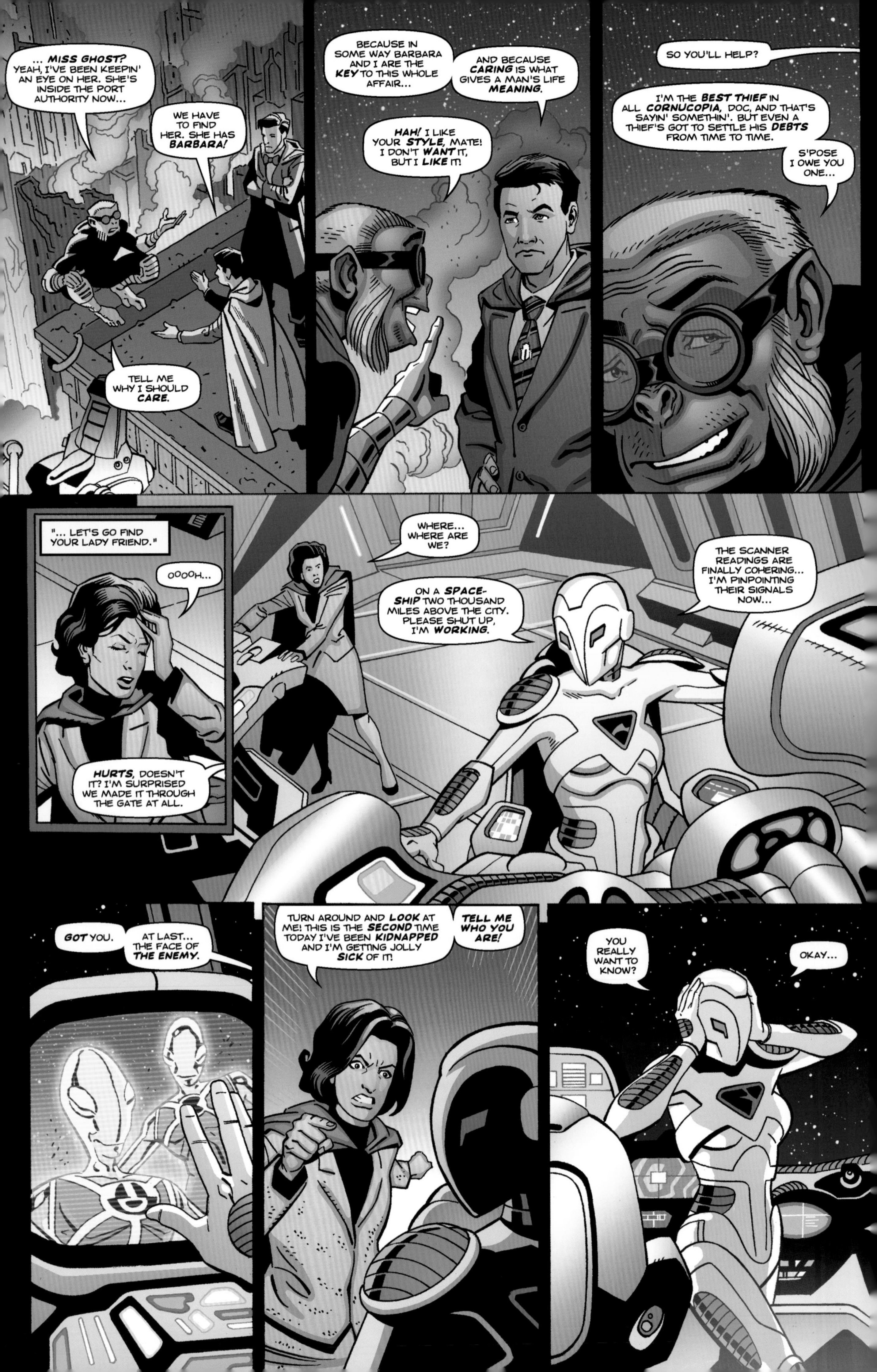
... MISS GHOST? YEAH, I'VE BEEN KEEPIN' AN EYE ON HER. SHE'S INSIDE THE PORT AUTHORITY NOW...
WE HAVE TO FIND HER. SHE HAS BARBARA!
TELL ME WHY I SHOULD CARE.
BECAUSE IN SOME WAY BARBARA AND I ARE THE KEY TO THIS WHOLE AFFAIR...
AND BECAUSE CARING IS WHAT GIVES A MAN'S LIFE MEANING.
HAH! I LIKE YOUR STYLE, MATE! I DON'T WANT IT, BUT I LIKE IT!
SO YOU'LL HELP?
I'M THE BEST THIEF IN ALL CORNUCOPIA, DOC, AND THAT'S SAYIN' SOMETHIN'. BUT EVEN A THIEF'S GOT TO SETTLE HIS DEBTS FROM TIME TO TIME.
S'POSE I OWE YOU ONE...
"... LET'S GO FIND YOUR LADY FRIEND."
OOOOH...
HURTS, DOESN'T IT? I'M SURPRISED WE MADE IT THROUGH THE GATE AT ALL.
WHERE... WHERE ARE WE?
ON A SPACE-SHIP TWO THOUSAND MILES ABOVE THE CITY. PLEASE SHUT UP, I'M WORKING.
THE SCANNER READINGS ARE FINALLY COHERING... I'M PINPOINTING THEIR SIGNALS NOW...
GOT YOU.
AT LAST... THE FACE OF THE ENEMY.
TURN AROUND AND LOOK AT ME! THIS IS THE SECOND TIME TODAY I'VE BEEN KIDNAPPED AND I'M GETTING JOLLY SICK OF IT!
TELL ME WHO YOU ARE!
YOU REALLY WANT TO KNOW?
OKAY...

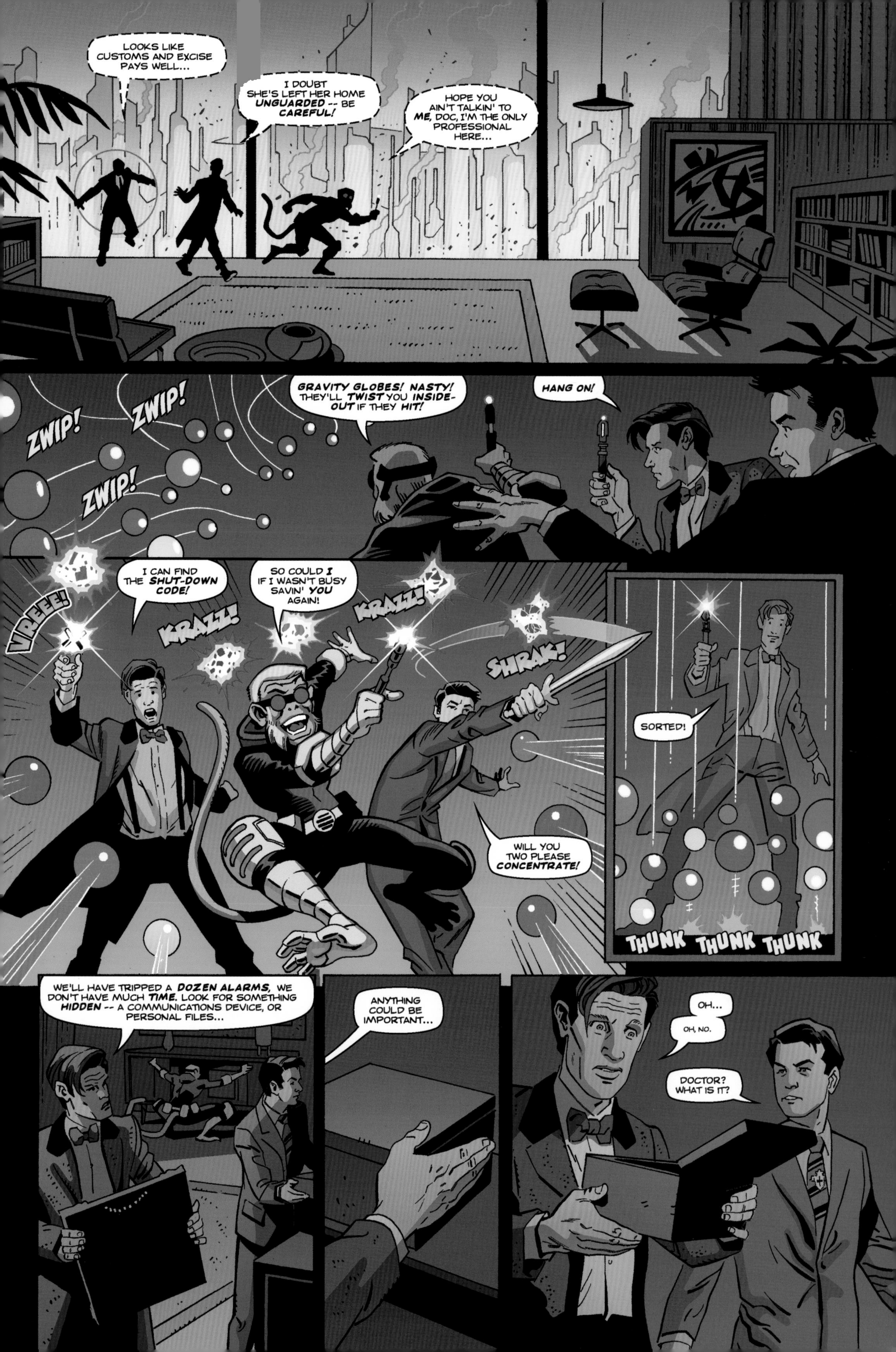
LOOKS LIKE CUSTOMS AND EXCISE PAYS WELL...
I DOUBT SHE'S LEFT HER HOME UNGUARDED -- BE CAREFUL!
HOPE YOU AIN'T TALKIN' TO ME, DOC, I'M THE ONLY PROFESSIONAL HERE...
ZWIP!
ZWIP!
ZWIP!
GRAVITY GLOBES! NASTY! THEY'LL TWIST YOU INSIDE-OUT IF THEY HIT!
HANG ON!
VREEE!
I CAN FIND THE SHUT-DOWN CODE!
KRAZZ!
SO COULD I IF I WASN'T BUSY SAVIN' YOU AGAIN!
KRAZZ!
SHRAK!
WILL YOU TWO PLEASE CONCENTRATE!
SORTED!
THUNK THUNK THUNK
WE'LL HAVE TRIPPED A DOZEN ALARMS, WE DON'T HAVE MUCH TIME. LOOK FOR SOMETHING HIDDEN -- A COMMUNICATIONS DEVICE, OR PERSONAL FILES...
ANYTHING COULD BE IMPORTANT...
OH...
OH, NO.
DOCTOR? WHAT IS IT?

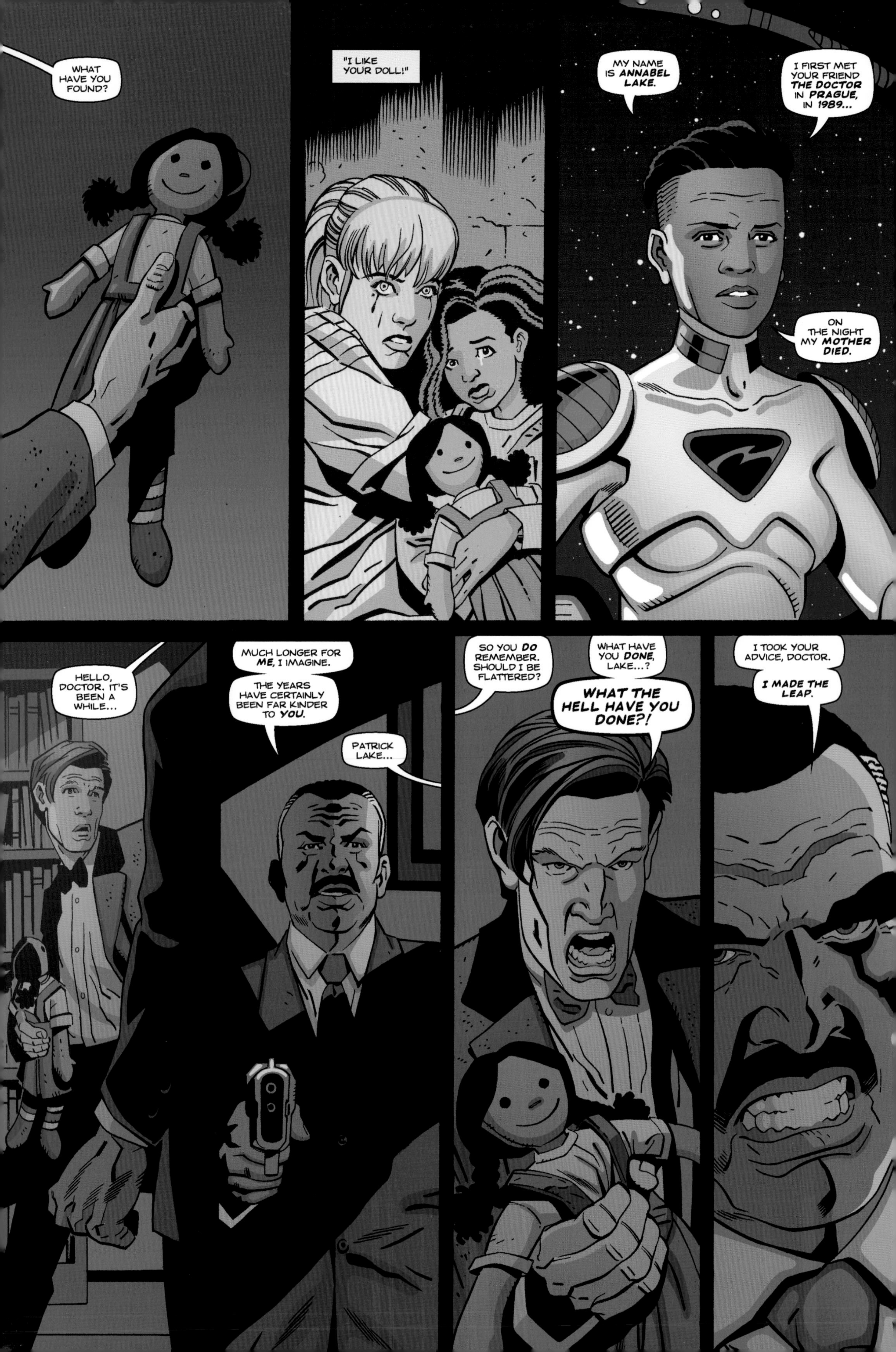
WHAT HAVE YOU FOUND?
"I LIKE YOUR DOLL!"
MY NAME IS ANNABEL LAKE.
I FIRST MET YOUR FRIEND THE DOCTOR IN PRAGUE, IN 1989...
ON THE NIGHT MY MOTHER DIED.
HELLO, DOCTOR. IT'S BEEN A WHILE...
MUCH LONGER FOR ME, I IMAGINE.
THE YEARS HAVE CERTAINLY BEEN FAR KINDER TO YOU.
PATRICK LAKE...
SO YOU DO REMEMBER. SHOULD I BE FLATTERED?
WHAT HAVE YOU DONE, LAKE...?
WHAT THE HELL HAVE YOU DONE?!
I TOOK YOUR ADVICE, DOCTOR.
I MADE THE LEAP.

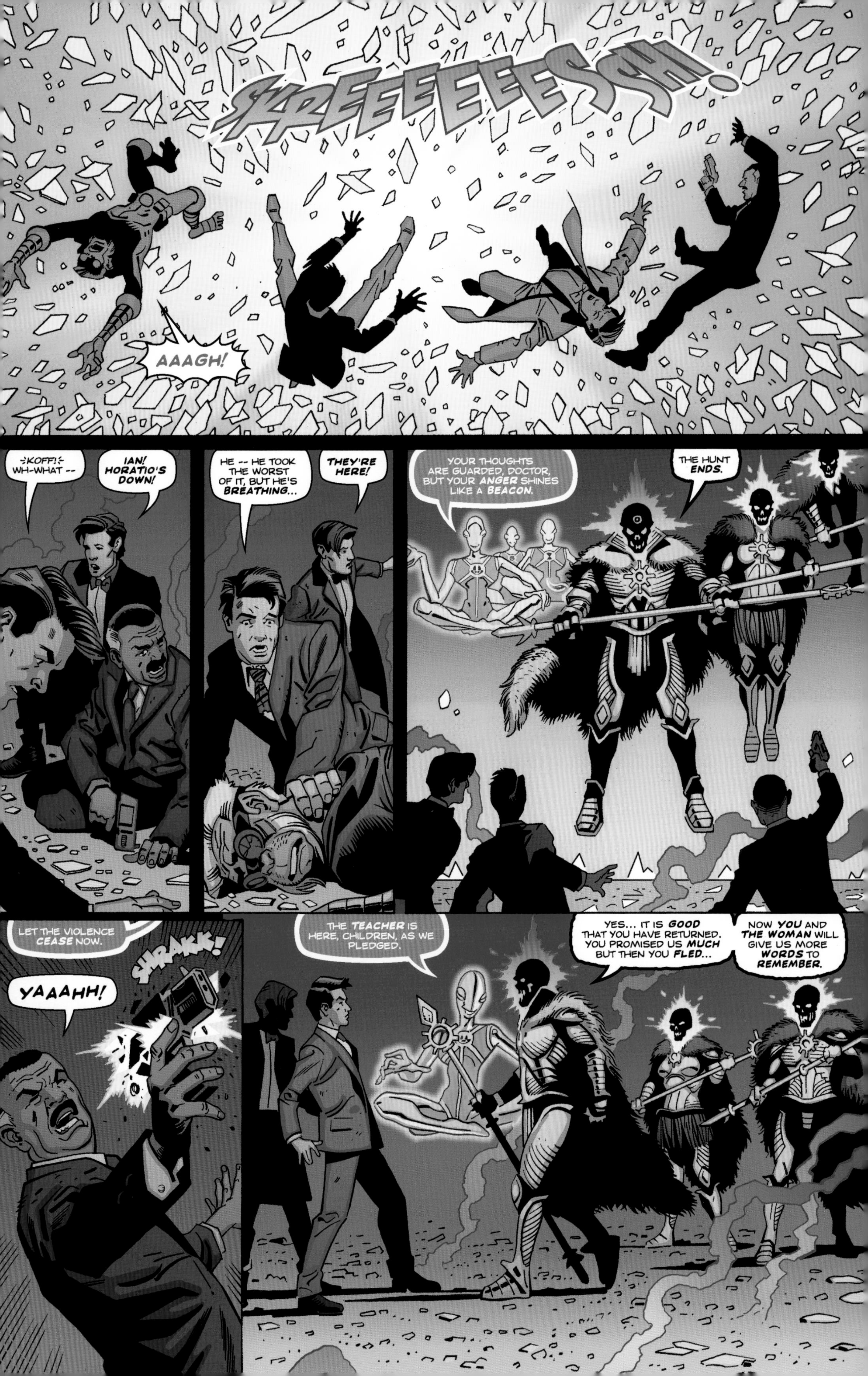

SKREEEEEESCH!
AAAGH!
-KOFF!- WH-WHAT --
IAN! HORATIO'S DOWN!
HE -- HE TOOK THE WORST OF IT, BUT HE'S BREATHING...
THEY'RE HERE!
YOUR THOUGHTS ARE GUARDED, DOCTOR, BUT YOUR ANGER SHINES LIKE A BEACON.
THE HUNT ENDS.
LET THE VIOLENCE CEASE NOW.
SHRAKK!
YAAAHH!
THE TEACHER IS HERE, CHILDREN, AS WE PLEDGED.
YES... IT IS GOOD THAT YOU HAVE RETURNED. YOU PROMISED US MUCH BUT THEN YOU FLED...
NOW YOU AND THE WOMAN WILL GIVE US MORE WORDS TO REMEMBER.

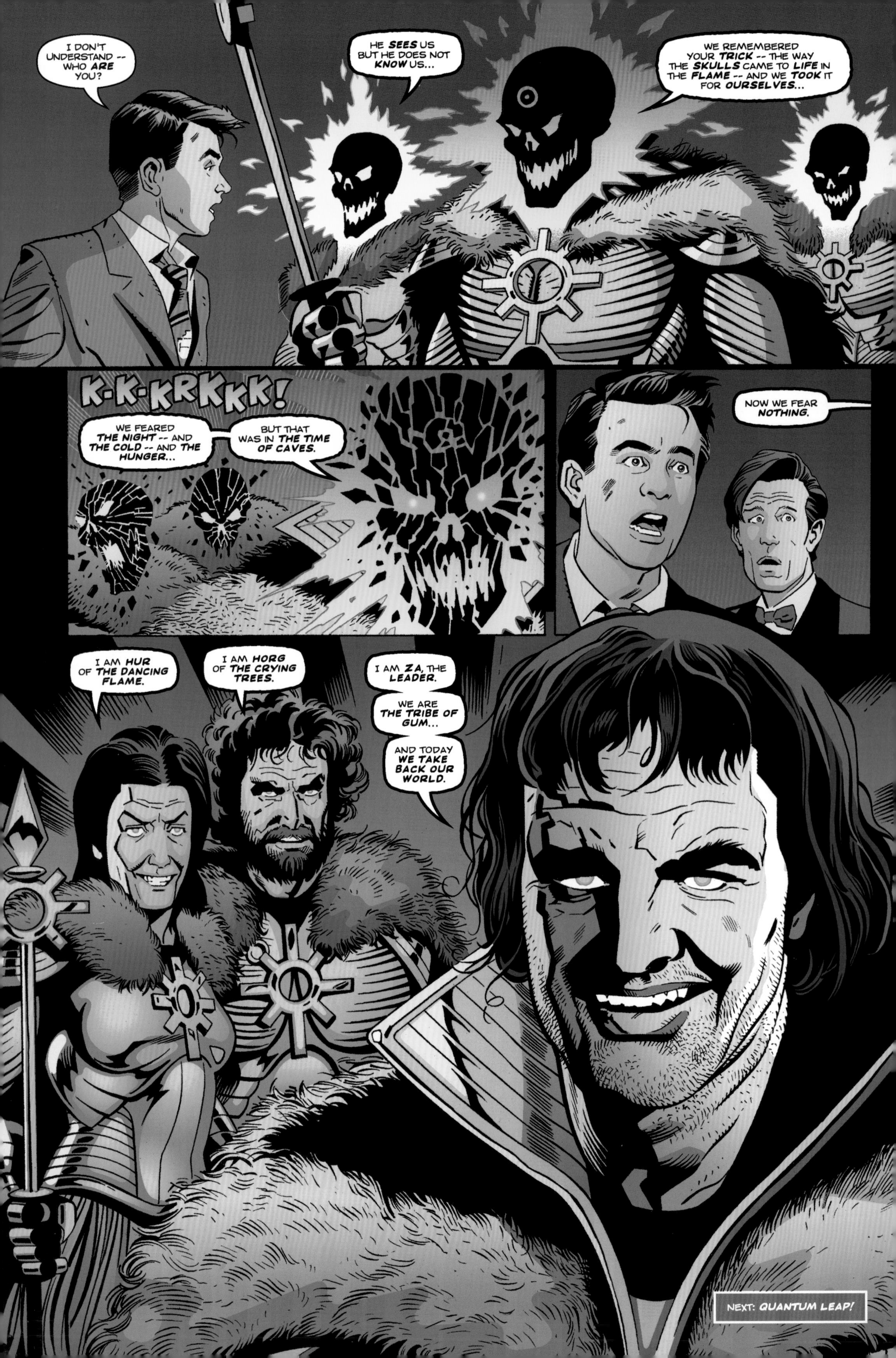
I DON'T UNDERSTAND -- WHO ARE YOU?
HE SEES US BUT HE DOES NOT KNOW US...
WE REMEMBERED YOUR TRICK -- THE WAY THE SKULLS CAME TO LIFE IN THE FLAME -- AND WE TOOK IT FOR OURSELVES...
K-K-KRKKK!
WE FEARED THE NIGHT -- AND THE COLD -- AND THE HUNGER...
BUT THAT WAS IN THE TIME OF CAVES.
NOW WE FEAR NOTHING.
I AM HUR OF THE DANCING FLAME.
I AM HORG OF THE CRYING TREES.
I AM ZA, THE LEADER.
WE ARE THE TRIBE OF GUM...
AND TODAY WE TAKE BACK OUR WORLD.
NEXT: QUANTUM LEAP!

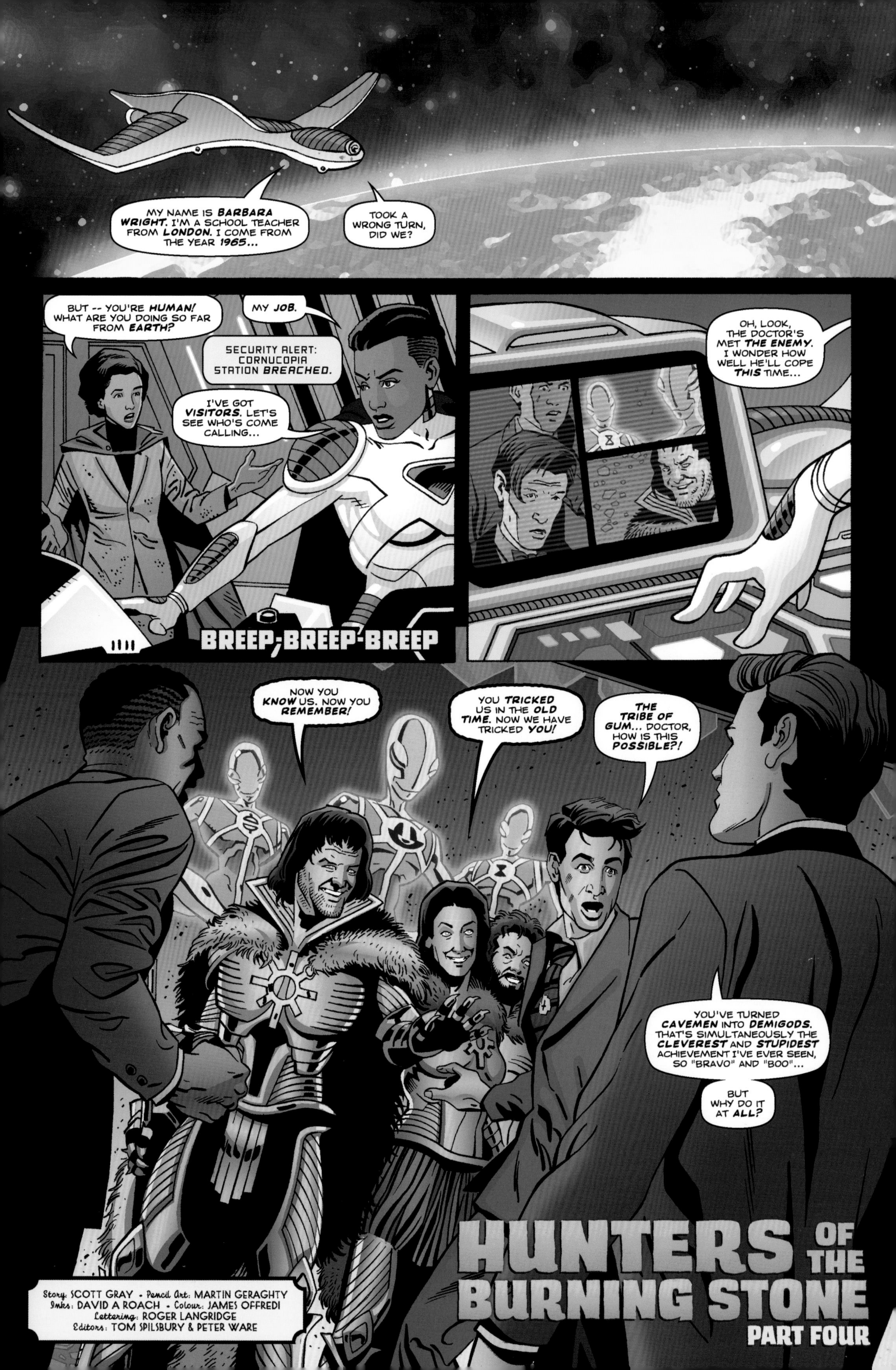
MY NAME IS BARBARA WRIGHT. I'M A SCHOOL TEACHER FROM LONDON. I COME FROM THE YEAR 1965...
TOOK A WRONG TURN, DID WE?
BUT -- YOU'RE HUMAN! WHAT ARE YOU DOING SO FAR FROM EARTH?
MY JOB.
SECURITY ALERT: CORNUCOPIA STATION BREACHED.
I'VE GOT VISITORS. LET'S SEE WHO'S COME CALLING...
BREEP-BREEP-BREEP
OH, LOOK, THE DOCTOR'S MET THE ENEMY. I WONDER HOW WELL HE'LL COPE THIS TIME...
NOW YOU KNOW US. NOW YOU REMEMBER!
YOU TRICKED US IN THE OLD TIME. NOW WE HAVE TRICKED YOU!
THE TRIBE OF GUM... DOCTOR, HOW IS THIS POSSIBLE?!
YOU'VE TURNED CAVEMEN INTO DEMIGODS. THAT'S SIMULTANEOUSLY THE CLEVEREST AND STUPIDEST ACHIEVEMENT I'VE EVER SEEN, SO "BRAVO" AND "BOO"...
BUT WHY DO IT AT ALL?
HUNTERS OF THE BURNING STONE
PART FOUR
Story: SCOTT GRAY • Pencil Art: MARTIN GERAGHTY
Inks: DAVID A ROACH • Colour: JAMES OFFREDI
Lettering: ROGER LANGRIDGE
Editors: TOM SPILSBURY & PETER WARE

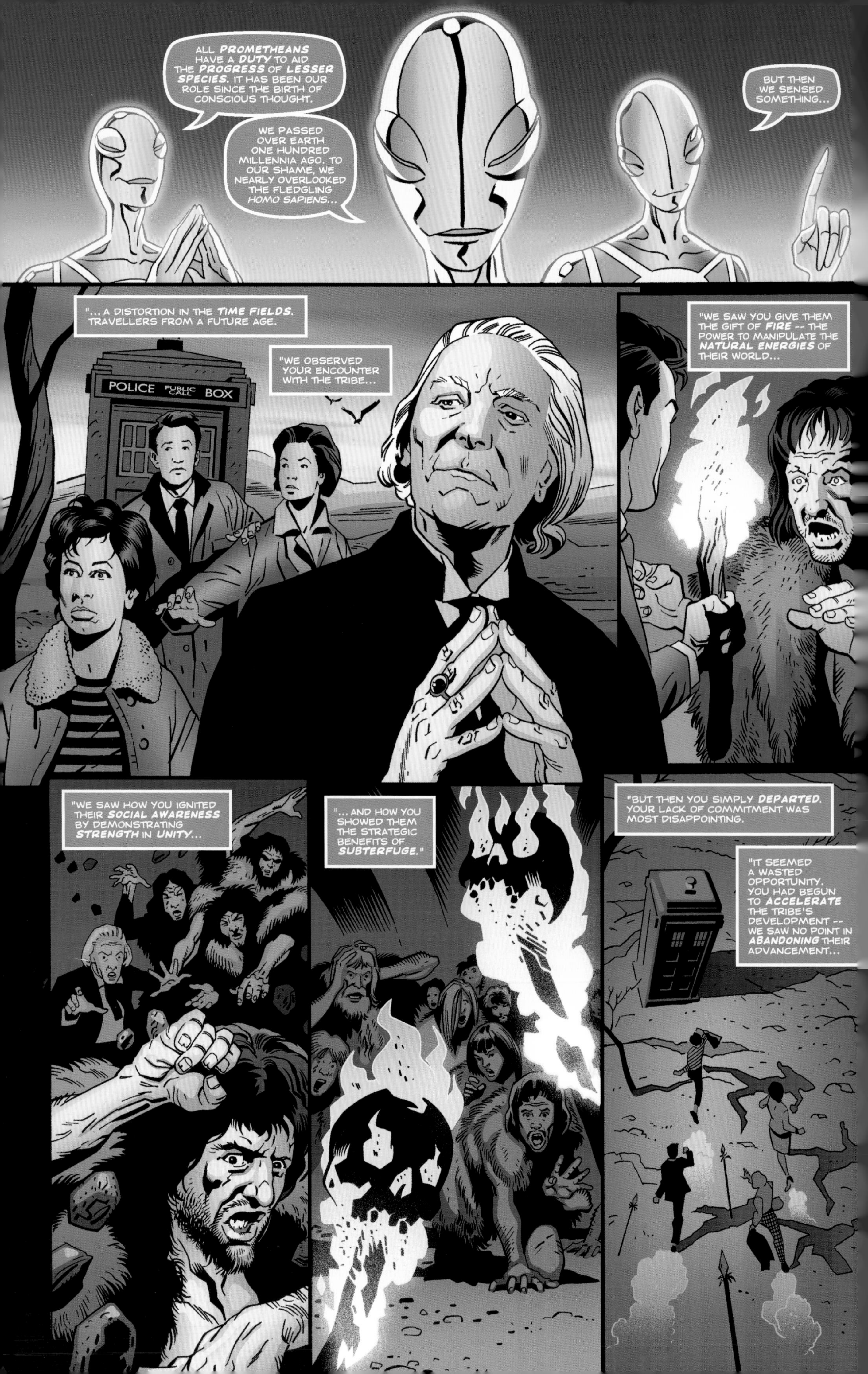
ALL PROMETHEANS HAVE A DUTY TO AID THE PROGRESS OF LESSER SPECIES. IT HAS BEEN OUR ROLE SINCE THE BIRTH OF CONSCIOUS THOUGHT.
WE PASSED OVER EARTH ONE HUNDRED MILLENNIA AGO. TO OUR SHAME, WE NEARLY OVERLOOKED THE FLEDGLING HOMO SAPIENS...
BUT THEN WE SENSED SOMETHING...
"... A DISTORTION IN THE TIME FIELDS. TRAVELLERS FROM A FUTURE AGE.
"WE OBSERVED YOUR ENCOUNTER WITH THE TRIBE...
POLICE PUBLIC CALL BOX
"WE SAW YOU GIVE THEM THE GIFT OF FIRE -- THE POWER TO MANIPULATE THE NATURAL ENERGIES OF THEIR WORLD...
"WE SAW HOW YOU IGNITED THEIR SOCIAL AWARENESS BY DEMONSTRATING STRENGTH IN UNITY...
"... AND HOW YOU SHOWED THEM THE STRATEGIC BENEFITS OF SUBTERFUGE."
"BUT THEN YOU SIMPLY DEPARTED. YOUR LACK OF COMMITMENT WAS MOST DISAPPOINTING.
"IT SEEMED A WASTED OPPORTUNITY. YOU HAD BEGUN TO ACCELERATE THE TRIBE'S DEVELOPMENT -- WE SAW NO POINT IN ABANDONING THEIR ADVANCEMENT...

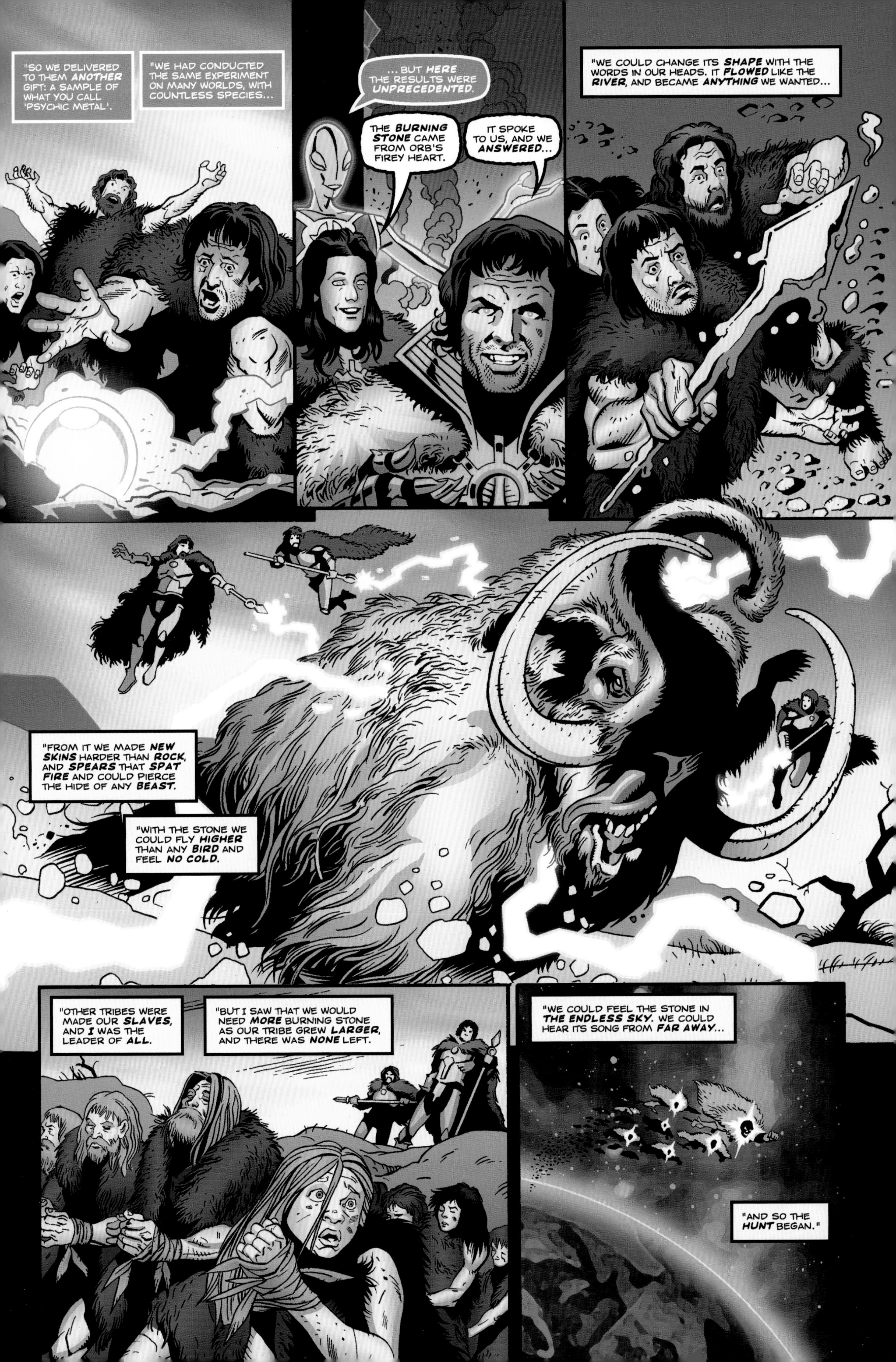
"SO WE DELIVERED TO THEM ANOTHER GIFT: A SAMPLE OF WHAT YOU CALL 'PSYCHIC METAL'.
"WE HAD CONDUCTED THE SAME EXPERIMENT ON MANY WORLDS, WITH COUNTLESS SPECIES...
... BUT HERE THE RESULTS WERE UNPRECEDENTED.
THE BURNING STONE CAME FROM ORB'S FIREY HEART.
IT SPOKE TO US, AND WE ANSWERED...
"WE COULD CHANGE ITS SHAPE WITH THE WORDS IN OUR HEADS. IT FLOWED LIKE THE RIVER, AND BECAME ANYTHING WE WANTED...
"FROM IT WE MADE NEW SKINS HARDER THAN ROCK, AND SPEARS THAT SPAT FIRE AND COULD PIERCE THE HIDE OF ANY BEAST.
"WITH THE STONE WE COULD FLY HIGHER THAN ANY BIRD AND FEEL NO COLD.
"OTHER TRIBES WERE MADE OUR SLAVES, AND I WAS THE LEADER OF ALL.
"BUT I SAW THAT WE WOULD NEED MORE BURNING STONE AS OUR TRIBE GREW LARGER, AND THERE WAS NONE LEFT.
"WE COULD FEEL THE STONE IN THE ENDLESS SKY. WE COULD HEAR ITS SONG FROM FAR AWAY...
"AND SO THE HUNT BEGAN."

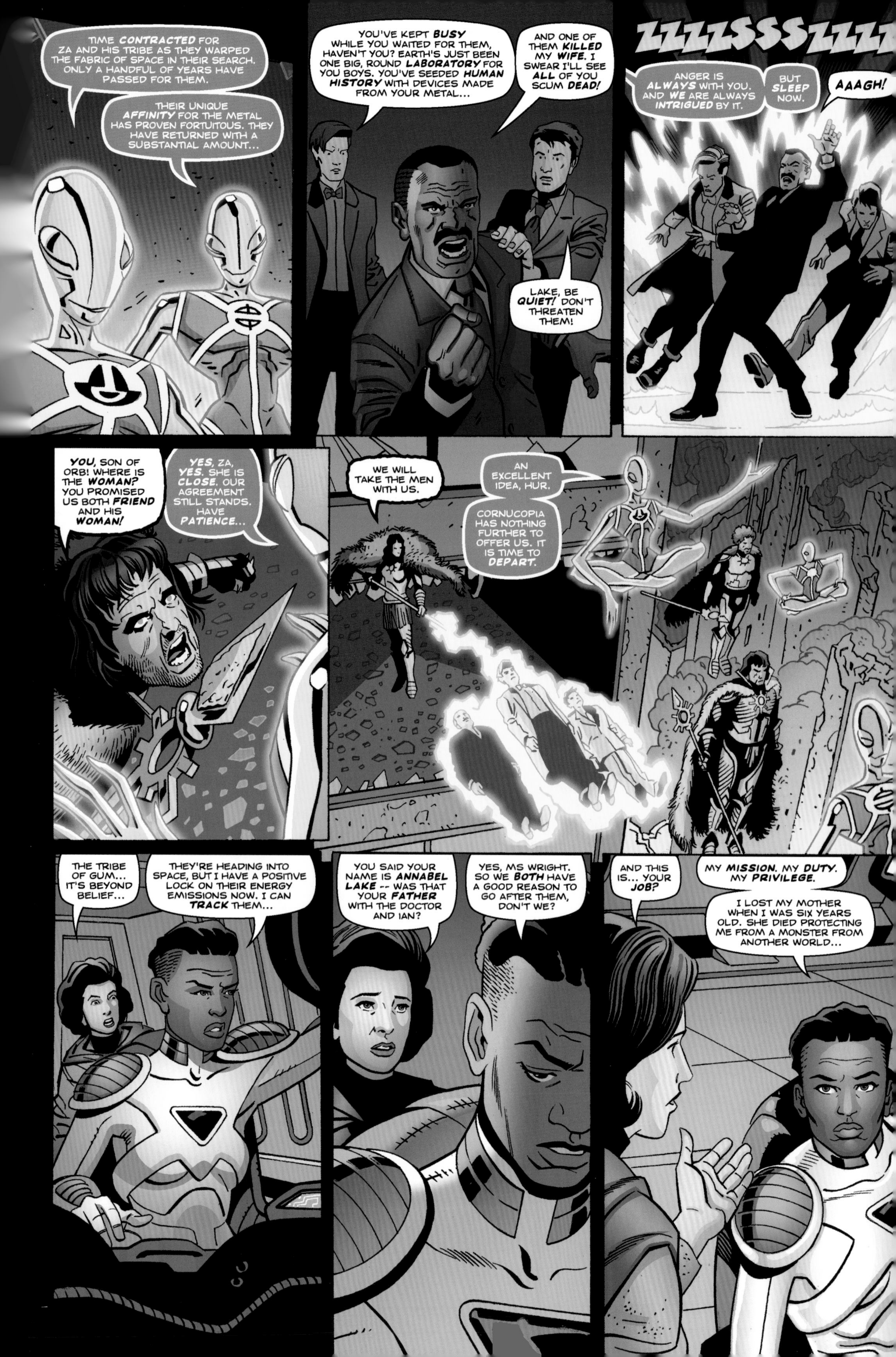
TIME CONTRACTED FOR ZA AND HIS TRIBE AS THEY WARPED THE FABRIC OF SPACE IN THEIR SEARCH. ONLY A HANDFUL OF YEARS HAVE PASSED FOR THEM.
THEIR UNIQUE AFFINITY FOR THE METAL HAS PROVEN FORTUITOUS. THEY HAVE RETURNED WITH A SUBSTANTIAL AMOUNT...
YOU'VE KEPT BUSY WHILE YOU WAITED FOR THEM, HAVEN'T YOU? EARTH'S JUST BEEN ONE BIG, ROUND LABORATORY FOR YOU BOYS. YOU'VE SEEDED HUMAN HISTORY WITH DEVICES MADE FROM YOUR METAL...
AND ONE OF THEM KILLED MY WIFE. I SWEAR I'LL SEE ALL OF YOU SCUM DEAD!
LAKE, BE QUIET! DON'T THREATEN THEM!
ZZZZSSSSZZZZ
ANGER IS ALWAYS WITH YOU. AND WE ARE ALWAYS INTRIGUED BY IT.
BUT SLEEP NOW.
AAAGH!
YOU, SON OF ORB! WHERE IS THE WOMAN? YOU PROMISED US BOTH FRIEND AND HIS WOMAN!
YES, ZA, YES. SHE IS CLOSE. OUR AGREEMENT STILL STANDS. HAVE PATIENCE...
WE WILL TAKE THE MEN WITH US.
AN EXCELLENT IDEA, HUR.
CORNUCOPIA HAS NOTHING FURTHER TO OFFER US. IT IS TIME TO DEPART.
THE TRIBE OF GUM... IT'S BEYOND BELIEF...
THEY'RE HEADING INTO SPACE, BUT I HAVE A POSITIVE LOCK ON THEIR ENERGY EMISSIONS NOW. I CAN TRACK THEM...
YOU SAID YOUR NAME IS ANNABEL LAKE -- WAS THAT YOUR FATHER WITH THE DOCTOR AND IAN?
YES, MS WRIGHT. SO WE BOTH HAVE A GOOD REASON TO GO AFTER THEM, DON'T WE?
AND THIS IS... YOUR JOB?
MY MISSION. MY DUTY. MY PRIVILEGE.
I LOST MY MOTHER WHEN I WAS SIX YEARS OLD. SHE DIED PROTECTING ME FROM A MONSTER FROM ANOTHER WORLD...

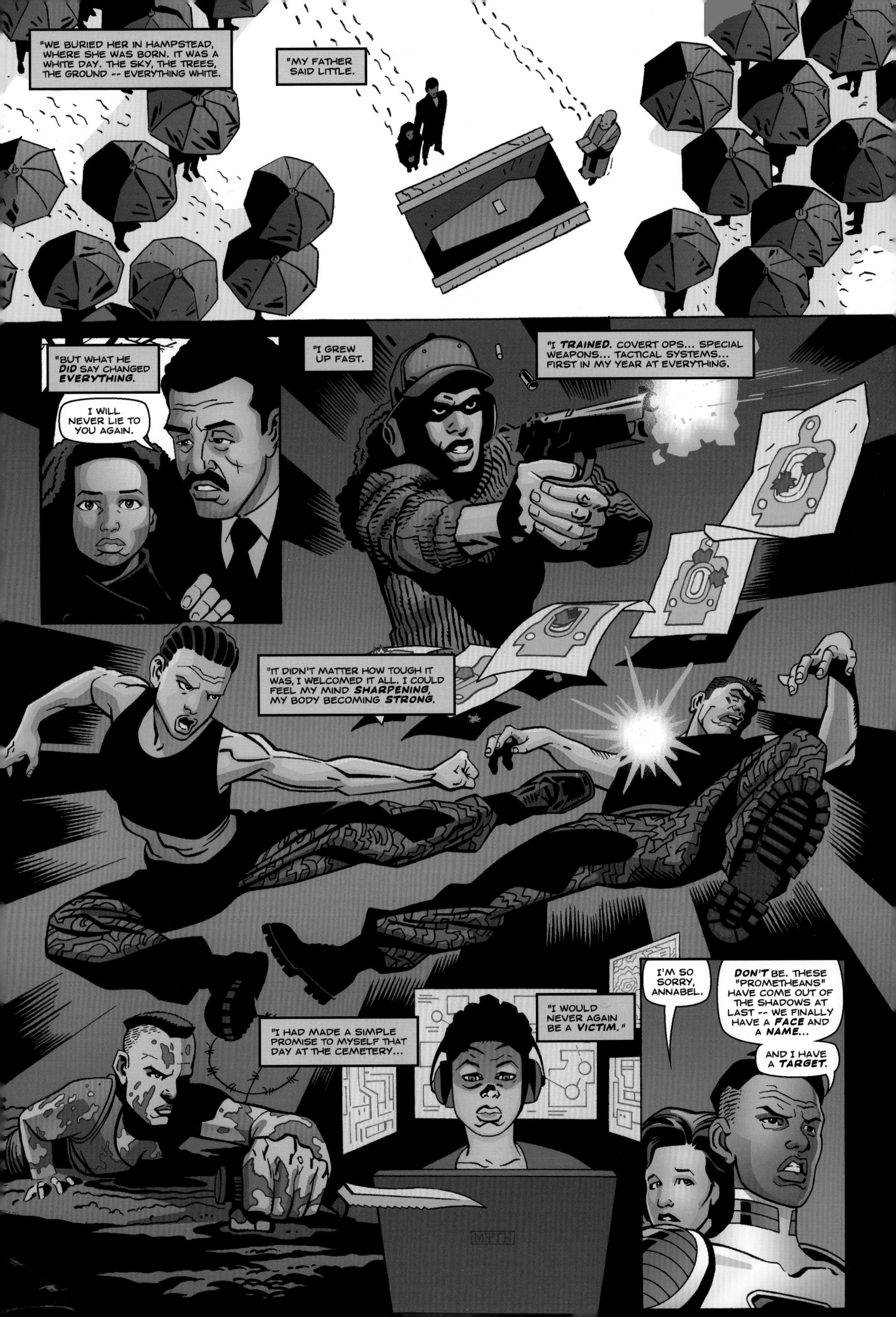

"WE BURIED HER IN HAMPSTEAD, WHERE SHE WAS BORN. IT WAS A WHITE DAY. THE SKY, THE TREES, THE GROUND -- EVERYTHING WHITE.
"MY FATHER SAID LITTLE.
"BUT WHAT HE DID SAY CHANGED EVERYTHING.
I WILL NEVER LIE TO YOU AGAIN.
"I GREW UP FAST.
"I TRAINED. COVERT OPS... SPECIAL WEAPONS... TACTICAL SYSTEMS... FIRST IN MY YEAR AT EVERYTHING.
"IT DIDN'T MATTER HOW TOUGH IT WAS, I WELCOMED IT ALL. I COULD FEEL MY MIND SHARPENING, MY BODY BECOMING STRONG.
"I HAD MADE A SIMPLE PROMISE TO MYSELF THAT DAY AT THE CEMETERY...
"I WOULD NEVER AGAIN BE A VICTIM."
I'M SO SORRY, ANNABEL.
DON'T BE. THESE "PROMETHEANS" HAVE COME OUT OF THE SHADOWS AT LAST -- WE FINALLY HAVE A FACE AND A NAME...
AND I HAVE A TARGET.
MYTH

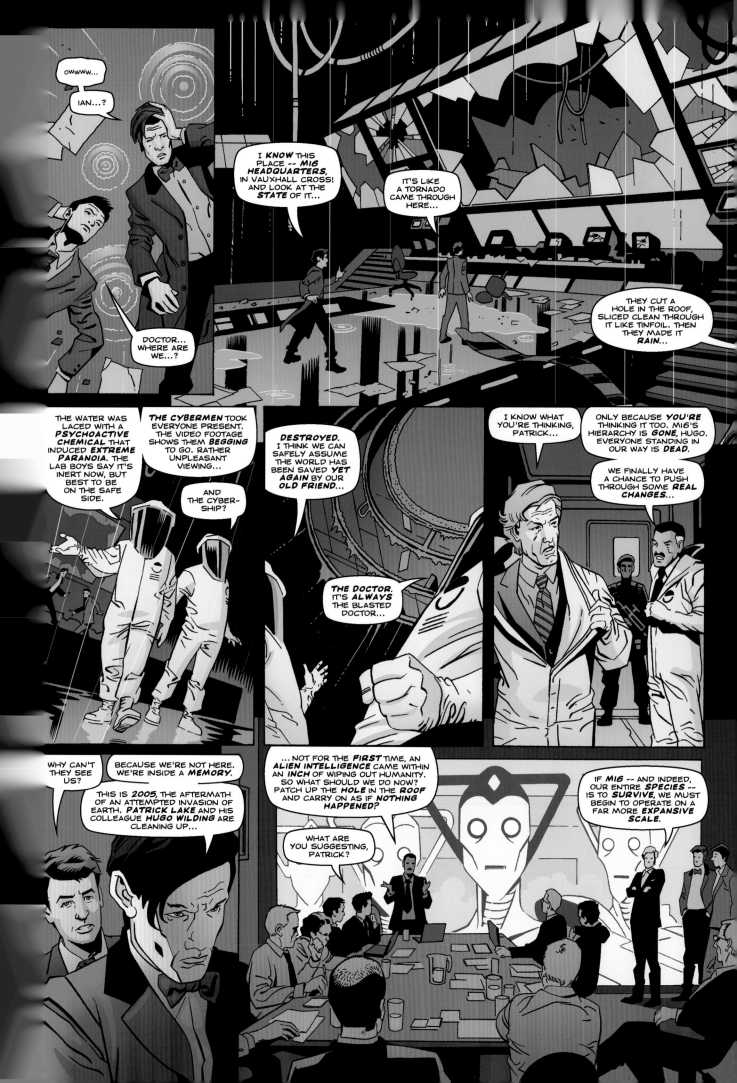

OWWWW...

IAN...?

DOCTOR... WHERE ARE WE...?

I *KNOW* THIS PLACE -- *M16 HEADQUARTERS*, IN VAUXHALL CROSS! AND LOOK AT THE *STATE* OF IT...

IT'S LIKE A TORNADO CAME THROUGH HERE...

THEY CUT A HOLE IN THE ROOF, SLICED CLEAN THROUGH IT LIKE TINFOIL. THEN THEY MADE IT *RAIN*...

THE WATER WAS LACED WITH A *PSYCHOACTIVE CHEMICAL* THAT INDUCED *EXTREME PARANOIA*. THE LAB BOYS SAY IT'S INERT NOW, BUT BEST TO BE ON THE SAFE SIDE.

THE CYBERMEN TOOK EVERYONE PRESENT. THE VIDEO FOOTAGE SHOWS THEM *BEGGING* TO GO. RATHER UNPLEASANT VIEWING...

AND THE CYBER-SHIP?

DESTROYED. I THINK WE CAN SAFELY ASSUME THE WORLD HAS BEEN SAVED *YET AGAIN* BY OUR *OLD FRIEND*...

THE DOCTOR. IT'S *ALWAYS* THE BLASTED DOCTOR...

I KNOW WHAT YOU'RE THINKING, PATRICK...

ONLY BECAUSE *YOU'RE* THINKING IT TOO, HUGO. M16'S HIERARCHY IS *GONE*. EVERYONE STANDING IN OUR WAY IS *DEAD*.

WE FINALLY HAVE A CHANCE TO PUSH THROUGH SOME *REAL CHANGES*...

WHY CAN'T THEY SEE US?

BECAUSE WE'RE NOT HERE. WE'RE INSIDE A *MEMORY*.

THIS IS *2005*, THE AFTERMATH OF AN ATTEMPTED INVASION OF EARTH. *PATRICK LAKE* AND HIS COLLEAGUE *HUGO WILDING* ARE CLEANING UP...

...NOT FOR THE *FIRST* TIME, AN *ALIEN INTELLIGENCE* CAME WITHIN AN *INCH* OF WIPING OUT HUMANITY. SO WHAT SHOULD WE DO NOW? PATCH UP THE *HOLE* IN THE *ROOF* AND CARRY ON AS IF *NOTHING* HAPPENED?

WHAT ARE YOU SUGGESTING, PATRICK?

IF *M16* -- AND INDEED, OUR ENTIRE *SPECIES* -- IS TO *SURVIVE*, WE MUST BEGIN TO OPERATE ON A FAR MORE *EXPANSIVE SCALE*.

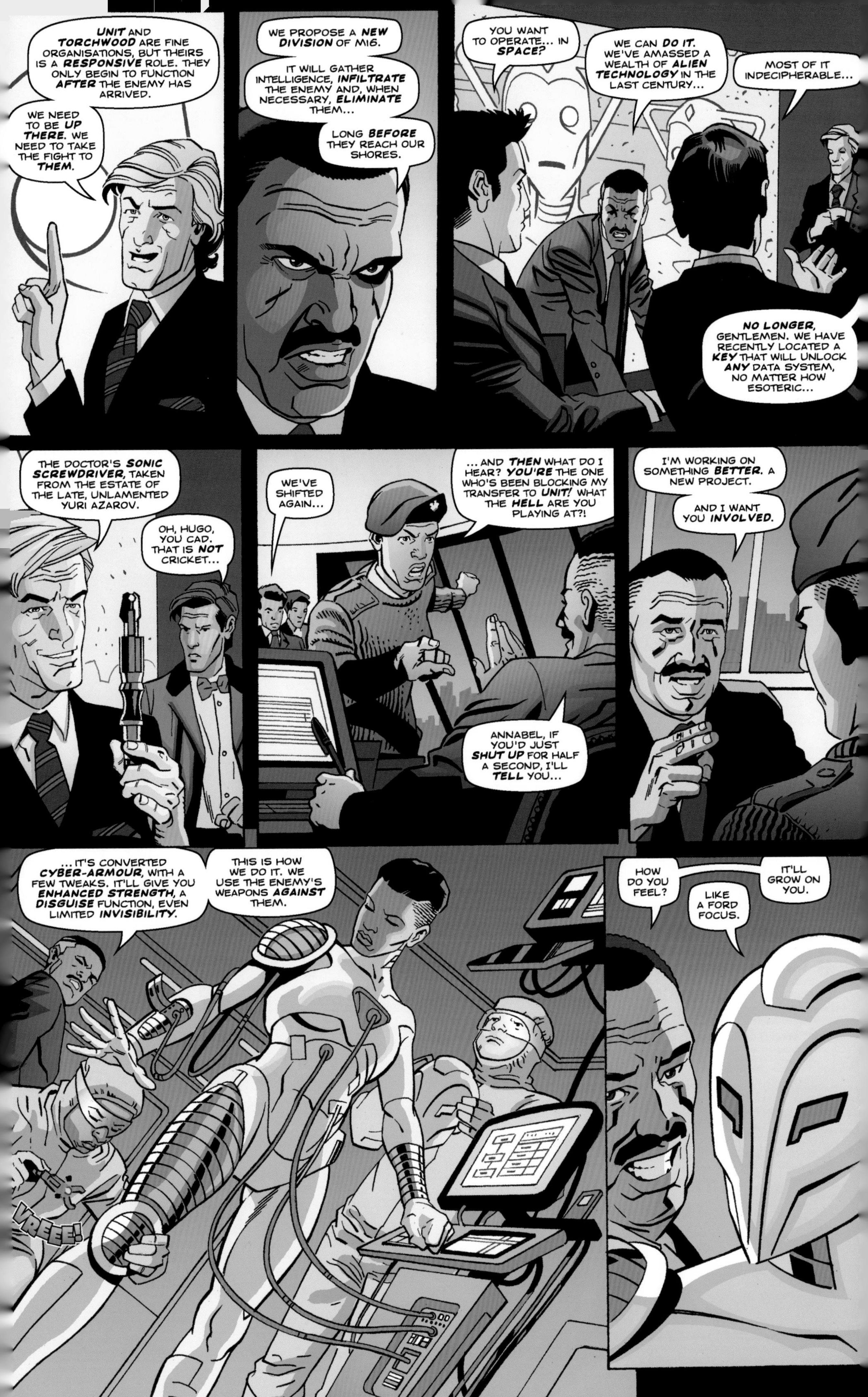
UNIT AND TORCHWOOD ARE FINE ORGANISATIONS, BUT THEIRS IS A RESPONSIVE ROLE. THEY ONLY BEGIN TO FUNCTION AFTER THE ENEMY HAS ARRIVED.
WE NEED TO BE UP THERE. WE NEED TO TAKE THE FIGHT TO THEM.
WE PROPOSE A NEW DIVISION OF MI6.
IT WILL GATHER INTELLIGENCE, INFILTRATE THE ENEMY AND, WHEN NECESSARY, ELIMINATE THEM...
LONG BEFORE THEY REACH OUR SHORES.
YOU WANT TO OPERATE... IN SPACE?
WE CAN DO IT. WE'VE AMASSED A WEALTH OF ALIEN TECHNOLOGY IN THE LAST CENTURY...
MOST OF IT INDECIPHERABLE...
NO LONGER, GENTLEMEN. WE HAVE RECENTLY LOCATED A KEY THAT WILL UNLOCK ANY DATA SYSTEM, NO MATTER HOW ESOTERIC...
THE DOCTOR'S SONIC SCREWDRIVER, TAKEN FROM THE ESTATE OF THE LATE, UNLAMENTED YURI AZAROV.
OH, HUGO, YOU CAD. THAT IS NOT CRICKET...
WE'VE SHIFTED AGAIN...
... AND THEN WHAT DO I HEAR? YOU'RE THE ONE WHO'S BEEN BLOCKING MY TRANSFER TO UNIT! WHAT THE HELL ARE YOU PLAYING AT?!
ANNABEL, IF YOU'D JUST SHUT UP FOR HALF A SECOND, I'LL TELL YOU...
I'M WORKING ON SOMETHING BETTER. A NEW PROJECT.
AND I WANT YOU INVOLVED.
... IT'S CONVERTED CYBER-ARMOUR, WITH A FEW TWEAKS. IT'LL GIVE YOU ENHANCED STRENGTH, A DISGUISE FUNCTION, EVEN LIMITED INVISIBILITY.
THIS IS HOW WE DO IT. WE USE THE ENEMY'S WEAPONS AGAINST THEM.
VREEE!
HOW DO YOU FEEL?
LIKE A FORD FOCUS.
IT'LL GROW ON YOU.

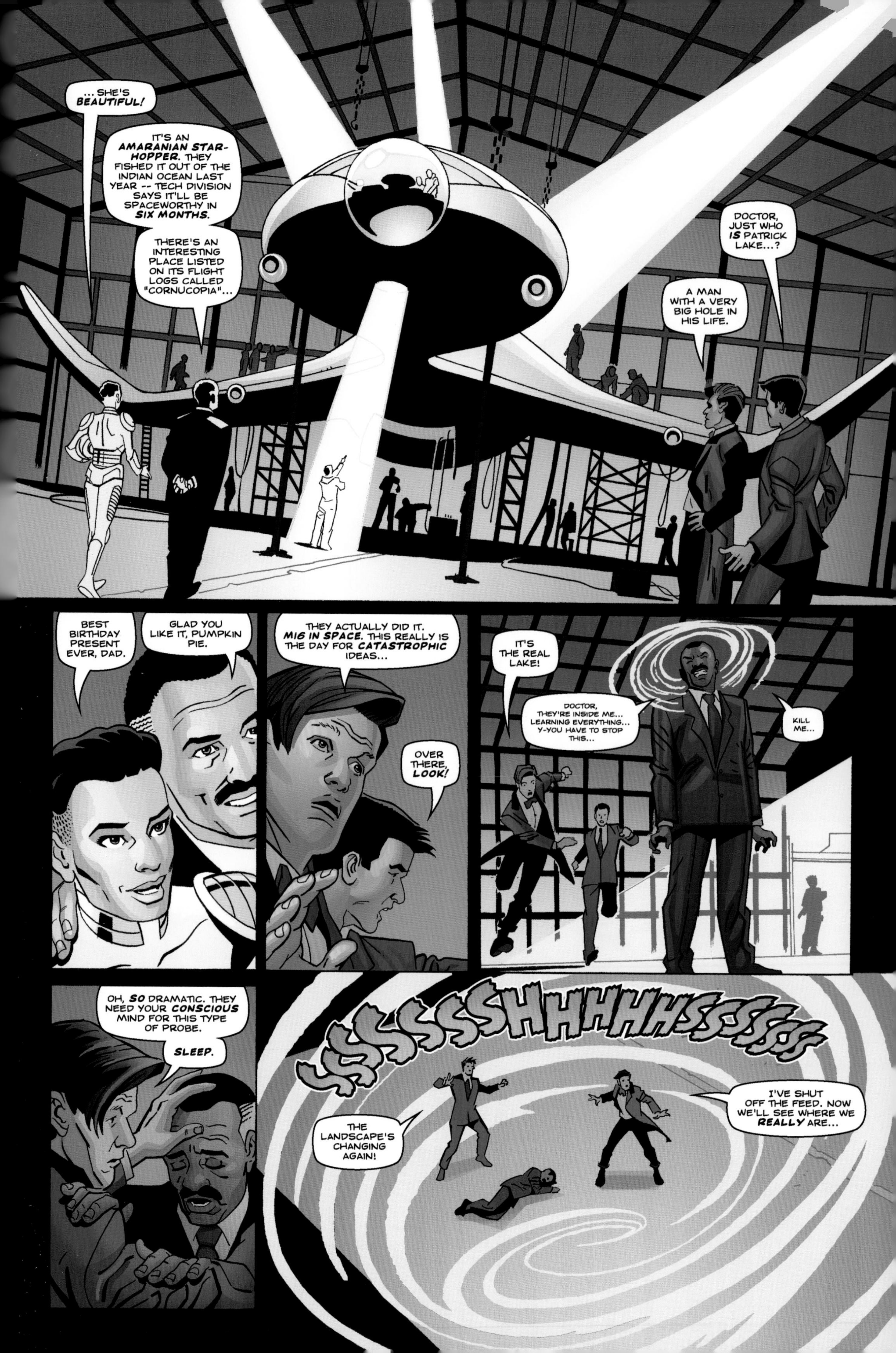
...SHE'S BEAUTIFUL!
IT'S AN AMARANIAN STAR-HOPPER. THEY FISHED IT OUT OF THE INDIAN OCEAN LAST YEAR -- TECH DIVISION SAYS IT'LL BE SPACEWORTHY IN SIX MONTHS.
THERE'S AN INTERESTING PLACE LISTED ON ITS FLIGHT LOGS CALLED "CORNUCOPIA"...
DOCTOR, JUST WHO IS PATRICK LAKE...?
A MAN WITH A VERY BIG HOLE IN HIS LIFE.
BEST BIRTHDAY PRESENT EVER, DAD.
GLAD YOU LIKE IT, PUMPKIN PIE.
THEY ACTUALLY DID IT. MI6 IN SPACE. THIS REALLY IS THE DAY FOR CATASTROPHIC IDEAS...
OVER THERE, LOOK!
IT'S THE REAL LAKE!
DOCTOR, THEY'RE INSIDE ME... LEARNING EVERYTHING... Y-YOU HAVE TO STOP THIS...
KILL ME...
OH, SO DRAMATIC. THEY NEED YOUR CONSCIOUS MIND FOR THIS TYPE OF PROBE.
SLEEP.
SSSSSSHHHHHSSSSSS
I'VE SHUT OFF THE FEED. NOW WE'LL SEE WHERE WE REALLY ARE...
THE LANDSCAPE'S CHANGING AGAIN!

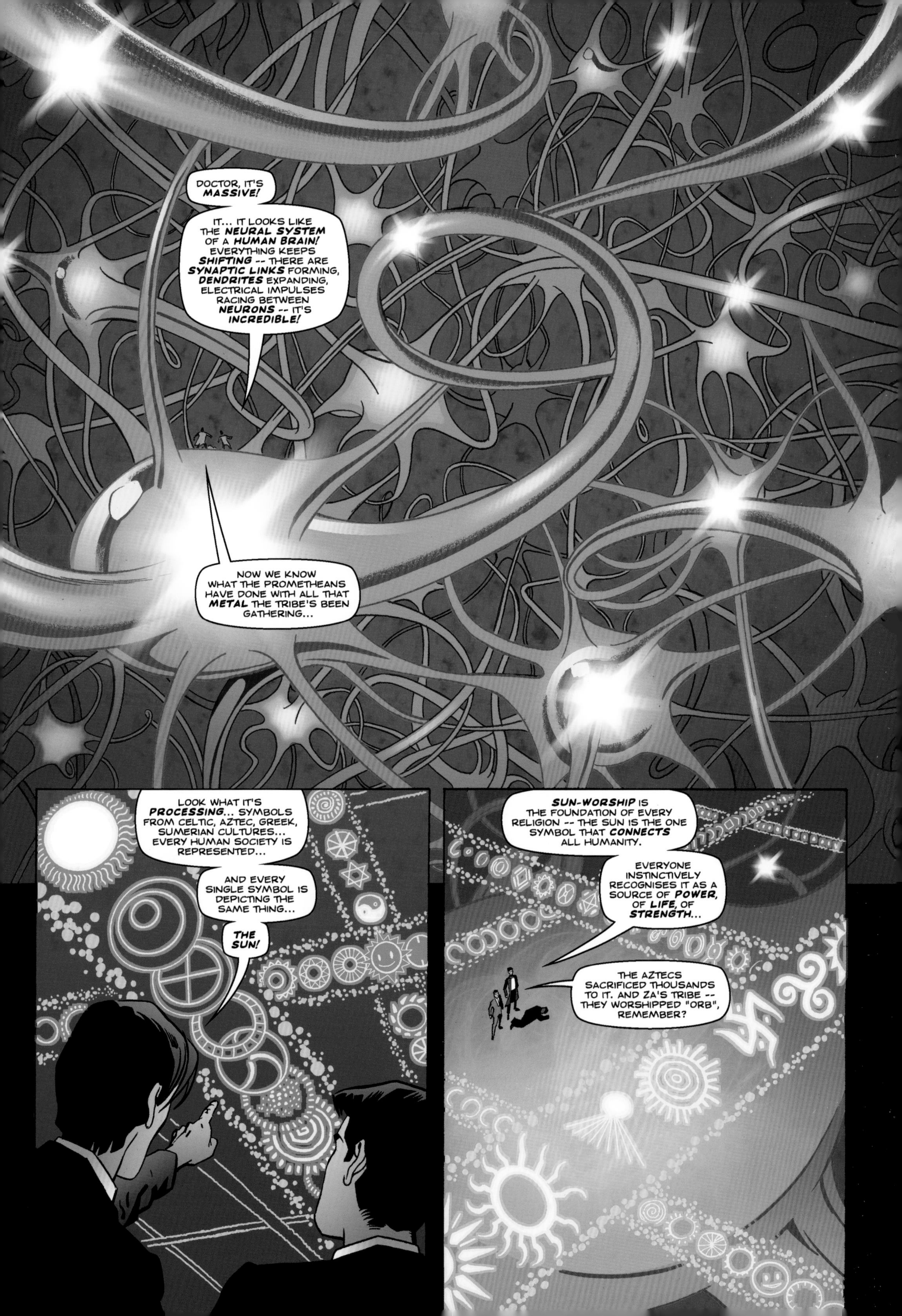

DOCTOR, IT'S MASSIVE!
IT... IT LOOKS LIKE THE NEURAL SYSTEM OF A HUMAN BRAIN! EVERYTHING KEEPS SHIFTING -- THERE ARE SYNAPTIC LINKS FORMING, DENDRITES EXPANDING, ELECTRICAL IMPULSES RACING BETWEEN NEURONS -- IT'S INCREDIBLE!
NOW WE KNOW WHAT THE PROMETHEANS HAVE DONE WITH ALL THAT METAL THE TRIBE'S BEEN GATHERING...
LOOK WHAT IT'S PROCESSING... SYMBOLS FROM CELTIC, AZTEC, GREEK, SUMERIAN CULTURES... EVERY HUMAN SOCIETY IS REPRESENTED...
AND EVERY SINGLE SYMBOL IS DEPICTING THE SAME THING...
THE SUN!
SUN-WORSHIP IS THE FOUNDATION OF EVERY RELIGION -- THE SUN IS THE ONE SYMBOL THAT CONNECTS ALL HUMANITY.
EVERYONE INSTINCTIVELY RECOGNISES IT AS A SOURCE OF POWER, OF LIFE, OF STRENGTH...
THE AZTECS SACRIFICED THOUSANDS TO IT. AND ZA'S TRIBE -- THEY WORSHIPPED "ORB", REMEMBER?

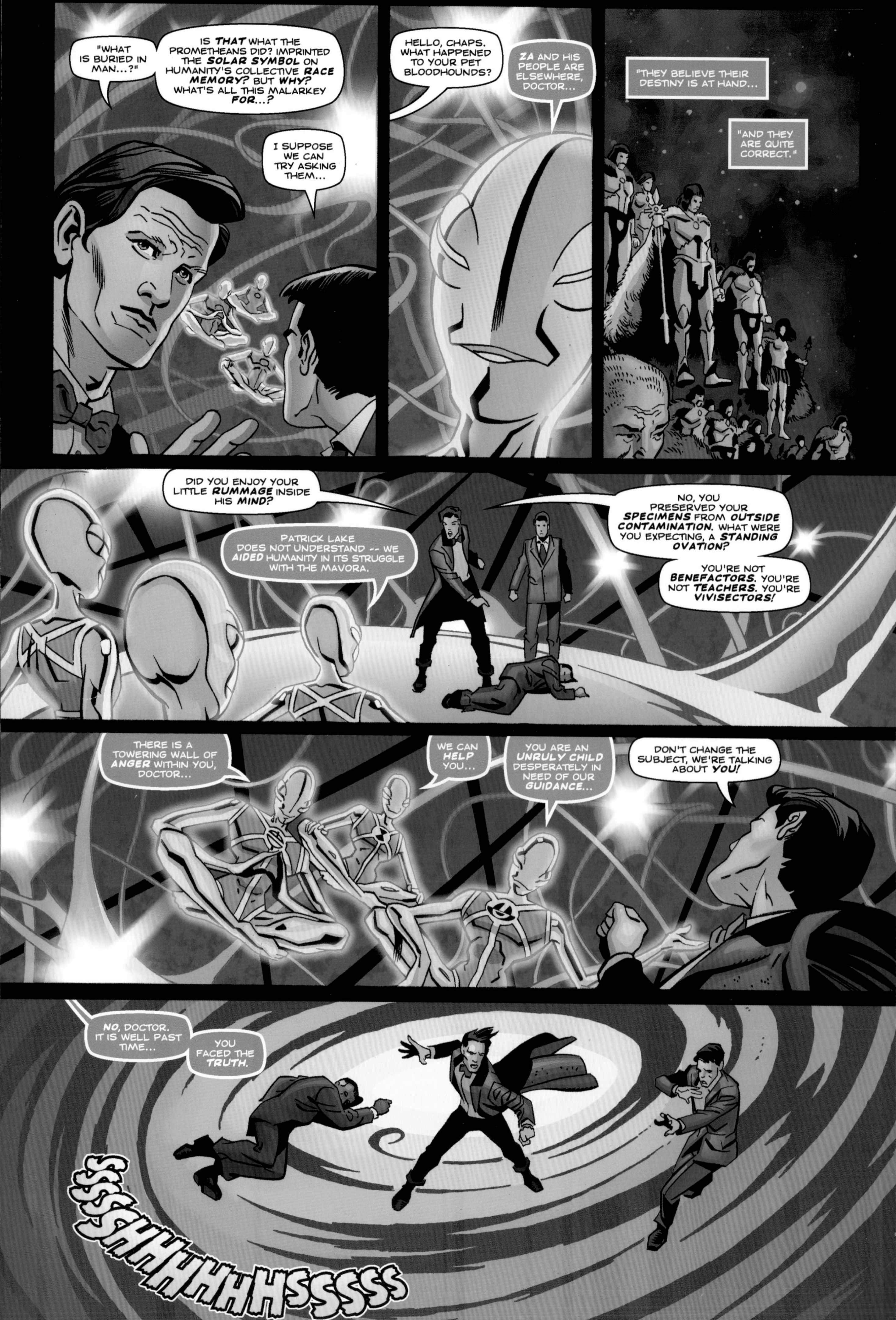
"WHAT IS BURIED IN MAN...?"
IS THAT WHAT THE PROMETHEANS DID? IMPRINTED THE SOLAR SYMBOL ON HUMANITY'S COLLECTIVE RACE MEMORY? BUT WHY? WHAT'S ALL THIS MALARKEY FOR...?
I SUPPOSE WE CAN TRY ASKING THEM...
HELLO, CHAPS. WHAT HAPPENED TO YOUR PET BLOODHOUNDS?
ZA AND HIS PEOPLE ARE ELSEWHERE, DOCTOR...
"THEY BELIEVE THEIR DESTINY IS AT HAND...
"AND THEY ARE QUITE CORRECT."
DID YOU ENJOY YOUR LITTLE RUMMAGE INSIDE HIS MIND?
PATRICK LAKE DOES NOT UNDERSTAND -- WE AIDED HUMANITY IN ITS STRUGGLE WITH THE MAVORA.
NO, YOU PRESERVED YOUR SPECIMENS FROM OUTSIDE CONTAMINATION. WHAT WERE YOU EXPECTING, A STANDING OVATION?
YOU'RE NOT BENEFACTORS. YOU'RE NOT TEACHERS. YOU'RE VIVISECTORS!
THERE IS A TOWERING WALL OF ANGER WITHIN YOU, DOCTOR...
WE CAN HELP YOU...
YOU ARE AN UNRULY CHILD DESPERATELY IN NEED OF OUR GUIDANCE...
DON'T CHANGE THE SUBJECT, WE'RE TALKING ABOUT YOU!
NO, DOCTOR. IT IS WELL PAST TIME...
YOU FACED THE TRUTH.
SSSSHHHHHHHSSSSS

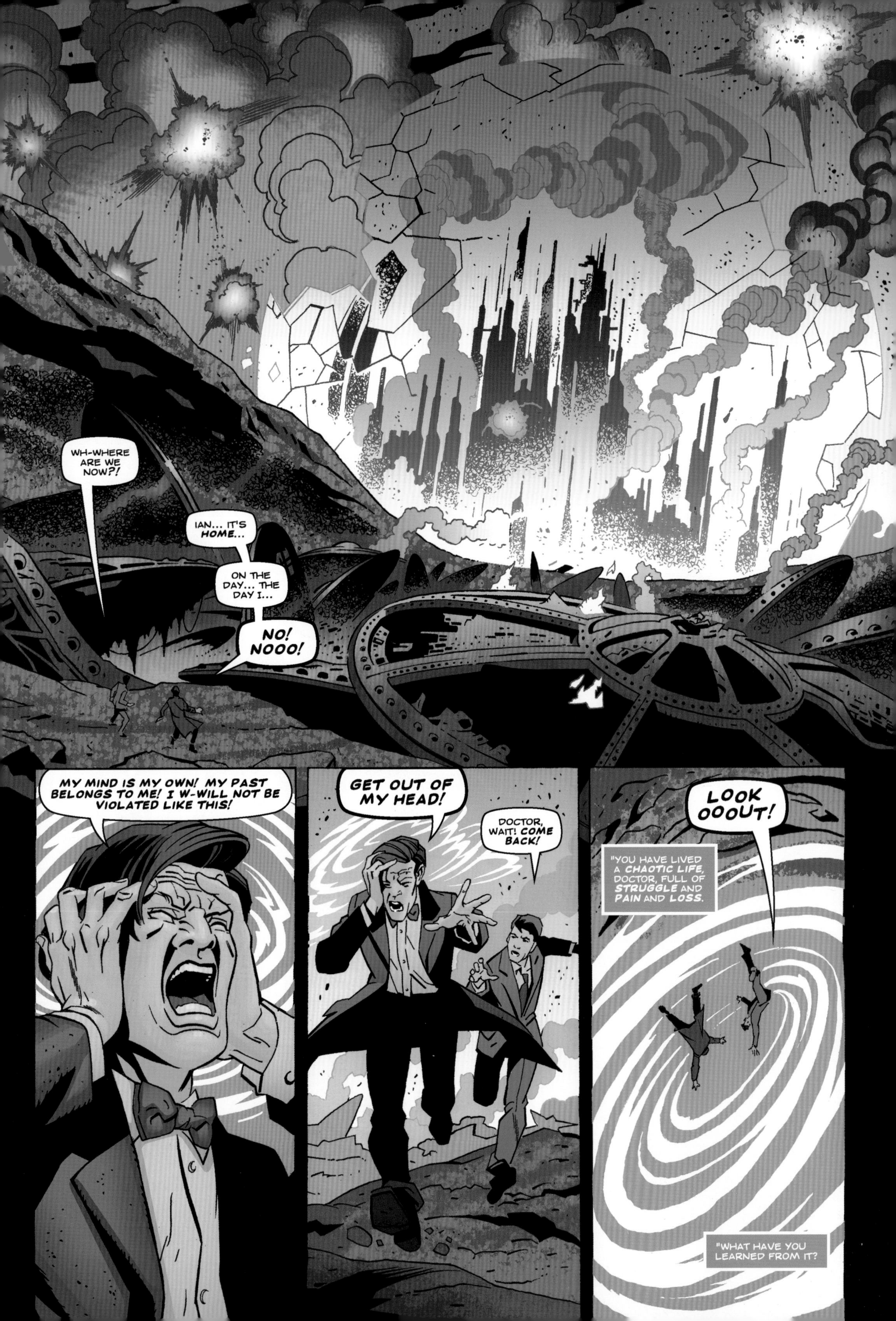
WH-WHERE ARE WE NOW?!
IAN... IT'S HOME...
ON THE DAY... THE DAY I...
NO! NOOO!
MY MIND IS MY OWN! MY PAST BELONGS TO ME! I W-WILL NOT BE VIOLATED LIKE THIS!
GET OUT OF MY HEAD!
DOCTOR, WAIT! COME BACK!
LOOK OOOUT!
"YOU HAVE LIVED A CHAOTIC LIFE, DOCTOR, FULL OF STRUGGLE AND PAIN AND LOSS.
"WHAT HAVE YOU LEARNED FROM IT?

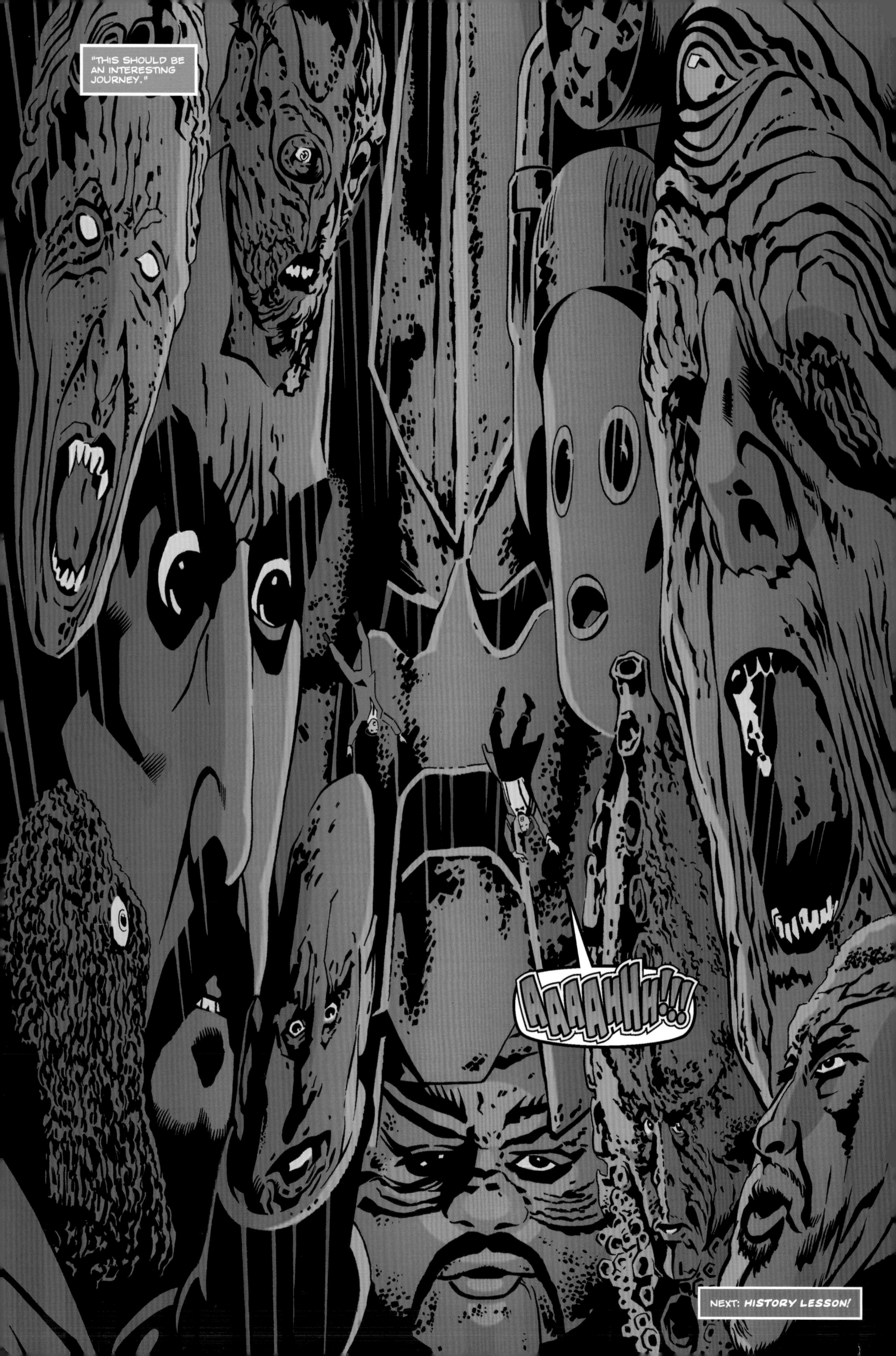
"THIS SHOULD BE AN INTERESTING JOURNEY."
AAAAHHH!!!
NEXT: HISTORY LESSON!

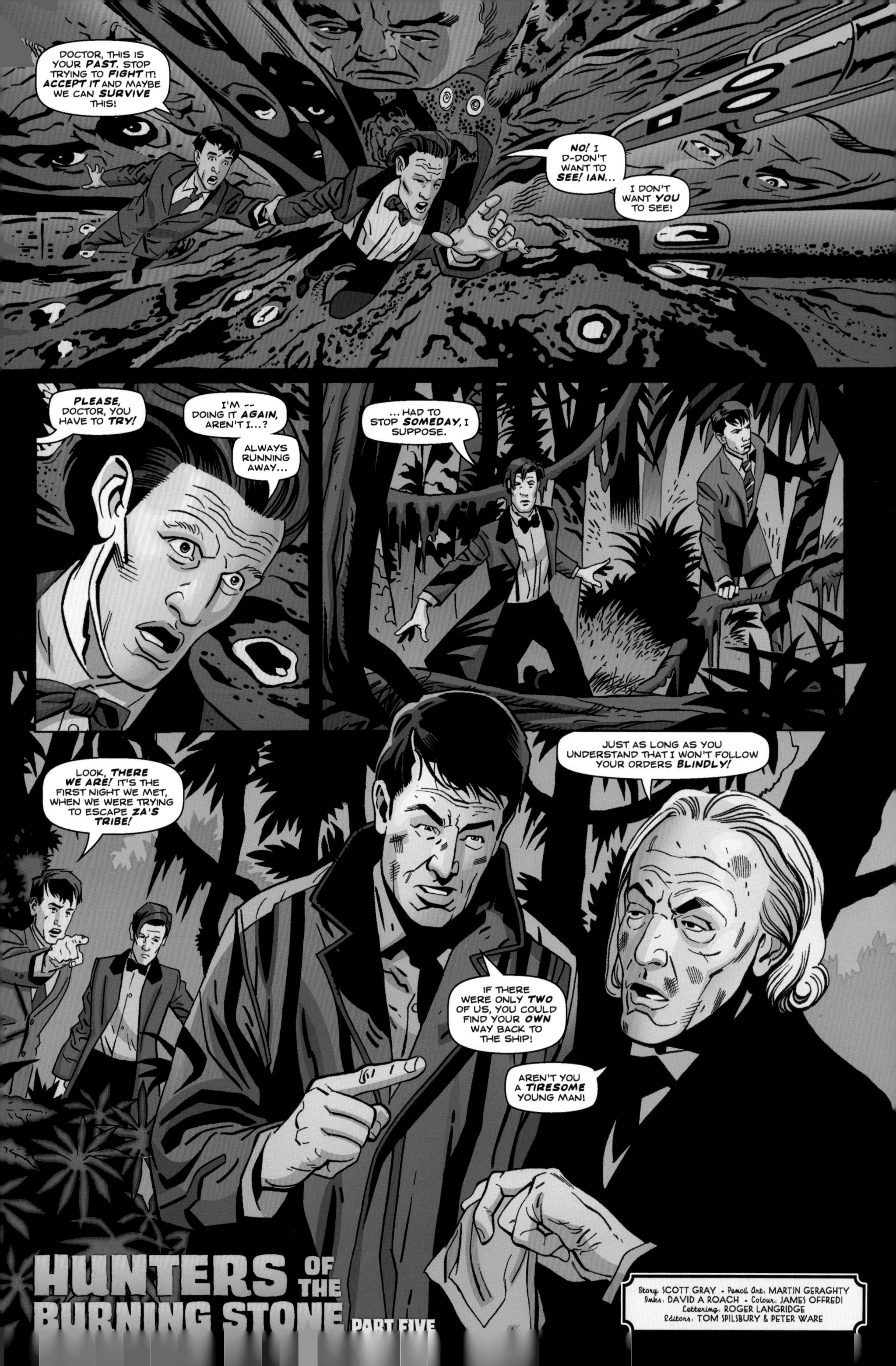
DOCTOR, THIS IS YOUR PAST. STOP TRYING TO FIGHT IT! ACCEPT IT AND MAYBE WE CAN SURVIVE THIS!
NO! I D-DON'T WANT TO SEE! IAN...
I DON'T WANT YOU TO SEE!
PLEASE, DOCTOR, YOU HAVE TO TRY!
I'M -- DOING IT AGAIN, AREN'T I...?
ALWAYS RUNNING AWAY...
...HAD TO STOP SOMEDAY, I SUPPOSE.
LOOK, THERE WE ARE! IT'S THE FIRST NIGHT WE MET, WHEN WE WERE TRYING TO ESCAPE ZA'S TRIBE!
JUST AS LONG AS YOU UNDERSTAND THAT I WON'T FOLLOW YOUR ORDERS BLINDLY!
IF THERE WERE ONLY TWO OF US, YOU COULD FIND YOUR OWN WAY BACK TO THE SHIP!
AREN'T YOU A TIRESOME YOUNG MAN!
HUNTERS OF THE BURNING STONE PART FIVE
Story: SCOTT GRAY • Pencil Art: MARTIN GERAGHTY
Inks: DAVID A ROACH • Colour: JAMES OFFREDI
Lettering: ROGER LANGRIDGE
Editors: TOM SPILSBURY & PETER WARE

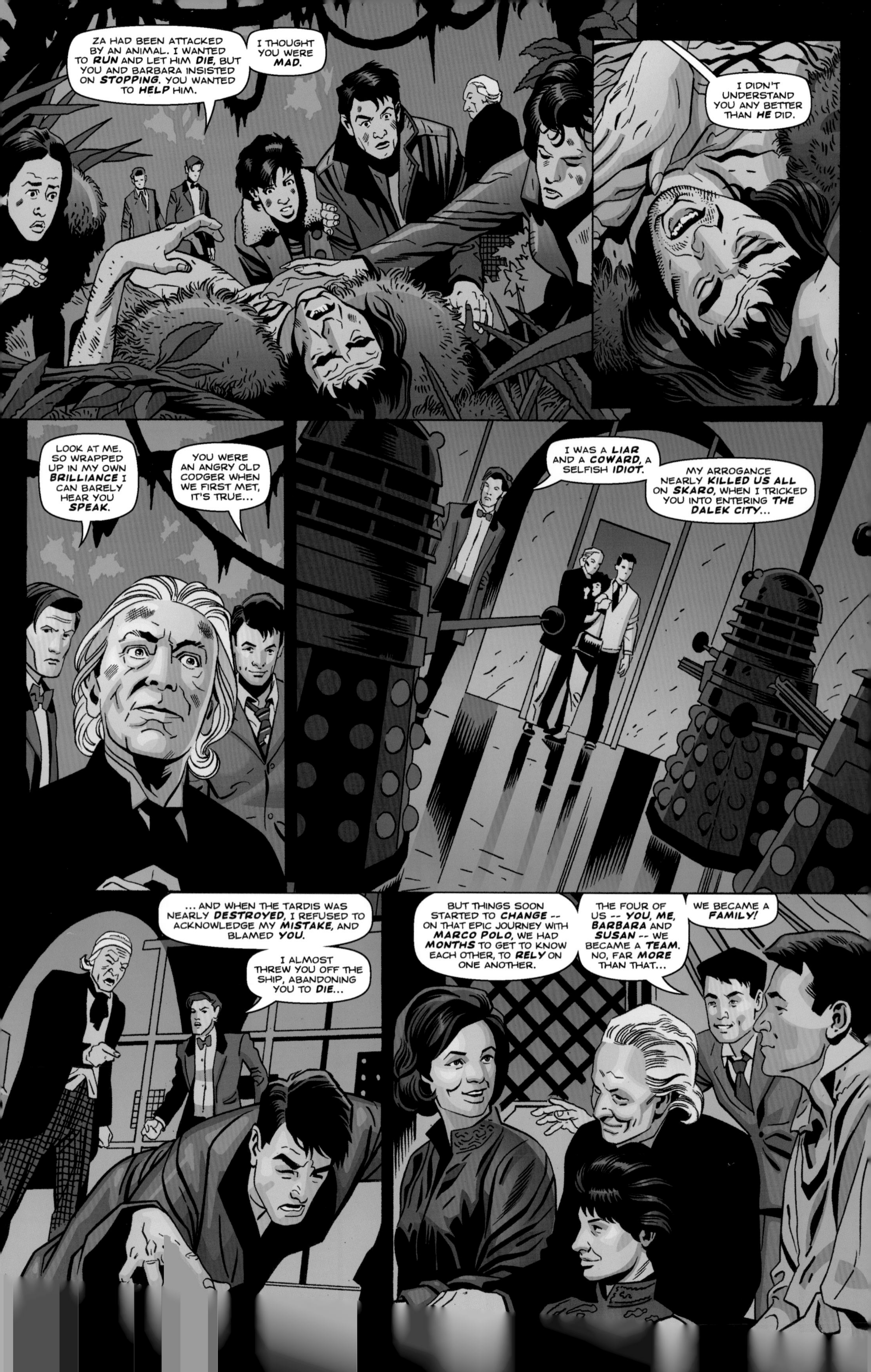
ZA HAD BEEN ATTACKED BY AN ANIMAL. I WANTED TO RUN AND LET HIM DIE, BUT YOU AND BARBARA INSISTED ON STOPPING. YOU WANTED TO HELP HIM.
I THOUGHT YOU WERE MAD.
I DIDN'T UNDERSTAND YOU ANY BETTER THAN HE DID.
LOOK AT ME. SO WRAPPED UP IN MY OWN BRILLIANCE I CAN BARELY HEAR YOU SPEAK.
YOU WERE AN ANGRY OLD CODGER WHEN WE FIRST MET, IT'S TRUE...
I WAS A LIAR AND A COWARD, A SELFISH IDIOT.
MY ARROGANCE NEARLY KILLED US ALL ON SKARO, WHEN I TRICKED YOU INTO ENTERING THE DALEK CITY...
...AND WHEN THE TARDIS WAS NEARLY DESTROYED, I REFUSED TO ACKNOWLEDGE MY MISTAKE, AND BLAMED YOU.
I ALMOST THREW YOU OFF THE SHIP, ABANDONING YOU TO DIE...
BUT THINGS SOON STARTED TO CHANGE -- ON THAT EPIC JOURNEY WITH MARCO POLO, WE HAD MONTHS TO GET TO KNOW EACH OTHER, TO RELY ON ONE ANOTHER.
THE FOUR OF US -- YOU, ME, BARBARA AND SUSAN -- WE BECAME A TEAM. NO, FAR MORE THAN THAT...
WE BECAME A FAMILY!

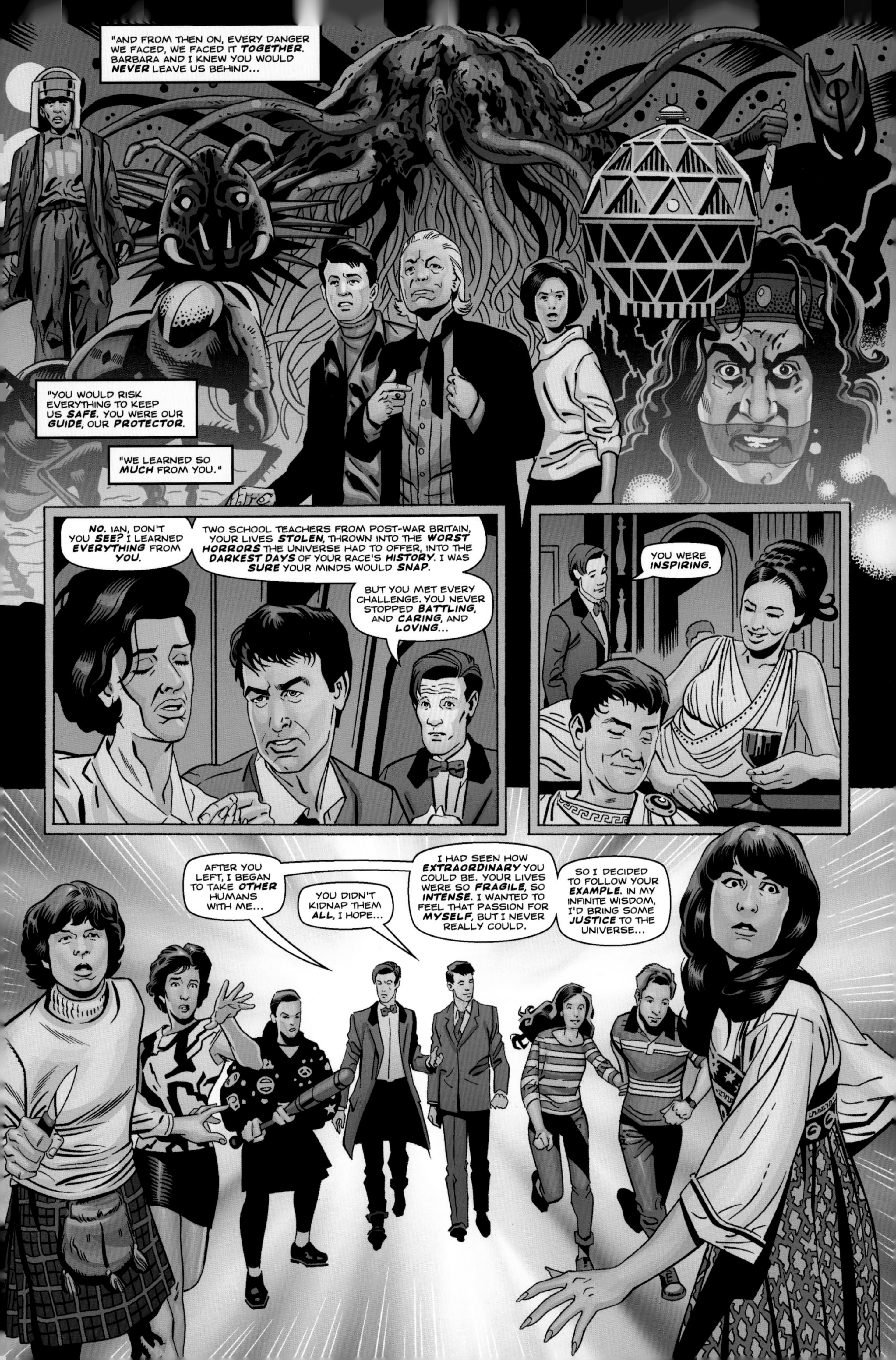
"AND FROM THEN ON, EVERY DANGER WE FACED, WE FACED IT TOGETHER. BARBARA AND I KNEW YOU WOULD NEVER LEAVE US BEHIND...
"YOU WOULD RISK EVERYTHING TO KEEP US SAFE. YOU WERE OUR GUIDE, OUR PROTECTOR.
"WE LEARNED SO MUCH FROM YOU."
NO. IAN, DON'T YOU SEE? I LEARNED EVERYTHING FROM YOU.
TWO SCHOOL TEACHERS FROM POST-WAR BRITAIN, YOUR LIVES STOLEN, THROWN INTO THE WORST HORRORS THE UNIVERSE HAD TO OFFER, INTO THE DARKEST DAYS OF YOUR RACE'S HISTORY. I WAS SURE YOUR MINDS WOULD SNAP.
BUT YOU MET EVERY CHALLENGE. YOU NEVER STOPPED BATTLING, AND CARING, AND LOVING...
YOU WERE INSPIRING.
AFTER YOU LEFT, I BEGAN TO TAKE OTHER HUMANS WITH ME...
YOU DIDN'T KIDNAP THEM ALL, I HOPE...
I HAD SEEN HOW EXTRAORDINARY YOU COULD BE. YOUR LIVES WERE SO FRAGILE, SO INTENSE. I WANTED TO FEEL THAT PASSION FOR MYSELF, BUT I NEVER REALLY COULD.
SO I DECIDED TO FOLLOW YOUR EXAMPLE. IN MY INFINITE WISDOM, I'D BRING SOME JUSTICE TO THE UNIVERSE...

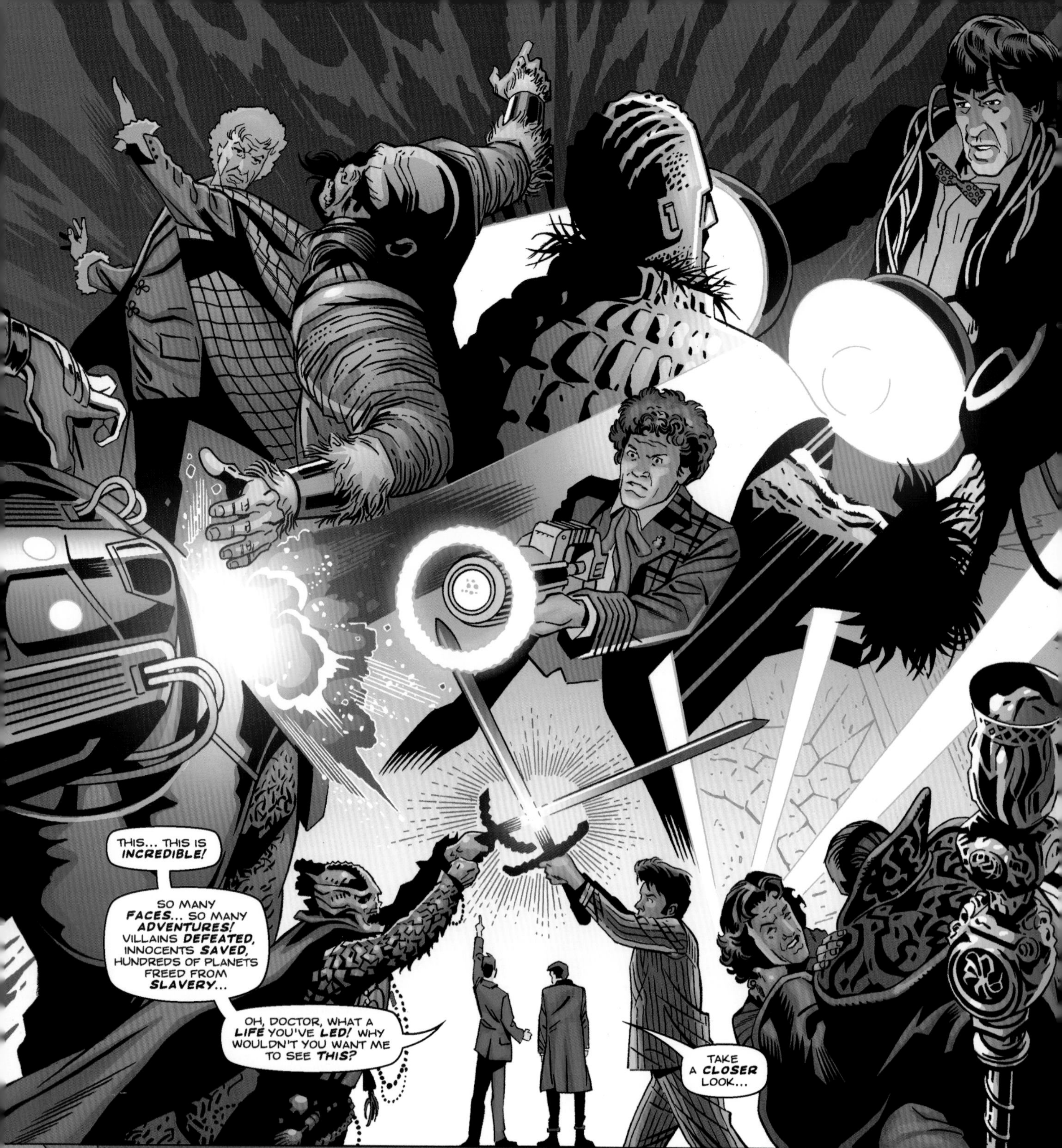
THIS... THIS IS INCREDIBLE!
SO MANY FACES... SO MANY ADVENTURES! VILLAINS DEFEATED, INNOCENTS SAVED, HUNDREDS OF PLANETS FREED FROM SLAVERY...
OH, DOCTOR, WHAT A LIFE YOU'VE LED! WHY WOULDN'T YOU WANT ME TO SEE THIS?
TAKE A CLOSER LOOK...

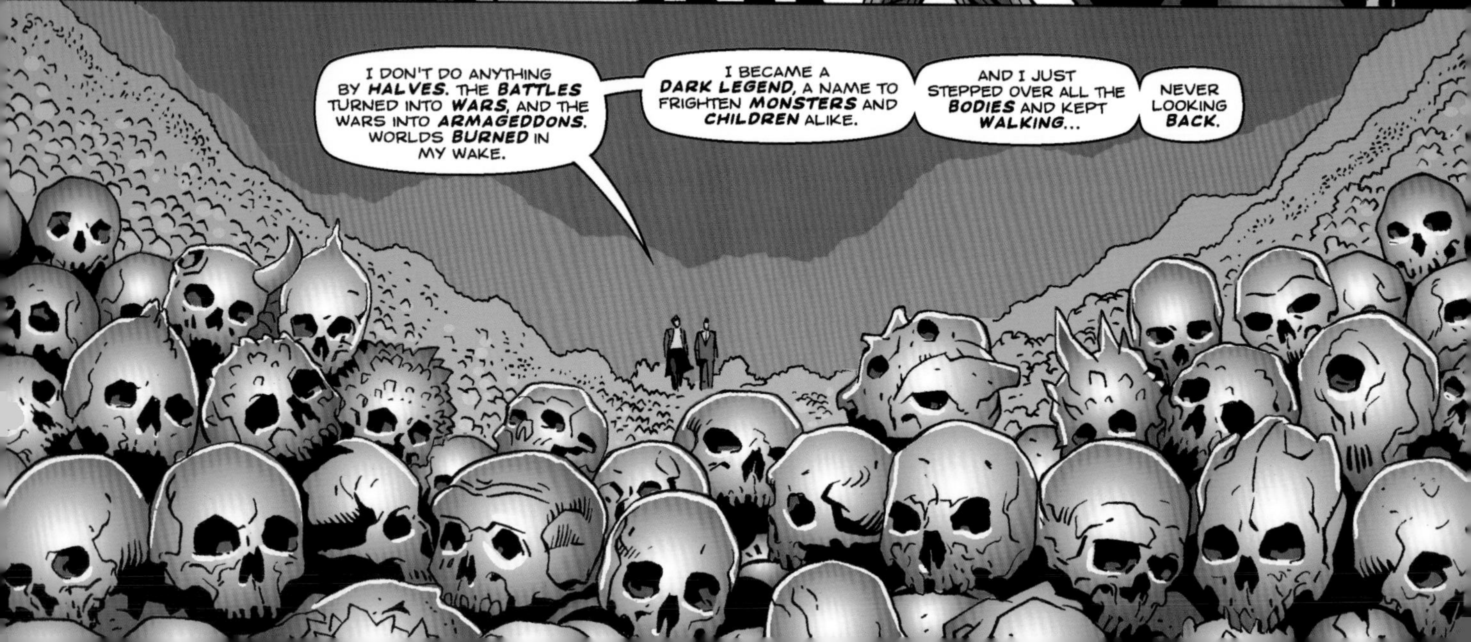
I DON'T DO ANYTHING BY HALVES. THE BATTLES TURNED INTO WARS, AND THE WARS INTO ARMAGEDDONS. WORLDS BURNED IN MY WAKE.
I BECAME A DARK LEGEND, A NAME TO FRIGHTEN MONSTERS AND CHILDREN ALIKE.
AND I JUST STEPPED OVER ALL THE BODIES AND KEPT WALKING...
NEVER LOOKING BACK.

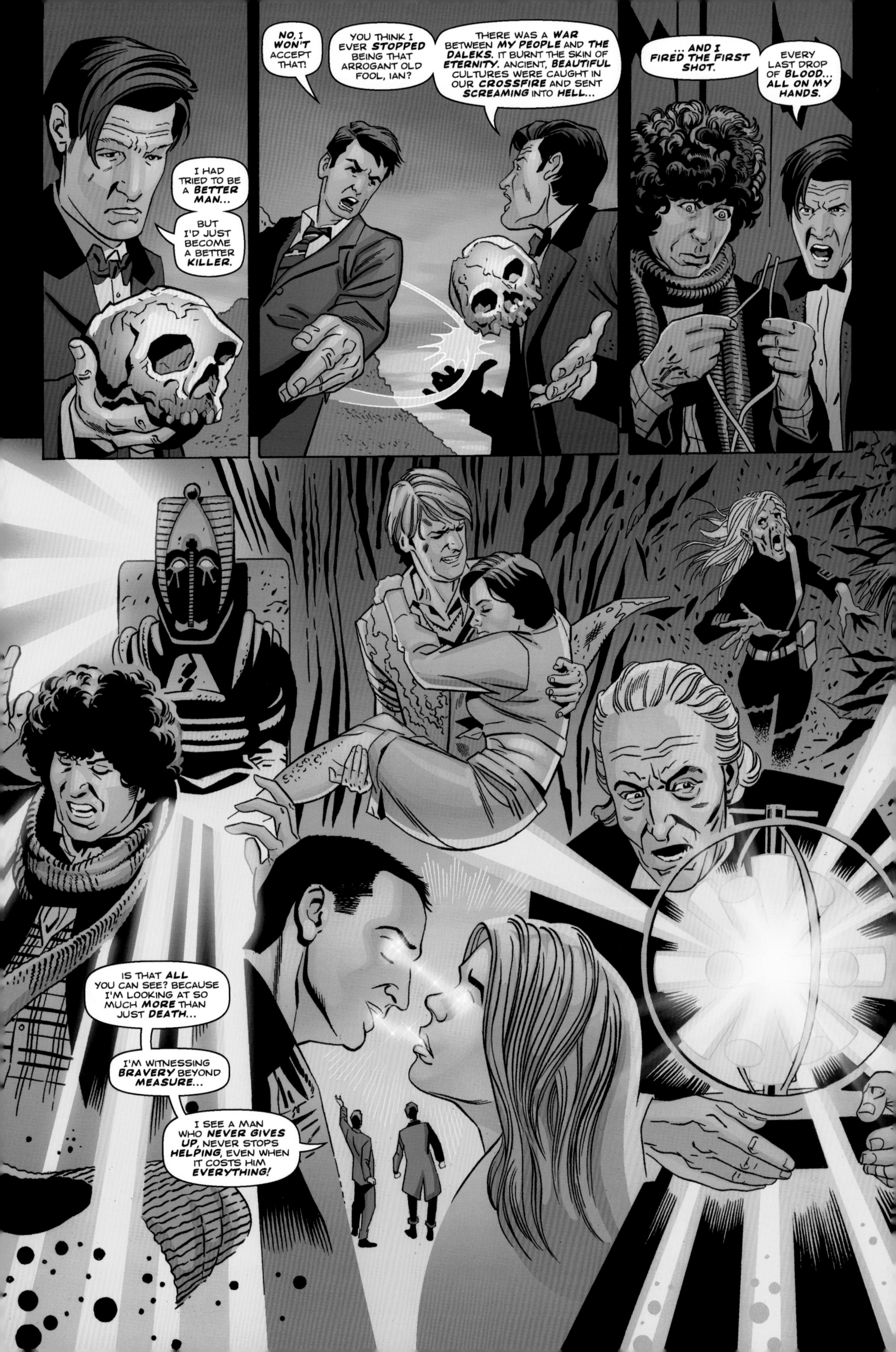
I HAD TRIED TO BE A BETTER MAN...
BUT I'D JUST BECOME A BETTER KILLER.
NO, I WON'T ACCEPT THAT!
YOU THINK I EVER STOPPED BEING THAT ARROGANT OLD FOOL, IAN?
THERE WAS A WAR BETWEEN MY PEOPLE AND THE DALEKS. IT BURNT THE SKIN OF ETERNITY. ANCIENT, BEAUTIFUL CULTURES WERE CAUGHT IN OUR CROSSFIRE AND SENT SCREAMING INTO HELL...
... AND I FIRED THE FIRST SHOT.
EVERY LAST DROP OF BLOOD... ALL ON MY HANDS.
IS THAT ALL YOU CAN SEE? BECAUSE I'M LOOKING AT SO MUCH MORE THAN JUST DEATH...
I'M WITNESSING BRAVERY BEYOND MEASURE...
I SEE A MAN WHO NEVER GIVES UP, NEVER STOPS HELPING, EVEN WHEN IT COSTS HIM EVERYTHING!

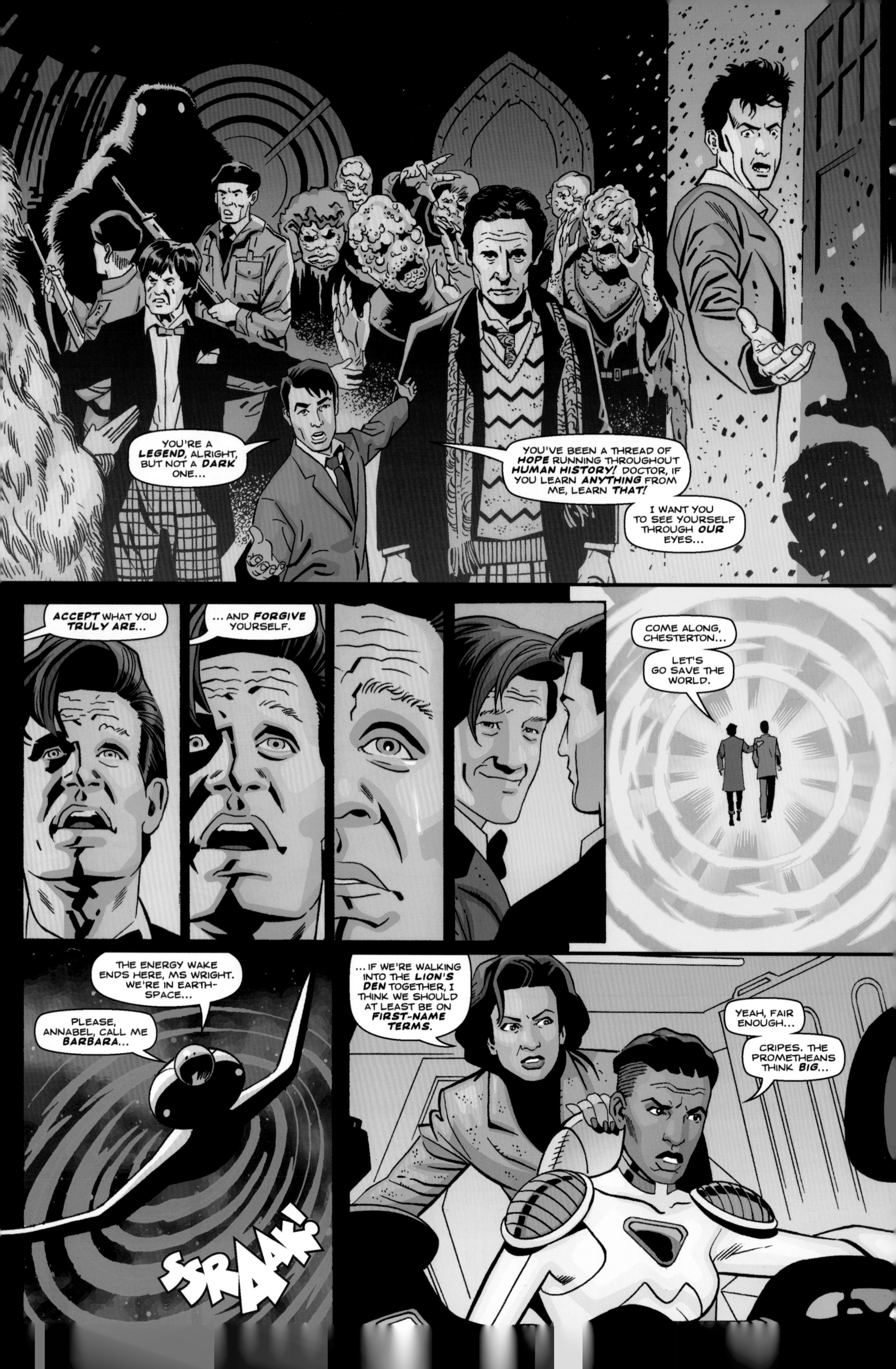
YOU'RE A LEGEND, ALRIGHT, BUT NOT A DARK ONE...
YOU'VE BEEN A THREAD OF HOPE RUNNING THROUGHOUT HUMAN HISTORY! DOCTOR, IF YOU LEARN ANYTHING FROM ME, LEARN THAT!
I WANT YOU TO SEE YOURSELF THROUGH OUR EYES...
ACCEPT WHAT YOU TRULY ARE...
... AND FORGIVE YOURSELF.
COME ALONG, CHESTERTON...
LET'S GO SAVE THE WORLD.
THE ENERGY WAKE ENDS HERE, MS WRIGHT. WE'RE IN EARTH-SPACE...
PLEASE, ANNABEL, CALL ME BARBARA...
SSRAAK!
... IF WE'RE WALKING INTO THE LION'S DEN TOGETHER, I THINK WE SHOULD AT LEAST BE ON FIRST-NAME TERMS.
YEAH, FAIR ENOUGH...
CRIPES. THE PROMETHEANS THINK BIG...

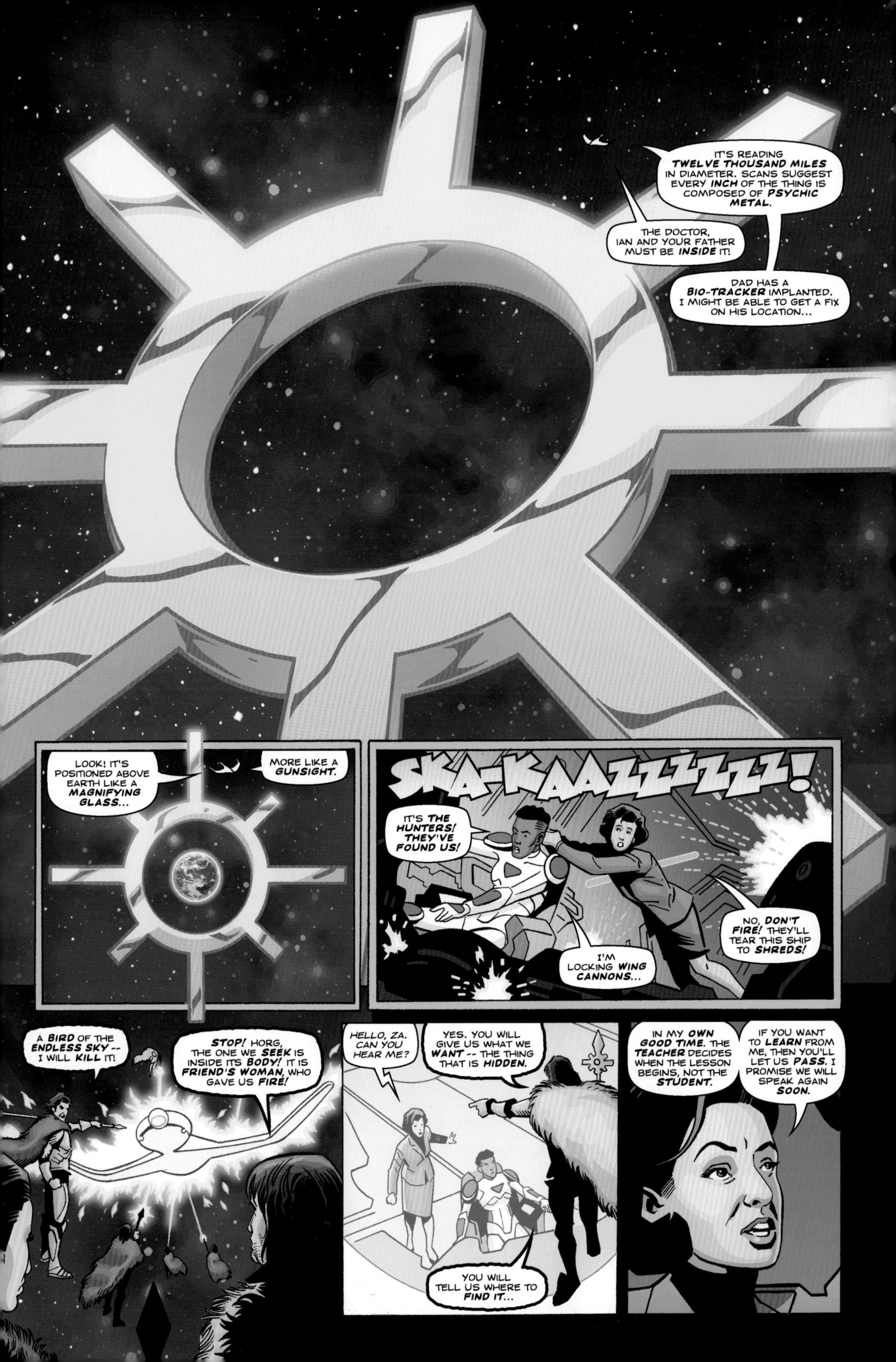
IT'S READING TWELVE THOUSAND MILES IN DIAMETER. SCANS SUGGEST EVERY INCH OF THE THING IS COMPOSED OF PSYCHIC METAL.
THE DOCTOR, IAN AND YOUR FATHER MUST BE INSIDE IT!
DAD HAS A BIO-TRACKER IMPLANTED. I MIGHT BE ABLE TO GET A FIX ON HIS LOCATION...
LOOK! IT'S POSITIONED ABOVE EARTH LIKE A MAGNIFYING GLASS...
MORE LIKE A GUNSIGHT.
SKA-KAAZZZZZZ!
IT'S THE HUNTERS! THEY'VE FOUND US!
I'M LOCKING WING CANNONS...
NO, DON'T FIRE! THEY'LL TEAR THIS SHIP TO SHREDS!
A BIRD OF THE ENDLESS SKY -- I WILL KILL IT!
STOP! HORG, THE ONE WE SEEK IS INSIDE ITS BODY! IT IS FRIEND'S WOMAN, WHO GAVE US FIRE!
HELLO, ZA. CAN YOU HEAR ME?
YES. YOU WILL GIVE US WHAT WE WANT -- THE THING THAT IS HIDDEN.
YOU WILL TELL US WHERE TO FIND IT...
IN MY OWN GOOD TIME. THE TEACHER DECIDES WHEN THE LESSON BEGINS, NOT THE STUDENT.
IF YOU WANT TO LEARN FROM ME, THEN YOU'LL LET US PASS. I PROMISE WE WILL SPEAK AGAIN SOON.

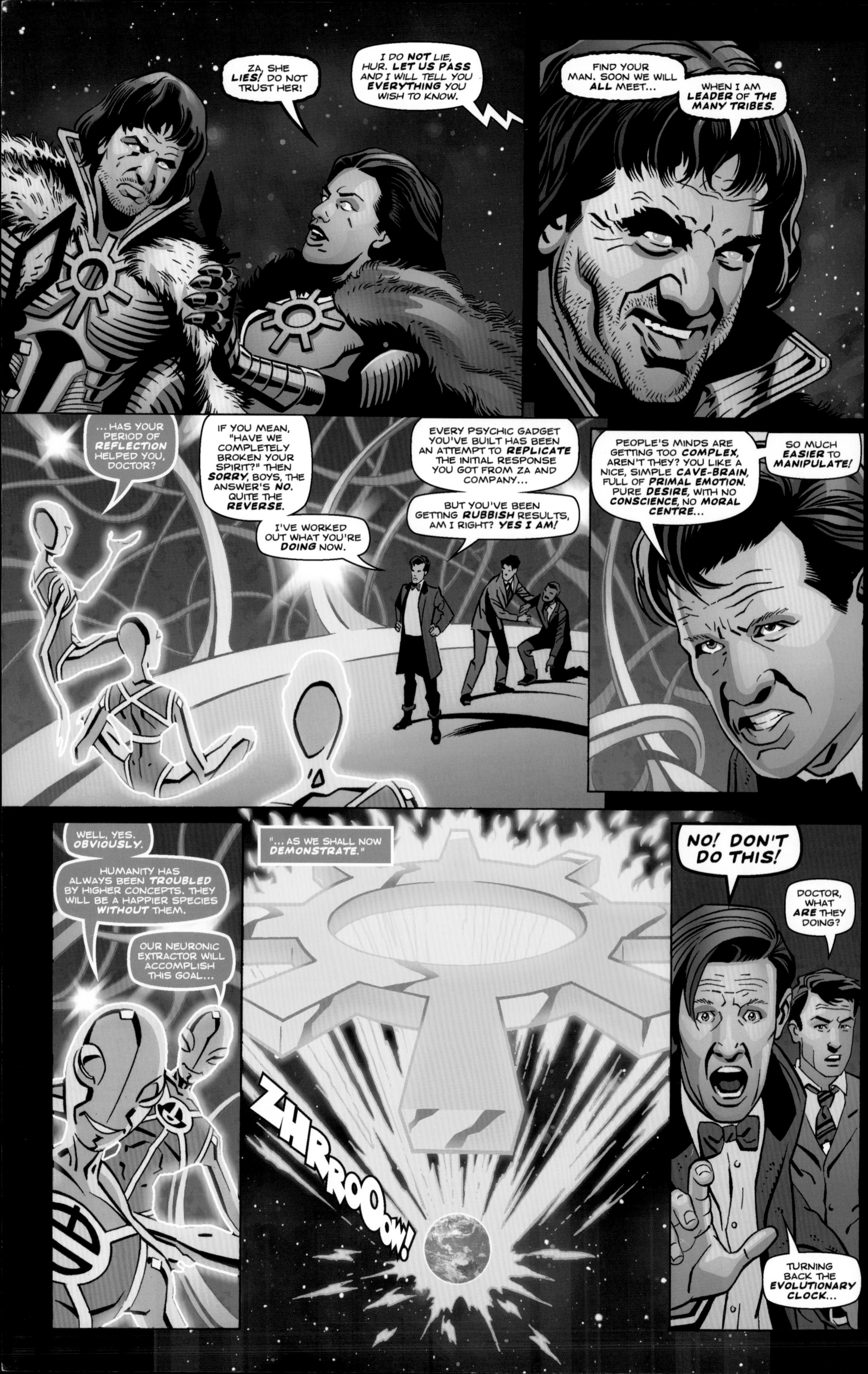
ZA, SHE LIES! DO NOT TRUST HER!
I DO NOT LIE, HUR. LET US PASS AND I WILL TELL YOU EVERYTHING YOU WISH TO KNOW.
FIND YOUR MAN. SOON WE WILL ALL MEET...
WHEN I AM LEADER OF THE MANY TRIBES.
...HAS YOUR PERIOD OF REFLECTION HELPED YOU, DOCTOR?
IF YOU MEAN, "HAVE WE COMPLETELY BROKEN YOUR SPIRIT?" THEN SORRY, BOYS, THE ANSWER'S NO. QUITE THE REVERSE.
I'VE WORKED OUT WHAT YOU'RE DOING NOW.
EVERY PSYCHIC GADGET YOU'VE BUILT HAS BEEN AN ATTEMPT TO REPLICATE THE INITIAL RESPONSE YOU GOT FROM ZA AND COMPANY...
BUT YOU'VE BEEN GETTING RUBBISH RESULTS, AM I RIGHT? YES I AM!
PEOPLE'S MINDS ARE GETTING TOO COMPLEX, AREN'T THEY? YOU LIKE A NICE, SIMPLE CAVE-BRAIN, FULL OF PRIMAL EMOTION. PURE DESIRE, WITH NO CONSCIENCE, NO MORAL CENTRE...
SO MUCH EASIER TO MANIPULATE!
WELL, YES. OBVIOUSLY.
HUMANITY HAS ALWAYS BEEN TROUBLED BY HIGHER CONCEPTS. THEY WILL BE A HAPPIER SPECIES WITHOUT THEM.
OUR NEURONIC EXTRACTOR WILL ACCOMPLISH THIS GOAL...
"...AS WE SHALL NOW DEMONSTRATE."
ZHRROOOOW!
NO! DON'T DO THIS!
DOCTOR, WHAT ARE THEY DOING?
TURNING BACK THE EVOLUTIONARY CLOCK...

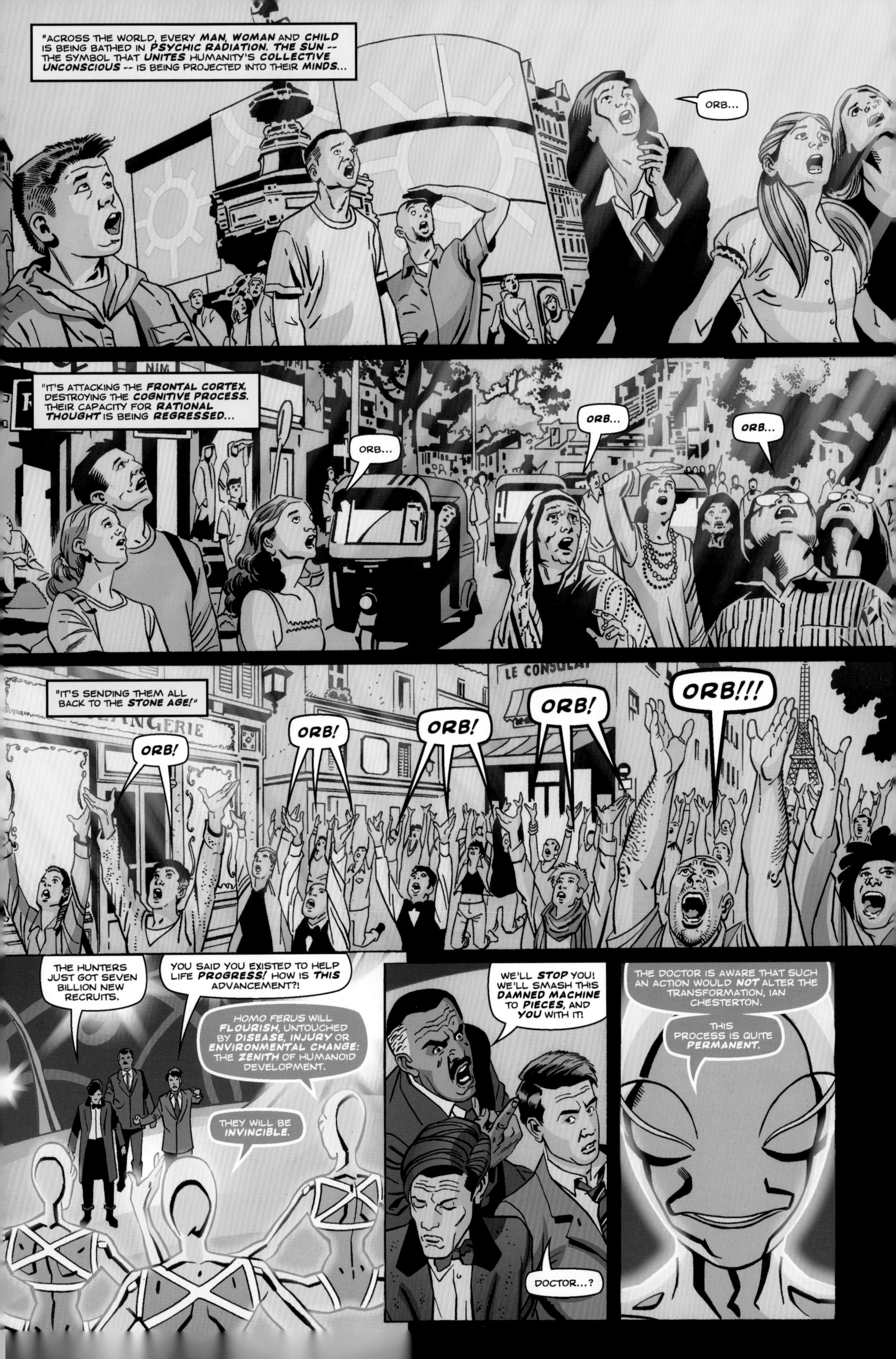
"ACROSS THE WORLD, EVERY MAN, WOMAN AND CHILD IS BEING BATHED IN PSYCHIC RADIATION. THE SUN -- THE SYMBOL THAT UNITES HUMANITY'S COLLECTIVE UNCONSCIOUS -- IS BEING PROJECTED INTO THEIR MINDS...
ORB...
"IT'S ATTACKING THE FRONTAL CORTEX, DESTROYING THE COGNITIVE PROCESS. THEIR CAPACITY FOR RATIONAL THOUGHT IS BEING REGRESSED...
ORB...
ORB...
ORB...
"IT'S SENDING THEM ALL BACK TO THE STONE AGE!"
ORB!
ORB!
ORB!
ORB!
ORB!!!
THE HUNTERS JUST GOT SEVEN BILLION NEW RECRUITS.
YOU SAID YOU EXISTED TO HELP LIFE PROGRESS! HOW IS THIS ADVANCEMENT?!
HOMO FERUS WILL FLOURISH, UNTOUCHED BY DISEASE, INJURY OR ENVIRONMENTAL CHANGE: THE ZENITH OF HUMANOID DEVELOPMENT.
THEY WILL BE INVINCIBLE.
WE'LL STOP YOU! WE'LL SMASH THIS DAMNED MACHINE TO PIECES, AND YOU WITH IT!
DOCTOR...?
THE DOCTOR IS AWARE THAT SUCH AN ACTION WOULD NOT ALTER THE TRANSFORMATION, IAN CHESTERTON.
THIS PROCESS IS QUITE PERMANENT.

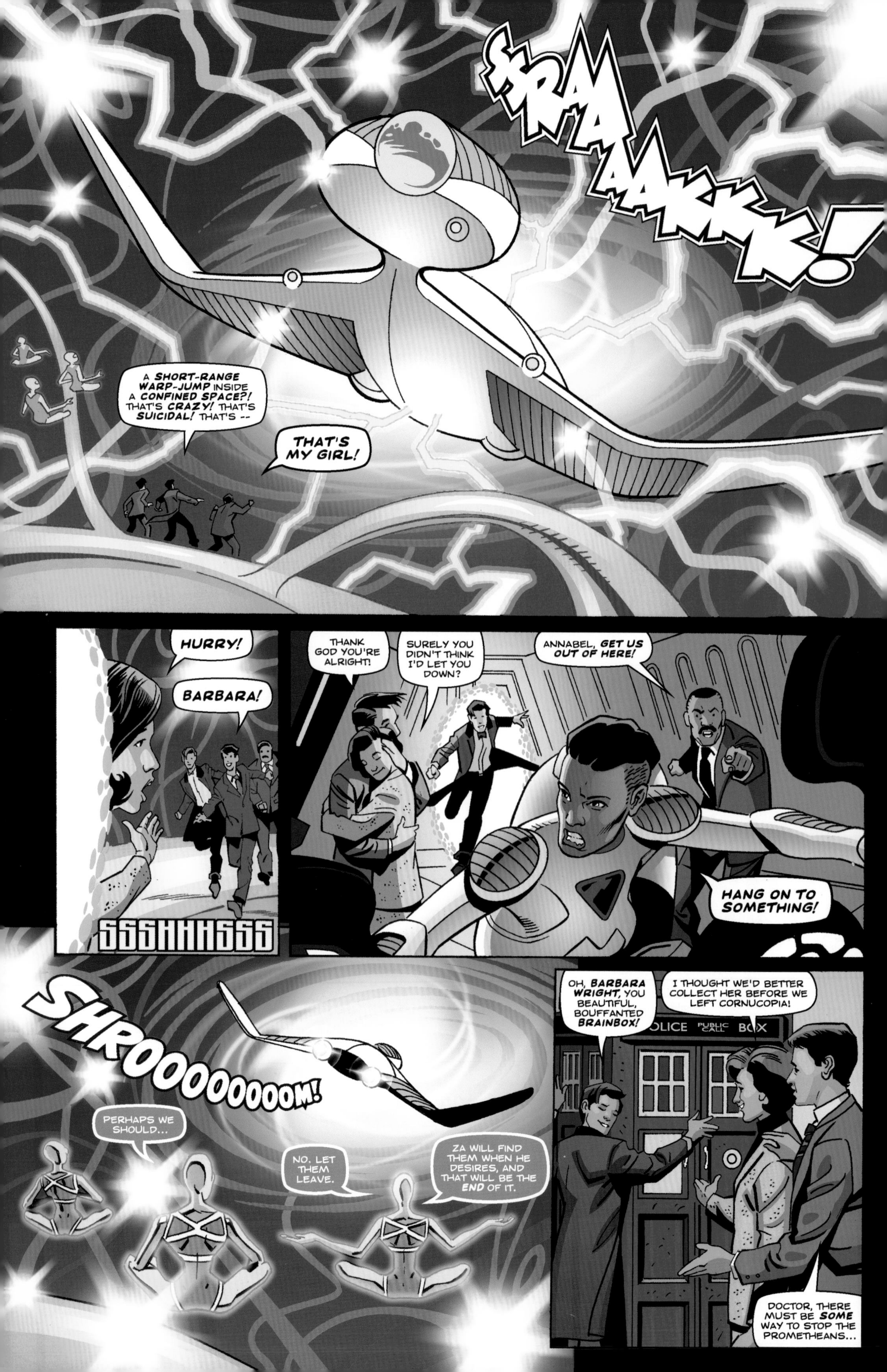
SKRAAAKKK!
A SHORT-RANGE WARP-JUMP INSIDE A CONFINED SPACE?! THAT'S CRAZY! THAT'S SUICIDAL! THAT'S --
THAT'S MY GIRL!
HURRY!
BARBARA!
SSSHHHSSS
THANK GOD YOU'RE ALRIGHT!
SURELY YOU DIDN'T THINK I'D LET YOU DOWN?
ANNABEL, GET US OUT OF HERE!
HANG ON TO SOMETHING!
SHROOOOOOOOOM!
PERHAPS WE SHOULD...
NO. LET THEM LEAVE.
ZA WILL FIND THEM WHEN HE DESIRES, AND THAT WILL BE THE END OF IT.
OH, BARBARA WRIGHT, YOU BEAUTIFUL, BOUFFANTED BRAINBOX!
I THOUGHT WE'D BETTER COLLECT HER BEFORE WE LEFT CORNUCOPIA!
OLICE PUBLIC CALL BOX
DOCTOR, THERE MUST BE SOME WAY TO STOP THE PROMETHEANS...

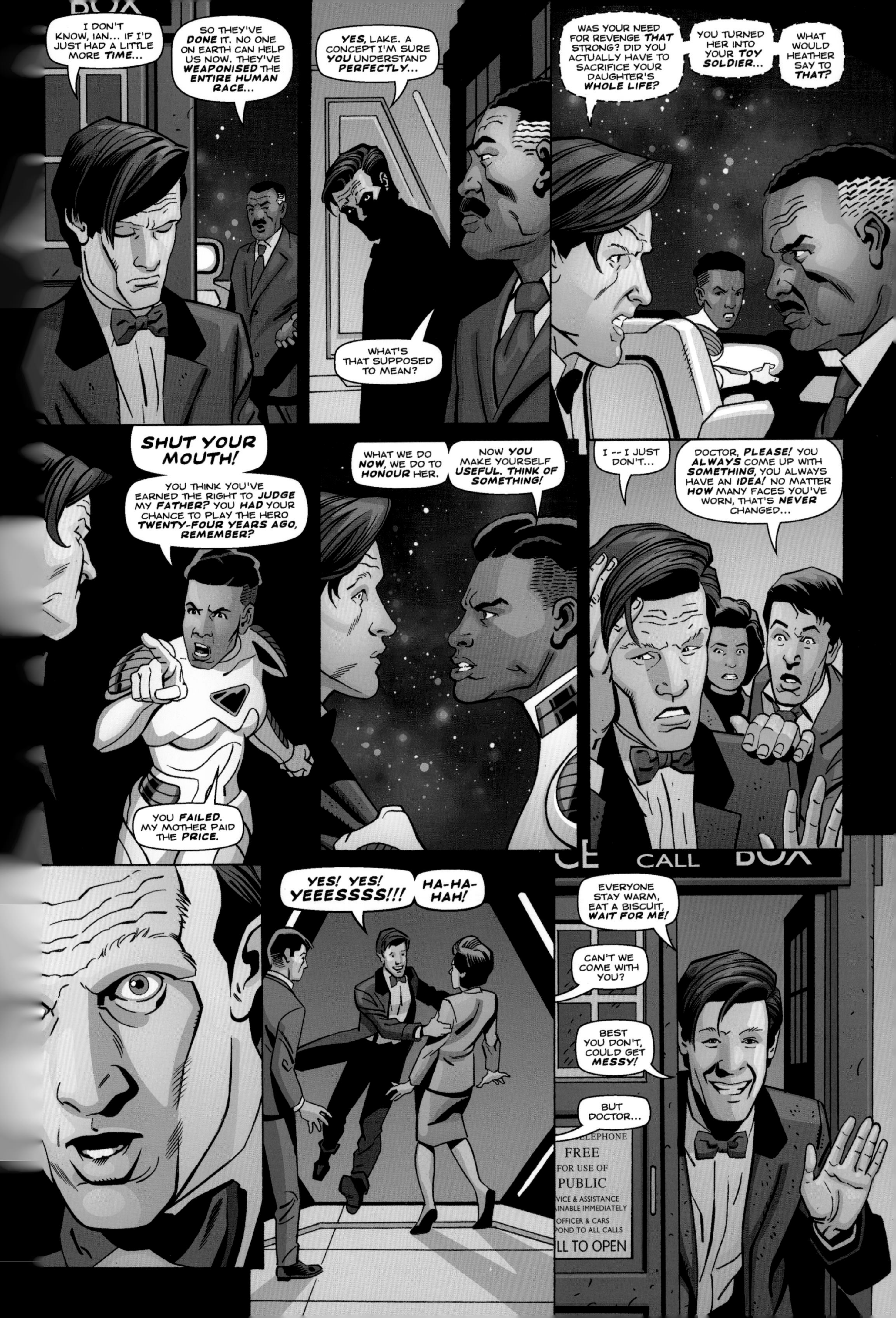

BOX
I DON'T KNOW, IAN... IF I'D JUST HAD A LITTLE MORE TIME...
SO THEY'VE DONE IT. NO ONE ON EARTH CAN HELP US NOW. THEY'VE WEAPONISED THE ENTIRE HUMAN RACE...
YES, LAKE. A CONCEPT I'M SURE YOU UNDERSTAND PERFECTLY...
WHAT'S THAT SUPPOSED TO MEAN?
WAS YOUR NEED FOR REVENGE THAT STRONG? DID YOU ACTUALLY HAVE TO SACRIFICE YOUR DAUGHTER'S WHOLE LIFE?
YOU TURNED HER INTO YOUR TOY SOLDIER...
WHAT WOULD HEATHER SAY TO THAT?
SHUT YOUR MOUTH!
YOU THINK YOU'VE EARNED THE RIGHT TO JUDGE MY FATHER? YOU HAD YOUR CHANCE TO PLAY THE HERO TWENTY-FOUR YEARS AGO, REMEMBER?
YOU FAILED. MY MOTHER PAID THE PRICE.
WHAT WE DO NOW, WE DO TO HONOUR HER.
NOW YOU MAKE YOURSELF USEFUL. THINK OF SOMETHING!
I -- I JUST DON'T...
DOCTOR, PLEASE! YOU ALWAYS COME UP WITH SOMETHING, YOU ALWAYS HAVE AN IDEA! NO MATTER HOW MANY FACES YOU'VE WORN, THAT'S NEVER CHANGED...
YES! YES! YEEESSSS!!!
HA-HA-HAH!
CE CALL BOX
EVERYONE STAY WARM, EAT A BISCUIT, WAIT FOR ME!
CAN'T WE COME WITH YOU?
BEST YOU DON'T, COULD GET MESSY!
BUT DOCTOR...
FREE
FOR USE OF
PUBLIC
VICE & ASSISTANCE
AINABLE IMMEDIATELY
OFFICER & CARS
POND TO ALL CALLS
LL TO OPEN

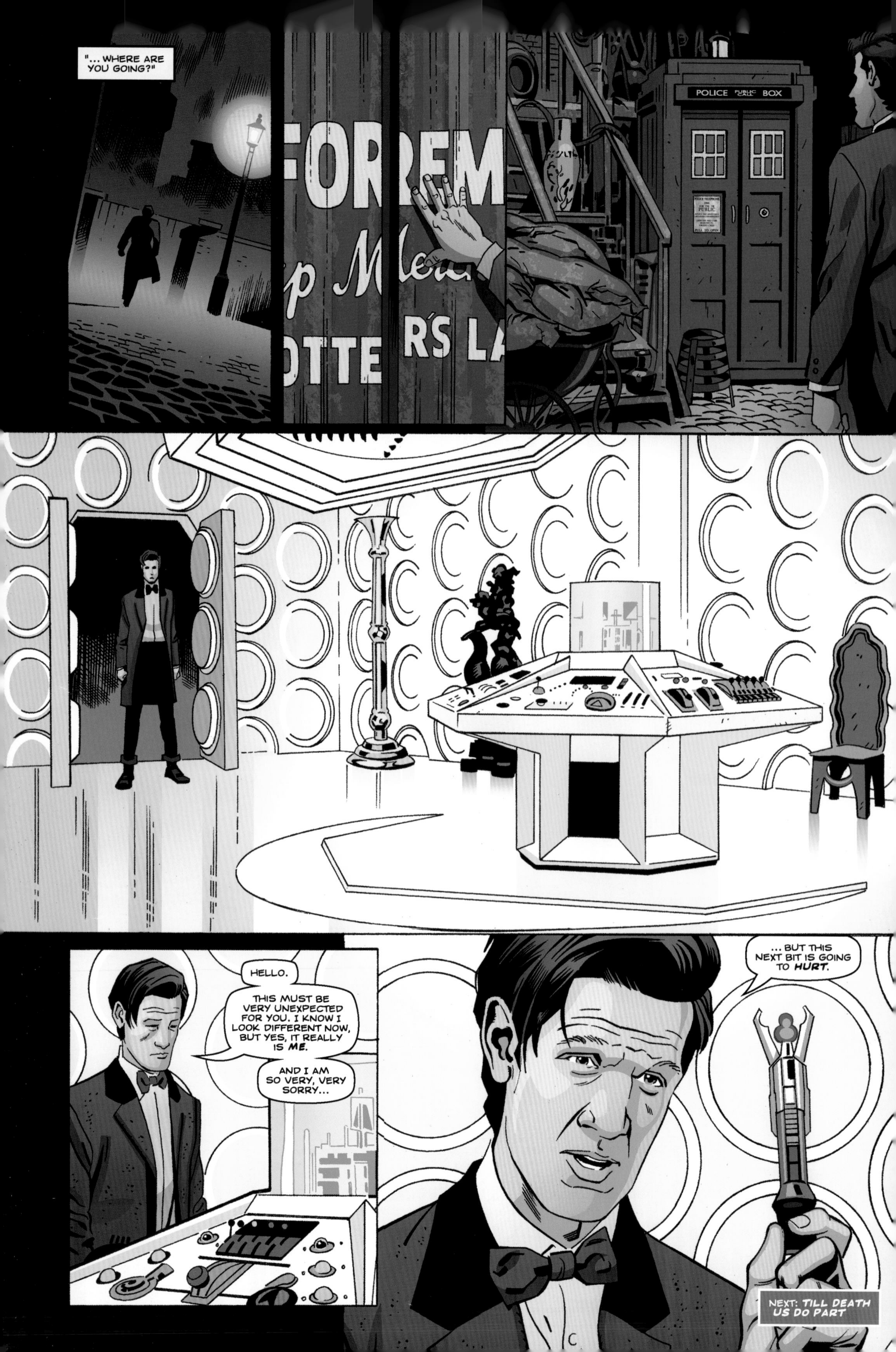
"... WHERE ARE YOU GOING?"
FOREM
OTTE
R'S LA
POLICE PUBLIC CALL BOX
HELLO.
THIS MUST BE VERY UNEXPECTED FOR YOU. I KNOW I LOOK DIFFERENT NOW, BUT YES, IT REALLY IS ME.
AND I AM SO VERY, VERY SORRY...
... BUT THIS NEXT BIT IS GOING TO HURT.
NEXT: TILL DEATH US DO PART

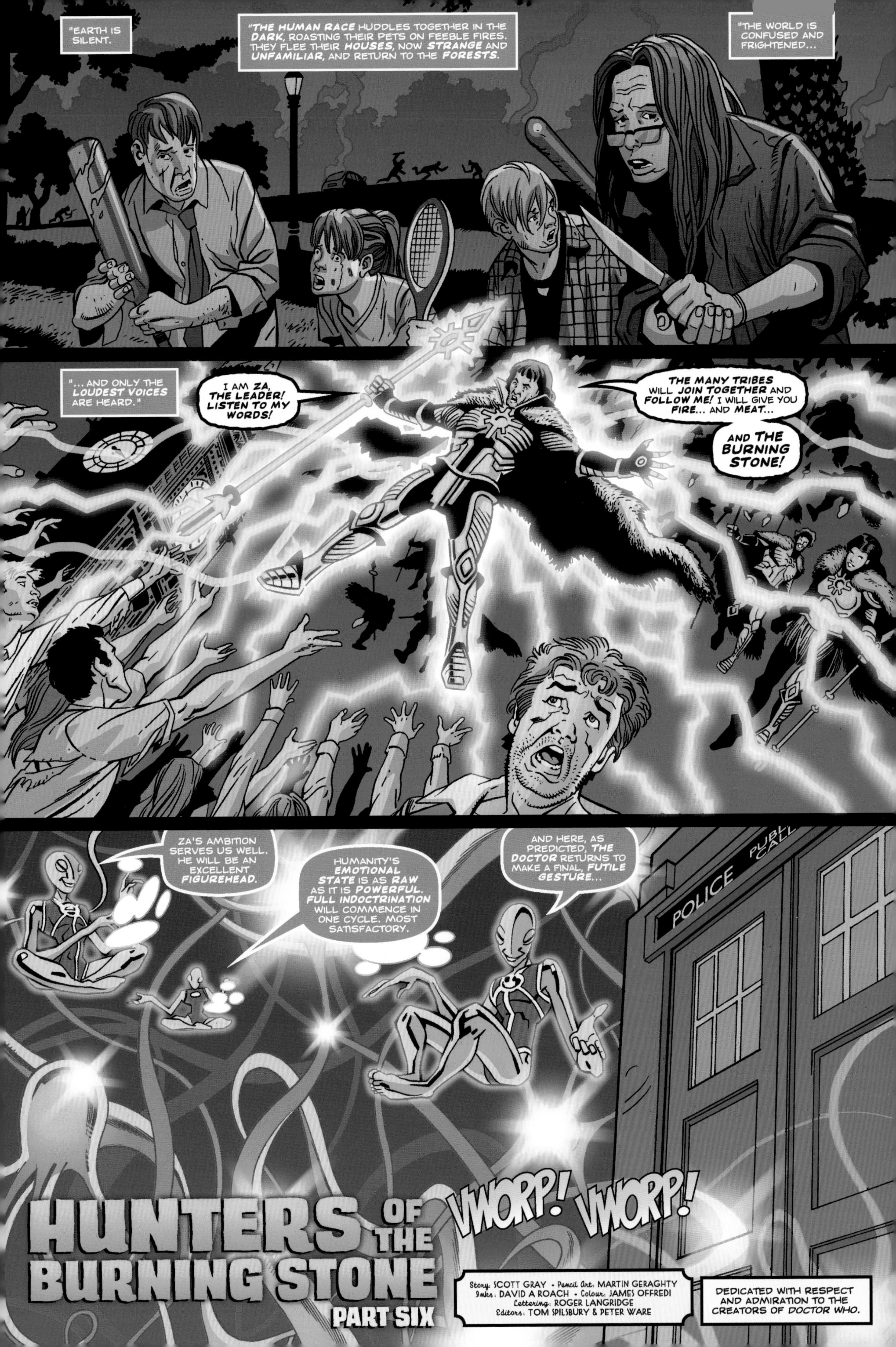
"EARTH IS SILENT.
"THE HUMAN RACE HUDDLES TOGETHER IN THE DARK, ROASTING THEIR PETS ON FEEBLE FIRES. THEY FLEE THEIR HOUSES, NOW STRANGE AND UNFAMILIAR, AND RETURN TO THE FORESTS.
"THE WORLD IS CONFUSED AND FRIGHTENED...
"...AND ONLY THE LOUDEST VOICES ARE HEARD."
I AM ZA, THE LEADER! LISTEN TO MY WORDS!
THE MANY TRIBES WILL JOIN TOGETHER AND FOLLOW ME! I WILL GIVE YOU FIRE... AND MEAT...
AND THE BURNING STONE!
ZA'S AMBITION SERVES US WELL. HE WILL BE AN EXCELLENT FIGUREHEAD.
HUMANITY'S EMOTIONAL STATE IS AS RAW AS IT IS POWERFUL. FULL INDOCTRINATION WILL COMMENCE IN ONE CYCLE. MOST SATISFACTORY.
AND HERE, AS PREDICTED, THE DOCTOR RETURNS TO MAKE A FINAL, FUTILE GESTURE...
POLICE PUBLIC CALL
VWORP! VWORP!
HUNTERS OF THE BURNING STONE
PART SIX
Story: SCOTT GRAY • Pencil Art: MARTIN GERAGHTY
Inks: DAVID A ROACH • Colour: JAMES OFFREDI
Lettering: ROGER LANGRIDGE
Editors: TOM SPILSBURY & PETER WARE
DEDICATED WITH RESPECT AND ADMIRATION TO THE CREATORS OF DOCTOR WHO.

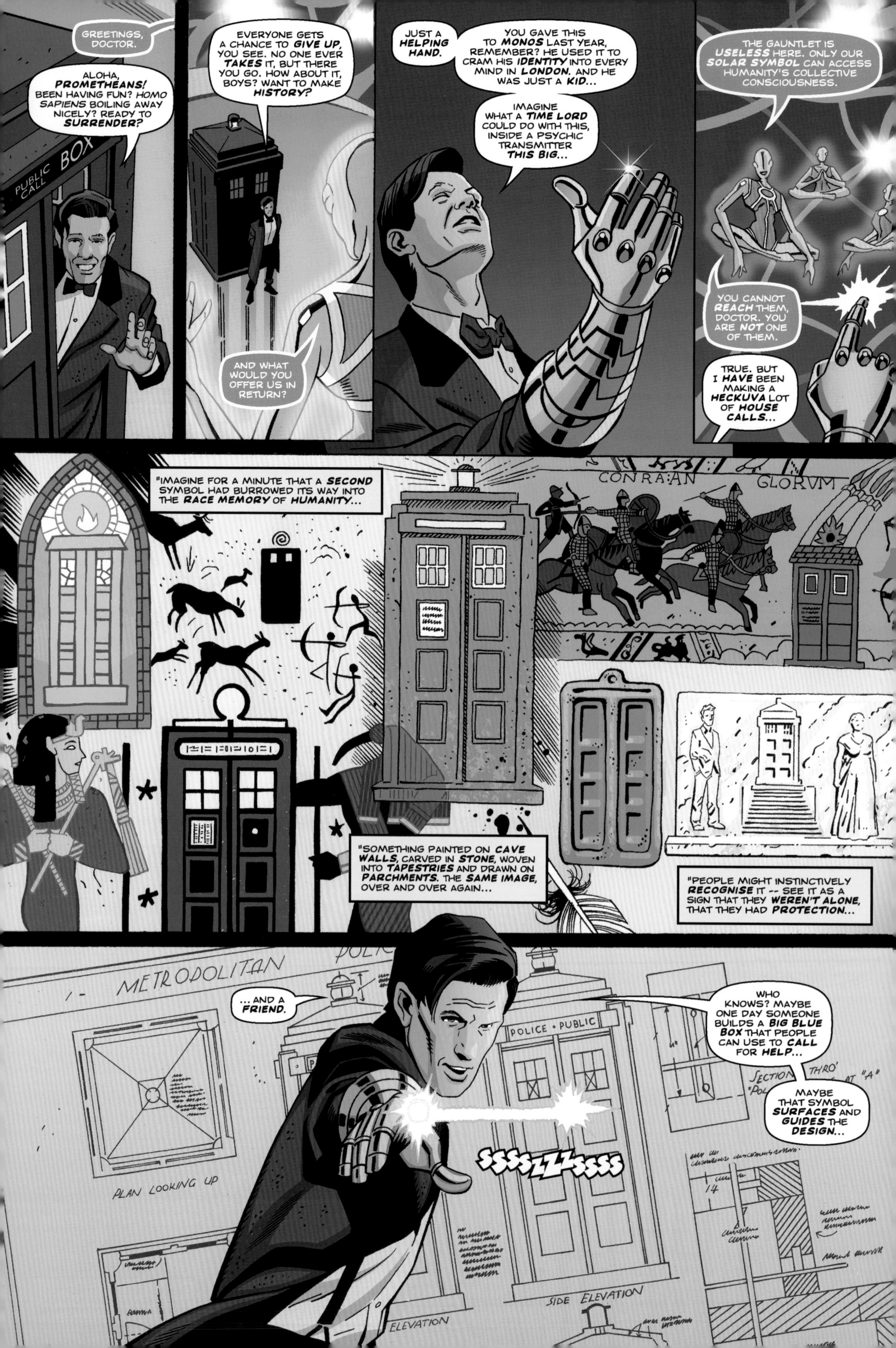
GREETINGS, DOCTOR.
ALOHA, PROMETHEANS! BEEN HAVING FUN? HOMO SAPIENS BOILING AWAY NICELY? READY TO SURRENDER?
PUBLIC CALL BOX
EVERYONE GETS A CHANCE TO GIVE UP, YOU SEE. NO ONE EVER TAKES IT, BUT THERE YOU GO. HOW ABOUT IT, BOYS? WANT TO MAKE HISTORY?
AND WHAT WOULD YOU OFFER US IN RETURN?
JUST A HELPING HAND.
YOU GAVE THIS TO MONOS LAST YEAR, REMEMBER? HE USED IT TO CRAM HIS IDENTITY INTO EVERY MIND IN LONDON. AND HE WAS JUST A KID...
IMAGINE WHAT A TIME LORD COULD DO WITH THIS, INSIDE A PSYCHIC TRANSMITTER THIS BIG...
THE GAUNTLET IS USELESS HERE. ONLY OUR SOLAR SYMBOL CAN ACCESS HUMANITY'S COLLECTIVE CONSCIOUSNESS.
YOU CANNOT REACH THEM, DOCTOR. YOU ARE NOT ONE OF THEM.
TRUE. BUT I HAVE BEEN MAKING A HECKUVA LOT OF HOUSE CALLS...
"IMAGINE FOR A MINUTE THAT A SECOND SYMBOL HAD BURROWED ITS WAY INTO THE RACE MEMORY OF HUMANITY...
CONRA:AN
GLORVM
"SOMETHING PAINTED ON CAVE WALLS, CARVED IN STONE, WOVEN INTO TAPESTRIES AND DRAWN ON PARCHMENTS. THE SAME IMAGE, OVER AND OVER AGAIN...
"PEOPLE MIGHT INSTINCTIVELY RECOGNISE IT -- SEE IT AS A SIGN THAT THEY WEREN'T ALONE, THAT THEY HAD PROTECTION...
METROPOLITAN
...AND A FRIEND.
POLICE · PUBLIC
WHO KNOWS? MAYBE ONE DAY SOMEONE BUILDS A BIG BLUE BOX THAT PEOPLE CAN USE TO CALL FOR HELP...
MAYBE THAT SYMBOL SURFACES AND GUIDES THE DESIGN...
SECTION THRO'
SSSSZZZSSSS
PLAN LOOKING UP
SIDE ELEVATION
ELEVATION

"...WOULDN'T *THAT* BE A LAUGH?"

RRRUUMBBLLE!

WHAT -- WHAT IS *THIS?* IDENTIFY! *IDENTIFY!*

NEURON PLATFORM IS *TRANSFORMING!* I REPEAT...

"NEURON PLATFORM IS *TRANSFORMING!*"

TOOK ME A LONG OLD WHILE... AND I NEEDED A LOT OF PRODDING...

BUT I *FINALLY* WORKED OUT WHAT WAS *BURIED IN MAN...*

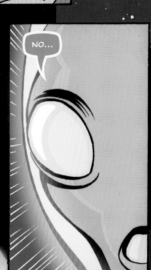

NO...

ME.

ZHRROOOW!

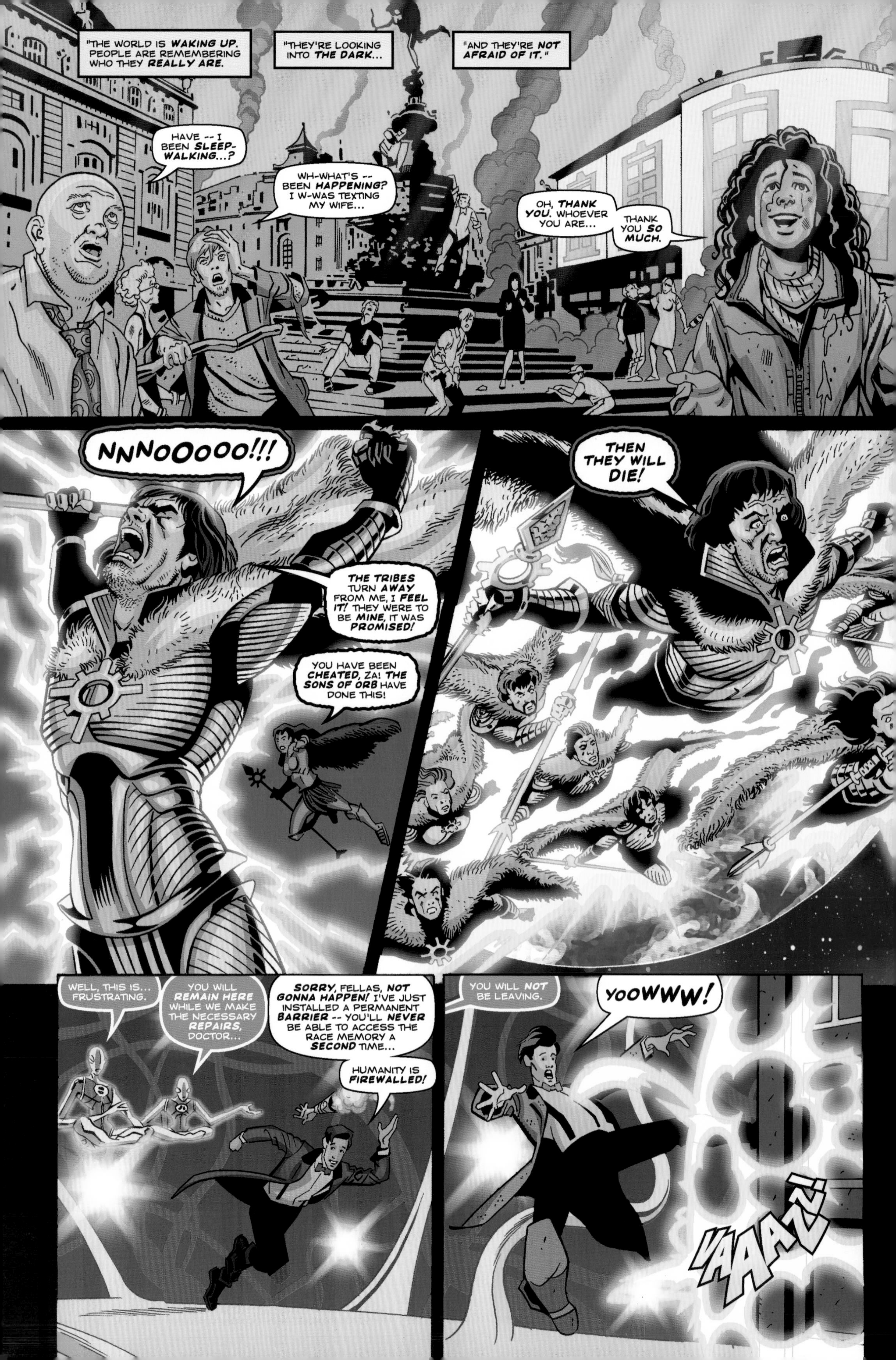
"THE WORLD IS WAKING UP. PEOPLE ARE REMEMBERING WHO THEY REALLY ARE.
"THEY'RE LOOKING INTO THE DARK...
"AND THEY'RE NOT AFRAID OF IT."
HAVE -- I BEEN SLEEP-WALKING...?
WH-WHAT'S -- BEEN HAPPENING? I W-WAS TEXTING MY WIFE...
OH, THANK YOU. WHOEVER YOU ARE...
THANK YOU SO MUCH.
NNNOOOOO!!!
THE TRIBES TURN AWAY FROM ME, I FEEL IT! THEY WERE TO BE MINE, IT WAS PROMISED!
YOU HAVE BEEN CHEATED, ZA! THE SONS OF ORB HAVE DONE THIS!
THEN THEY WILL DIE!
WELL, THIS IS... FRUSTRATING.
YOU WILL REMAIN HERE WHILE WE MAKE THE NECESSARY REPAIRS, DOCTOR...
SORRY, FELLAS, NOT GONNA HAPPEN! I'VE JUST INSTALLED A PERMANENT BARRIER -- YOU'LL NEVER BE ABLE TO ACCESS THE RACE MEMORY A SECOND TIME...
HUMANITY IS FIREWALLED!
YOU WILL NOT BE LEAVING.
YOOWWW!
VAAAÑ

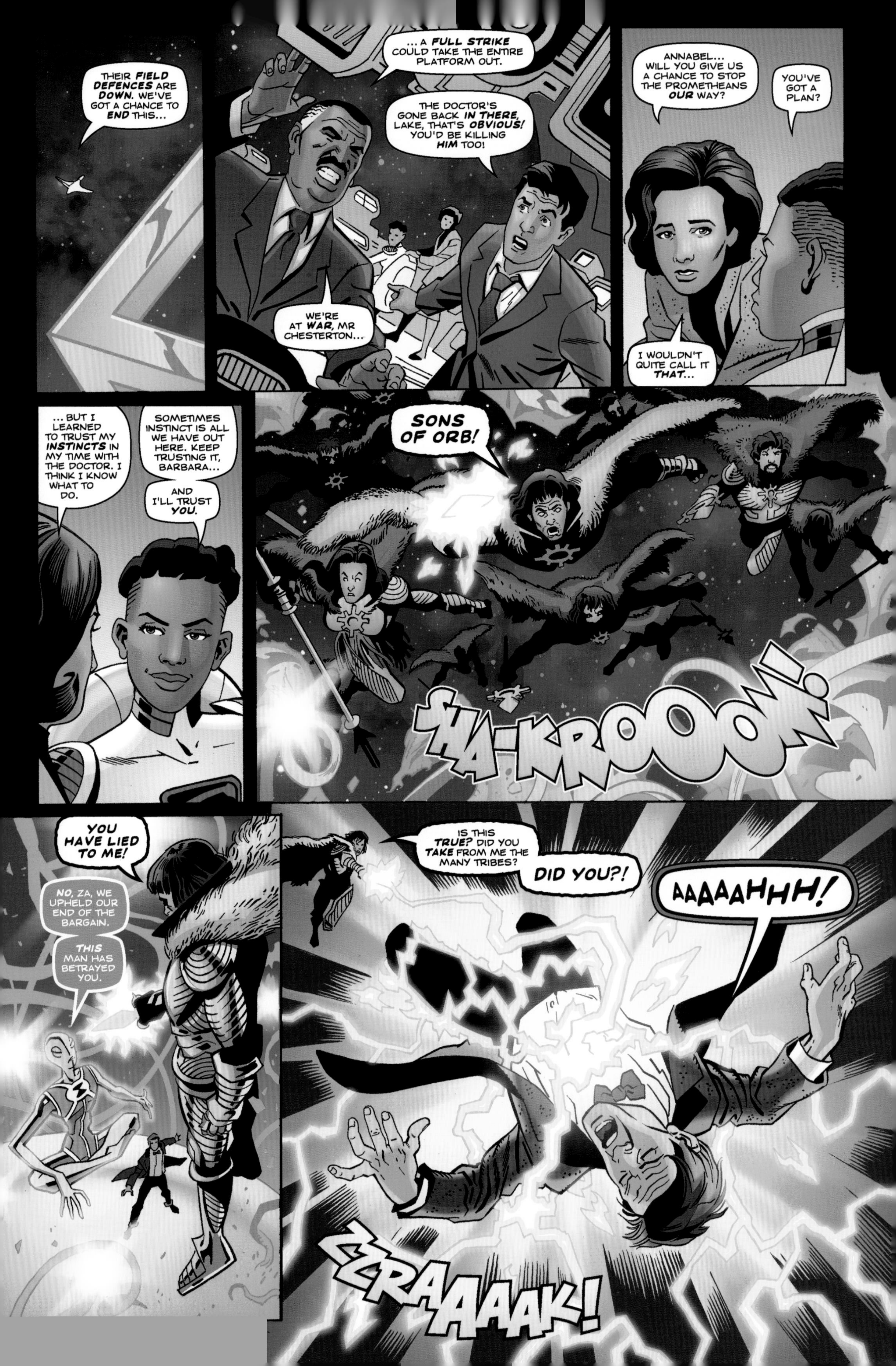
THEIR FIELD DEFENCES ARE DOWN. WE'VE GOT A CHANCE TO END THIS...
...A FULL STRIKE COULD TAKE THE ENTIRE PLATFORM OUT.
THE DOCTOR'S GONE BACK IN THERE, LAKE, THAT'S OBVIOUS! YOU'D BE KILLING HIM TOO!
WE'RE AT WAR, MR CHESTERTON...
ANNABEL... WILL YOU GIVE US A CHANCE TO STOP THE PROMETHEANS OUR WAY?
YOU'VE GOT A PLAN?
I WOULDN'T QUITE CALL IT THAT...
...BUT I LEARNED TO TRUST MY INSTINCTS IN MY TIME WITH THE DOCTOR. I THINK I KNOW WHAT TO DO.
SOMETIMES INSTINCT IS ALL WE HAVE OUT HERE. KEEP TRUSTING IT, BARBARA...
AND I'LL TRUST YOU.
SONS OF ORB!
SHA-KROOOM!
YOU HAVE LIED TO ME!
NO, ZA, WE UPHELD OUR END OF THE BARGAIN.
THIS MAN HAS BETRAYED YOU.
IS THIS TRUE? DID YOU TAKE FROM ME THE MANY TRIBES?
DID YOU?!
AAAAAHHH!
ZZRAAAAK!

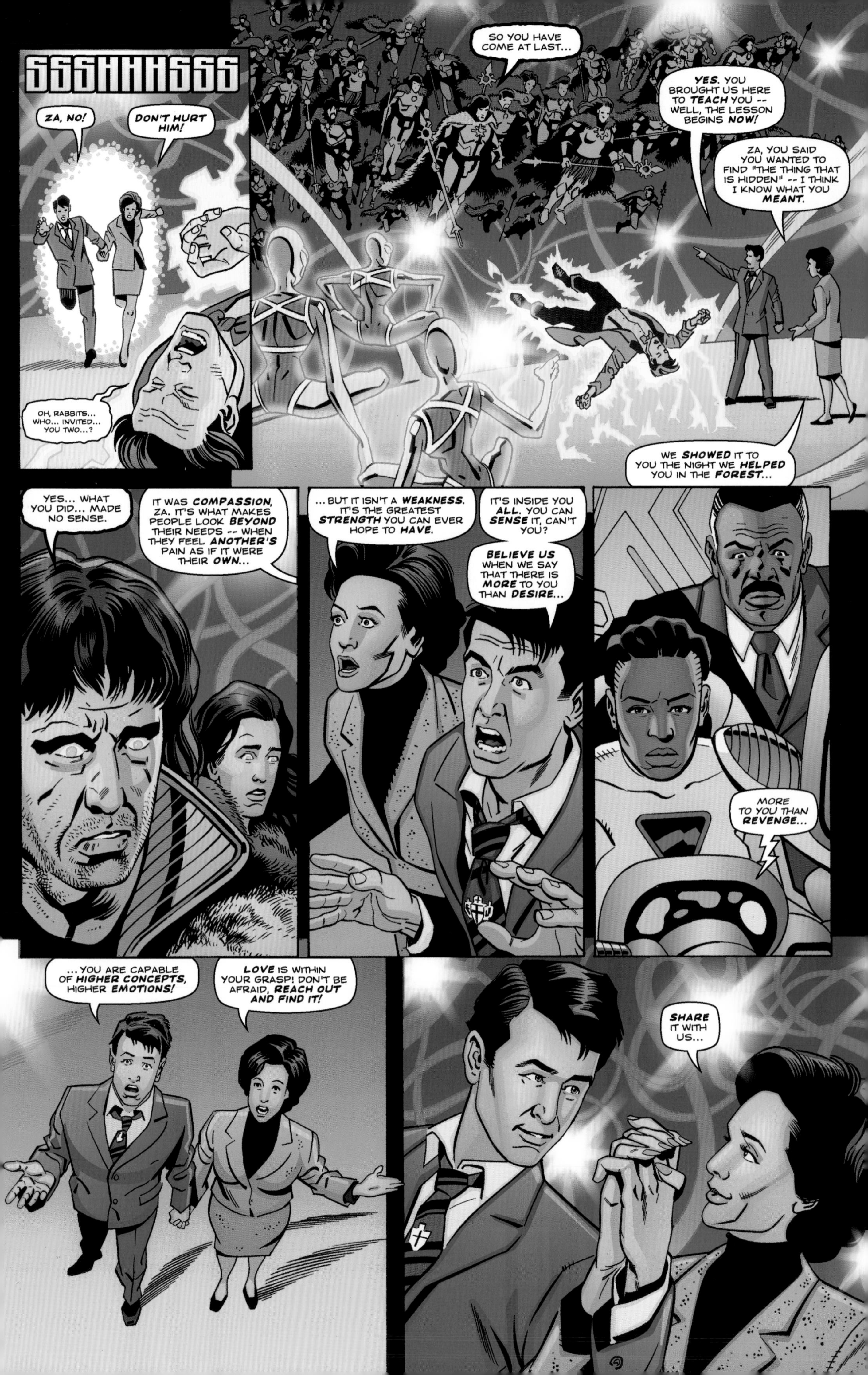
SSSHHHSSS
ZA, NO!
DON'T HURT HIM!
OH, RABBITS... WHO... INVITED... YOU TWO...?
SO YOU HAVE COME AT LAST...
YES. YOU BROUGHT US HERE TO TEACH YOU -- WELL, THE LESSON BEGINS NOW!
ZA, YOU SAID YOU WANTED TO FIND "THE THING THAT IS HIDDEN" -- I THINK I KNOW WHAT YOU MEANT.
WE SHOWED IT TO YOU THE NIGHT WE HELPED YOU IN THE FOREST...
YES... WHAT YOU DID... MADE NO SENSE.
IT WAS COMPASSION, ZA. IT'S WHAT MAKES PEOPLE LOOK BEYOND THEIR NEEDS -- WHEN THEY FEEL ANOTHER'S PAIN AS IF IT WERE THEIR OWN...
...BUT IT ISN'T A WEAKNESS. IT'S THE GREATEST STRENGTH YOU CAN EVER HOPE TO HAVE.
IT'S INSIDE YOU ALL. YOU CAN SENSE IT, CAN'T YOU?
BELIEVE US WHEN WE SAY THAT THERE IS MORE TO YOU THAN DESIRE...
MORE TO YOU THAN REVENGE...
...YOU ARE CAPABLE OF HIGHER CONCEPTS, HIGHER EMOTIONS!
LOVE IS WITHIN YOUR GRASP! DON'T BE AFRAID, REACH OUT AND FIND IT!
SHARE IT WITH US...

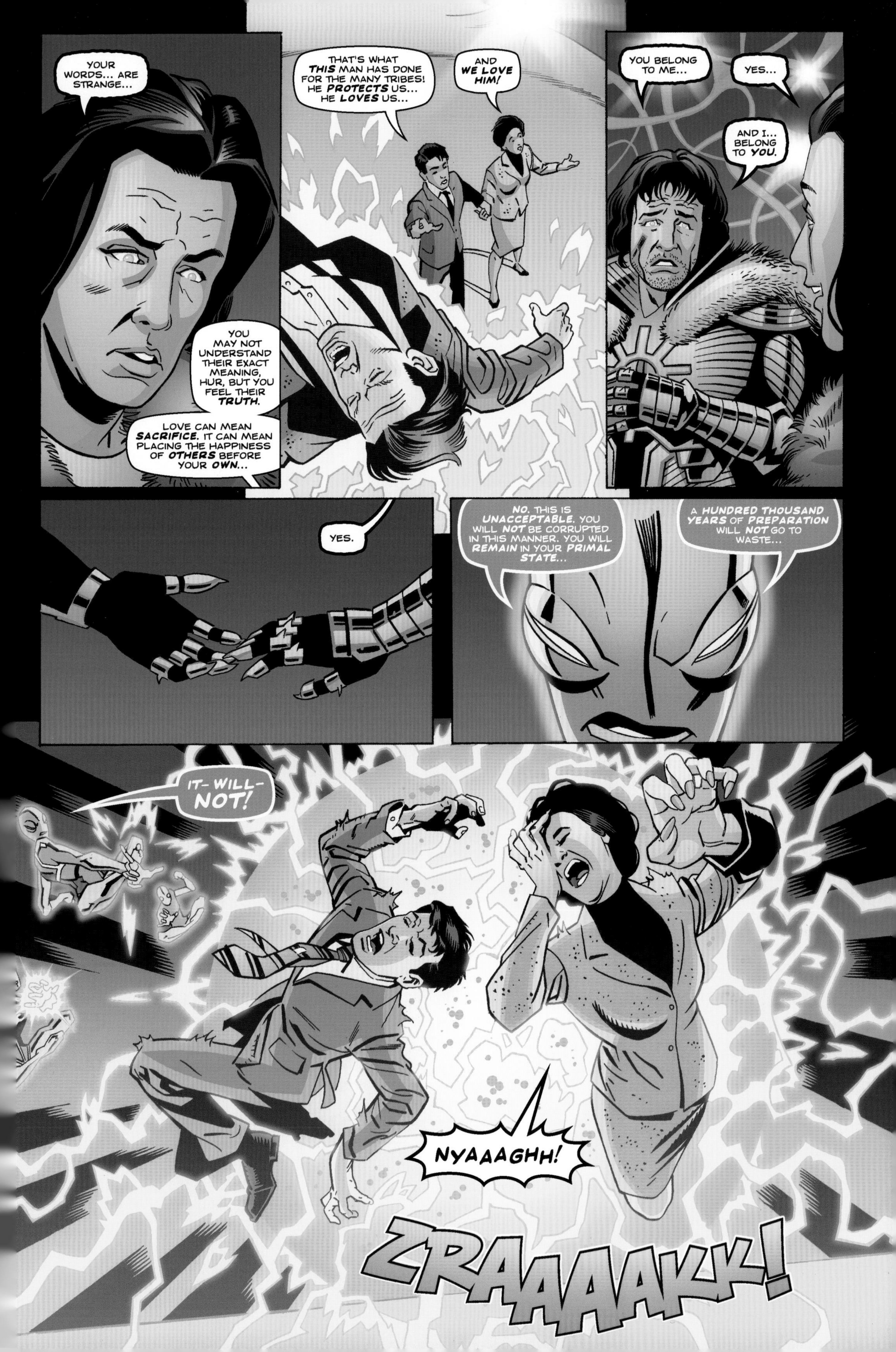

YOUR WORDS... ARE STRANGE...
YOU MAY NOT UNDERSTAND THEIR EXACT MEANING, HUR, BUT YOU FEEL THEIR TRUTH.
LOVE CAN MEAN SACRIFICE. IT CAN MEAN PLACING THE HAPPINESS OF OTHERS BEFORE YOUR OWN...
THAT'S WHAT THIS MAN HAS DONE FOR THE MANY TRIBES! HE PROTECTS US... HE LOVES US...
AND WE LOVE HIM!
YOU BELONG TO ME...
YES...
AND I... BELONG TO YOU.
YES.
NO. THIS IS UNACCEPTABLE. YOU WILL NOT BE CORRUPTED IN THIS MANNER. YOU WILL REMAIN IN YOUR PRIMAL STATE...
A HUNDRED THOUSAND YEARS OF PREPARATION WILL NOT GO TO WASTE...
IT- WILL- NOT!
NYAAAGHH!
ZRAAAAKK!

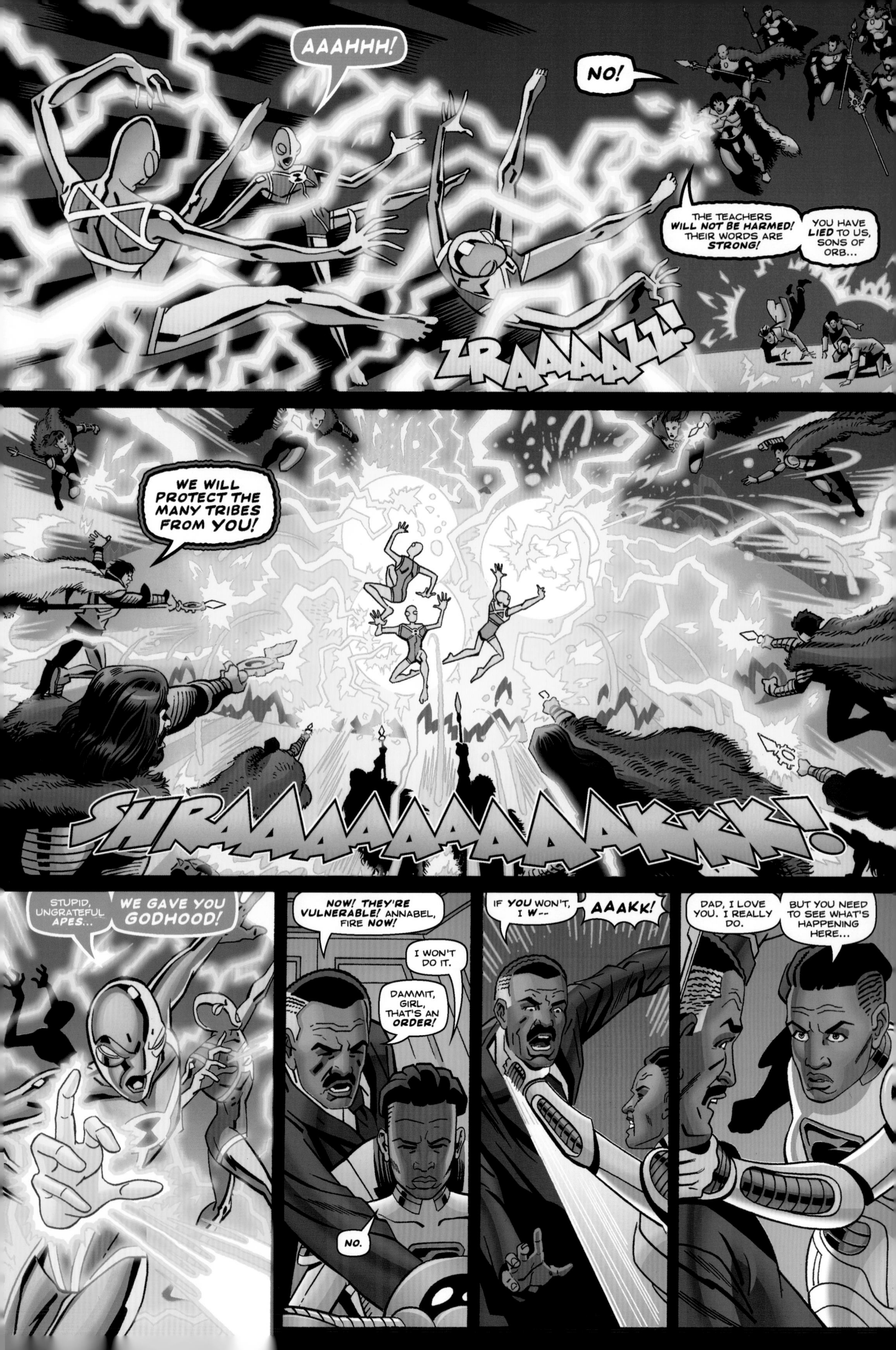
AAAHHH!
NO!
THE TEACHERS WILL NOT BE HARMED! THEIR WORDS ARE STRONG!
YOU HAVE LIED TO US, SONS OF ORB...
ZRAAAAZZ!
WE WILL PROTECT THE MANY TRIBES FROM YOU!
SHRAAAAAAAAKKK!
STUPID, UNGRATEFUL APES...
WE GAVE YOU GODHOOD!
NOW! THEY'RE VULNERABLE! ANNABEL, FIRE NOW!
I WON'T DO IT.
DAMMIT, GIRL, THAT'S AN ORDER!
NO.
IF YOU WON'T, I W--
AAAKK!
DAD, I LOVE YOU. I REALLY DO.
BUT YOU NEED TO SEE WHAT'S HAPPENING HERE...

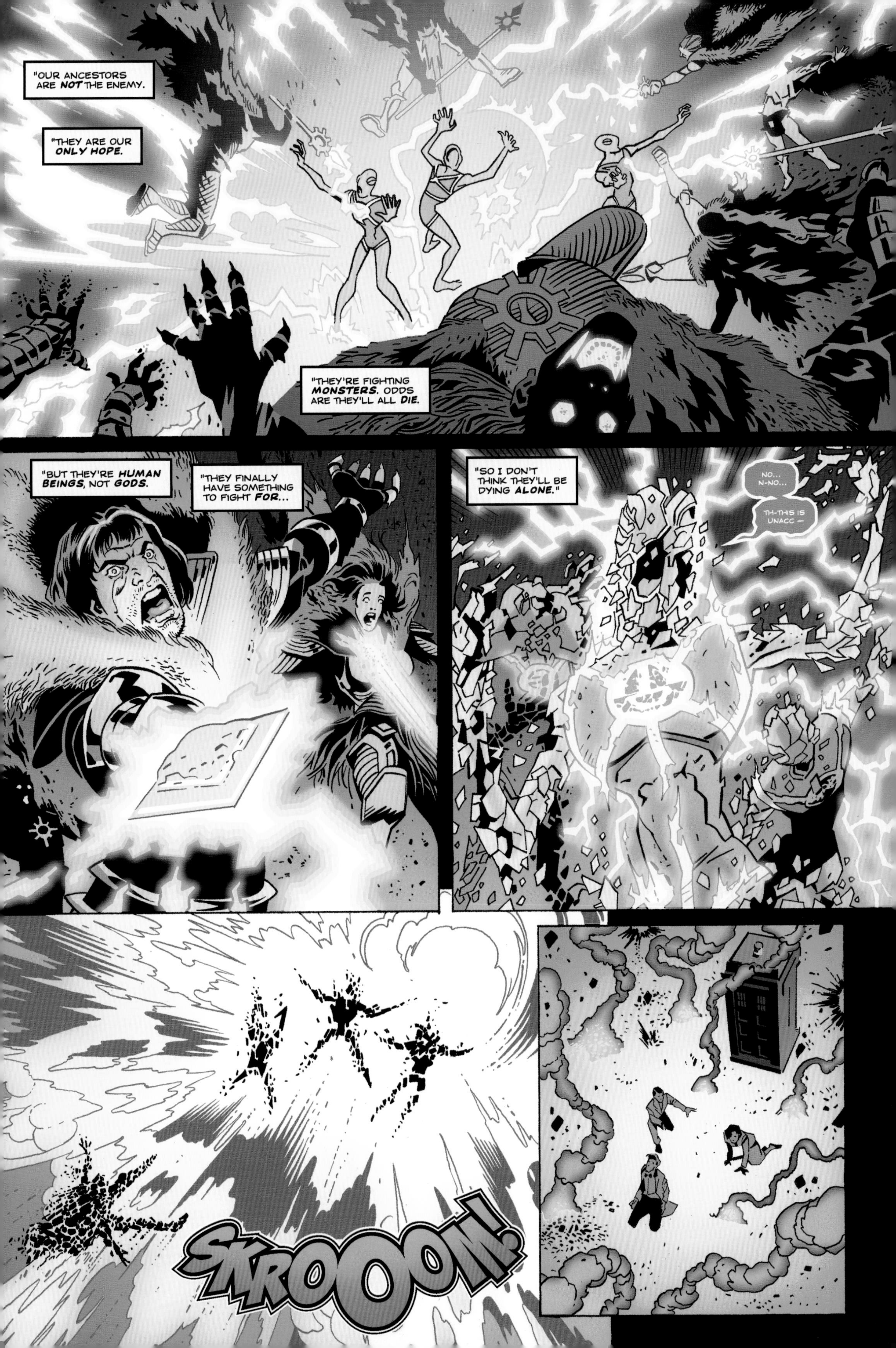
"OUR ANCESTORS ARE NOT THE ENEMY.
"THEY ARE OUR ONLY HOPE.
"THEY'RE FIGHTING MONSTERS. ODDS ARE THEY'LL ALL DIE.
"BUT THEY'RE HUMAN BEINGS, NOT GODS.
"THEY FINALLY HAVE SOMETHING TO FIGHT FOR...
"SO I DON'T THINK THEY'LL BE DYING ALONE."
NO... N-NO...
TH-THIS IS UNACC —
SKROOOOM!

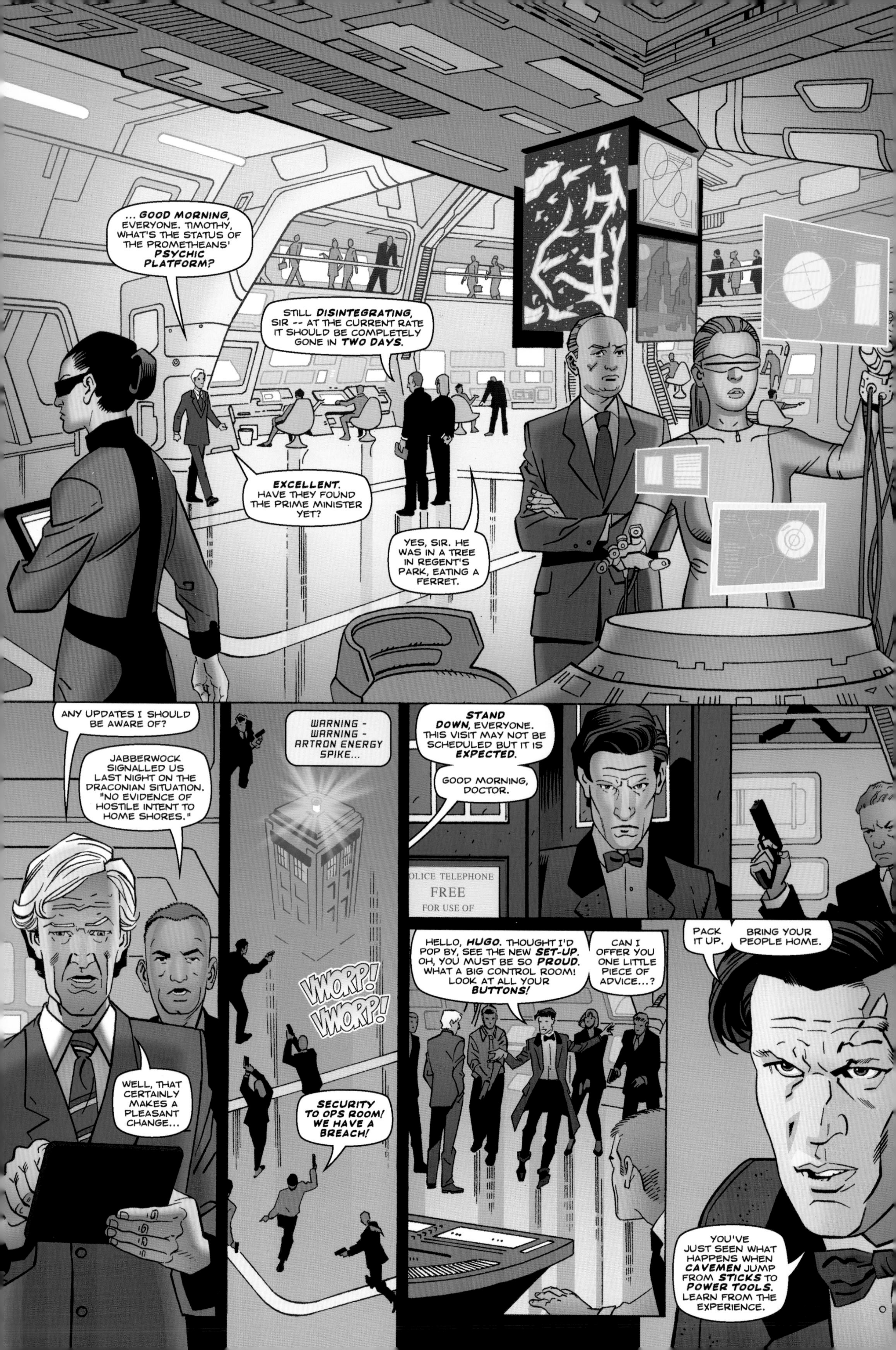

... GOOD MORNING, EVERYONE. TIMOTHY, WHAT'S THE STATUS OF THE PROMETHEANS' PSYCHIC PLATFORM?
STILL DISINTEGRATING, SIR -- AT THE CURRENT RATE IT SHOULD BE COMPLETELY GONE IN TWO DAYS.
EXCELLENT. HAVE THEY FOUND THE PRIME MINISTER YET?
YES, SIR. HE WAS IN A TREE IN REGENT'S PARK, EATING A FERRET.
ANY UPDATES I SHOULD BE AWARE OF?
JABBERWOCK SIGNALLED US LAST NIGHT ON THE DRACONIAN SITUATION. "NO EVIDENCE OF HOSTILE INTENT TO HOME SHORES."
WELL, THAT CERTAINLY MAKES A PLEASANT CHANGE...
WARNING - WARNING - ARTRON ENERGY SPIKE...
VWORP! VWORP!
SECURITY TO OPS ROOM! WE HAVE A BREACH!
STAND DOWN, EVERYONE. THIS VISIT MAY NOT BE SCHEDULED BUT IT IS EXPECTED.
GOOD MORNING, DOCTOR.
OLICE TELEPHONE
FREE
FOR USE OF
HELLO, HUGO. THOUGHT I'D POP BY, SEE THE NEW SET-UP. OH, YOU MUST BE SO PROUD. WHAT A BIG CONTROL ROOM! LOOK AT ALL YOUR BUTTONS!
CAN I OFFER YOU ONE LITTLE PIECE OF ADVICE...?
PACK IT UP.
BRING YOUR PEOPLE HOME.
YOU'VE JUST SEEN WHAT HAPPENS WHEN CAVEMEN JUMP FROM STICKS TO POWER TOOLS. LEARN FROM THE EXPERIENCE.

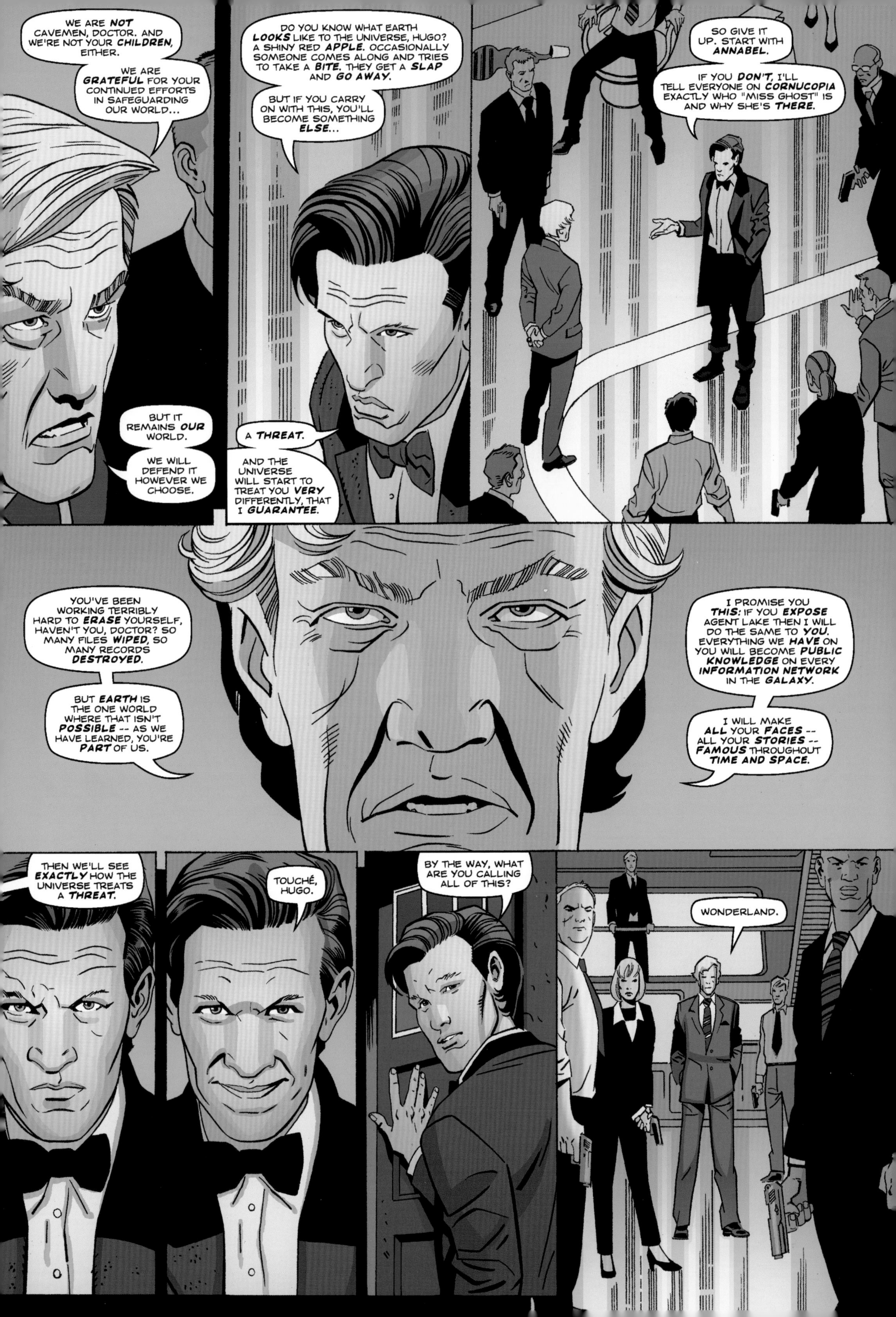
WE ARE NOT CAVEMEN, DOCTOR. AND WE'RE NOT YOUR CHILDREN, EITHER.
WE ARE GRATEFUL FOR YOUR CONTINUED EFFORTS IN SAFEGUARDING OUR WORLD...
BUT IT REMAINS OUR WORLD.
WE WILL DEFEND IT HOWEVER WE CHOOSE.
DO YOU KNOW WHAT EARTH LOOKS LIKE TO THE UNIVERSE, HUGO? A SHINY RED APPLE. OCCASIONALLY SOMEONE COMES ALONG AND TRIES TO TAKE A BITE. THEY GET A SLAP AND GO AWAY.
BUT IF YOU CARRY ON WITH THIS, YOU'LL BECOME SOMETHING ELSE...
A THREAT.
AND THE UNIVERSE WILL START TO TREAT YOU VERY DIFFERENTLY, THAT I GUARANTEE.
SO GIVE IT UP. START WITH ANNABEL.
IF YOU DON'T, I'LL TELL EVERYONE ON CORNUCOPIA EXACTLY WHO "MISS GHOST" IS AND WHY SHE'S THERE.
YOU'VE BEEN WORKING TERRIBLY HARD TO ERASE YOURSELF, HAVEN'T YOU, DOCTOR? SO MANY FILES WIPED, SO MANY RECORDS DESTROYED.
BUT EARTH IS THE ONE WORLD WHERE THAT ISN'T POSSIBLE -- AS WE HAVE LEARNED, YOU'RE PART OF US.
I PROMISE YOU THIS: IF YOU EXPOSE AGENT LAKE THEN I WILL DO THE SAME TO YOU. EVERYTHING WE HAVE ON YOU WILL BECOME PUBLIC KNOWLEDGE ON EVERY INFORMATION NETWORK IN THE GALAXY.
I WILL MAKE ALL YOUR FACES -- ALL YOUR STORIES -- FAMOUS THROUGHOUT TIME AND SPACE.
THEN WE'LL SEE EXACTLY HOW THE UNIVERSE TREATS A THREAT.
TOUCHÉ, HUGO.
BY THE WAY, WHAT ARE YOU CALLING ALL OF THIS?
WONDERLAND.

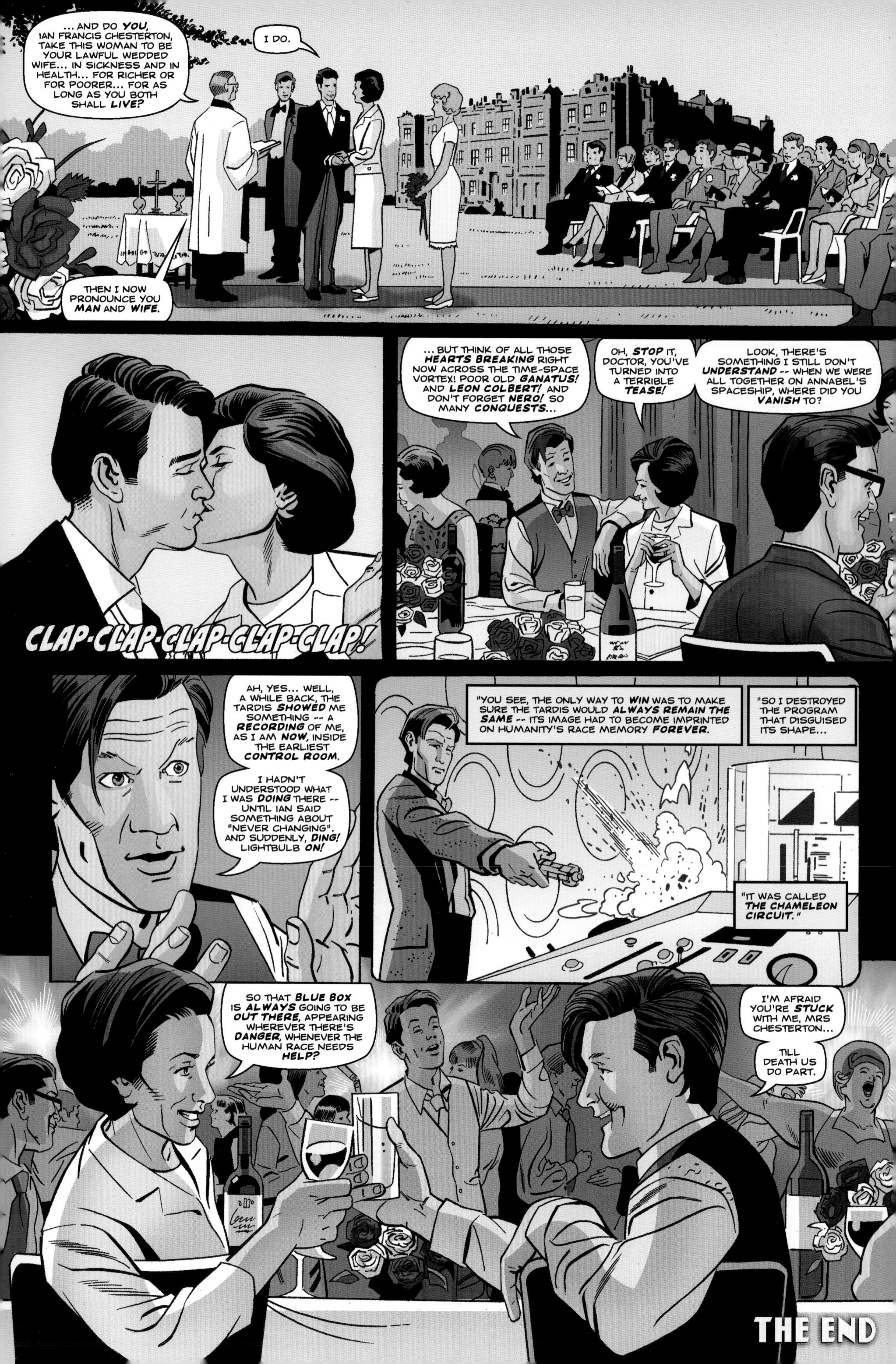
...AND DO YOU, IAN FRANCIS CHESTERTON, TAKE THIS WOMAN TO BE YOUR LAWFUL WEDDED WIFE... IN SICKNESS AND IN HEALTH... FOR RICHER OR FOR POORER... FOR AS LONG AS YOU BOTH SHALL LIVE?
I DO.
THEN I NOW PRONOUNCE YOU MAN AND WIFE.
CLAP-CLAP-CLAP-CLAP-CLAP!
...BUT THINK OF ALL THOSE HEARTS BREAKING RIGHT NOW ACROSS THE TIME-SPACE VORTEX! POOR OLD GANATUS! AND LEON COLBERT! AND DON'T FORGET NERO! SO MANY CONQUESTS...
OH, STOP IT, DOCTOR, YOU'VE TURNED INTO A TERRIBLE TEASE!
LOOK, THERE'S SOMETHING I STILL DON'T UNDERSTAND -- WHEN WE WERE ALL TOGETHER ON ANNABEL'S SPACESHIP, WHERE DID YOU VANISH TO?
AH, YES... WELL, A WHILE BACK, THE TARDIS SHOWED ME SOMETHING -- A RECORDING OF ME, AS I AM NOW, INSIDE THE EARLIEST CONTROL ROOM.
I HADN'T UNDERSTOOD WHAT I WAS DOING THERE -- UNTIL IAN SAID SOMETHING ABOUT "NEVER CHANGING". AND SUDDENLY, DING! LIGHTBULB ON!
"YOU SEE, THE ONLY WAY TO WIN WAS TO MAKE SURE THE TARDIS WOULD ALWAYS REMAIN THE SAME -- ITS IMAGE HAD TO BECOME IMPRINTED ON HUMANITY'S RACE MEMORY FOREVER.
"SO I DESTROYED THE PROGRAM THAT DISGUISED ITS SHAPE...
"IT WAS CALLED THE CHAMELEON CIRCUIT."
SO THAT BLUE BOX IS ALWAYS GOING TO BE OUT THERE, APPEARING WHEREVER THERE'S DANGER, WHENEVER THE HUMAN RACE NEEDS HELP?
I'M AFRAID YOU'RE STUCK WITH ME, MRS CHESTERTON...
TILL DEATH US DO PART.
THE END

COMMENTARY

THE BROKEN MAN

Scott Gray

This story began life in an idle phone conversation with writer/artist Dan McDaid in (I guess) 2011. I'm sure Dan and I started with an in-depth discussion of page layout, panel progression and composition, but once that was out of the way, we quickly moved on to the important stuff: industry gossip and our current favourite comics, TV shows and movies. We were both big fans of *Luther*, the crime series created by Neil Cross (now a *Doctor Who* writer). If you haven't seen it and you're a) old enough to watch post-watershed TV and b) like your post-watershed TV a little on the strange side, then look out for it. We loved the dark, surreal nature of the show. London had been transformed into a bizarre playground only one step removed from Gotham City, preyed on by killers with insane motivations and terrifying personas. Lumpen TV critics moaned about the 'outlandish' plots, missing the point by several light-years – this was TV bordering on the hallucinogenic. Most of all, Dan and I admired the lead actor, Idris Elba, who generated a physical presence that you just don't see very often on the small screen – he was very obviously a movie star in the making. I said something like, "Idris Elba really needs to be in a *Doctor Who* sometime, before he gets too expensive," and Dan agreed.

Of course, budget isn't really a problem for the **Doctor Who Magazine** comic strip, so I began to imagine a character Mr Elba could play. I came up with Elias Drake, a super-cool secret agent active in Britain in the 1960s. He'd operate in a world of mad scientists, psychedelic discos and beautiful assassins, very much in the vein of *The Avengers*, *The Saint* and *The Prisoner*. Elias meets the Doctor, Amy and Rory in a stately country house filled with pop art backdrops. They're mingling at a party with a series of eccentric figures in fancy dress. The guests begin to get knocked off one-by-one in suitably bizarre fashion via a series of deadly booby traps. Elias and the Doctor team up to uncover the colourful villain who for once is human – there would be no alien element at all. I was imagining Elias as a character who could return at a future date. Maybe we could even chart his career through the decades as he rose through the ranks of whatever fictional spy group he was part of (I was probably planning a silly acronym).

I didn't get very far. It all felt phony, too obviously derivative, too *Austin Powers*. I came to the conclusion that this kind of pastiche doesn't sit well in *Doctor Who*. A story set on Earth needs to have a reasonably realistic environment for it to work. That magical collision between the mundane and the cosmic is vital: we need shop-window dummies that are actually robotic killers; a telephone box that's a disguised time machine; black cats that are really teleporting aliens. But all of that strangeness only works if the world it's invading is recognisable. The familiar turned inside-out lies right at the heart of the series – that's been true from the very first scene. If the Doctor and friends landed in a groovy 1960s fantasy world that had only ever really existed in the minds of Brian Clemens and Patrick McGoohan, then that juxtaposition wouldn't be there; it would be just one group of fantasy archetypes colliding with another. It would be a hollow experience. We needed some reality.

So I had a rethink: Elias Drake got a new name that didn't sound quite so made-up, he was placed in a world that was a lot better researched, and he was given a wife and daughter who could provide him with some much-needed emotional weight.

Below: Martin Geraghty's first character sketch of Patrick Lake, inspired by the actor Idris Elba.

no Goatee

Patrick

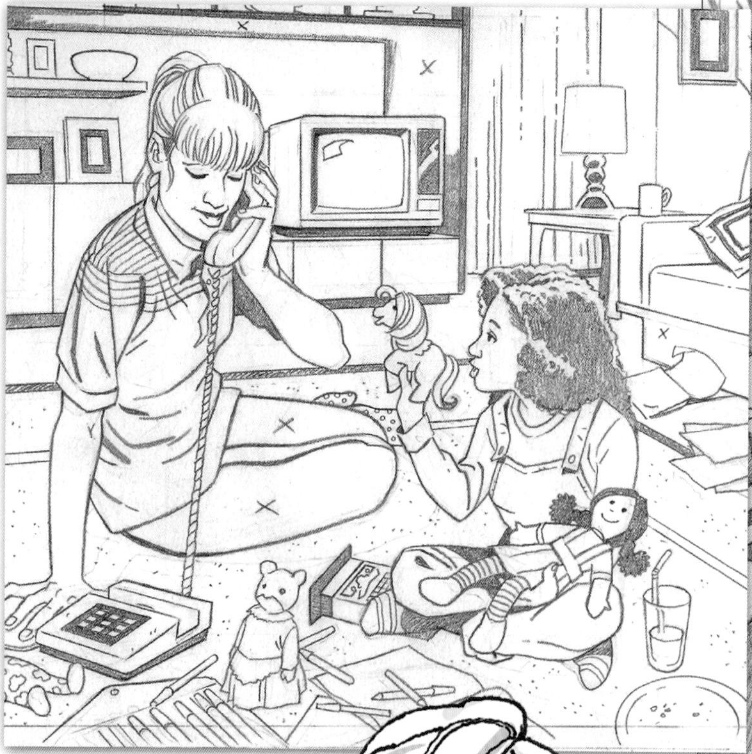

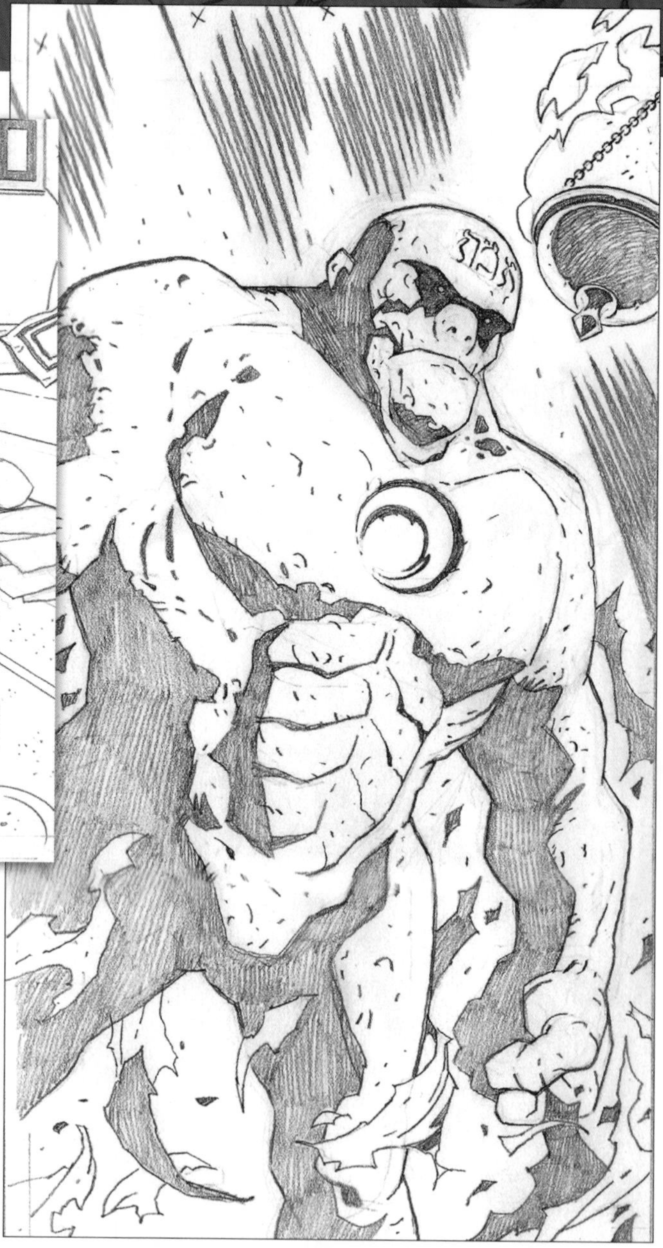

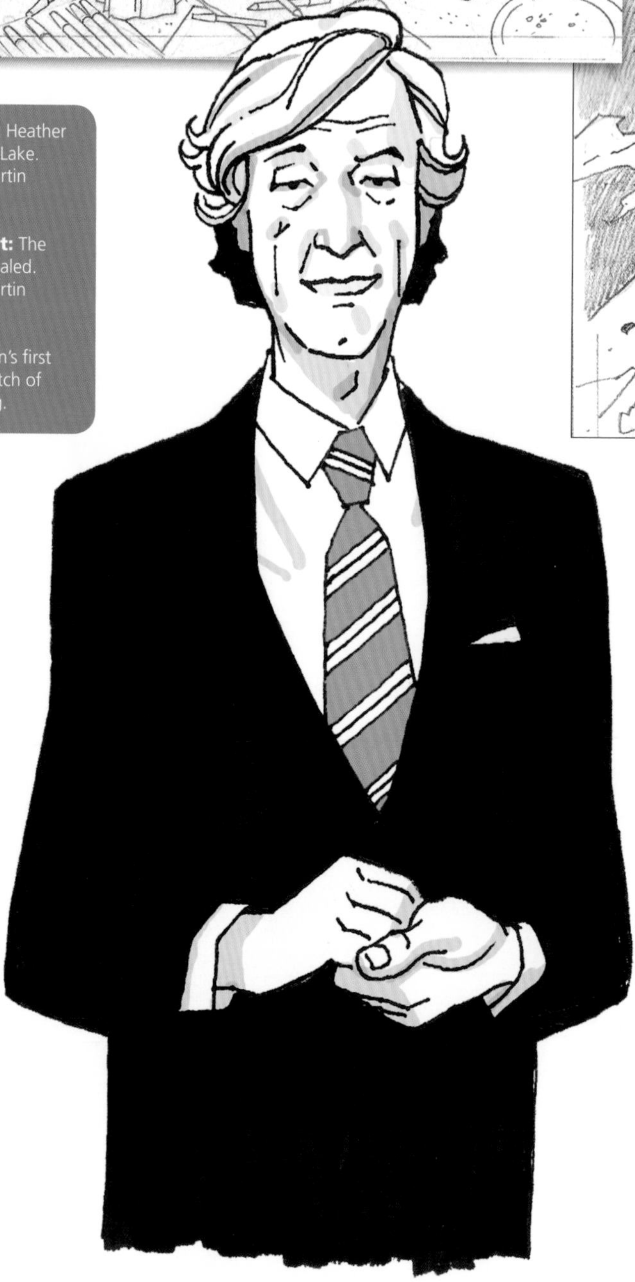

Above left: Heather and Annabel Lake. Pencils by Martin Geraghty.

Above right: The Golem is revealed. Pencils by Martin Geraghty.

Right: Martin's first character sketch of Hugo Wilding.

While I was thinking this through, the idea of Wonderland, or 'Space MI6', was taking root. Earth may have UNIT and Torchwood to defend it, but as Hugo Wilding says in *Hunters of the Burning Stone*, those groups have to sit around and wait for the enemy to arrive. An organisation capable of operating beyond Earth, just as MI6 operates outside Britain, seemed like the logical next step. *The Sarah Jane Adventures* story *Enemy of the Bane* had established the Black Archive; a UNIT warehouse where salvaged alien devices were stored and examined. We had also seen UNIT adapting a Sontaran teleport system in the *Doctor Who* story *The Stolen Earth*, and Torchwood had used a spaceship as a weapon in *The Christmas Invasion*. Those pesky humans were clearly starting to play with the big toys now, whether the Doctor liked it or not – where would that lead?

I was also remembering where Martin Geraghty and I had left MI6 back in 2005 in the **DWM** comic story *The Flood* – with all their top people dead and a big hole in the roof of their HQ. I kept wondering what would happen the next day – how would the survivors react to such a devastating attack? Would they just shrug their shoulders and go back to monitoring Al-Qaeda? That seemed unlikely – in fact, it seemed *unthinkable*. Political and ideological conflicts would suddenly seem like minor problems compared with vast alien empires hovering overhead. So what changes would they make?

The Broken Man is very much a stealth origin story for Wonderland; it sets up the characters I knew I'd be playing with in our 'season finale'. They all fell into place quite quickly. I knew Patrick Lake would be a man who'd refuse to accept the reality of anything outside his own experience, and that failure of imagination would lead to disaster. I knew he'd have a colleague with a rather more flexible perspective. I knew Patrick would have a loving wife who knew nothing of his real job, and I immediately realised that she would die at the story's end, thereby setting Patrick on a long, hard, dark road. And I knew he'd be taking his daughter along with him.

All of that was settled on very early, back while I was scripting *The Chains of Olympus*. I'd love to say that the storyline followed just as smoothly, but ohhh, no, my friends. That's just not my style *at all*. I stumbled around for a good long while. I had no setting for these characters, no time or place. For Annabel to be an adult in the present day, the story would have to be set in the late 1980s or early 1990s to feature her as a child. I needed a political hot-spot for Patrick to be operating in, and considered both Apartheid-era South Africa and Hong Kong. But Eastern Europe quickly jumped to the front of the queue; the fall of the Soviet Union had easily been the biggest historical event taking place while I was growing up, and I had clear memories of watching it unfold on the news. Protesters in the snow, tanks in the streets, people cheering on top of the Berlin Wall – yeah, that was the ticket...

Czechoslovakia soon became the Soviet state of choice. I found a terrific reference book on Soviet history which gave me a good grounding in the era (I have since lost it and can't remember the title, my apologies to the author). I went hunting for as much information on the Czech capital, Prague, as I could find. I'd never been there but I was happy to hear that Martin had visited it. A good omen! I picked up several books, including Citbor Rybar's *Jewish Prague* which was invaluable.

Everyone contributing to the visuals did an astonishing job. Martin, David Roach, James Offredi and Roger Langridge all seemed to connect like never before, all complementing each others' talents. That scene-setting image of Patrick walking across Charles Bridge, with that grim title hanging in the air as the snow falls, made me realise how lucky I was to have this team in place. By the time they got to the knockout Joseph-chasing-the-Doctor sequence in the same chapter I was jumping for joy. Martin did a superb job tackling the copious amount of reference material needed for a story set in a foreign country in the recent past. I got to grips with Google Maps and realised I could take a virtual walk around the areas of Prague specified in the story – that was a huge help.

You may have noticed that Patrick really doesn't look anything like Idris Elba. Martin came up with some excellent sketches but we quickly realised there was a credibility problem: Patrick Lake had to be believable as an accountant-turned-informer in order to con Yuri Azarov. Idris Elba does *not* look like an accountant. At all. Patrick's face and physique were therefore softened to make him more convincing. He stayed black, though, even though that meant he stood out like a sore thumb in a pre-immigrant, all-white Prague. I reasoned that that would actually help him with Yuri – first by drawing his attention to Patrick, and then because Yuri wouldn't believe that anyone so distinctive in appearance would be used as a spy.

Prague was home to a classic myth: the Golem. If there's one thing that *Doctor Who* loves to do, it's take a nice, unsuspecting piece of folklore and give it a sci-fi makeover. I couldn't resist using the Golem but held back revealing its presence for as long as I could. The image of a sinister giant wrapped up in bandages, trench coat and a big hat appealed so much, coming as it did from the terrific robot baddies the Cybernauts in *The Avengers*. Maybe I couldn't set a story in the world of John Steed and Emma Peel but I could still pilfer from them.

The Golem's disguise also connected neatly to an observation made by Socrates in *The Chains of Olympus*: the Doctor often relies on assumed knowledge instead of applying proper logical analysis. I knew he would look at Joseph and think "servo-robot", not bothering to consider any other explanation – and because of that, the readers would do the same. After all, the Doctor's never wrong, is he? Well, yes he is, quite often if you stop to think about it. But of course, in a sense, the Doctor isn't really mistaken – the Golem *is* a robot, the very first one in history, in fact. He's just built out of clay instead of steel.

Below: Martin Geraghty's first inked illustration of Yuri and Joseph.

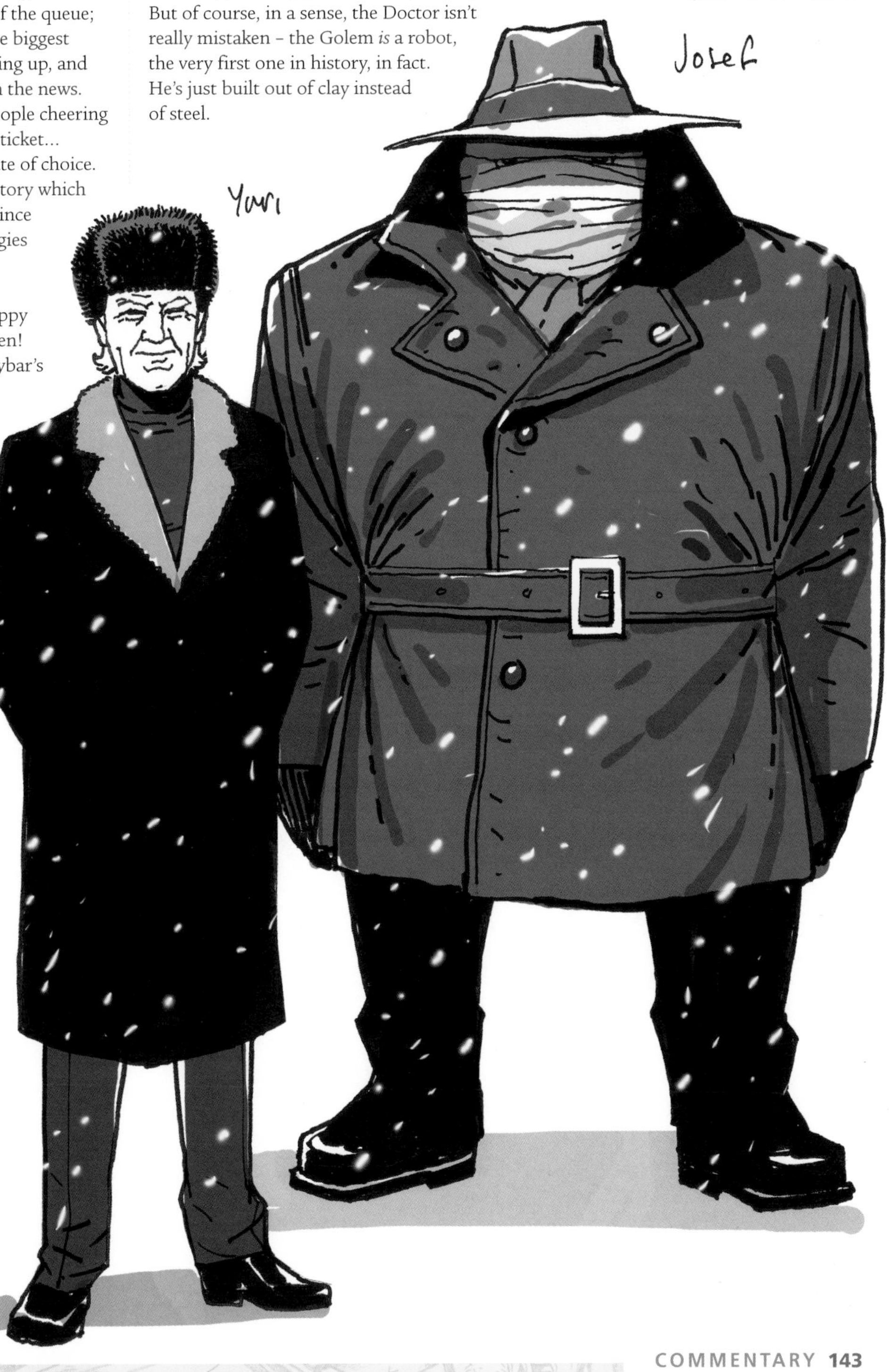
Josef
Yuri

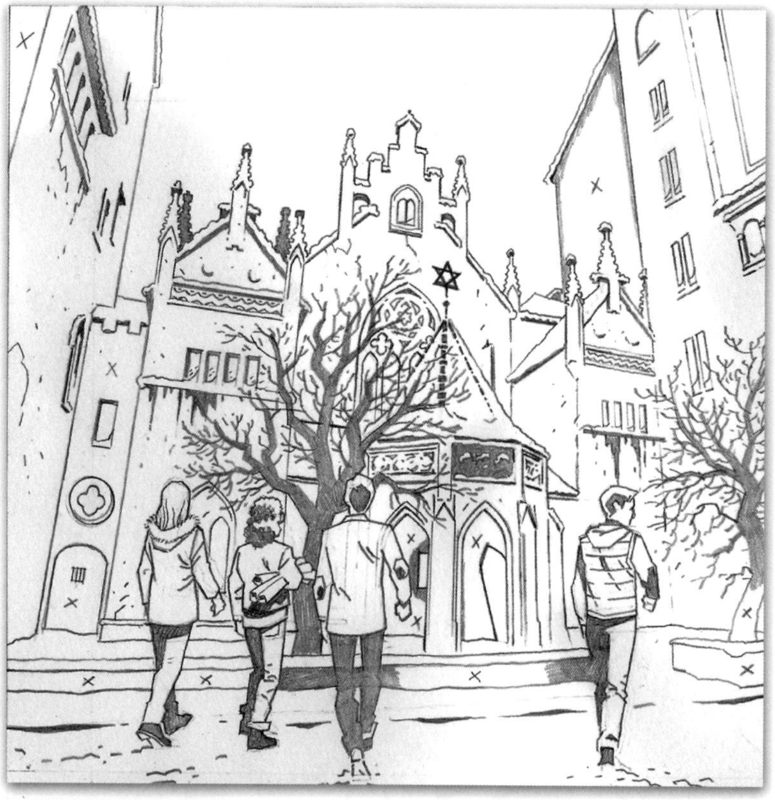

Yuri creating an army of Golems at the climax: a new workers' army for the reborn Soviet Union.

The Old Jewish Cemetery and Saul Hoffman's home, the Maisel Synagogue, are real. When the Nazis occupied Prague they shipped in Jewish artefacts they had looted from across Europe and placed them there. They were planning to turn it into 'a museum for an extinct race'. Some things you just can't make up.

Gerhard Frankel was fictional but Rabbi Judah Loew ben Bezalel was a major figure in Jewish history. His statue stands at Prague's New Town Hall. The attacks on the Jewish ghetto in the sixteenth century were also real, and started me thinking about the danger of a well-placed lie, and how it can act like a lit match on a wood pile. The Golem had 'emet' – 'truth' – written on its forehead. The slogan of the 1989 Czech democracy movement had been 'Pravda Vitezi' – 'Truth Prevails'. Those two facts clicked together and gave me the starting-point for the villains – they would be liars.

'Mavora' is a lake in New Zealand – it was just one of those times when you see a good name on a signpost and make a note of it before it vanishes forever. I had jotted down the notion of a two-dimensional alien race in my ever-present notebook a few months earlier. They had been inspired by the floor tiles in the bathroom – they were patterned, and I kept seeing weird, distorted faces in them (but everyone does that, right...?). I imagined thousands of 2-D creatures, all different colours, all assembled in a giant grid in space. I had initially seen them as comedic in nature and hesitated to use them here as villains. But with so many supporting characters in the story, and Yuri Azarov dominating as the central baddie, I knew there wouldn't be enough space left for an elaborate alien race. "Just make them hungry squares," I told myself.

I found another reference source online: a woman had posted a diary of her days as a high school student in Prague, taking part in the demonstrations. It's true that no one died in the Czech protests, but they were far from peaceful – the people behind the 'Velvet Revolution' still suffered plenty of brutality. Many protesters had been killed in previous demonstrations across Eastern Europe. The Czech people expected the same would happen again,

Above: The Doctor and friends approach the Maisel Synagogue. Pencil art by Martin Geraghty.

Below: The Prague riots of the sixteenth century. Pencils by Martin Geraghty.

The Doctor's also correct when he says that 'robot' (or more precisely 'robota') is a word first invented in Prague by the author Karel Capek in his play *RUR*, or *Rossum's Universal Robots*, first performed in 1921. The story is set in the near future when robot workers are being manufactured on an island factory. They rise up and exterminate humanity, but at the end begin to exhibit positive human emotions. It's interesting to note that Capek's robots are created out of a synthetic organic material, and are really closer to what we would call clones today. For a while I toyed with a much stronger connection between the play and the story's plot. I could easily see

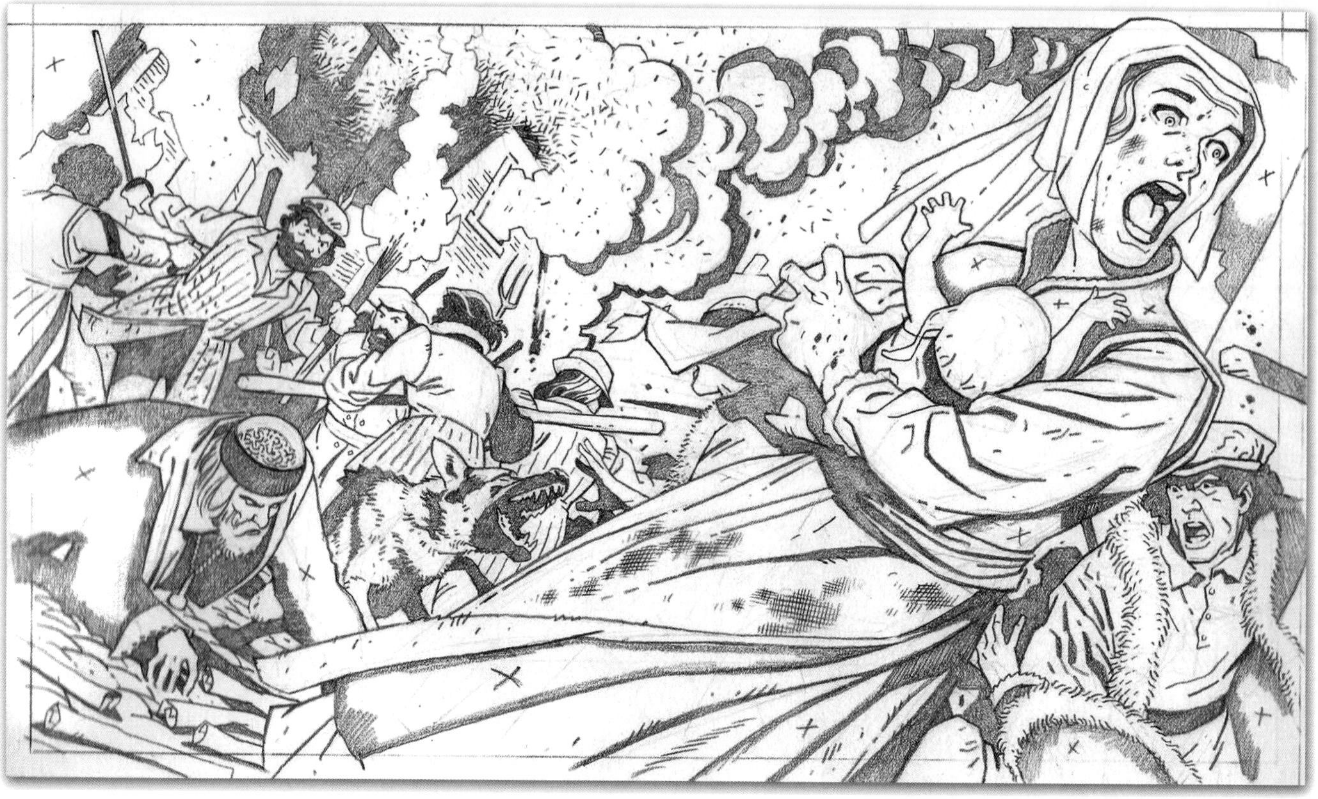

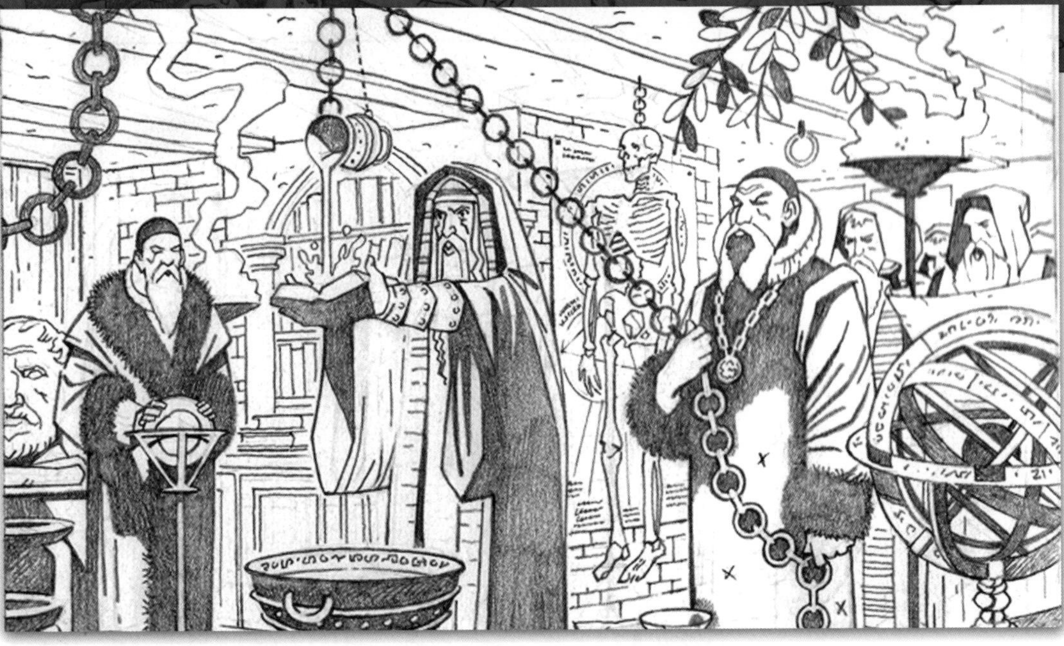

Left: Rabbi Loew and colleagues. Pencil art by Martin Geraghty.

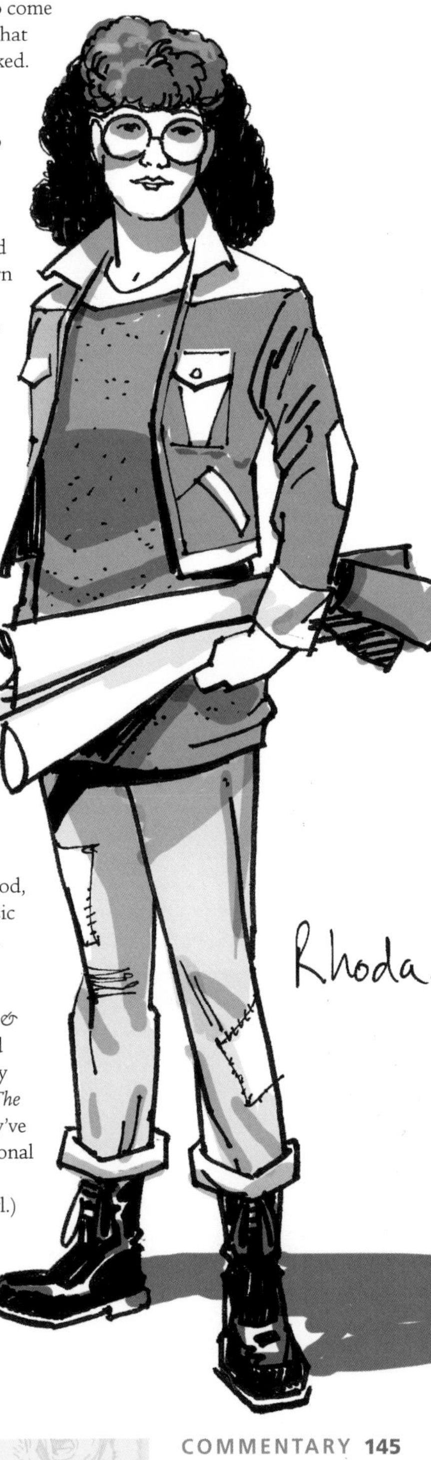
Rhoda.

Below: Martin's first inked sketch of Rhoda Hoffman.

but they still marched out into the streets armed only with placards, candles and hope. The bravery they displayed was inspiring, and I wanted to pay my respects to them with the feisty Rhoda Hoffman.

Joining us in the **DWM** office around this point was John Ainsworth, who had been brought in to create the US-targeted magazine *Doctor Who Insider*. John was an old friend and he brought with him years of experience script-editing and directing Big Finish's *Doctor Who* audios. He had a strong understanding of story structure and joined resident editors Tom Spilsbury and Peter Ware as a third pair of eyes overseeing the comic strip. He influenced the story's conclusion: I had originally just put a big funnel of energy inside the crypt that the Mavora were using as a power source. Joseph tries to destroy it and dies, leaving Heather to step in, become the new Golem and sacrifice herself. It was all a bit nebulous and confusing and nobody liked it. John suggested that an intelligent villain would be a far more effective final threat, and so the Mavora Queen was born.

Heather Lake proved to be the toughest hurdle in the whole story. It's a cliché to say that characters come to life and start dictating events in a story, but occasionally a character will take on a life of her own. Heather had to be sympathetic, loving and admirable, and so inevitably I ended up liking her. But Heather had been designed from the start to die – that was really her purpose in the story. She was doomed from the first page.

Doctor Who has a bite to it, a sharp edge that has to be addressed from time to time: it can't always be just faceless extras and villains who die. Sometimes bad things happen to good people. But in plotting out this story, I honestly felt like a murderer. I felt *terrible*. I had never experienced a reaction like it before. I consoled myself with the thought that when it was finished I would at least have produced something sincere.

To make matters worse, I had this horrible image stuck in my head: a weeping Annabel clutching her mother's body at the end of the story. That felt like I was crossing a line – we were moving from a sad conclusion to something else entirely, something unspeakably traumatic. I discussed it with Tom and Pete, trying to find a way around it. Ultimately, the Doctor saved us. I reasoned that if there was any way he could spare Annabel the fear she was experiencing, then he would do it. So Annabel slept through the final few pages, and the immediate trauma belonged to Patrick alone.

Another stumbling block was explaining how Yuri could end up in control of the Golem. I just couldn't get my head around it: here was a man who had spent his whole life dealing in lies, betrayal and murder. How could he make a connection with a creature built for justice, that only responded to truth? I spent weeks trying to come up with some bit of stupid techno-babble that would sound convincing, but nothing worked.

I had forgotten a critical, fundamental rule in writing for this genre: the villain *never* thinks he's the villain. Yuri is the hero of his own life story, and he can justify every single piece of nastiness he's ever carried out with one word: patriotism. He believes in the Soviet Union, he's convinced that it's the only thing stopping the Western powers from overrunning Europe, and anything he does to preserve it is therefore right and true. It seems so obvious now but that thought took *ages* to surface. When it did, I had my man fully-formed.

I had briefly considered another way to polish Yuri off at the end: he'd be packing his bags, trying to get out of Prague, when he is confronted by a shadowy figure – another KGB agent Yuri simply calls 'Vlad'. The agent guns him down for his betrayal. Any resemblance to the current Russian president would I'm sure have been *entirely* coincidental...

I was very sorry that Saul never got to meet the Golem. That felt like a big missed opportunity. I imagined Saul's awe would have soon been replaced by righteous anger when he realised that Prague's protector had let them down when the Nazis invaded. That would have been a good, meaty scene! But lack of space and the basic momentum of the story didn't allow for it.

I loved writing for Amy and Rory here, they brought some much-needed comedy into the story. *The Chains of Olympus*, *Sticks & Stones* and *The Cornucopia Caper* (all printed in our previous volume) were set when they were travelling full-time with the Doctor. *The Broken Man*, however, takes place after they've returned to Earth and are now only occasional adventurers. (That's how Amy can get the lipstick through the post from her little girl.)

I'm very proud of *The Broken Man*, I think it's one of the strongest stories produced for **DWM** in recent times. It was a lot of hard work for everyone concerned but the results were worth it. I hope you agree.

Above: Martin's finished pencil art and initial layout for Part Two's cliffhanger.

Below: The first colour study of the Mavora by Martin Geraghty.

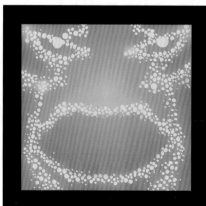

Martin Geraghty Artist

I'd only just arrived in an isolated cottage out on the picturesquely bleak North Yorkshire moors for a weekend break when Scott called to brief me on my forthcoming assignment: a period espionage thriller set behind the Iron Curtain with the enticing prospect of my having to draw the character of a young KGB agent called Vladimir Putin. I've genuinely only just remembered this fact as I've sat down to type this commentary so I've no idea why the current Russian president didn't show up in the final script. I'd like to think Scott thought better of it after being followed to his car one evening by a burly man with a steel-tipped umbrella.

Right from Page One we are introduced to major characters who will have a very serious impact on the Doctor's life a few stories on. Scott described Patrick as looking like Idris Elba, but as you can see, this didn't quite work out and he ended up looking like no one in particular. I always waiver over making characters look like recognisable actors (cue chorus of "We know, it looks nothing like Matt Smith!"). I think it could be something to do with the time-consuming aspect of having yet another actor you are constantly having to refer to for visual reference. Alan Barnes asked me twice to cast Helen Mirren as a character in stories penned by him and twice I failed miserably. If you've a copy of *Endgame* floating about I'll let you guess which characters they could be.

Anyway, *The Broken Man* was a marvellous story to work on, chock-full of imagery that I could really have fun with. I've visited Prague in winter on a few occasions and it's wonderfully evocative; all black silhouettes and claw-like branches against leaden skies. And, with the exception of Rhoda's late-80s get-up, it's practically impossible, visually, to tell what period our story is set – in architectural terms it's virtually a city in stasis.

All the staples of the genre are firmly in place: the fur-hatted villain and his scary trench-coated henchman; illicit meetings in deserted parks; brown envelopes stuffed with money changing hands as a telephoto lens clicks away amidst the all-pervading air of a people suppressed. Amazing to think that, stripped of the plot's science-fiction trappings, this was a reality only a generation ago in a now-popular holiday destination. And of course, when trying to recreate a genuine location I did my utmost to present the city as faithfully as I could within the confines of the available visual material. As always, when given stories set in reality, research is the absolute cornerstone of my approach.

Amongst many highlights for me as an artist on this story, the most fun was probably the Doctor being chased through the deserted streets by the huge, implacable character of Joseph, who visually brings to mind the Cybernauts from *The Avengers*. The mood music that I listened to during the entire drawing process on this tale was Alberto Iglesias' soundtrack to the recent *Tinker, Tailor, Soldier, Spy* movie adaptation, which worked really well for me in getting the requisite tone.

Revisiting these pages now 18 months on, I'm immensely proud of the work I did on them in the service of Scott's exciting, pitch-perfect script, and James O's colouring work is absolutely bang-on the money, with the Warhol-inspired Pop Art stylings of the Mavora providing a wonderful contrast to the bleak locale for Part Three's spectacular cliffhanger. Scott's seemingly innate ability to create villains that resolutely belong in the comic strip medium shows no sign of abating.

He finishes the tale off in grim fashion with the last page bringing to mind the Seventh Doctor cradling Ace in *Ground Zero*, all those years ago.

And it's clear that there will be far-reaching implications for the Doctor...

Imaginary Enemies

Scott Gray Writer

It was Christmas! I had never written a Christmas story before, but they were becoming a semi-regular tradition at **DWM**. Jonathan Morris and Rob Davis had given us *The Professor, the Queen and the Bookshop* two years earlier; a brilliant tribute to CS Lewis. It had viewed the Doctor, Amy and Rory through a fantasy prism, exploring the idea of what *Doctor Who* might have looked like if Lewis had created it. The story had been a big hit with the readership.

So I had a hard act to follow.

Celebrating the Yuletide wasn't the most important element of the story, though: we were saying goodbye to the Ponds. Amy and Rory had left the TV series three months earlier in *The Angels Take Manhattan*, and we had reached the point in the strip when we also had to wish them good luck and send them on their way. The last time the comic strip had presented a 'farewell' story for a companion was Donna Noble's departure in *Time of My Life*. This had also been produced by Jonathan Morris and Rob Davis, and it had been another exceptional story – equal parts hilarious and heartbreaking. Again, the readers had *loved* it.

So really, I had *two* hard acts to follow. (Thanks a *bunch*, boys.)

My first thought was to do another tribute story. There hadn't been just one Doctor in my childhood, there had been *two* – and the possibility that their worlds could overlap got me excited. Like millions of kids I had loved the books of Theodor Giesel, better known as Dr Seuss. My appreciation only increased when I started reading them again with my children. I had noticed that the main character in *The Cat in the Hat* had a certain Doctorish quality to him; the Cat was a flamboyant, anarchic figure who pops up out of the blue, drags a couple of ordinary kids into an adventure, pulls all manner of bizarre inventions out of nowhere and generally causes seventeen different kinds of havoc – and then cheerfully disappears at the end. It would be an easy task to recast Matt Smith's Doctor as a Cat-like character.

The working title was *The Doc and the Klok*. I was envisioning the whole thing illustrated as a Dr Seuss pastiche with no word balloons, only captions. A young brother and sister wake on Christmas morning and run to their parents' bedroom. They find two crying babies in the bed, but no sign of their mum and dad. Downstairs they find a large blue present wrapped up in the living room. Bursting out of it comes the magical figure of the Doc, who has come in search of adventure. The Doc and the kids find a new clock on the wall with a sinister face. The Klok is alive and can manipulate time – it has regressed the kids' parents to babies. The Klok releases a swarm of various nasty monsters that run riot throughout the house. The Doc lifts up his fez to reveal two tiny helpers, Pond #1 and Pond #2. They help him and the kids capture the monsters, restore the parents to adulthood and defeat the Klok.

The final page would be a sudden stylistic shift back to 'reality'. The two children are fast asleep in their beds. The Doctor has his hands on their foreheads. He's been telling them the Seuss-style story. He informs the shaken parents that that's how they'll always remember the terrifying events of the night – as a silly bedtime story; an amusing dream. The horrific truth of the Klok and his monsters has been turned into something they'll be able to cope with. The Doctor turns to leave. The parents thank him and ask about the two people he put into the story, "Pond #1 and Pond #2" – who were they? The Doctor sadly tells them that they were "friends from long ago..."

Above: Amelia, Mels and Rory try to outrun the goblins! Pencil art by Mike Collins.

Below: The classic *The Cat in the Hat* by Dr Seuss, published by Random House.

It wasn't bad, but it wasn't making me do cartwheels either. I could see a couple of big problems. There was the notion of asking an artist to draw 11 pages of a 12-page story in someone else's style. I knew people who could do it – Roger Langridge in particular had demonstrated many times a chameleonic ability to channel the styles of classic cartoonists, and he would have been the first person I'd have phoned. But... it felt cheeky somehow. Disrespectful. A professional artist wants to bring his own vision to a story, not parrot someone else's. A pastiche that lasted two or three pages might have been fine, but a whole story? The idea made me itch.

An equally big problem was the simple fact that I was devising a 'farewell to the Ponds' story that didn't actually have them in it. Which... y'know... didn't seem like a particularly great idea.

THE CAT IN THE HAT
By Dr. Seuss

So I had a re-think. I wanted a story that would put Amy and Rory firmly centre-stage; never an easy thing to do when there's an eccentric 1000-year-old alien time-traveller hogging the spotlight. I pondered doing a story without the Doctor, with Amy and Rory back on Earth, living in London, getting on with their lives, but it didn't excite. It was only when I started thinking of it as a Christmas story *first* that I made some progress – it's a time of magic, snow, presents and of course... *children!*

Depicting Amy and Rory as kids immediately appealed. Caitlin Blackwood (Karen Gillan's real-life cousin, fact-fans) had been a wonderful young Amelia, and it seemed a sweet idea to put her back in the comic strip after her appearance in *The Professor, the Queen and the Bookshop*, only this time in 'proper' continuity. And of course, if

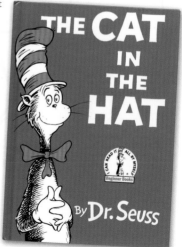

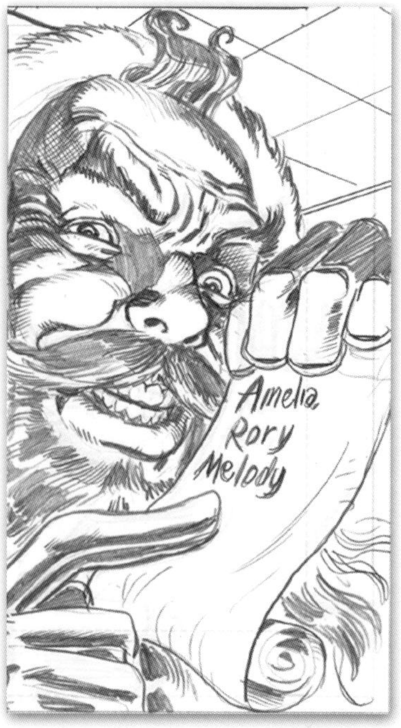
Amelia
Rory
Melody

Amelia was going to be there then her best friend had to make an appearance too...

River Song provokes extreme reactions, and I'm sure Steven Moffat (and she) wouldn't want it any other way. People either love her or loathe her – I happily sit in the former camp. Her earlier incarnation Mels seemed to me to be almost as fun, but we only got a brief glimpse of her in *Let's Kill Hitler*. *The Impossible Astronaut* had established that the Ponds' little girl had super-strength (she broke out of the NASA suit, remember?), and I immediately seized on that. I had been a fan of Astrid Lindgren's character Pippi Longstocking when I was a boy, so Mels gave me the chance to tip my hat to the other 'Strongest Girl in the World'. Mike Collins generously provided me with possibly the best fight scene ever done in the **DWM** strip; fluid, dynamic and very funny.

The villains were originally going to be the 'Overdogs' – three humanoid canines who were attempting to curry favour with the Trickster, the time-twisting villain seen in several episodes of *The Sarah Jane Adventures*. There had also been a reference to the Trickster in the *Doctor Who* story *Turn Left* which featured the Time Beetle as part of the 'Pantheon of Discord'. I liked the sound of that – I inferred that there was an entire society of creatures that delighted in altering reality and causing chaos. The Overdogs were three fairly thick brothers who were trying to join the Pantheon, using Amelia, Rory and Mels as their audition piece for the Trickster. I messed around with them for a couple of weeks but they failed to inspire. I replaced them with 'Atnas Sualc' (yes, really), a sinister sorcerer who was Santa's evil twin brother. Better, but still not there...

Then the gods smiled on me: I stumbled across an online reference to Krampus, a genuine piece of Germanic folklore. I had never heard of him but he's been big news in Scandanavia for centuries. Krampus is the companion to Saint Nicholas; basically the Anti-Santa. A red-skinned demonic figure, Krampus follows Santa around and nicks the presents he's deposited, sometimes replacing them with lumps of coal. The really naughty children are just grabbed in their sleep, thrown into his sack and carried off, never to be seen again. (Can't think why *he* didn't get adopted by Coca-Cola.) Krampus' flipped white/red colour scheme was my tribute to DC's Professor Zoom, *aka* the evil Reverse Flash, whose costume is the exact opposite of the Flash's.

I wanted to start the story with a comic drawn by a child, in pencils and coloured in crayon. It would show how Amelia met the Doctor that first night in *The Eleventh Hour.* Then a sneering Veronica would be revealed holding it up – it's been drawn by Amelia. Veronica gleefully tears the comic in half. Lack of page-space prohibited that, so I had Veronica decapitate a doll of the Doctor instead.

There's a friendliness to Mike Collins' artwork, a welcoming quality, that made him the perfect fit for this story. Mike is a master at drawing children too. It's all there: the innocence, the cruelty, the fear and the fun. And his Krampus was just *amazing* – somehow managing to be both comical and creepy as hell. I knew it was vital that Amelia and Rory not remember Krampus and company at the end. Amy's life was clearly long and tough, with no allies to support her belief that the Doctor was real. That meant Rory couldn't have any experience of aliens as a boy.

The final page came early in the plotting and gave me the confidence to edge along, as painfully as ever, until I had a complete story. I knew it would work, and be one of those great images that can really only work in comics. On TV the montage would only have been seen fleetingly. On paper the reader could examine each of those photos for as long as they liked. Mike and David did an exemplary job depicting the Ponds' unfolding post-Doctor life. I knew that the montage would get a strong reaction from the readership but it wasn't a manipulative move – I was a huge fan of both characters and was going to miss them as dearly as anyone. If you cried at that last page, then you weren't alone – I shed a few tears too.

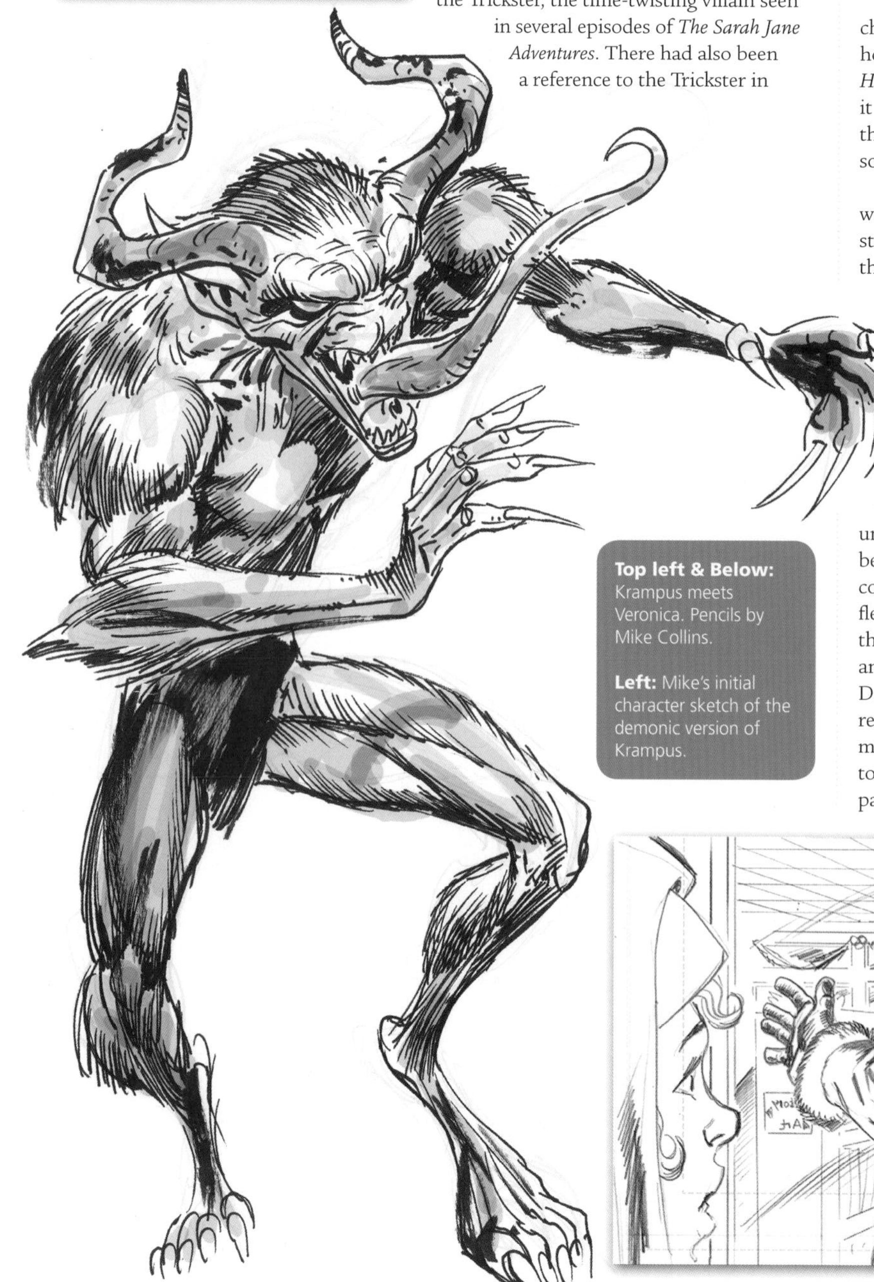

Top left & Below: Krampus meets Veronica. Pencils by Mike Collins.

Left: Mike's initial character sketch of the demonic version of Krampus.

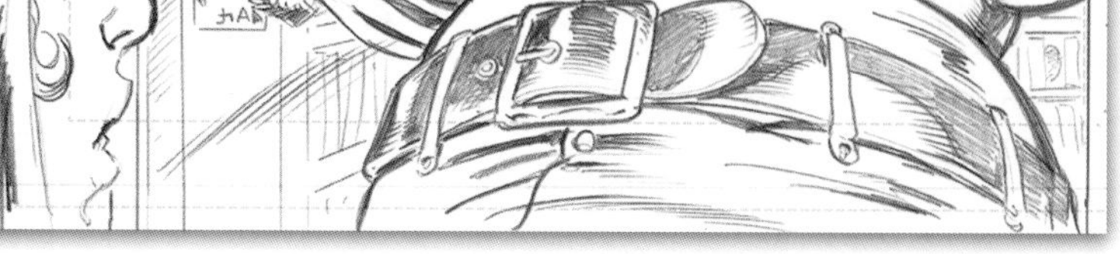

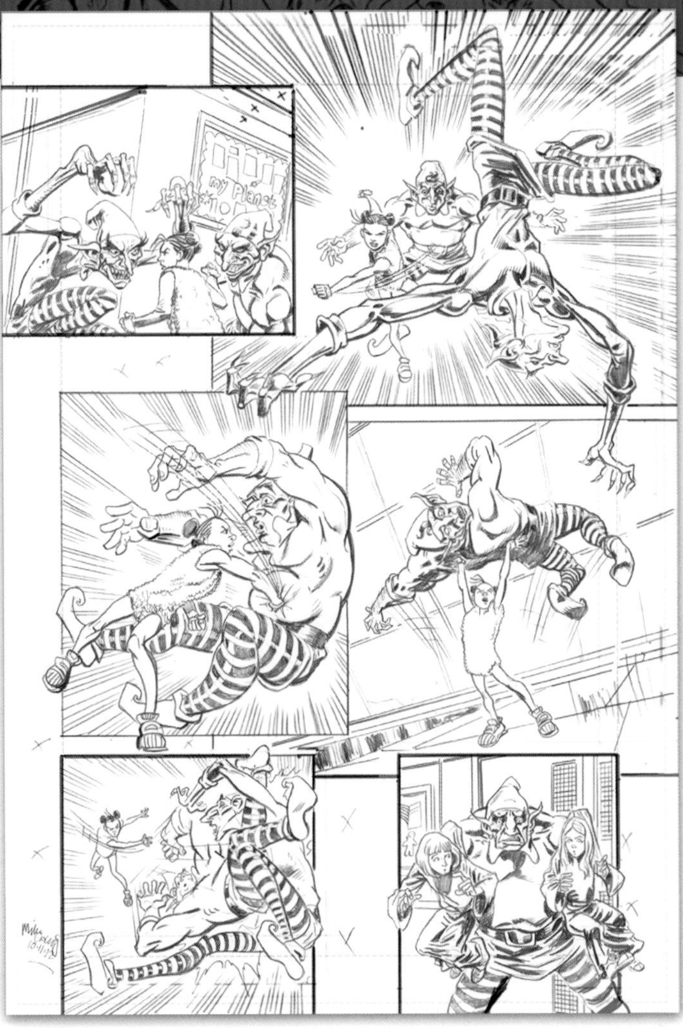

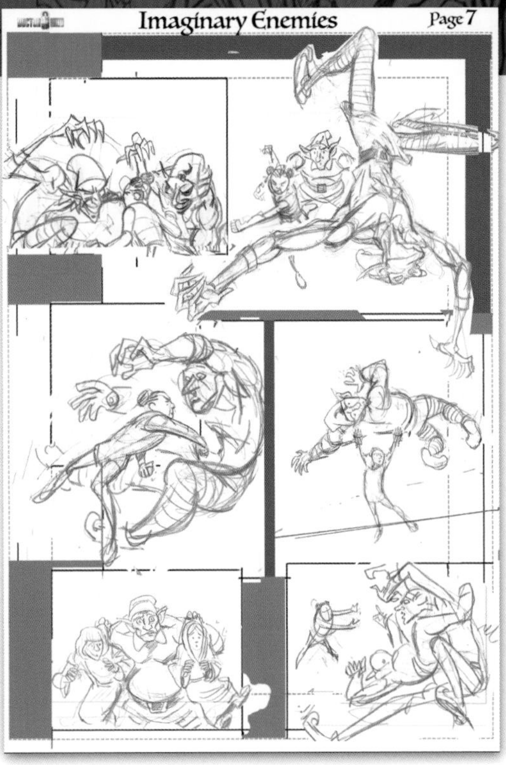
Imaginary Enemies
Page 7

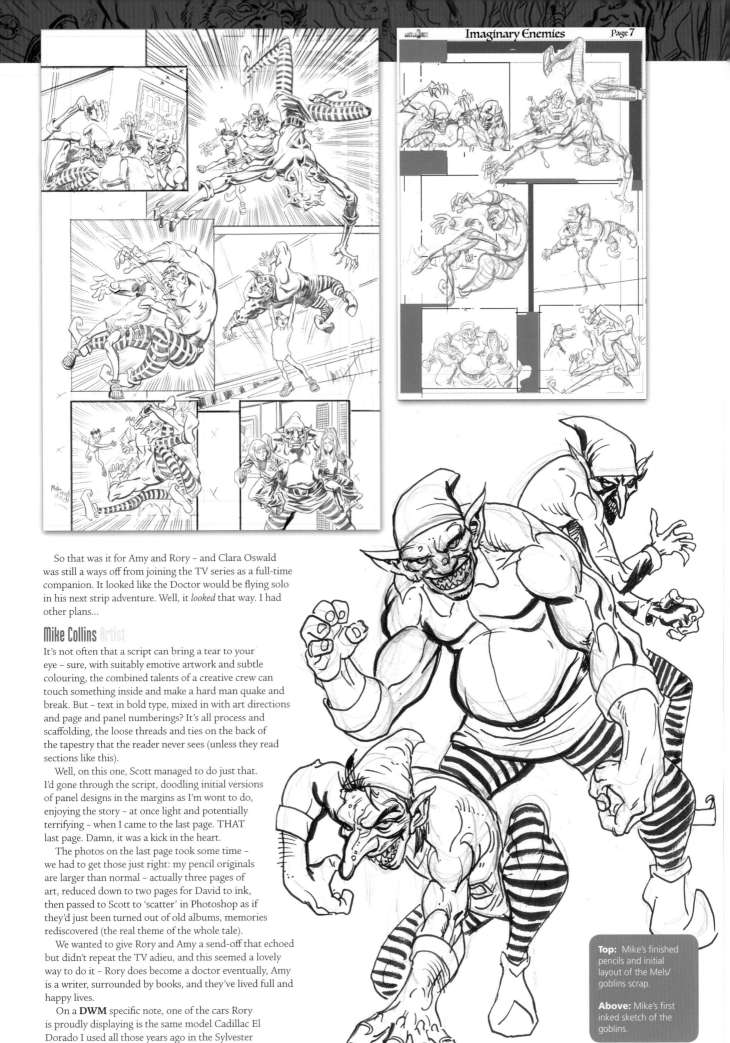

So that was it for Amy and Rory – and Clara Oswald was still a ways off from joining the TV series as a full-time companion. It looked like the Doctor would be flying solo in his next strip adventure. Well, it *looked* that way. I had other plans...

Mike Collins Artist

It's not often that a script can bring a tear to your eye – sure, with suitably emotive artwork and subtle colouring, the combined talents of a creative crew can touch something inside and make a hard man quake and break. But – text in bold type, mixed in with art directions and page and panel numberings? It's all process and scaffolding, the loose threads and ties on the back of the tapestry that the reader never sees (unless they read sections like this).

Well, on this one, Scott managed to do just that. I'd gone through the script, doodling initial versions of panel designs in the margins as I'm wont to do, enjoying the story – at once light and potentially terrifying – when I came to the last page. THAT last page. Damn, it was a kick in the heart.

The photos on the last page took some time – we had to get those just right: my pencil originals are larger than normal – actually three pages of art, reduced down to two pages for David to ink, then passed to Scott to 'scatter' in Photoshop as if they'd just been turned out of old albums, memories rediscovered (the real theme of the whole tale).

We wanted to give Rory and Amy a send-off that echoed but didn't repeat the TV adieu, and this seemed a lovely way to do it – Rory does become a doctor eventually, Amy is a writer, surrounded by books, and they've lived full and happy lives.

On a **DWM** specific note, one of the cars Rory is proudly displaying is the same model Cadillac El Dorado I used all those years ago in the Sylvester

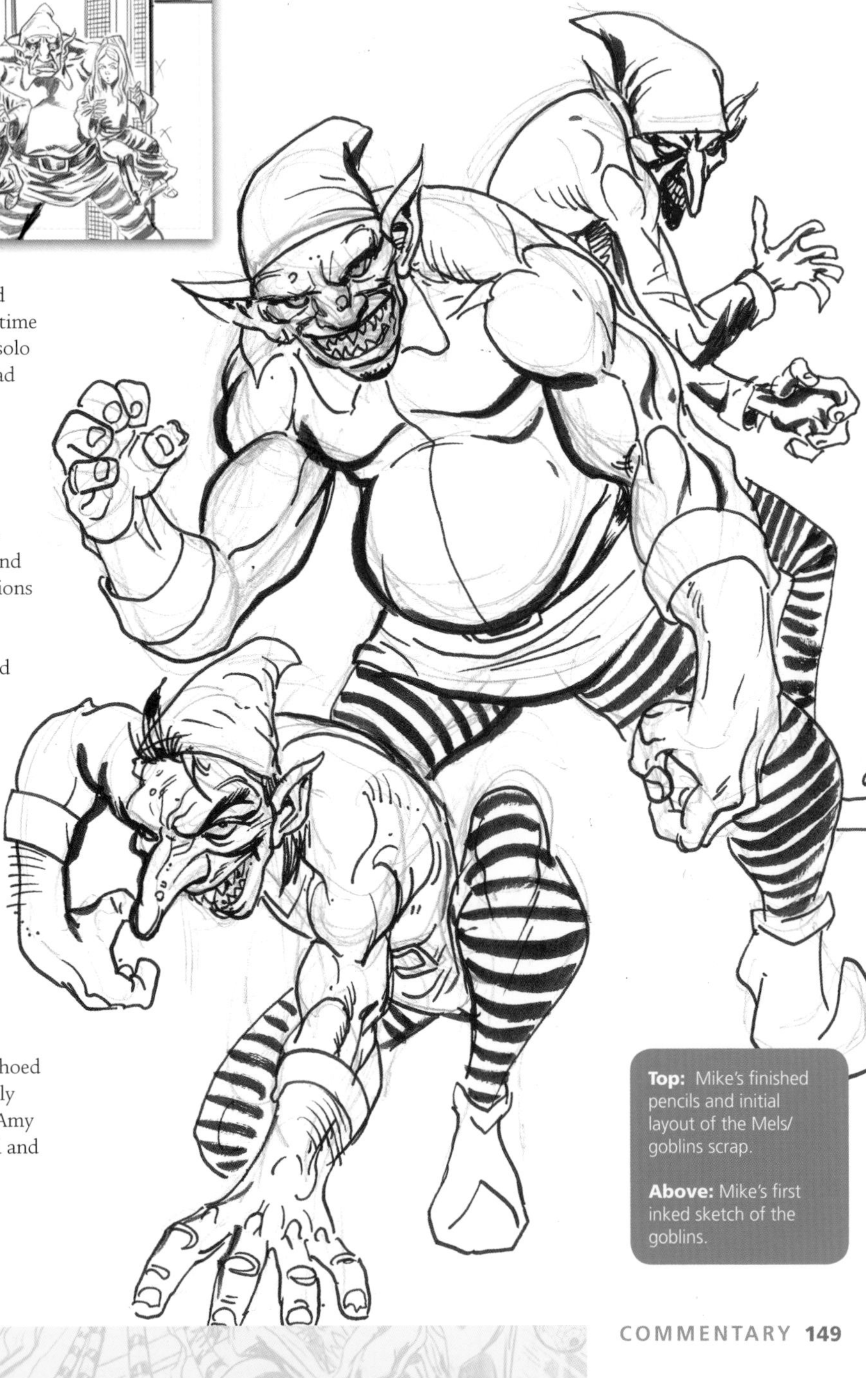

Top: Mike's finished pencils and initial layout of the Mels/goblins scrap.

Above: Mike's first inked sketch of the goblins.

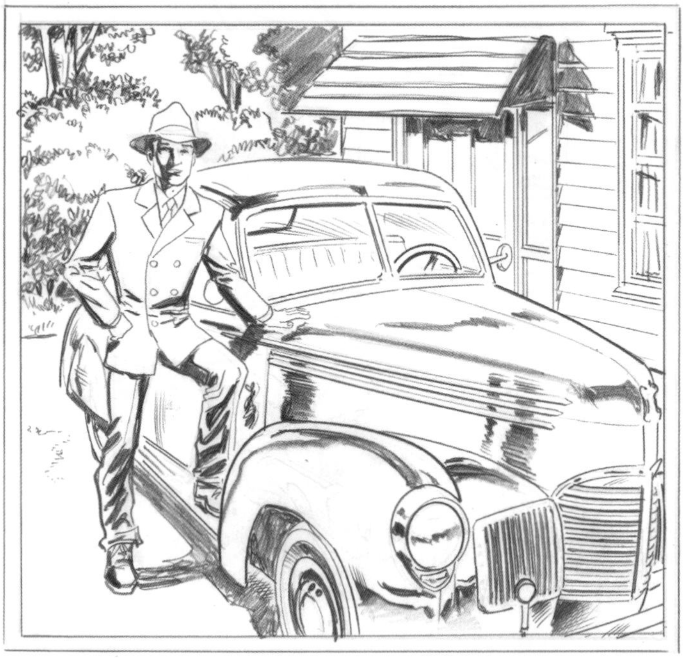

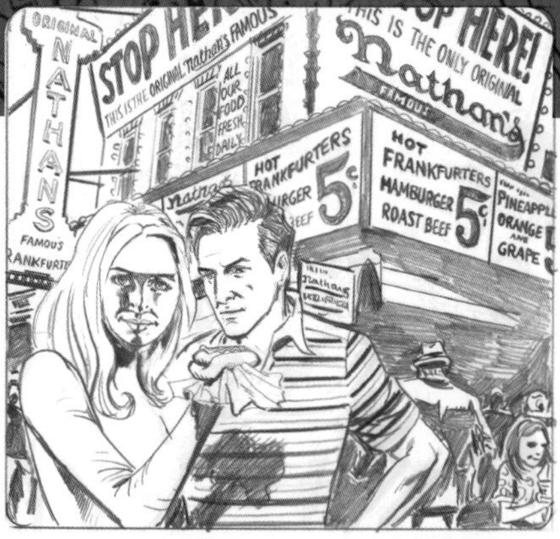
STOP HERE!
THIS IS THE ONLY ORIGINAL
Nathan's
FAMOUS
HOT
FRANKFURTERS
HAMBURGER
ROAST BEEF
5¢
PINEAPPLE
ORANGE
GRAPE
ORIGINAL
NATHANS
FAMOUS
FRANKFURTERS

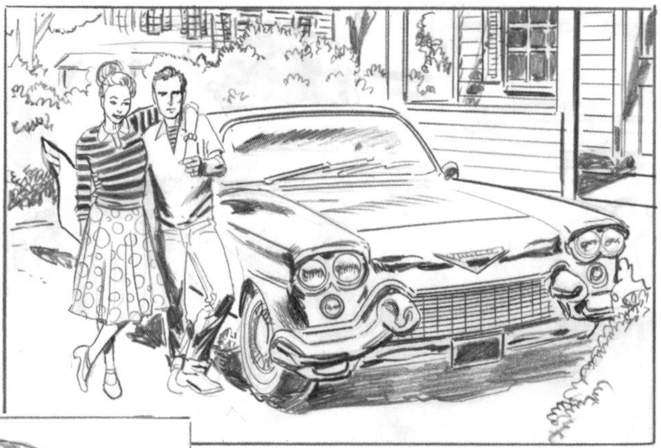

Above & right: Mike's pencil art for the Amy and Rory 'photos'.

Below: Mike's first colour sketch of Mels as the "Sheep of Doom"!

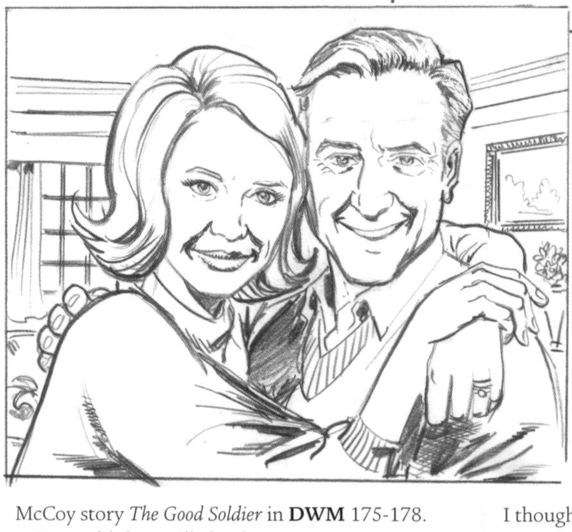

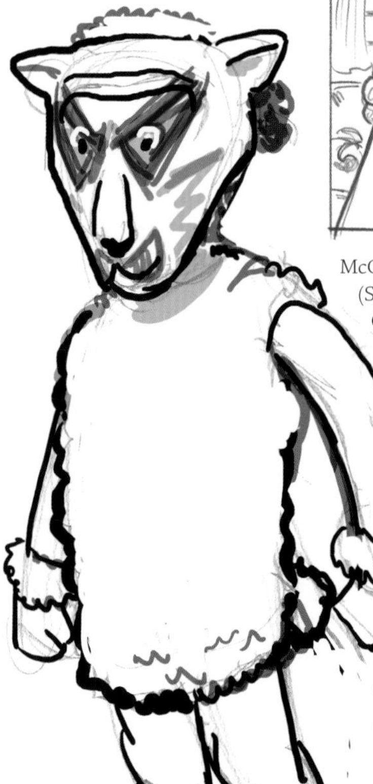

McCoy story *The Good Soldier* in **DWM** 175-178. (So could that really be the TARDIS, its Chameleon Circuit working briefly?)

So in timey-wimey style, that's the final page discussed, what of the body of the tale? The adventures of three kids versus an evil Santa Claus? Like *The Lodger* back in the Tenth Doctor's run, I knew this was a story the readership of **DWM** would either adore or hunt us through the streets of Cardiff, demanding blood for straying so far from the *Doctor Who* formula. Like that fabulous little Gareth Roberts tale (which of course went on to be an Eleventh Doctor TV episode), the readership embraced the sentiment in the way it was intended; celebratory and sad.

The evil elves were a joy to create, and I could do a whole series of Sheep Mel's adventures, taking out bad guys and cruel schoolgirls. I'm pretty sure Scott would be up for writing it too!

Scott apologised to me for spoiling the end of *The Angels Take Manhattan* (one of the upsides/downsides of working on the **DWM** strip is that – because of production time – if it's relevant to the story, we get to know things before they air) which meant I then had to hide that last page from my daughters who were looking forward to seeing Amy and Rory's continuing adventures...

My daughters are key to my approach on this story: re-watching *Let's Kill Hitler*, I couldn't spot a clear exterior shot of Rory, Mels and Amy's primary school. Now, it's no secret that pretty much all the 'London' locations in *Doctor Who* are actually here in Cardiff where, coincidentally, myself and long-time **DWM** inker David A Roach both live. I've used several local locations in stories, keeping with this theme (for instance, the street in *FAQ* is one I walk down to the train station on the way to my studio in Cardiff Bay each morning).

So, for the primary school in this story I thought it would be a nice touch to use a school I was all-too familiar with – the one my own daughters had gone too, Eglwys Wen. (Curiously, in one of those odd juxtapositions that Cardiff itself is hard-wired with, as we're part of the wider Marvel family, the site also contained Welsh language primary Ysgol Gymraeg Melin Gruffydd where Ioan Gruffudd – movie Fantastic Four's Mr Fantastic – attended!)

For me, this added to the poignancy that Scott's story echoed with – my daughters have long left (my eldest is now a primary school teacher herself, though on the other side of Cardiff), but as the school is in our village, I still visit occasionally to give talks. The corridors that Mels, Amy and Rory run down, the classrooms they huddle in, are a mix of those briefly seen on TV and those seen by me on a daily basis while my girls went there.

Shortly after the comic saw print, I'd committed to one of my periodic visits to the old school, to take a class on drawing monsters and heroes – something I started while my girls were there and I've carried on ever since – and was able to present the original art of page one, featuring the outside of the school, as a gift.

Ironically, the summer before, while I was drawing the strip, the building had had a facelift and the frontage had been changed so much, the art was – like the strip it featured in – already an echo of a time gone, a snatch of a memory, of school days passed. Sad, but somehow in keeping with the story we'd drawn.

Hunters of the Burning Stone

Scott Gray Writer

Doctor Who was having a birthday. A really big one. But I was ready for the party... almost. I had been preparing this story for 15 months, establishing characters, planting seeds, dropping hints. However, when the time came to actually sit down and properly plot the whole thing out scene-by-scene, I did my usual thing: I froze. So many characters! So many settings! So many cliffhangers! Where to begin?

Right at the start of his excellent book *The Writer's Tale*, former *Doctor Who* showrunner Russell T Davies talks about the 'Maybe': the area of potential story ideas that all writers explore as they begin work. Trouble is, the Maybe for *Doctor Who* is pretty much an infinite space. Maybe your story is set in present-day Madrid. Maybe it's in a parallel universe. Maybe it's in prehistoric Brighton or a burger bar on Jupiter or the Land of Fiction. Maybe your villain is a giant hedgehog or Genghis Khan or the living embodiment of sarcasm. Maybe, maybe, maybe...

I felt the pressure of presenting the **DWM** strip's 50th anniversary story. It *had* to be special. I knew several of the basic beats: the Doctor would be forced to go on a journey of self-discovery and do the one thing that truly scares him: look in the mirror. I knew the image of the TARDIS, embedded in humanity's collective psyche, would prove crucial to his victory. I had the Prometheans established very early on, back when I was plotting *The Chains of Olympus*. I was always aware of exactly what was 'buried in Man'. But that was all stuff for the climax. It didn't help me get started. I wanted to explore every possible path the storyline could take and that paralysed me for a long while. I was stuck in the Maybe.

Tom and Pete had given me a rough (and ultimately correct) idea of when Amy and Rory were going to be leaving the TV series. I did my sums and concluded early on that they probably wouldn't still be around when our 'season finale' arrived. That's why the pair weren't present at two key story arc moments: when the Doctor gets that cryptic message in the TARDIS at the end of *Sticks & Stones* and when he confronts Miss Ghost at the conclusion of *The Cornucopia Caper*. This had to be a personal mystery for the Doctor to solve.

I had been very proud of the end of *Sticks & Stones*; it was a scene that played to the medium's strengths. A novel would have been obligated to describe what the Doctor was seeing on the monitor. It wouldn't have worked on TV either, as Matt Smith's voice on the monitor would have instantly given the game away. It could *only* work in a comic. I was also pleased with the time-twisting element to Miss Ghost's face-off with the Doctor in *The Cornucopia Caper*, with her repeating the question, "What is buried in Man?" that she had heard as a child in Prague, even though the Doctor (and the reader) had yet to experience it.

Hunters just *had* to be drawn by Martin Geraghty – he's been the backbone of the **DWM** strip for an age-and-a-half, always giving it every ounce of his talent and inspiration. His love for *Doctor Who* is boundless and he poured it into every single panel of this story. Martin, David Roach and James Offredi were bouncing off each other in all sorts of wonderful directions here – those amazing montages in Part Five... the relived scenes from *100,000 BC*... the Hunters' attack in Part Two... and of course, *that* cliffhanger in Part One...

Ian and Barbara's presence was the last element of the story to

Below: The first pencil sketches of Annabel in her armour by Scott Gray.

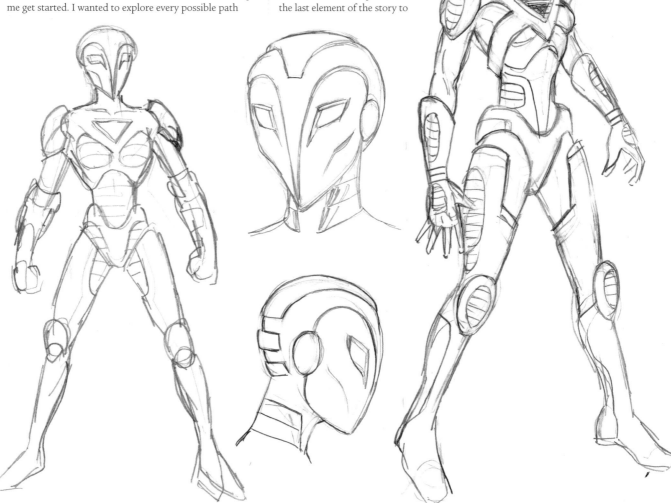

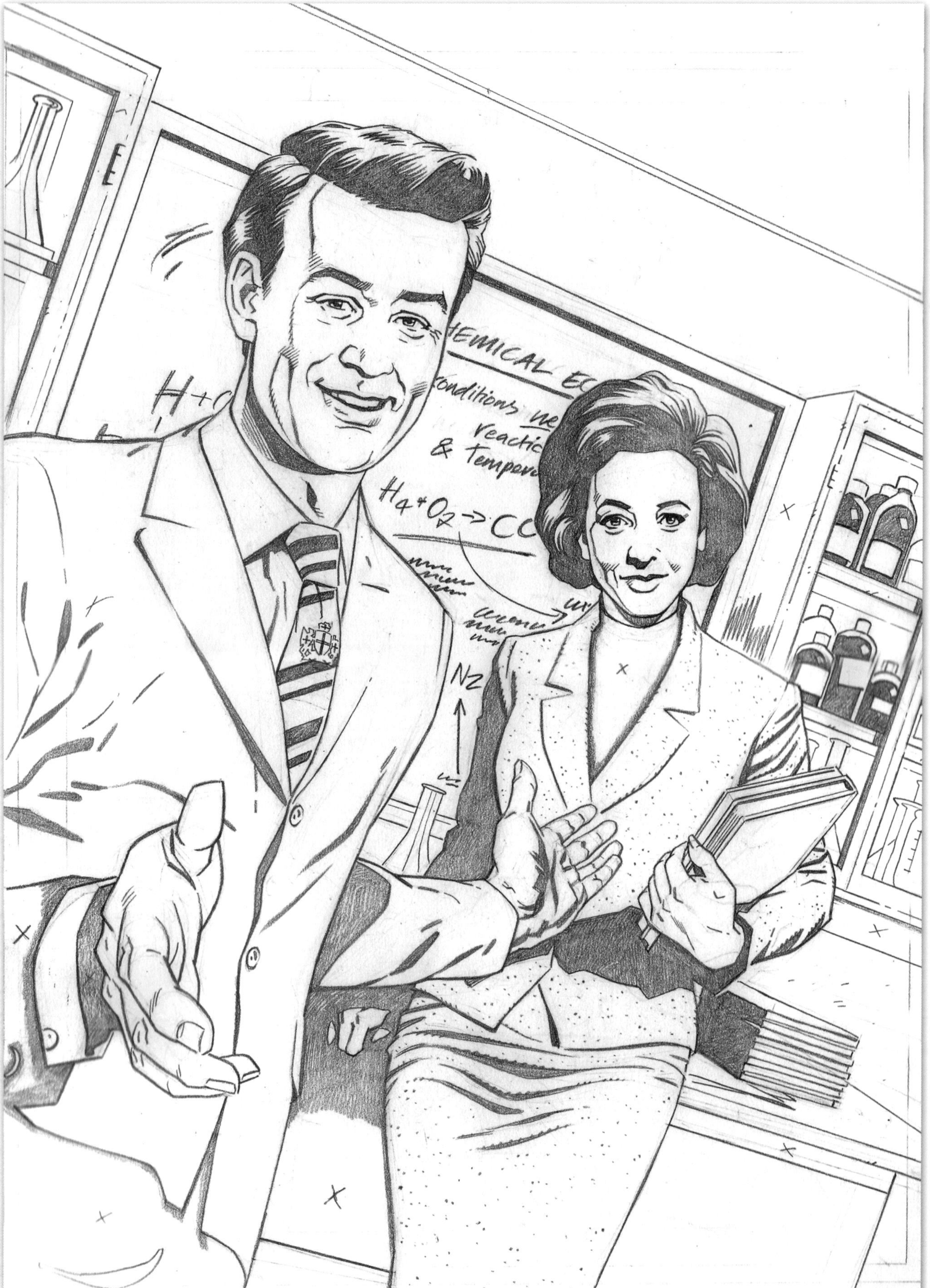

take shape. When it first came to mind I quickly dismissed it as too indulgent. But... they just kept sneaking back! Their return wasn't something I would have seriously considered at any other time in the comic strip, but this was the 50th anniversary. All bets were off. I realised that, if done properly, it could lead to something with genuine resonance. The **DWM** strip had stayed the distance – we had been around for decades, we had earned the right to do something that big. I also wanted a surprise that would make the fans sit up and take notice, something that the TV series couldn't possibly duplicate. There was no recasting necessary, no *Forrest Gump* CGI trickery needed; we could simply take William Russell and Jacqueline Hill, looking like they had just stepped off the set of *The Chase*, and put them inside the modern TARDIS to meet Matt Smith. That's the magic of comics – time travel is simple.

I watched all of the TV stories that featured Ian and Barbara and took plenty of notes. I also looked out for good close-up shots that Martin might be able to use as reference. I knew he'd rise to the challenge of capturing them both, and so he did. His first full-page pencil illo of the pair was an instant classic, and got everyone in the office buzzing.

There's a school of thought that Ian and Barbara have never been bettered as companions in *Doctor Who*'s history, and I wouldn't argue with that. They are detailed, intelligent characters that possess a maturity and credibility never again equalled in the series. They're portrayed with depth by two accomplished actors who have a natural rapport. No matter how limited the set, no matter how basic the special effect, William Russell and Jacqueline Hill played every scene with utter conviction and integrity. They kept *Doctor Who* tethered to reality as it set sail through a universe of imagination. Their performances were so distinct that I had their voices locked in my head from the beginning. The first six pages of Part Two were the easiest and most enjoyable to write in the whole story; I just sat back and listened to the three characters talk to each other.

But I had originally planned a completely different way of introducing Ian and Barbara. The story would have opened on the snowy plains of the Antarctic. An expedition is investigating a mysterious, gigantic pyramid. Ian and Barbara are part of the team but their identities are concealed from the reader by hoods, scarves and goggles. They've been drawn there by some kind of psychic summoning – strange dreams, whispering in their heads, that sort of thing. The Doctor arrives in another part of the pyramid (which looks just like the one in *The Cornucopia Caper* – it's another Promethean spacecraft) and is attacked by monstrous guards. It's a trap! The other people in the expedition are all killed and the Doctor is wounded. He's carried to safety by the only two survivors. They remove their headgear on the last page to reveal – gasp! – Ian and Barbara!

I quite liked this for a Part One – nice setting, plenty of action – but there were problems. For a start, I realised that keeping Ian and Barbara's identities a secret throughout the chapter was going to get very awkward very quickly. I wanted their speech patterns to be as close as possible to the TV series, and all this pair *ever* seemed to do was refer to each other by name!

"How are you feeling, Barbara?"

"Much better, thanks, Ian."

"That's a relief. Barbara, there's something I need to tell you..."

"Yes, Ian, what is it?" *etc, etc, etc...*

These two getting through 11 pages without *once* calling each other by name seemed about as likely as me winning the Booker Prize.

But there was a larger issue: I wanted Ian and Barbara living a normal life. That had been their goal when they left the Doctor and I wanted to stay true to that. Having them already actively involved in the adventure felt wrong. But

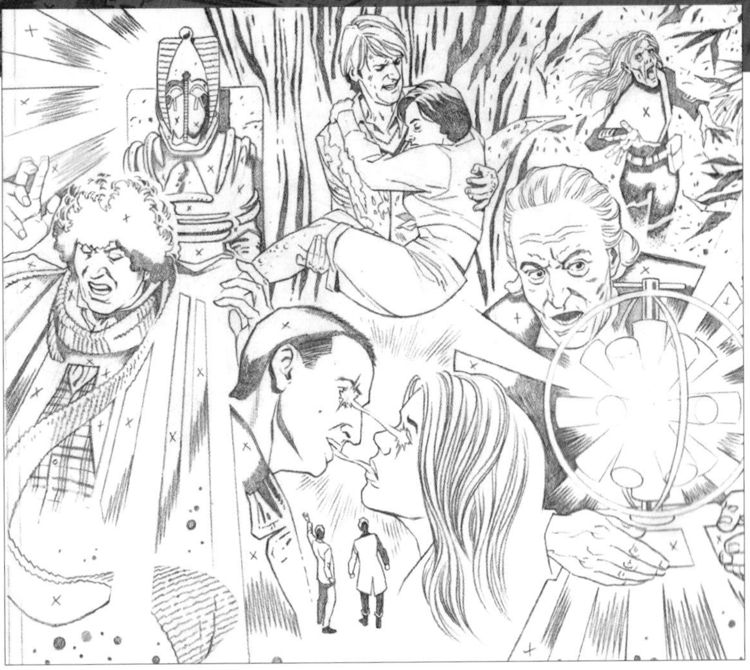

Opposite page: Ian and Barbara are revealed! Pencil art by Martin Geraghty.

Above: A montage of the Doctor's sacrifices. Pencil art by Martin Geraghty.

I wanted that revelatory full-page cliffhanger too – how to get both? I circled around that one for a couple of weeks. Then one evening I took my daughter to an open night at a local secondary school, and that sparked the notion of placing Ian and Barbara in a very familiar setting that would turn out to be false. So Martin got to recreate Coal Hill School, complete with those two whispering girls in the hallway!

There seems to be a general attitude in *Doctor Who* fandom that the opening episode, *An Unearthly Child*, is fantastic – which it certainly is – but the three episodes that follow aren't much cop. 'Just a bunch of cavemen grunting and waving clubs' seems to be the standard description. Almost everyone seems to wish that the Doctor and company had just jumped straight to Skaro for the first story. But almost everyone is wrong.

I admit I'd always gone along with received wisdom on this one, but there's a big difference between watching a TV story and *studying* it. Upon looking at it carefully, my opinion of *100,000 BC* shifted 180 degrees. It was *brilliant!*

Here's the thing: this is *exactly* the story that was needed to launch *Doctor Who*. Anthony Coburn's script is tight, tense, and focuses on the four leads like no other tale. Coburn keeps them together for almost the entire time. He forces them to interact under extreme pressure, giving us a strong understanding of how their relationships will develop in the coming months. We witness Ian and the Doctor's rivalry, Barbara and Ian's respect for one another, Susan's innocence and courage, and the Doctor's callous, domineering nature. The foursome gradually begin to work together in order to survive, hinting at the teamwork that will follow. If this had been a more standard, plot-heavy adventure with the leads getting split up, kidnapped and pushed into alternating storylines, we wouldn't have had anything like that level of focus. Skaro, the Thals and the Daleks would have grabbed the viewers' attention, pushing the regulars into the background before we'd had a chance to get to know them. *100,000 BC* was an essential character piece.

And the Tribe of Gum is anything but a bunch of grunting savages. Za and Hur are a fascinating couple, grappling with their primitive politics, constantly struggling to maintain authority over the Tribe. Then there's Old

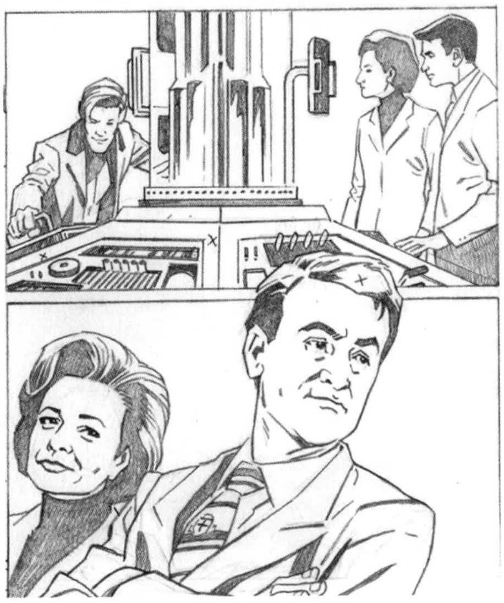

Below: The Doctor, Ian and Barbara, back in the TARDIS! Pencils by Martin Geraghty.

Above: The Doctor returns to 76 Totter's Lane. Pencil art by Martin Geraghty.

Below: Martin's initial pencil sketches of the Prometheans.

Mother and her fear of what uncontrollable power might bring down on her people: "Fire will kill us all in the end." What a *superb* line, written in the shadow of the Cold War. Kal is the scheming outsider who sees a vulnerable group ripe for the taking, with only one man standing in his way. Supporting them all is the sarcastic Horg who plays Za off against Kal, secure in the knowledge that they both want his daughter – which means he'll be okay. They're all strong, believable figures. Coburn's themes of betrayal, survival, politics and compassion expertly interweave to make this a subtle, powerful story, one too often unfairly dismissed.

The brilliant scene where Barbara abandons their chance for escape and stops to help Za led directly to the climax of *Hunters*, of course. The fact that the Hartnell Doctor seems just as uncomprehending of Barbara's motivation as Za and Hur is astonishing in hindsight. It's often been commented upon that when *Doctor Who* began, Ian and Barbara were the true heroes of the series, with the Doctor acting as a selfish, deceitful, sometimes even malevolent, foil. As the characters race back to the TARDIS at the climax of *100,000 BC*, Barbara stumbles and falls – and the Doctor *runs right over her!* While this level of initial nastiness had been discussed in books and magazine articles, I had never seen it addressed within an actual story. I thought the Doctor's slow evolution into a hero would be a fitting subject to address in the anniversary story.

The idea of the TARDIS being a part of humanity's collective consciousness came from real world events, bizarrely enough. In 1998 the BBC and the London Metropolitan Police got into a legal battle over ownership of the police box trademark. The BBC argued that the image was now far more associated with *Doctor Who* than with the London Met and they therefore had a right to use it for merchandising purposes. The Beeb won, and from that day on, the police box became the TARDIS in the eyes of the legal world. The Doctor fought the law, and the law lost.

I thought that was *fascinating!* It's the only case I can think of where a fictional construct has supplanted the object it's based on in the public consciousness. I'd love to know exactly when the cultural tipping-point occurred – when did we go from the TARDIS looking like a police box to police boxes looking like the TARDIS? Whenever it happened, it's undeniable; when Joe Public comes across a police box today he only sees a time/space machine. That's quite an achievement. *Doctor Who* fan (and TARDIS connoisseur) Jason Lythgoe-Hay lent us a copy of the original police box designs drawn by Gilbert MacKenzie Trench OBE in 1929, and Martin used them as a background image in Part Six.

Revealing the Doctor to be responsible for jamming the TARDIS' Chameleon Circuit was a plot twist I would never have dreamed of using under normal circumstances. I knew in a sense I was tinkering with the entire history of the series. That was *huge!* But this was a special occasion. Like Ian and Barbara's return, it was big and audacious and we needed that. And besides, the twist had flowed organically from events in the story – it wasn't something I'd set out to do at the start.

When Tom and Pete read the story outline they both had the same question: why had the TARDIS chosen that particular moment at the end of *Sticks & Stones* to show the Doctor the recording of himself inside the original control room? It had been centuries since it had occurred, after all. I actually had an answer! The climax to *Sticks & Stones* involved the Doctor deliberately zapping a core program – the telepathic circuit. That sparks a memory in the TARDIS of the last time the Doctor had performed a similar act of vandalism back in Totter's Yard in 1963, so she shows it to him.

I steered Martin badly off-course with my initial description of the Prometheans. I'd thought it might be fun to base them on those kinds of godlike beings that Captain Kirk frequently encountered in the original *Star Trek* – the ones who always seemed to be eternally wise and powerful and wear sparkly togas. They annoyed the *hell* out of me. Jumped-up pillocks, the lot of them! I wanted the Prometheans to look like the smuggest race in the universe, and asked Martin to give them big heads, togas, and no legs (to suggest an above-it-all, levitating laziness). He complied, but the result lacked any menace at all! It was my mistake – we backtracked and turned them into malevolent Greys instead.

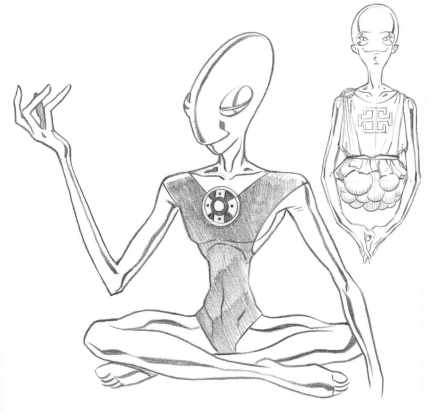

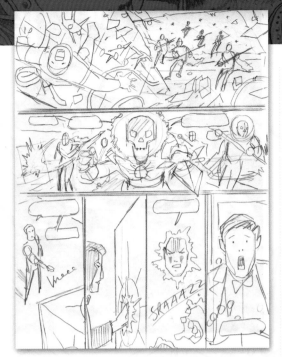

I loved Martin's version of the adult Annabel Lake. That first reveal, her face so tough and so vulnerable, was perfect. My starting point for the character was that she was a mirror image of Amy Pond, but a tragically distorted one. Young Amelia meets the Doctor on an amazing night brimming with glowing phone boxes, giant eyeballs and fish fingers and custard. The brief encounter leaves her with a burning, lifelong desire to recapture that magic. Annabel also meets the Doctor as a child but on a very different kind of night – one composed of giant monsters, underground prisons and the death of her mother. The Doctor isn't a magical figure for Annabel; he's a harbinger of horror. I designed her armour for use in *The Cornucopia Caper*, but didn't tell Dan McDaid who she was. (Many entertaining guesses followed.)

Two Marvel titles had given me an eternal love for spy stories in comics. *Shang-Chi, Master of Kung Fu* by Doug Moench and Paul Gulacy is one of the highwater marks of 1970s comics, featuring for my money the most spectacular fight scenes ever devised for the medium. It's never been reprinted due to copyright complications (it features characters from Sax Rohmer's Fu Manchu novels), but I *beg* you, go look for the back issues. That series led me to its chief inspiration: the 1960s comic *Nick Fury, Agent of SHIELD* by Jim Steranko. Saturated with super-science, pop art and beautiful women, it's been a major influence on generations of creators. Nick Fury was driving an invisible car 34 years before James Bond got one. Comics don't come any cooler! Both titles fed directly into the concept of Wonderland.

I love UNIT as much as any *Doctor Who* daftie, but I've noticed in recent years that it's become an awfully cosy set-up. Every time those soldiers roll up in their land rovers, an officer will jump out, proudly salute the Doctor and tell him how he's studied his file all his life and what an honour it is to meet him and would he care for a cup of tea, please? UNIT seems to be comprised solely of *Doctor Who* fans these days, always happy to accept his authority. That's very nice for the Doctor, I'm sure, but it made me wonder if there could be room for another type of organisation, one that would have a decidedly different attitude to our hero. Wonderland are not the Doctor's cheerleaders. They look at him and see a man who could be an asset in some situations, a liability in others. If they're going to be his allies then it'll be on their terms, not his. If they become his enemies then they'll be very dangerous ones indeed.

I had started off with a different set of human pawns in mind for the Prometheans to manipulate: the Aztecs! Another brilliant story from William Hartnell's era, John Lucarotti's *The Aztecs* put Barbara into a fantastic

scenario: mistaken for a god by an Aztec priest, she is forced to continue the charade in order to safeguard the TARDIS crew's lives. But once in a position of power she attempts to alter history and banish the Aztec practice of human sacrifice. The story gave us a moral quandary for Barbara, action for Ian, even romance for the Doctor. It also provided us with a very memorable villain whom I was keen to bring back: the High Priest of human sacrifice, Tlotoxl – a man who could be argued is really the hero of the story! Seen from his perspective, *The Aztecs* changes dramatically: here's a man who has dedicated his life to the survival of his people by showing deference to their gods. He encounters an alien (Barbara) whom he realises is an imposter. She attempts to destroy his society – and he defeats her! Tlotoxl had been a superb adversary, played with Shakespearian relish by John Ringham. He looked amazing in his facial make-up, something that I knew would translate well into comics. Tlotoxl would have a personal score to settle with Barbara, leading to all sorts of intense scenes. Very promising, and there was more too...

I'd always been intrigued by the mention of the architect Topau (the father of proud warrior Ixta) in *The Aztecs*. He was an unseen character who had disappeared years earlier inside his own temple. I wondered if perhaps the Prometheans had delighted in his artistry and spirited him away, putting him to work designing their spaceships. (That was why the Ziggurat in *The Cornucopia Caper* looked like an inverted Aztec temple.) Of course, Topau would have to encounter Ian, and learn from the Prometheans that he had killed his son in a duel... Good stuff!

The Aztecs were sun-worshippers, so that tied in neatly with the Prometheans' plan. It was easy to imagine scores of super-powered Aztec warriors descending on both

Above: The Hunters attack! Martin's initial layout and finished pencil art.

HUNTERS OF THE BURNING STONE

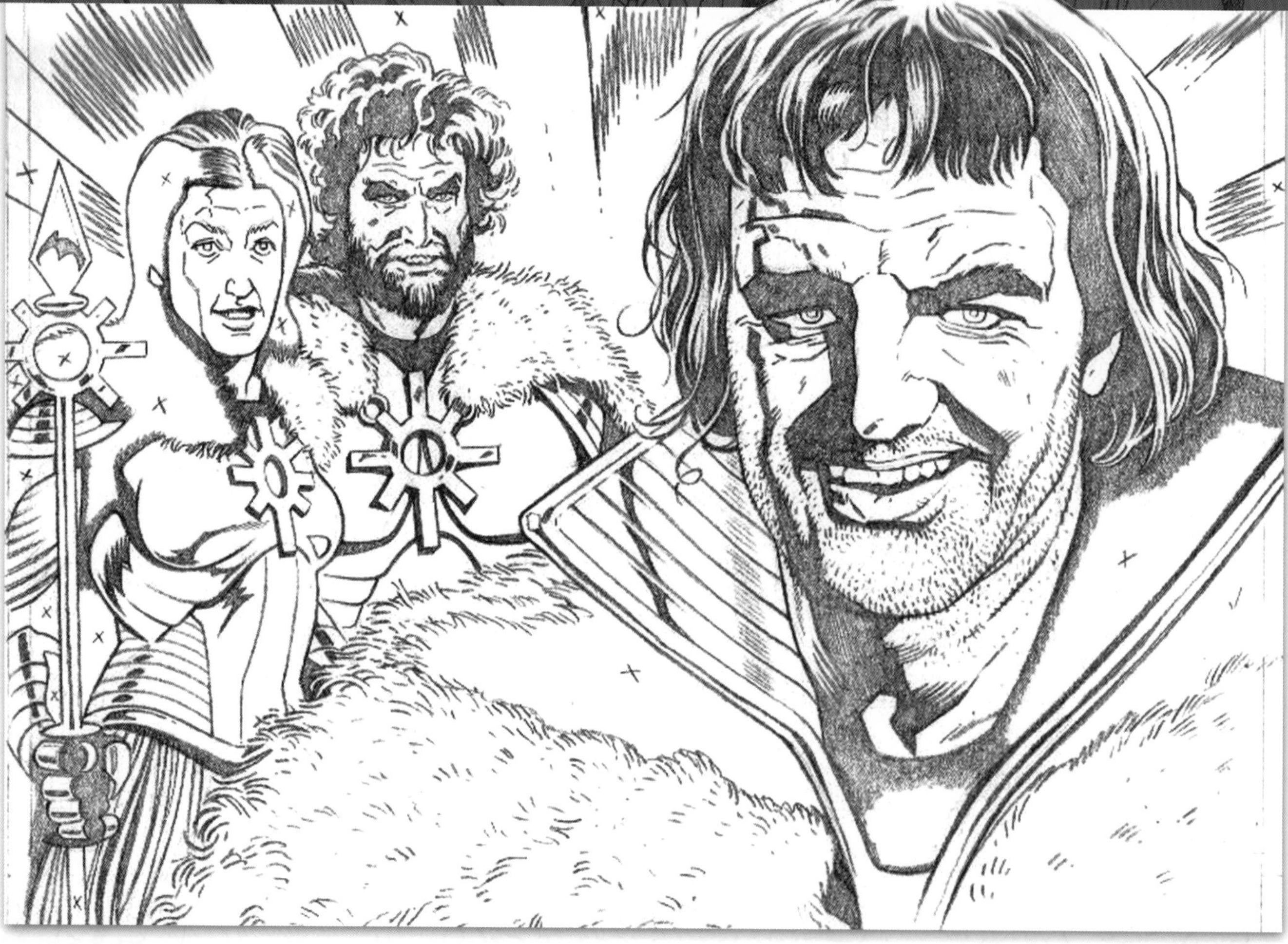

Above: Hur, Horg and Za are revealed at the end of Part Three. Pencils by Martin Geraghty.

Cornucopia and Earth in all their feathered finery – Martin would have had a ball with that!

But as tempting as all that was, the Tribe of Gum were also thumping on the door, and they weren't going away. Making *Hunters* a direct sequel to the very first *Doctor Who* adventure felt so pure, so *primal*. I knew Part Three's cliffhanger revelation would be just as jaw-dropping as Part One's. Also, starting the Prometheans' experiment on humanity at the dawn of man felt like a much stronger concept than seeing them manipulate the already highly-advanced Aztec society. And the more I thought about Za and Hur, the more important they became to the story – they would be nice counterparts to Ian and Barbara. Once the skull motif came to mind, it was a done deal – the Tribe had the gig. I was desperate to keep their identities a secret until the end of Part Three. It felt incredibly obvious to me: the Hunters carried spears, wore fur, used only a basic vocabulary and had flaming skulls for faces! I suspect if I had made any direct connection between them and Ian and Barbara early on then some readers would have twigged, so I kept the Hunters focused on their precious psychic metal.

And as for their design – well, Mr Geraghty really went to town on that one, didn't he? Absolutely jaw-dropping!

People often ask writers to discuss their influences. There's a natural tendency to list the works and creators that have inspired and excited, but there's a flip-side: it's just as important to understand when something *doesn't* work, when someone fails to deliver. Those are influences too. They teach us what *not* to do.

Which brings me to *Skyfall*.

Bear with me. This'll make sense in a bit.

I've had a life-long love of the James Bond films. They may stumble from time-to-time but taken as a whole, the series has consistently offered an exciting world of intrigue, action and humour – a world we know isn't real but is so well-crafted that we don't care, featuring a magnificent hero we can follow with confidence. *Skyfall* was released when I was in the middle of planning the whole Wonderland set-up, so I went to see it hoping for some inspiring big-screen spy action.

Skyfall begins with James Bond chasing a mercenary across Istanbul. The baddie has stolen a hard drive containing the identities of scores of Western agents working undercover. Bond battles the mercenary atop a train but is accidentally shot by a fellow agent, Eve Moneypenny. He falls into a river, apparently dead. Cue opening credits and a fab song from Adele. So far, so good.

But then we jump weeks ahead. The main villain, Silva, cracks the encryption on the hard drive and begins to expose the agents. Their covers are blown and they are captured and executed.

So where's James Bond? Lying on a beach, drinking Heineken.

It turns out that Bond has survived the bullet, but couldn't be bothered to carry on with his mission. He reveals that his feelings were hurt when M ordered Moneypenny to take the shot, because M didn't trust him to defeat the mercenary on the train. Aw, diddums, 007. It isn't until MI6 headquarters gets blown to bits that Bond decides to end his holiday and go back to London. It takes him about 30 minutes to identify the mercenary, who then leads him to Silva. So by wallowing on a beach, filled with self-pity, Bond has given Silva the one thing he needed: time to break the encryption. The blood of those undercover agents is on Bond's hands, a fact neither he nor anyone else in the film acknowledges.

That alone would make *Skyfall* a wretched affair. *But then it gets worse!*

Crazy old Silva is gunning for M. Through an absurdly convoluted scheme (which relies on the 'genius' Q taking a laptop belonging to a villain with near-supernatural hacking abilities and plugging it into the MI6 server), Silva escapes captivity and goes after her. But Bond has a cunning plan to protect his boss. He whisks M away from all her bodyguards and takes her to a remote house in the middle of Scotland.

And then he tells Silva where they are.

It's a *trap*, see? All Silva has are two squads of highly-trained mercenaries, machine guns, explosives and a big helicopter. But James Bond has a shotgun and Albert Finney! Silva doesn't stand a chance!

Uh-oh. Maybe he does. Silva kills M. He succeeds. Bond fails.

And James Bond doesn't fail, for the first time in 50 years of movie adventure, because the villain is brilliant. No, he fails because James Bond has suddenly become a sulky, unprofessional, incompetent *baboon*.

That's not just bad writing. That's vandalism. That's *betrayal*.

It's supposed to work like this: the creators of popular characters are their gods. JK Rowling can do whatever she likes to Harry Potter - that's her absolute right. But for writers who are lucky enough to be handed classic characters that have outlived their creators - fictional figures so powerful they can entertain generation after generation - the deal is different. Those writers are *custodians*. They have a duty to respect what has gone before, to recognise the original intent of the creators, to understand the characters' legacies, strengths and values. Be it Sherlock Holmes, Captain America or Winnie the Pooh, those writers must honour the fundamental traits of the character. If they don't - if they just toss aside all the elements that make them impressive and unique and instead write whatever the hell they want, even if it's the exact *opposite* of what the creator intended - then they are arrogant idiots.

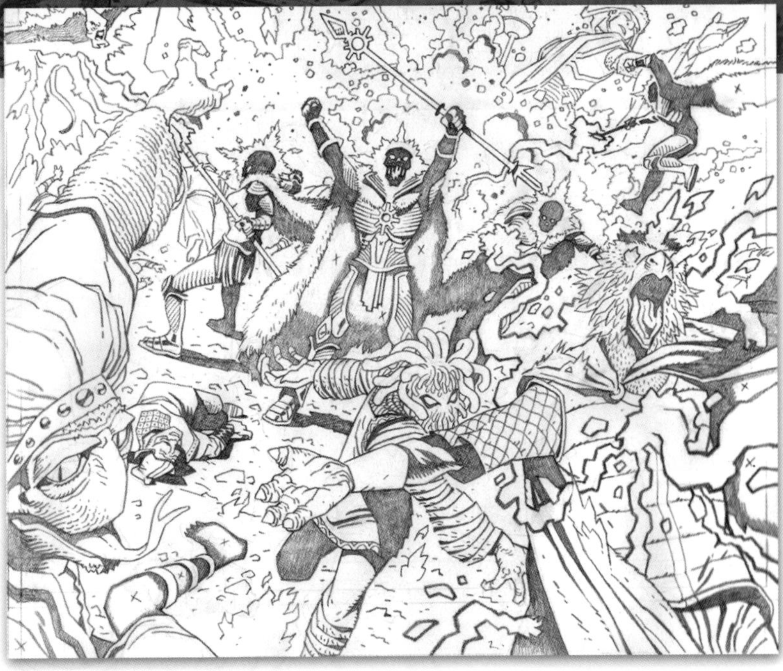

After seeing *Skyfall* so badly fail James Bond, I dearly wanted *Hunters of the Burning Stone* to pay proper tribute to the Doctor. Anniversary stories are supposed to be *celebrations*. I wanted the story to exemplify all the qualities that make the Doctor such an inspiring character. He'd be ingenious, compassionate, funny, resourceful and courageous. By no means perfect, of course - capable of error and anger - but still humanity's champion. The greatest science-fiction hero ever created. Full-stop.

Writing Yuri Azarov in *The Broken Man* had reminded me that a good villain never thinks of himself as a villain. This

Above: The Hunters arrive on Cornucopia. Pencils by Martin Geraghty.

Below: Martin's initial inked character sketches of Hur and Za.

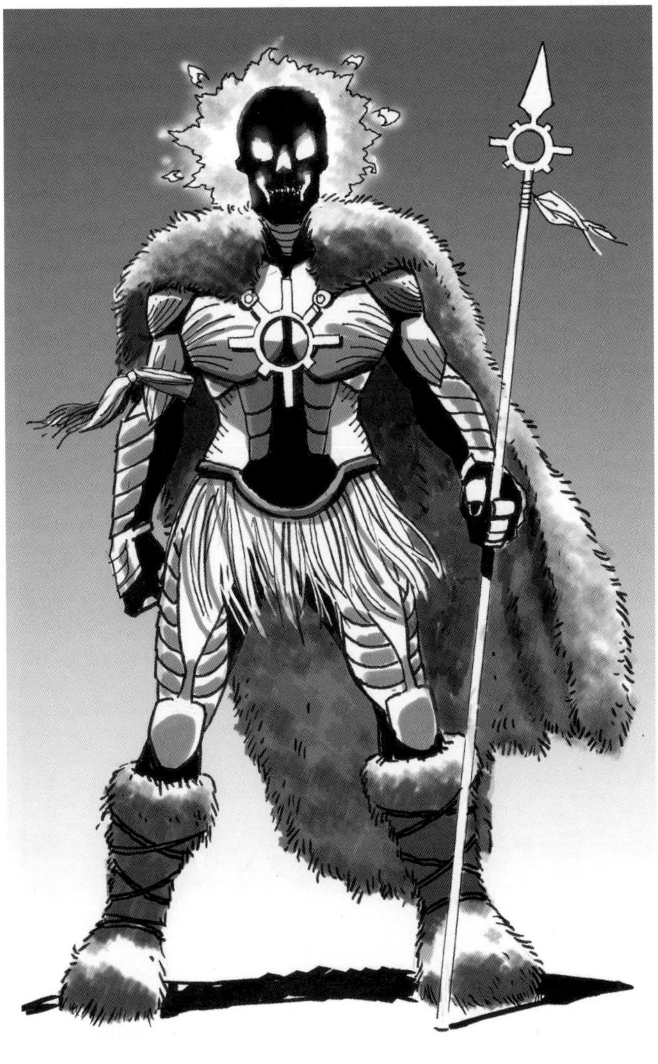

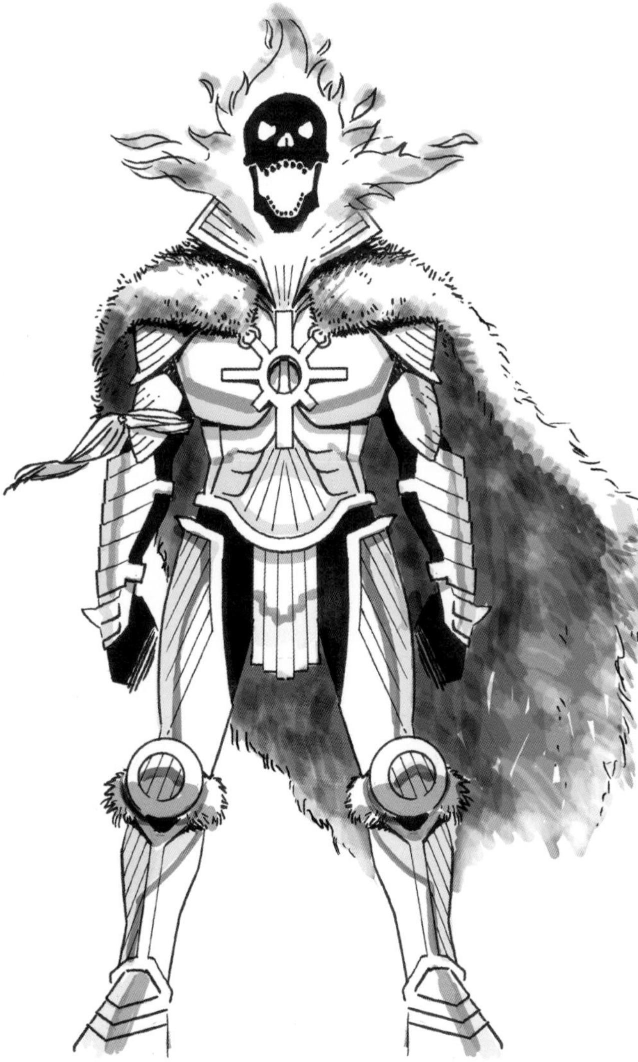

Above: Ian and the Doctor witness the last day of the Time War on Gallifrey. Pencil art by Martin Geraghty.

Below: Ian and the Doctor take a trip through the Doctor's memories. Pencils by Martin Geraghty.

led me to an important conclusion: the reverse perspective was equally valid. A true hero never sees himself as a hero. If you asked the Doctor to describe himself, he might say "explorer" or "scientist" or "great dancer". Catch him on a darker day and he might even say "destroyer". But "hero"? No. Unthinkable. Heroes are people who just get on with the job, regardless of the risk to themselves: a nurse in a casualty ward, a journalist in a fascist country, a fireman in an inferno. Heroes put other people first because that's just how they roll – and that's the Doctor. People who *believe* they're heroes are invariably self-absorbed monsters. They're the ones who need applause, who *demand* it. The most extreme examples often end up running countries (always into the ground) with their face on every poster, expecting the masses to cheer at every wave of their hand.

Exploring the nature of the Doctor's heroism took me back to the TV story *Amy's Choice*. The Doctor, Amy and Rory are trapped inside two deadly realities by the mysterious Dream Lord, a being who seems to know a great deal about the Doctor. The Doctor has deduced the Dream Lord's true identity, however, and at one point makes a very telling observation…

"There's only one person in the universe who hates me as much as you do."

At the story's conclusion (spoiler alert) it is revealed that the Dream Lord is in fact an aspect of the Doctor himself – a dark piece of his own consciousness.

That made me sit up. So the Doctor *hates* himself? Really? Not just the odd twinge of self-loathing from time to time – he hates himself *more than anyone else in the universe?* If you stop to think about it, that's a stupendously long list. The Doctor hates himself more than the Master? More than Davros? More than the Black Guardian or Fenric or Beep the Meep?

This was news to me. I certainly hadn't noticed any evidence of this in twentieth-century *Doctor Who*. Back then the Doctor seemed to be quite pleased with himself. He was usually a very happy fella, living his life by his own rules. What had happened to change that? It had to be the Time War; that often-mentioned but never-witnessed cataclysmic dust-up between the Time Lords and the Daleks. The Doctor had clearly ended it, and been (more or less) the sole survivor. He was carrying so much anger and sorrow and shame on an unimaginable level. Matt Smith had commented in several interviews that he believed the Doctor is forever moving forward, never stopping to look back, because of his grim past. One remark Matt made was particularly stark…

"I think the Doctor's got a lot of blood on his hands… I think if he didn't travel the universe he'd probably end up hanging himself."

So the Doctor was in a far more fragile state than I'd realised. But whatever the consequences of the Time War, however many deaths the Doctor has brought about, it's fair to say that the effect he's had on the universe has been infinitely more positive than negative. He's saved far more lives than he's ever ended. He's about hope, not despair. He represents mercy, not revenge. But would such a moral man, tormented by guilt, see it that way? No. The Prometheans' mental probe would have crushed him if he'd walked through it on his own. Luckily, he had a friend along for the journey.

Simply put, Ian Chesterton and Barbara Wright are the Doctor's teachers. They have an understanding of the Doctor that few other companions can match. (Oh, I am *so* loving using the present tense here!) They showed him how to be a hero and they gave him his love for humanity – because *they* are humanity at its finest.

Having them marry at the end seemed the only possible conclusion. I know there are plenty of fans that subscribe to the 'just good friends' theory, but to them I say: what show were *you* watching? The notion that after *The Chase* they gave each other a quick hug and then went their separate ways just seems ludicrous to me. These two had bonded over months of facing danger, horror, beauty and wonder together. They had seen each other at their bravest and weakest, and gained an understanding of one another that most couples take a lifetime to achieve.

My introduction to Ian and Barbara came long before I watched any TV episodes. It was via the Target novel *Doctor Who and the Crusaders* by David Whitaker (the show's first story editor). There's a terrific prologue set aboard the TARDIS where he describes the subtle changes that Ian and Barbara have undergone since meeting the Doctor…

"But always her eyes turned to Ian and their hands were ready to reach out and touch, for, whatever world of the future enmeshed them, they knew their destinies were bound up in each other – the one sure thing fixed and unalterable, in the ever-changing life of the Doctor."

David Whitaker was the man who carefully shaped the characters' development over that all-important first year of *Doctor Who*. If *he* says they were in love, then that's good enough for me!

Martin Geraghty Artist

"There are some technical issues we need to go through before you get cracking on this one" (or words to that effect) wrote Scott to me at the onset of **DWM**'s comic strip love-letter to the show's 50th anniversary. Arguably the biggest storyline the mag had produced in its long history? Hmm, maybe.

"So I'll probably be drawing some elements as overlays or James will be colouring something up in negative so I'll have to bear that in mind then," I naïvely thought at the time.

"No, we're changing the whole shape of the mag so there'll be less top and bottom."

This caused a bit of to-ing and fro-ing between artist and editor, believe me. When people mention "technical issues" to me, be it during my day job, or when I've got a plumber round, I tend to zone out because I'm not a technical person. In fact I'm a hopeless luddite, so I was forever being instructed by Scott to add more artwork round the edges, as the graphic novel version of this story would have to be the same height and width as previous volumes. So, basically you now have the "Exclusive Directors Cut!" version in your hands, "including previously unseen material!" such as a bit more of people's legs and extra rooftops.

Anyway, enough of that technical blather! What you really want to know is, what was it like drawing an epic saga that reunites the Doctor with his first two human companions, pits him once more against the Tribe of Gum and takes him on a journey into the inner recesses of his Id and a soul-draining trawl through his entire TV life-story?

"Bloomin' marvellous" comes the answer from a lifelong *Doctor Who* fan.

I'll not say it was an easy ride. I'd not experienced such sleepless nights on the strip since *The Flood* – the scale and importance of this story knocked even the Eighth Doctor's epic swan-song into a cocked hat and the deadlines here were punishing – the Christmas break always hammers schedules into the ground and this was no exception. I think I was having to turn episodes round in about three weeks at one stage and believe me, at the tempo I usually work at, that is going some. Life really did have to take a back seat for six months on this one.

But still, what a story to be involved in! What a celebration – Scott declined to tell me what Part One's cliffhanger was going to be until I received the finished script and I think I actually giggled when I read the panel description. Surely one of the absolute all-time greats of the comic strip, and a sheer delight to see the reaction it got from readers, young and old alike. Again, this is something that just couldn't be done by the TV show, no matter how technically superb the production values now are. Ian was easier to capture than Barbara to be honest; Jacqueline Hill's face has an elusive quality that continually evaded me. I eventually started lightboxing screen-grabs which I rarely do, and even then they didn't look like her! Very odd.

I really could wax lyrical about this one for pages – don't worry, I'll resist – but writing from the point of view of a comic artist as well as a *Doctor Who* fan, each episode delivered in spades everything that makes me both of those things. At times it smacked the same giddy hit as when waiting for *The Five Faces of Doctor Who* season back in the winter of 81, or saving up a month's-worth of paper round wages to buy *Revenge of the Cybermen* on VHS or seeing Doctor Five giving Lethbridge-Stewart his memories back. And no random kisses to the past here but flashbacks tailored to the script with absolute precision within a plot that ticks like a Swiss watch. A truly worthy way to celebrate the show's mythos, as well as on a personal note, for me to commemorate my 20th anniversary year on the strip with the same writer who started me off in the first place! (Insert gag about people doing less time for committing murder here!)

Oh, and of *course* Ian and Barbara got married!

So, that was our bit to celebrate 50 years of a TV legend, I hope you all liked it. I'm considering letting someone else draw the centenary story… ●

Above: A montage of villainy from the William Hartnell era. Pencil art by Martin Geraghty.

Below: The Doctor at the controls of the TARDIS. Pencils by Martin Geraghty.

DOCTOR WHO COMIC COLLECTIONS

Volume One of the Fourth Doctor's comic strip adventures, containing five digitally restored stories:

THE IRON LEGION, CITY OF THE DAMNED, THE STAR BEAST, THE DOGS OF DOOM and **THE TIME WITCH!**

Featuring work from **Dave Gibbons, Pat Mills, John Wagner** and **Steve Moore**

164 pages | b&w | softcover
£14.99 | $24.95
ISBN 1-9041 59-37-0

Volume Two of the Fourth Doctor's comic strip adventures, containing 10 digitally restored stories:

DRAGON'S CLAW, THE COLLECTOR, DREAMERS OF DEATH, THE LIFE BRINGER, WAR OF THE WORDS, SPIDER-GOD, THE DEAL, END OF THE LINE, THE FREE-FALL WARRIORS, JUNKYARD DEMON and **THE NEUTRON KNIGHTS!**

164 pages | b&w | softcover
£14.99 | $24.95
ISBN 1-9041 59-81-8

The Fifth Doctor's complete comic strip run, containing six digitally restored stories:

THE TIDES OF TIME, STARS FELL ON STOCKBRIDGE, THE STOCKBRIDGE HORROR, LUNAR LAGOON, 4-DIMENSIONAL VISTAS and **THE MODERATOR!**

Featuring art from **Dave Gibbons**

228 pages | b&w | softcover
£14.99 | $24.95
ISBN 1-9041 59-92-3

Volume One of the Sixth Doctor's comic strip adventures containing seven digitally restored adventures:

THE SHAPE SHIFTER, VOYAGER, POLLY THE GLOT, ONCE UPON A TIME LORD, WAR-GAME, FUNHOUSE and **KANE'S STORY/ABEL'S STORY/ THE WARRIOR'S STORY/ FROBISHER'S STORY!**

172 pages | b&w softcover
£15.99 | $31.95
ISBN 978-1-905239-71-9

Volume Two of the Sixth Doctor's comic strip adventures containing the following digitally restored adventures:

EXODUS, REVELATION!, GENESIS!, NATURE OF THE BEAST, TIME BOMB, SALAD DAZE, CHANGES, PROFITS OF DOOM, THE GIFT and **THE WORLD SHAPERS!**

188 pages | b&w | softcover
£15.99 | $31.95
ISBN 978-1-905239-87-0

Volume One of the Seventh Doctor's comic strip adventures containing 11 digitally restored stories:

A COLD DAY IN HELL!, REDEMPTION!, THE CROSSROADS OF TIME, CLAWS OF THE KLATHI!, CULTURE SHOCK!, KEEPSAKE, PLANET OF THE DEAD, ECHOES OF THE MOGOR!, TIME AND TIDE, FOLLOW THAT TARDIS! and **INVADERS FROM GANTAC!**

PLUS an introduction and commentary by former strip editors **Richard Starkings** and **John Freeman**

188 pages | b&w | softcover
£15.99 | $31.95 | ISBN 978-1-84653-410-2

Volume Two of the Seventh Doctor's complete comic strip adventures from the pages of **DWM** and *The Incredible Hulk Presents*. Contains 14 complete stories:

NEMESIS OF THE DALEKS, STAIRWAY TO HEAVEN, ONCE IN A LIFETIME, HUNGER FROM THE ENDS OF TIME!, WAR WORLD!, TECHNICAL HITCH, A SWITCH IN TIME!, THE SENTINEL!, WHO'S THAT GIRL!, THE ENLIGHTENMENT OF LI-CHEE THE WISE, SLIMMER!, NINEVEH!, TRAIN-FLIGHT, DOCTOR CONKERER!
and also the adventures of Abslom Daak in
ABSLOM DAAK... DALEK KILLER and **STAR TIGERS!**

PLUS a massive behind-the-scenes feature, including commentaries from the writers, artists and editors, cut scenes, pencil art, design sketches, and much, much more.

196 pages | b&w | softcover
£16.99 | $24.99 | ISBN 978-1-84653-531-4

CLASSIC STRIP ADVENTURES

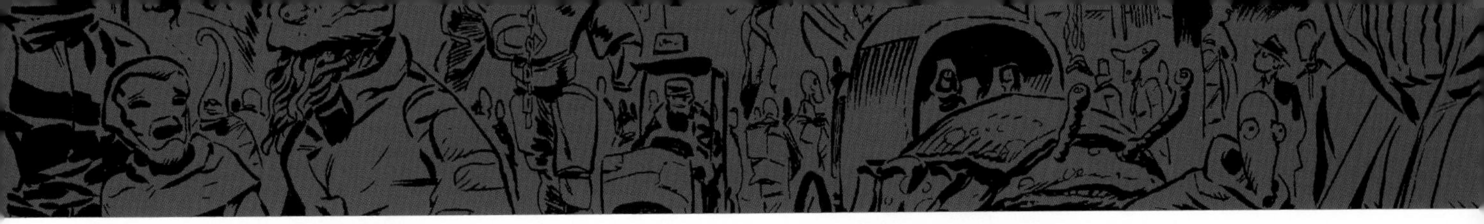

THE COMPLETE EIGHTH DOCTOR

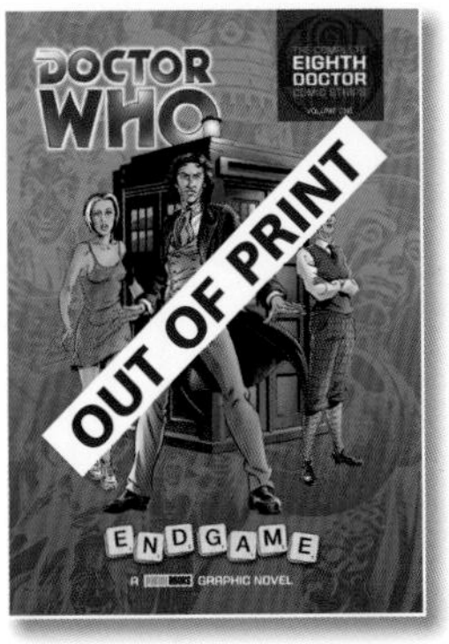
DOCTOR WHO
EIGHTH DOCTOR
OUT OF PRINT
ENDGAME

Volume One of the Eighth Doctor's complete comic strip adventures, containing eight digitally restored stories: **ENDGAME**, **THE KEEP**, **FIRE AND BRIMSTONE**, **TOOTH AND CLAW**, **THE FINAL CHAPTER**, **WORMWOOD**, **A LIFE OF MATTER AND DEATH** and **BY HOOK OR BY CROOK**!

PLUS a 16-page behind-the-scenes feature with unused story ideas, character designs and an authors' commentary on all the strips!

228 pages | b&w | softcover
£14.99 | $24.95 | ISBN 1-9052 39-09-2

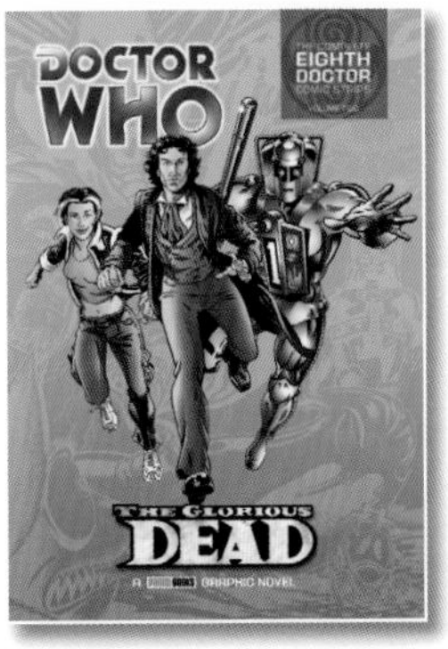
DOCTOR WHO
EIGHTH DOCTOR
THE GLORIOUS DEAD

Volume Two of the Eighth Doctor's complete comic strip adventures, containing eight digitally restored stories: **THE FALLEN, UNNATURAL BORN KILLERS, THE ROAD TO HELL, COMPANY OF THIEVES, THE GLORIOUS DEAD, THE AUTONOMY BUG, HAPPY DEATHDAY** and **TV ACTION**!

PLUS a six-page behind-the-scenes feature and two classic 1980s strips featuring Kroton the Cyberman: **THROWBACK** and **SHIP OF FOOLS**!

244 pages | b&w | softcover
£15.99 | $26.50 | ISBN 1-9052 39-44-0

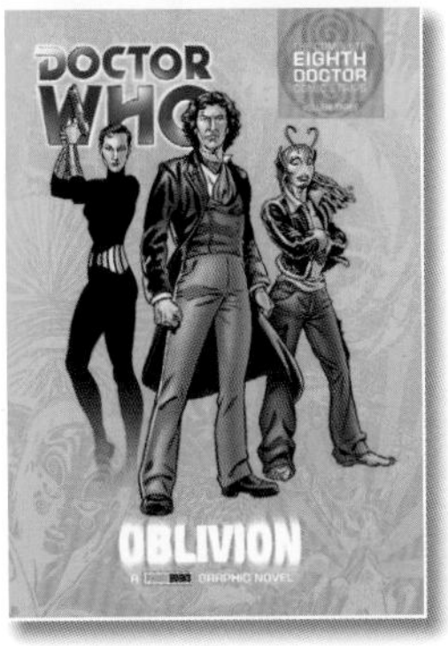
DOCTOR WHO
EIGHTH DOCTOR
OBLIVION

Volume Three of the Eighth Doctor's complete comic strip adventures, containing eight digitally restored stories: **OPHIDIUS**, **BEAUTIFUL FREAK**, **THE WAY OF ALL FLESH**, **CHILDREN OF THE REVOLUTION**, **ME AND MY SHADOW**, **UROBOROS** and **OBLIVION**!

PLUS a massive 22-page behind-the-scenes feature, bonus strip **CHARACTER ASSASSIN** and a newly-extended conclusion to Dalek strip **CHILDREN OF THE REVOLUTION**!

228 pages | full colour | softcover
£15.99 | $26.50 | ISBN 1-905239-45-9

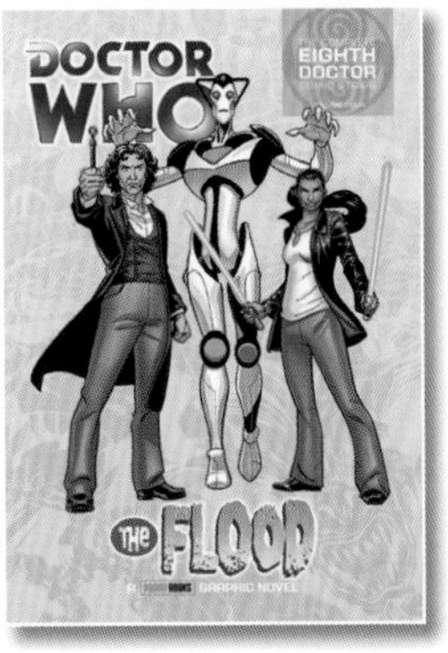
DOCTOR WHO
EIGHTH DOCTOR
THE FLOOD

Volume Four of the Eighth Doctor's complete comic strip adventures, containing eight digitally restored stories: **WHERE NOBODY KNOWS YOUR NAME, THE NIGHTMARE GAME, THE POWER OF THOUERIS!, THE CURIOUS TALE OF SPRING-HEELED JACK, THE LAND OF HAPPY ENDINGS, BAD BLOOD, SINS OF THE FATHERS** and **THE FLOOD**!

PLUS a massive 28-page behind-the-scenes feature, and a newly-extended conclusion to **THE FLOOD!**

228 pages | full colour | softcover
£15.99 | $26.50 | ISBN 978-1-905239-65-8

THE COMPLETE TENTH DOCTOR

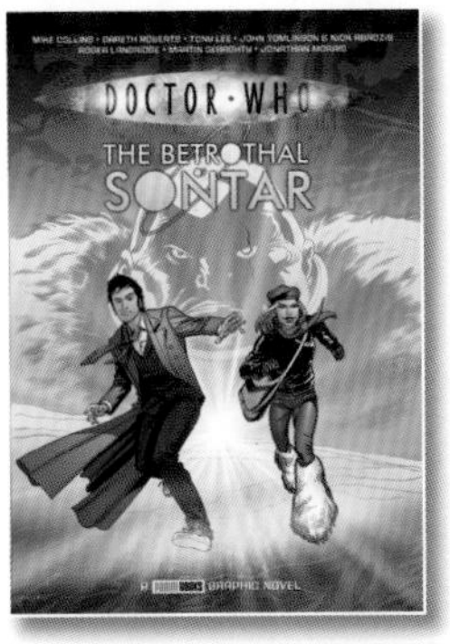
DOCTOR WHO
THE BETROTHAL OF SONTAR

Volume One of the Tenth Doctor's complete comic strip adventures from the pages of **DWM**, containing eight complete stories:

THE BETROTHAL OF SONTAR, **THE LODGER**, **F.A.Q.**, **THE FUTURISTS**, **INTERSTELLAR OVERDRIVE**, **OPERA OF DOOM!**, **THE GREEN-EYED MONSTER** and **THE WARKEEPER'S CROWN**!

PLUS a massive 15-page behind-the-scenes feature, including commentaries from the writers, artists and editors, cut scenes, pencil art, design sketches, and more.

180 pages | full colour softcover
£15.99 | $31.95
ISBN 978-1-905239-90-0

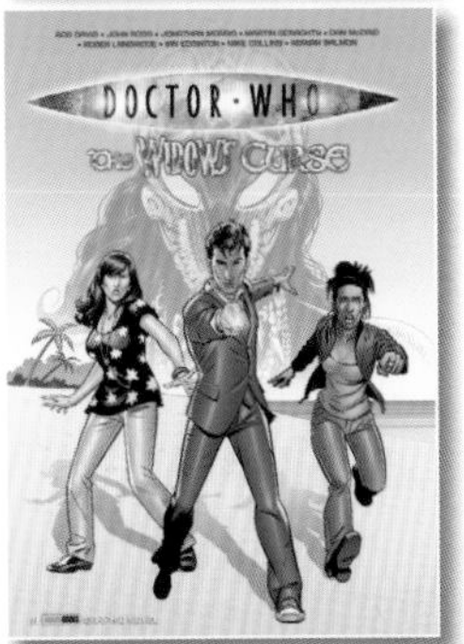
DOCTOR WHO
THE WIDOW'S CURSE

Volume Two of the Tenth Doctor's complete comic strip adventures from the pages of **DWM**, containing nine complete stories:

THE WOMAN WHO SOLD THE WORLD, **BUS STOP!**, **THE FIRST**, **SUN SCREEN**, **DEATH TO THE DOCTOR!**, **UNIVERSAL MONSTERS**, **THE WIDOW'S CURSE**, **THE IMMORTAL EMPEROR** and **THE TIME OF MY LIFE**!

PLUS a massive behind-the-scenes feature, including commentaries from the writers and artists, design sketches and more.

220 pages | full colour | softcover
£15.99 | $31.95
ISBN 978-1-84653-429-4

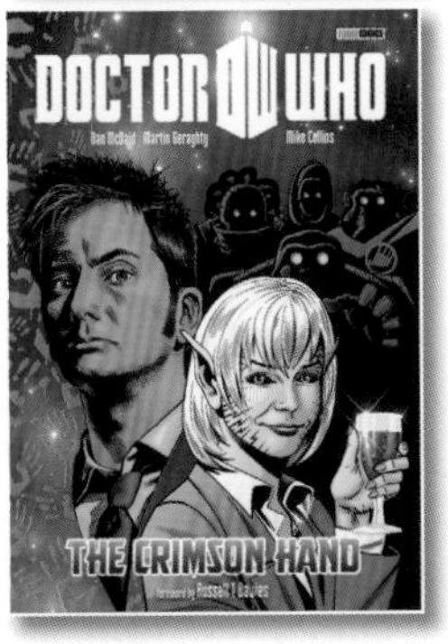
DOCTOR WHO
THE CRIMSON HAND

Volume Three of the Tenth Doctor's complete comic strip adventures from the pages of **DWM**, containing 10 complete stories:

HOTEL HISTORIA, **SPACE VIKINGS!**, **THINKTWICE**, **THE STOCKBRIDGE CHILD**, **MORTAL BELOVED**, **THE AGE OF ICE**, **THE DEEP HEREAFTER**, **ONOMATOPOEIA**, **GHOSTS OF THE NORTHERN LINE** and **THE CRIMSON HAND**!

PLUS a massive behind-the-scenes feature, including commentaries from the writers and artists, design sketches and more.

260 pages | full colour | softcover
£15.99 | $31.95
ISBN 978-1-84653-451-5

THE ELEVENTH DOCTOR

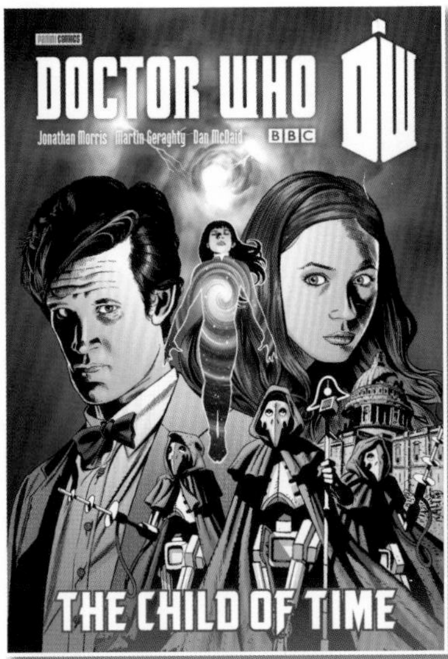
DOCTOR WHO
BBC
THE CHILD OF TIME

Volume One of the Eleventh Doctor's complete comic strip adventures from the pages of **DWM**, containing nine complete stories:

SUPERNATURE, **PLANET BOLLYWOOD!**, **THE GOLDEN ONES**, **THE PROFESSOR**, **THE QUEEN AND THE BOOKSHOP**, **THE SCREAMS OF DEATH**, **DO NOT GO GENTLE INTO THAT GOOD NIGHT**, **FOREVER DREAMING**, **APOTHEOSIS** and **THE CHILD OF TIME**!

PLUS a massive behind-the-scenes feature, including commentaries from the writers, artists and editors, cut scenes, pencil art, design sketches, and much, much more.

244 pages | full colour | softcover
£16.99 | $24.99
ISBN 978-1-84653-460-7

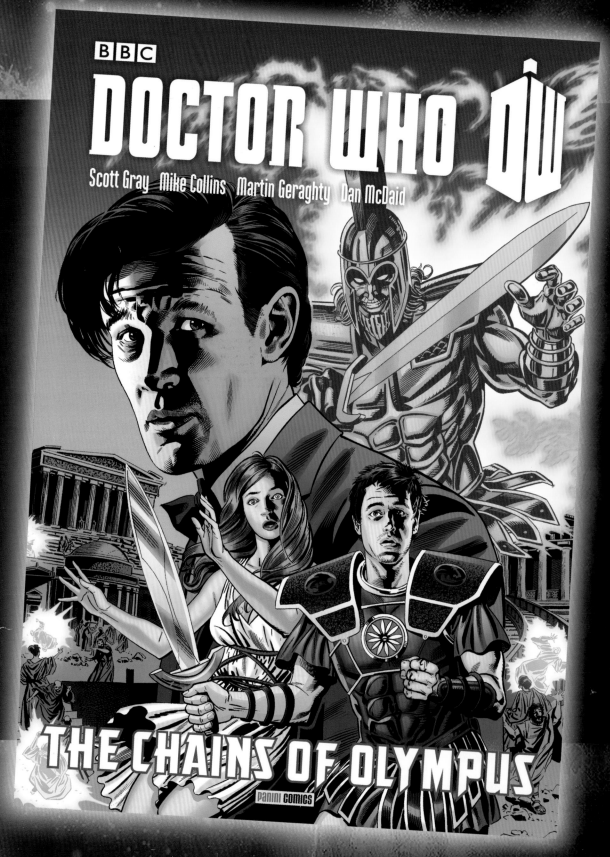